Intuit® QuickBooks® Fundamentals Learning Guide 2014 / 2015

Find instructions for 2014 / 2015 software, the 2015 QuickBooks Accountant desktop software, and 2014 and 2015 student data files to be compatible with what software you may be using in the classroom.

Product Name	Intuit QuickBooks Fundamentals Learning Guide 2014/2015 ISBN: 978-0-9911002-3-1
Trademarks	Intuit, the Intuit logo, QuickBooks, QuickBooks Pro, QuickBase, Quicken, TurboTax, ProSeries, Lacerte, EasyStep, and QuickZoom, among others, are registered trademarks and/or registered service marks of Intuit Inc. in the United States and other countries. QuickBooks ProAdvisor is a trademark and/or service mark of Intuit Inc. in the United States and other countries. Other parties' trademarks or service marks are the property of their respective owners and should be treated as such. Terms, conditions, features, service offerings, prices, and hours referenced in this document are subject to change without notice. We at Intuit are committed to bringing you great online services through QuickBooks. Occasionally, we may decide to update our selection and change our service offerings, so please check www.quickbooks.com for the latest information, including pricing and availability, on our products and services.
Copyright	© 2014 Intuit, Inc. All rights reserved.
Disclaimer	This material is intended as a learning aid for QuickBooks software users. Under no circumstances shall the author or publisher be liable for any damages, including any lost profits, lost data or other indirect damages arising out of anything written in this document or expressed directly or indirectly by the author or publisher.
Developed and Written By	Bonnie Biafore

Education Program

Welcome to the Intuit Family!

We hope that you enjoy learning or refreshing your QuickBooks skills with the **Intuit QuickBooks Fundamentals Learning Guide 2014/2015.**

Make sure you take full advantage of the step by step instruction, review questions and in-depth business case scenarios as you use **QuickBooks Accountant trial software,** the same full version software that professionals use. Plus, you'll find a **special offer on the next page just for current students** to purchase their own copy of QuickBooks for up to 70% off retail pricing.

The **Intuit Education Program** is committed to providing educators and students with the tools and resources needed to integrate QuickBooks into the classroom. Today, over 5 million small businesses are using QuickBooks, the #1 best-selling accounting software.* *Ask us today about QuickBooks Online, the #1 cloud accounting solution by small businesses and accounting professionals!*

Teachers tell us that the main reason they incorporate QuickBooks in the classroom is that it helps their students get jobs! We realize that having this real world experience gives students a competitive edge day 1 on the job.

Check out our tools for educators to help you get started, or enhance what you are already doing in the classroom:

- **Free Instructor Tools!** This includes an instructor guide to complement this Intuit QuickBooks Fundamentals Learning Guide, Solutions to Problem Sets and more.

- **QuickBooks Software Site License for the Computer Lab in Mac or PC.** Whether you have 10-25-50 or more students going through the computer lab, we have multi-user licenses for academic institutions at great discounts for educators.

- **Examples of How Teachers are Using QuickBooks in the Classroom Today.** We love to share and hear from you! We know every class is different, and we want you to decide what's best for your class. QuickBooks is used in so many ways in the classroom. Some examples include use in an entrepreneurial class as the 'back bone' of student's mock businesses, in a dedicated computer class with QuickBooks certification using a flipped classroom format, as well as in a Financial Accounting Class for some homework exercises to provide that practical experience.

Learn more today and please visit us at intuitaccountants.com/LearnQuickBooks or call 1-866-570-3843.

We look forward to making your next year in the classroom or in the workforce a success!

The Intuit Education Program Team

* Based on NPD Retail Tracking Service for retail sales from May 2011-May 2012.

Table of Contents

Chapter 2
Managing Expenses 33

Chapter 3
Sales and Income 69

Chapter 4
More Customer Transactions and Reports 109

Chapter 5
Bank Reconciliation and Bank Transactions........................... 135

Chapter 6

Chapter 7

Chapter 8
Tracking Inventory 235

Preface

The Intuit QuickBooks Fundamentals Learning Guide 2014/2015 introduces you to QuickBooks, Intuit's powerful, yet easy-to-use accounting software for small business. With the help of this book, you'll learn how to use many of the features available in the desktop version of QuickBooks Accountant for Windows.

This guide focuses on QuickBooks Accountant for Windows, but you can complete most of the exercises using QuickBooks Premier or QuickBooks Pro. (For brevity, this guide refers to QuickBooks Accountant for Windows simply as QuickBooks.) Although this guide doesn't specifically cover QuickBooks Enterprise Solutions, much of this material works with Enterprise Solutions editions.

> Note: This guide does not cover QuickBooks Online or QuickBooks Pro for Mac.

Using This Book

The instructions and screen captures in this book were prepared using QuickBooks Accountant 2015. The instructions identify differences between QuickBooks 2014 and 2015 editions and features that are new to QuickBooks 2015. If you use an edition other than QuickBooks Accountant 2015, you may notice your screens and some of the steps you perform vary slightly from the ones in this book.

This guide contains 13 chapters and a final case study. Each chapter uses explanations and hands-on tutorials to present a major aspect of managing a business's finances. You can work through each chapter's hands-on tutorials to obtain experience with QuickBooks. The review questions at the end of each chapter help test your knowledge. The exercises at the end of each chapter provide additional hands-on experience using QuickBooks to perform common bookkeeping tasks. Chapter 14, Company Startup Case Study, is a final exercise that covers topics from every chapter in the book.

Because each chapter and its accompanying exercises are based on a sample company file that you restore from this guide's CD, you can complete the chapters in any order.

> Note: If you plan to use QuickBooks features that integrate with Microsoft Office, such as importing and exporting data to Excel, you need to have Microsoft Office installed on your computer.

Using the QuickBooks Student Trial

The QuickBooks Accountant 2015 Student Trial included on this guide's CD is a full-featured version of QuickBooks. You can install it on your computer to use as you study this guide and complete the exercises.

> Tip: QuickBooks Accountant can toggle to other versions of QuickBooks including Pro, Premier, and Premier industry editions. You can explore any QuickBooks edition by toggling within your trial software.

To install QuickBooks Accountant 2015, insert the software CD into your computer's CD or DVD drive, and then follow the on-screen instructions. When prompted, fill in the License Number and Product Number printed on the yellow sticker adhered to the plastic CD sleeve at the back of this book. After the installation is complete, you must register your copy of QuickBooks. You can use this trial version for 140 days after installation.

Using the Exercise Files

The CD that accompanies this book contains exercise files you use as you work through chapter tutorials and the end-of-chapter exercises.

Installing the Exercise Files

To install the exercise files from this book's CD to your computer, follow these steps:

1. Insert the CD into your computer's CD or DVD drive.

2. Copy the folder on the CD to the folder where you want to store the files on your computer's hard drive.

   If you are using a computer in a classroom or lab, ask your instructor where you should store your exercise files.

3. Eject the CD from the drive and store it in a safe place.

Restoring Portable Files

Each chapter uses a separate company file for the chapter's computer practice. In addition, each exercise at the end of a chapter uses a separate exercise file. These files are QuickBooks portable company files, so you must restore them to regular company file format before you can work with them. See the section, Restoring a Portable Company File, on page 7 to learn how to restore a portable file.

At the beginning of each chapter and before each exercise, you will see a note that tells you which exercise file to use for that work. To ensure that your file matches the book's screen captures and instructions, you must restore the specified exercise file before beginning to work on a chapter or exercise. Here is an example of one of these notes:

> Note: For the computer practice in this chapter, restore the sample file, sample_product-based business 2015 (Portable).QBM. (Or, if you are using QuickBooks 2014, restore sample_product-based business 2014 (Portable).QBM.)

In each chapter, steps you should perform are prefaced with the heading:

Computer Practice

Some sections present material that you should understand, but you shouldn't perform the steps in your exercise file. In that case, you'll see a note like this:

> Note: Do not perform these steps. They are for reference only.

QuickBooks Certification

This book can help you prepare to take the QuickBooks User Certification Exam. After passing the exam, you become an Intuit QuickBooks Certified User, which validates your QuickBooks knowledge. For more information and to find testing center locations, go to http://www.certiport.com/quickbooks.

Acknowledgements

I want to thank the incredible team that helped me with this book. Without them, this Learning Guide wouldn't exist. My thanks and gratitude go out to:

- Trevor Matheson for introducing me to the Intuit Education Program Team.

- Katelyn Brown for editing the manuscript, capturing screen images, checking for accuracy, and so much more.

- Michael Cobb (Real World Training) for reviewing the manuscript and correcting my technical errors.

- Chris Devlin for copy editing and eagle-eyed proofreading.

- Scott Baird for setting up our production environment, laying out the final manuscript, and preparing the index.

- Everyone on the Intuit team, including Sharon Markowitz, Dax Parreno, and Lisa Schwartz for helping bring this project to fruition.

I hope you enjoy learning QuickBooks with the help of the Intuit QuickBooks Fundamentals Learning Guide 2014/2015.

Bonnie Biafore
October 2014

Chapter 1

Introducing QuickBooks

Topics

This chapter covers the following topics:

- QuickBooks Products
- Working with QuickBooks Files
- Creating and Restoring Backup Files
- Touring the QuickBooks User Interface
- Introducing QuickBooks Transactions
- QuickBooks Help
- A Brief Introduction to Accounting

QuickBooks acts as both a bookkeeping/accounting program and a financial management tool. Once you set up your company file and record your financial transactions, the program helps you track and manage income, expenses, inventory, job costing, receivables, payables, and much more. With QuickBooks reports, you can evaluate your organization's performance and make informed business decisions.

QuickBooks is designed so you can keep your books even if you haven't mastered the debits and credits of double-entry accounting. However, you need to use its features properly to ensure that your financial records are correct. To do that, you need to understand how QuickBooks works, how company files are set up, how to perform bookkeeping tasks with the program's features, and finally how to retrieve information about your business from your QuickBooks company file.

This chapter begins with an introduction to the basics of QuickBooks. You'll learn about the QuickBooks product line. You'll also learn how to work with QuickBooks company files. Then, you'll get to know a little bit about the program's interface, how to record transactions, and how to obtain QuickBooks help. Finally, the chapter concludes with a brief overview of what you need to know about accounting to use QuickBooks properly.

> Note: For the computer practice in this chapter, restore the sample file, *sample_product-based business 2015 (Portable).QBM.* (Or, if you are using QuickBooks 2014, restore *sample_product-based business 2014 (Portable).QBM.*)

QuickBooks Products

The QuickBooks product line represents a broad set of accounting and bookkeeping tools that are easy to learn. Financial tools, such as general ledger, accounts receivable, accounts payable, inventory, sales tax, and financial reporting are built into QuickBooks products. In addition, Intuit offers many optional, fee-based products and services, such as payroll services, merchant account services, and time-tracking products that integrate with QuickBooks.

QuickBooks Editions

QuickBooks comes in several product editions to satisfy different needs and budgets: QuickBooks Online, QuickBooks Pro, QuickBooks Premier, QuickBooks Accountant, and QuickBooks Enterprise Solutions. In addition, QuickBooks Premier and Enterprise Solutions editions offer six industry-specific editions: General Business, Contractor, Manufacturers & Wholesaler, Nonprofit, Professional Services, and Retail.

> Note: All QuickBooks editions support multiple simultaneous users. However, to access a company file in multi-user mode, each user must run the same version of QuickBooks.

This book covers QuickBooks Pro, non-industry-specific QuickBooks Premier, and QuickBooks Accountant, because these editions are the most commonly used. This book does not cover QuickBooks Enterprise Solutions, although it is easy to learn once you've mastered Pro, Premier, or Accountant. Also, the book does not cover QuickBooks Online, which is a web-based product that looks and works differently than the editions covered in this book. To compare all QuickBooks editions, see www.quickbooks.com.

QuickBooks Releases

Initially, you install a specific version of QuickBooks, such as QuickBooks 2014 or 2015. After a version is released for sale, users may uncover errors in the software. When that happens, Intuit corrects the errors and updates the program with patches distributed via the Internet. Each patch represents a release of the QuickBooks program.

To see which software release you have installed, launch QuickBooks, and then press F2 or Ctrl+1. At the top of the *Product Information* window, you'll see the label "Product" followed by the QuickBooks product and release, such as "QuickBooks Accountant 2015 Release R1P".

To install the latest maintenance release, on the *Help* menu, choose *Update QuickBooks*. Then, follow the instructions on the *Update QuickBooks* dialog box's screens to download and install maintenance releases into QuickBooks.

> Note: This book is based on QuickBooks Accountant 2015 release R1P. If your computer is running a newer release (a higher release number, such as R3P), you may see slight differences compared to the descriptions and screens in this book.

Sample Files

This book uses the sample files that come with QuickBooks: Rock Castle Construction is set up as a product-based business and Larry's Landscaping represents a service-based business. These sample files demonstrate most of QuickBooks features and provide a safe way to experiment with QuickBooks.

As you work through the examples and exercises in this book, think about how you can apply QuickBooks' features to your own organization.

The QuickBooks 2014/2015 Learning Guide provides portable files for these sample files for both QuickBooks 2014 and 2015 on the CD that accompanies this book so you can restore the version you want to work with. To learn how to restore portable files, refer to the section, "Restoring Portable Company Files."

Working with QuickBooks Files

It's important to understand the different types of QuickBooks files and the purpose of each one. QuickBooks has three primary types of files, which can be opened by choosing *Open or Restore Company* on the *File menu*:

- **Working files (company files):** These are the files you use for your day-to-day work, such as recording transactions and running reports. These working files have a file type of QuickBooks Company File and a ".qbw" file extension (for QuickBooks working).

- **Portable company files:** These files (file extension ".qbm") are compact versions of your working files, intended for exchanging files between computers. You must restore a portable file (page 7) to a working file before you can use it. Do not use portable files to back up your data.

- **Backup files:** These files (file extension ".qbb" for QuickBooks backup) are compressed data files and are used to minimize loss of your financial information. You must restore a backup file to a working company file before you can use it. See page 8 for more information on creating and restoring backup files.

QuickBooks also offers the Accountant's Copy feature, which enables an accounting professional to review and work on a special copy of a client's company file while the client simultaneously works on the original company file. The client can then merge the accountant's changes into the company file. Refer to QuickBooks Help for information on the Accountant's Copy.

Creating a New File

QuickBooks offers four ways to create a new company file: Express Start, Detailed Start, Company Based on an Existing Company, and converting from other accounting software. Express Start is a relatively quick method for creating a new company file. However, an organized approach helps produce a company file that is set up properly for your needs. Chapter 13 covers file setup in detail. That way, you can apply what you've learned in earlier chapters to make decisions during the setup process.

Opening a QuickBooks Sample File

QuickBooks includes sample company files that you can use to experiment with the program's features without endangering your organization's QuickBooks data.

> Note: The CD that accompanies this book includes portable files for the QuickBooks sample files used in this material. You can restore these portable files to obtain a sample file that works with QuickBooks 2014 or QuickBooks 2015, depending on which version you run. If you restore these portable files, you open the sample files using *Open or Restore Company*, described in the next section.

Computer Practice

Follow these steps to open a sample file:

1. To launch QuickBooks, double-click the program icon on your desktop or select the QuickBooks entry from the Windows Start menu.

    QuickBooks will either display the *No Company Open* window (Figure 1-2) or open the last company file you worked on. The *No Company Open* window appears if you are launching QuickBooks for the first time or you closed your company file before exiting your last Quick-Books session. If you did not close the last company file you worked on before exiting your QuickBooks session, the program opens that company file.

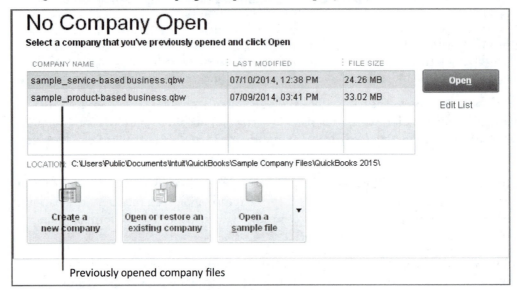

Figure 1-1 No Company Open Window

2. If the *No Company Open* window does not appear, on the *File* menu, choose *Close Company*. If QuickBooks asks if you want to back up your file, click *No*.

3. When the *No Company Open* window appears, click the "Open a sample file" button, and then choose *Sample product-based business* from the drop-down list.

    The *QuickBooks Information* screen (shown in Figure 1-2) appears.

4. To open the sample file, click *OK*.

    If an Accountant Center or External Accountant message appears, turn off the *Show window when opening a company file* checkbox, and then click the X at the *Accountant Center window's* top right corner.

The sample file is open and ready for you to begin exploring.

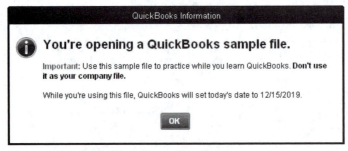

Figure 1-2 Sample File Information Screen

Opening a QuickBooks Company File

If you work with more than one company, you'll have a QuickBooks company file for each one. You can switch from one company file to another at any time. QuickBooks provides easy access to company files you've worked with before. You can also open any company file with a few more clicks.

Here is an easy way to open a company file that you've worked on previously:

1. On the *File* menu, choose *Open Previous Company*.

2. On the submenu that appears, choose the company file you want to open.

> Tip: You can change the number of company files that appear in the *Open Previous Company* submenu. On the *File menu*, choose *Open Previous Company*, and then on the submenu, choose *Set number of previous companies*. (This entry is grayed out if no company file is open.) In the box, type the number of company files you want to see in the submenu (up to 20), and then click *OK*.

If the company file you want to open doesn't appear on the *Open Previous Company* submenu, follow these steps instead:

1. On the *File* menu, choose *Open or Restore Company*.

2. In the *Open or Restore Company* dialog box, select the *Open a company file* option, and then click *Next*.

3. In the *Open a Company* dialog box, navigate to the folder that contains the company file you want to open. In the *Name* list, click the company file name, and then click *Open*.

> Note: If you use QuickBooks Accountant or Enterprise Solutions, you can open two company files at the same time (On the *File* menu, choose *Open Second Company*.) However, the activities you can perform in the second file are very limited. Unless you want to open the file to look for information, it's best to use the *Open Previous Company* or *Open or Restore Company* menu entry to open a company file.

Closing a QuickBooks File

You don't have to explicitly save a company file. QuickBooks saves the information you enter as you work. The program also closes the company file that's open when you open another company file or close the QuickBooks program. If you want to close a company file, on the *File* menu, choose *Close Company*.

Closing the QuickBooks Program

Because QuickBooks saves your data as you work, you can simply close the program. To exit QuickBooks, on the *File* menu, choose *Exit* (or click the X at the program window's top-right corner).

Creating and Restoring Portable Company Files

Portable company files are compressed company data files that are small enough to send to others (via email or on a USB flash drive, for example). For example, the exercise files that accompany this book are portable company files that you restore.

> Tip: If you send a company file to someone else to work on or transfer it from your desktop computer to your laptop, be sure to transfer the file back to your computer, so you always work on the up-to-date company file. The only exception to this rule is if you send your accountant an Accountant's Copy (see page 3). In that case, when your accountant sends the updated copy back, you can merge the changes from the Accountant's Copy into your company file.

Creating a Portable Company File

To create a portable company file, follow these steps:

1. On the *File* menu, choose *Create Copy*.

2. In the *Save Copy or Backup* dialog box, select the *Portable company file* option, as shown in Figure 1-3, and then click *Next*.

3. In the *Save Portable Company File* dialog box, navigate to the folder where you want to save the file.

   QuickBooks automatically fills in the *File name* box with the company file name followed by "(Portable)". You can edit the name if you wish.

Figure 1-3 Create Portable Company File

4. Click *Save*.

5. In the *Close and reopen* message box, click *OK*.

   QuickBooks closes all the open windows and creates the portable file.

6. In the message box that tells you where QuickBooks has saved the portable file, click *OK*.

    The program reopens its windows and you can resume working on your company file. The file extension for a portable file is .qbm, such as *sample_portable_file.qbm*. That way, you can identify a portable file even if it doesn't contain the word "portable" in its name.

Restoring a Portable Company File

Here are the steps to restoring a portable company file to a regular QuickBooks company file:

Computer Practice

1. On the *File* menu, choose *Open or Restore Company*.

2. In the *Open or Restore Company* dialog box, select the *Restore a portable file* option, as shown in Figure 1-4, and then click *Next*.

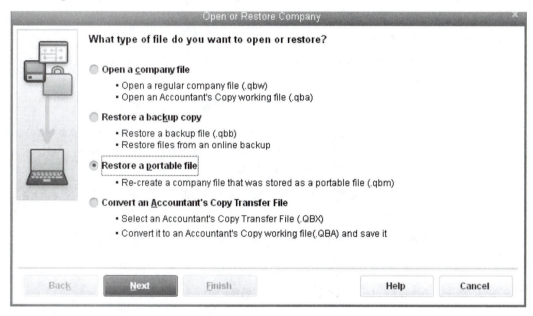

Figure 1-4 Restore a Portable Company File

3. In the *Open Portable Company File* dialog box, navigate to the folder that contains the portable company file that you want to restore.

    If you don't know where this book's portable company files are located on your computer, ask your instructor.

4. In the file list, click the file you want to restore *sample_product-based business 2015 (Portable). qbm*. Or, if you are using QuickBooks 2014, restore *sample_product-based business 2014 (Portable).qbm.*, and then click *Open*.

    The next screen tells you that you need to choose where you want to store the company file that QuickBooks creates from the portable company file. Click *Next*.

5. In the *Save Company File as* dialog box, shown in Figure 1-5, navigate to the folder where you want to restore the file.

    If you don't know where to restore the file, ask your instructor.

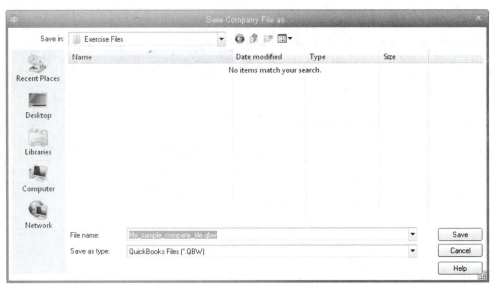

Figure 1-5 Choose Location to Restore File

6. In the *File name* box, edit the file name if you want to use a different file name for the restored file, such as adding "*_Restored*" to the name. Then, click *Save*.

   If QuickBooks asks you to update your company file, click *Yes*.

   While QuickBooks restores the portable company file to a regular company file, the *Working* message box shows the restoration progress. (If you restore a sample file, you must first click *OK* in the sample file *QuickBooks Information* message box.)

7. When the process is complete, click *OK* in the message box that tells you the portable company file has been opened successfully.

Now, your company file is open and ready for you to begin work.

Creating and Restoring Backup Files

Your financial information is important and you don't want to lose it. To prevent or minimize data loss, you should regularly back up your company files. Although you may back up all the data on your computer with dedicated backup software, you can also create backup files within QuickBooks as an added level of security. For example, if you spend several hours on a task, you can create a backup file immediately to protect your data until your nightly system backup runs. That way, if your computer's hard drive fails or another disaster occurs, you can restore your backup to another computer and resume your work. You can also set up scheduled backups within QuickBooks.

Note: Don't create portable company files to use as backup files. Backup files contain more information about your company than portable files do.

Creating a Backup File

You can back up a company file immediately or set up a backup schedule so QuickBooks automatically creates your backups on the days and times you specify.

To create a backup, follow these steps:

1. On the *File* menu, choose *Create Copy*.

2. In the *Save Copy or Backup* window (see Figure 1-3), choose *Backup copy*, and then click *Next*.

3. On the next screen, choose the *Local backup* option to store the backup file on your computer, a network drive, or a removable storage device, such as a DVD or USB flash drive. Click *Next*.

   If you subscribe to Intuit's fee-based online backup service, select the *Online backup* option.

4. In the *Backup Options* dialog box, shown in Figure 1-6, click *Browse*.

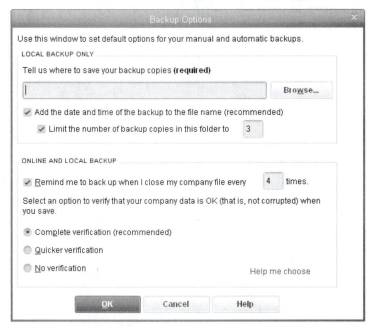

Figure 1-6 Backup Options

5. In the *Browse for Folder* dialog box, select the folder where you want to store your backup file (see Figure 1-7). Click *OK*.

   Store backup files in a safe location, ideally on a drive other than the one that contains your working company file. That way, if your company file is damaged *and* your hard drive fails, you can still recover your data from your backup file.

Figure 1-7 Backup Location

6. In the *Backup Options* dialog box, click *OK*.

7. In the *Create Backup* screen, shown in Figure 1-8, you can create an immediate backup or set up a backup schedule. To set up a schedule, select the *Only schedule future backups* option, and then click *Next*.

    To save a backup immediately, select the *Save it now* option, and then click *Finish*. When the backup is complete, you see the *QuickBooks Information* message box that tells you the filename and folder location for the backup.

Figure 1-8 Setting up a Backup Schedule

8. In the *Save Copy or Backup* screen, click *New* below the *Back Up on a Schedule* table, shown in Figure 1-9.

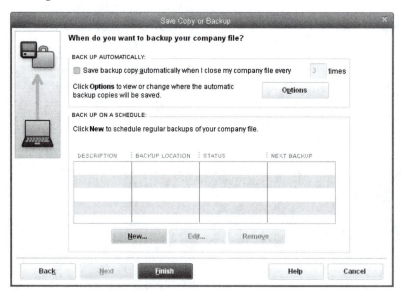

Figure 1-9 Create a Backup Schedule

9. In the *Schedule Backup* dialog box (Figure 1-10), type a name for the backup schedule, such as Nightly or Weekly. Click *Browse* to select the backup folder.

10. In the *Start time* boxes, choose the time when you want QuickBooks to create the backup file. Turn on the day checkboxes to specify which days you want the program to create a backup.

11. After you specify the schedule settings, click *OK* to close the *Schedule Backup* dialog box.

Figure 1-10 Defining the Backup Schedule

12. In the *Store Windows Password* window that opens, type your Windows username and password, and then click *OK*.

    The new schedule appears in the *Back Up on a Schedule* table.

13. In the *Save Copy or Backup* dialog box, click *Finish*. In the message box that tells you the backups have been scheduled, click *OK*.

Your backup schedule is ready. When the next day and time that you designated arrives, QuickBooks creates a backup file of your company file. The file extension for QuickBooks backup files is .qbb, for example, *sample_file_backup.qbb*.

Restoring a Backup File

If you need to restore a QuickBooks backup file, follow these steps:

1. On the *File* menu, choose *Open or Restore Company*.

2. In the *Open or Restore Company* dialog box, select the *Restore a backup copy* option, and then click *Next*.

3. On the next *Open or Restore Company* screen, select the *Local backup* option, and then click *Next*.

    If you want to restore a backup file created through Intuit's fee-based online backup service, select the *Online backup* option instead.

4. In the *Open Backup Copy* window, navigate to the folder that contains the backup file you want to restore. Select the file in the list, and then click *Open*.

    The next screen tells you that you have to choose the location where you want to restore the file. Click *Next*.

5. In the *Save Company File As* dialog box, navigate to the folder where you want to restore the file.

    Choose a folder such as the folder for all working company files or a folder for a specific client's company file.

6. If you don't want to overwrite your existing company file, in the *File name* box, be sure to edit the file name.

> Tip: If you aren't sure whether you should overwrite a file, edit the restored file's name. For example if you change the restored file name from *sample_company_file.qbw* to *sample_company_file_restored.qbw*, QuickBooks won't overwrite your original file.

7. Click *Save*.

    QuickBooks restores the backup file as a regular company file in the folder you specified. The restored file has a file extension of .qbw, such as *sample_company_file_restored.qbw*.

8. If a *Confirm Save As* message box warns you that a file already exists and asks if you want to replace it, QuickBooks is asking if you want to overwrite the existing company file. If you don't want to overwrite your working company file, click *No*. Back in the *Save Company File* as dialog box, change the name in the *File name* box, and then click *Save*.

    If your original company file is damaged and you want to replace it, click *Yes*. In the *Delete Entire File* dialog box, type *YES* in the text box to confirm that you want to delete the file. Then, click *OK*.

After the backup file is restored to a company file, a message box tells you the file has been restored successfully.

Touring the QuickBooks User Interface

QuickBooks has several features that help you get to the tasks you want to perform or view the information you need. The *Home Page*, QuickBooks Centers, menus, the icon bar, and shortcut keys provide easy access to bookkeeping tasks, regardless where you are in the program. At the same time, QuickBooks Centers, *Snapshots*, the *Insights* page, and the *Calendar* show financial information in various ways. As you work, you might end up with several QuickBooks windows open at the same time. You can manage these windows to make your work easier. This section introduces these features, so you can work productively in QuickBooks.

The Home Page

The QuickBooks *Home Page* (Figure 1-11) shows the overall workflow of your bookkeeping tasks. Tasks related to purchasing appear in the *Vendors* pane; sales-related tasks are in the *Customers* pane; and employee tasks show up in the *Employees* pane. Workflow arrows between task icons show the typical sequence of performing bookkeeping tasks, but you don't have to perform the tasks in that order or use every icon that appears.

The *Home Page's Company* and *Banking* sections include other features you use frequently, such as *Chart of Accounts* in the *Company* section and *Write Checks* in the *Banking* section.

The icons that appear on the *Home Page* depend on the preferences you chose when you created your company file. For example, the *Employees* panel won't appear if you told QuickBooks you don't have employees. Other settings determine whether you see icons, such as *Purchase Orders* or *Sales Receipts*.

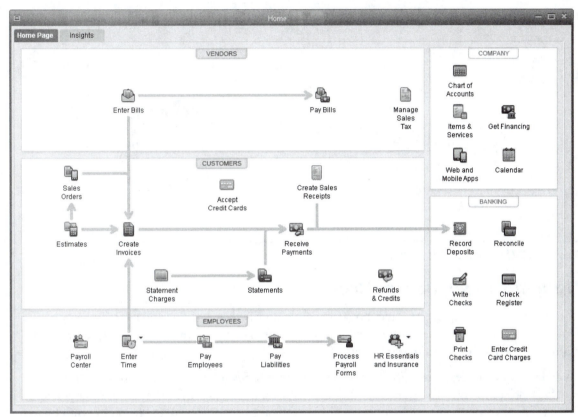

Figure 1-11 The Home Page

The Insights Tab

The *Insights* tab (new in QuickBooks 2015) appears to the right of the *Home Page* tab at the *Home Page* window's top-left corner. The *Insights* tab (Figure 1-12) provides a high-level view of the company's financial activity. Initially, the top panel displays a *Profit & Loss* graph that shows income, expenses, and profit by month. Click the left or right arrow on either side of the panel to display other high-level graphs, such as *Top Customers by Sales*.

The bottom half of the tab displays information about income and expenses. The colored bars in the *Income* section show the totals for unpaid invoices, overdue invoices, and payments received in the past 30 days. The *Expenses* pie chart helps identify your most prevalent expenses.

You can look at details by clicking within the *Insights* graphs. For example, clicking a month's bar in the *Profit & Loss* graph runs a *Profit & Loss Detail* report for that month. Click a horizontal bar in the *Income* section to open *Income Tracker* to that category of invoice.

Figure 1-12 The Insights Tab

Using the Menu Bar and Icon Bar

The menu bar at the top of the QuickBooks main window is always visible and contains every QuickBooks feature. But the *Favorites* menu and the icon bar are two methods for keeping your most frequently-used features within easy reach.

To add your favorite features to the *Favorites* menu, choose *Favorites*, and then choose *Customize Favorites*. Select an entry you want to add to the *Favorites* menu, and then click *Add*. After you add items to the *Favorites* menu, you can access them by choosing *Favorites* on the menu bar, and then choosing the entry you want.

The icon bar, which appears on the left side of the QuickBooks' main window, makes it easy to access the programs features. Initially, it contains shortcuts to popular windows, such as *Income Tracker*, QuickBooks Centers (labeled Customers, Vendors, and Employees), *Create Invoices* (labeled Invoice), and *Enter Bills* (labeled Bill).

You can streamline your work by adding your favorite features to the *My Shortcuts* section of the icon bar. You can also remove entries or rearrange the order in which the shortcuts appear.

To learn how to customize the icon bar, search *QuickBooks Help* for *icon bar*, and then choose the *Use the Icon Bar* topic.

QuickBooks Centers

QuickBooks Centers (Customer, Vendor, Employee, and so on) provide quick access to common tasks and information. You can view and create transactions, such as invoices in the *Customer Center* (Figure 1-13) and bills in the *Vendor Center*. Each center also displays information, such as names and addresses, contact, to-do items, notes, and more.

The *Customer*, *Vendor*, and *Employee Centers* have two tabs on the left:

- The first tab (*Customers & Jobs*, *Vendors*, or *Employees* depending on which center you open) contains the corresponding *Name* list. You can click an entry in this list to view and edit information about that customer, vendor, or employee. For example, you can look at a customer's transactions, review notes added to the customer's record, and then look up contact information to give the customer a call. (If your company has turned on payroll, the *Employee Center* also contains a separate tab for the *Payroll Center*.)

- The *Transactions* tab lists the transaction types related to the center, such as Invoices, Sales Receipts, and Received Payments in the *Customer Center*, and Bills and Bill Payments in the *Vendor Center*. This tab is helpful when you want to view transactions for all customers, vendors, or employees.

> Note: You can customize the information that appears in centers. For example, you can filter the customer list on the *Customers & Jobs* tab to show only customers with open balances. Or you can filter a customer's transactions to show only open invoices for this fiscal year.

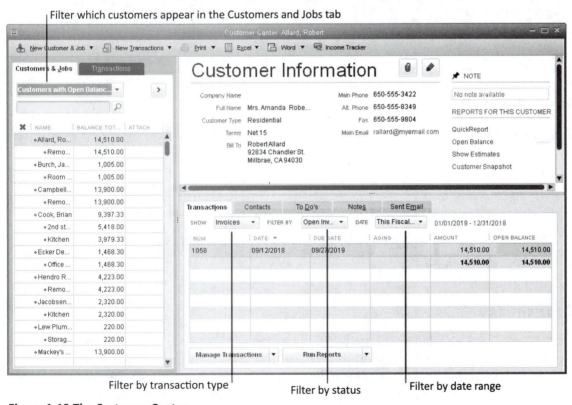

Figure 1-13 The Customer Center

Income Tracker

The *Income Tracker* window (Figure 1-14) displays a high-level view of income as well as the transactions that contribute to the totals you see. At the top of the window, horizontal bars display totals for unbilled income, open invoices, overdue invoices, and customer payments during the past 30 days. The table below the bars lists income transactions. You can filter the list by clicking one of the bars at the top. For example, clicking the *Overdue* box filters the table to show only overdue invoices. You can also filter by clicking the drop-down lists immediately above the table.

In addition, you can take action on transactions in the table. For example, click the down arrow in an open invoices *Action* cell and you can choose to receive payment on that invoice, print the row, or email the row.

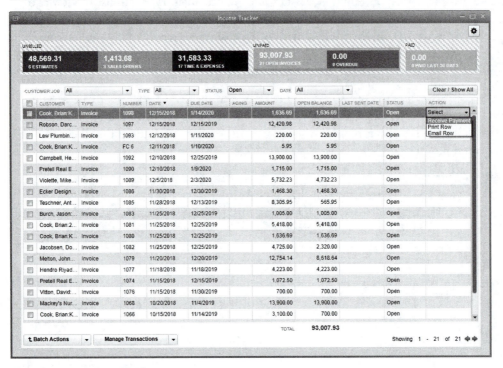

Figure 1-14 Income Tracker

Computer Practice

1. In the icon bar, click *Income Tracker*.

2. In the *Income Tracker* window, click the *Open Invoices* bar at the top of the window.

3. Click the *Action* cell for one of the invoices, and then choose *Receive Payment*.

4. Close the *Receive Payment* window by clicking the X at the window's top right.

5. Close the *Income Tracker* window.

Snapshots

The *Company Snapshot* window (Figure 1-15) summarizes various aspects of your company's finances, like income and expense trends, account balances, customers who owe you money, best-selling items, expense breakdown, and reminders. To open the *Company Snapshot* window, on the *Company* menu, choose *Company Snapshot* or click the *Snapshots* entry in the icon bar. Then, click the *Company*, *Payments*, or *Customer* tab to display overall company info, Accounts Receivable and payment info, or customer info, respectively.

You can choose the views you want to see. To add or remove views on a tab, click the tab, and then click *Add Content*.

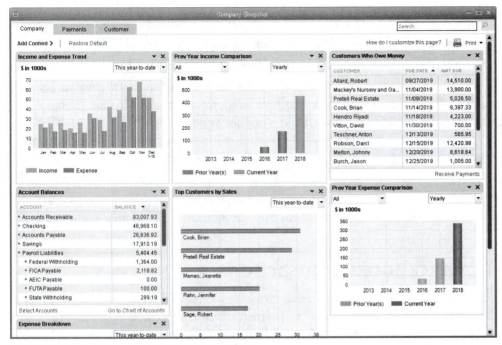

Figure 1-15 The Company Snapshot Window

Calendar

The *Calendar* window (see Figure 1-16) shows when transactions and to-dos were recorded or are due. (The *Entered* date is the transaction date entered in the transaction form, not the date that someone created the transaction.) You can use the *Calendar* to see which to-dos are coming up or are past due. You can also view past due or almost due transactions. To open the *Calendar*, in the icon bar, click *Calendar*, or on the *Company* menu, choose *Calendar*.

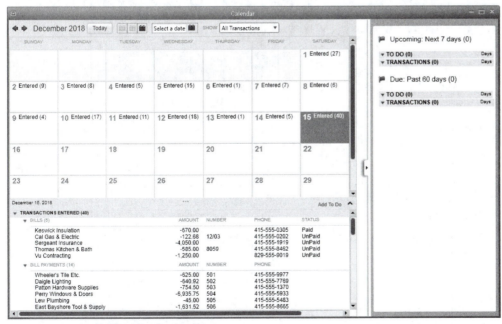

Figure 1-16 The Calendar Window

Working with Windows

You can set up QuickBooks to display one window at a time (on the *View* menu, choose *One Window*). If you do that, each window you open appears in front of the other open windows.

If you want to keep windows open to make them easy to access or you need to compare values between two windows, you can tell QuickBooks to display multiple windows (on the *View* menu, choose *Multiple Windows*). Multiple windows in QuickBooks work like windows in other programs. Click a window to bring it to the front. Click the buttons at the window's upper right to minimize, maximize, or close it. Drag the title bar to reposition it. Drag its edges or corners to resize it.

Whether you use one window or multiple windows, you can switch between windows from the menu bar (choose *Window*, and then choose the name of the window you want to look at). You can also click *Open Windows* in the middle section of the icon bar, and then click the window you want.

Introducing QuickBooks Transactions

In QuickBooks, transactions document your financial activities: buying and selling products and services, paying bills, invoicing customers, depositing payments, writing checks, and so on. This section provides a brief introduction to the QuickBooks features you use to record transactions. You'll learn how to record different types of transactions in the remaining chapters of this book.

Transaction Forms

QuickBooks forms look much like their corresponding paper forms. Here's an example of the form you use to record a bill from a vendor (Figure 1-17).

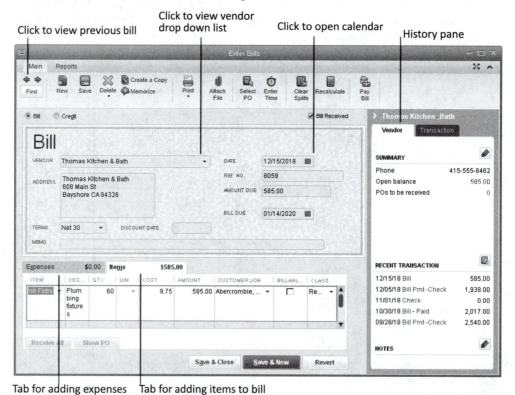

Figure 1-17 The Enter Bills Window

Computer Practice

Follow these steps to explore this form:

1. On the *Home Page*, click *Enter Bills*.

2. In the *Enter Bills* window, click the left arrow at the window's top-left corner to display the previous bill that was entered.

3. Click the down arrow in the *Vendor* box to display the vendor drop-down list.

4. Click the calendar icon next to the *Date* box to view the calendar.

5. If you make any changes to the bill, click *Revert* to undo those changes.

6. Close the *Enter Bills* window.

When you record a transaction in a QuickBooks transaction window, the program does the accounting for you in the background. For example, when you record a bill, QuickBooks updates your accounts payable account to show how much you owe the vendor. Then when you pay the bill, QuickBooks reduces the amount in the accounts payable account and vendor balance to reflect the payment you made. It increases the appropriate expense account to show what you spent money on.

> Tip: On the transaction window's right, the *History* section provides a summary of recent activity related to this vendor or customer. For example, click the link shown in blue text to the right of the *Open balance* label to see the transactions that contribute to your open balance with the vendor. In the *Recent Transactions* list, click the blue link to open the transaction in its corresponding transaction window.

Lists

QuickBooks lists can help you work quickly and accurately. By picking from lists instead of typing, you can enter values quickly and consistently. And when you fill in fields when you create a customer, vendor, employee, or other record, QuickBooks automatically pulls that information into the transactions you create. For example, when you choose a vendor in the *Enter Bills* window, the program fills in the name, address, payment terms, and other values from the vendor record (as shown in Figure 1-17).

Some lists appear on the *Lists* menu, such as the *Chart of Accounts List*, *Item List*, *Terms List*, and *Price Level List*. To open a list window for one of these lists, on the *Lists* menu, choose the list you want. (A few lists are one level deeper. To open these lists, on the *Lists* menu, choose *Customer & Vendor Profile Lists*, and then choose the list you want.) The *Customer & Job List*, *Vendor List*, and *Employee List* appear in their respective centers (see page 15).

Accounts

Accounts come in various types to track your business finances: what you earn, what you spend, how much you owe to others, how much others owe you, and so on. The chart of accounts is a list of all the accounts you use to categorize your finances.

The *Chart of Accounts* is initially sorted by account number if you turn on account numbers (see Figure 1-18). Typical account numbering groups different types of accounts within number ranges. The *Balance Total* column shows balances for accounts that appear on the Balance Sheet: asset, liability, and equity accounts (except for Retained Earnings).

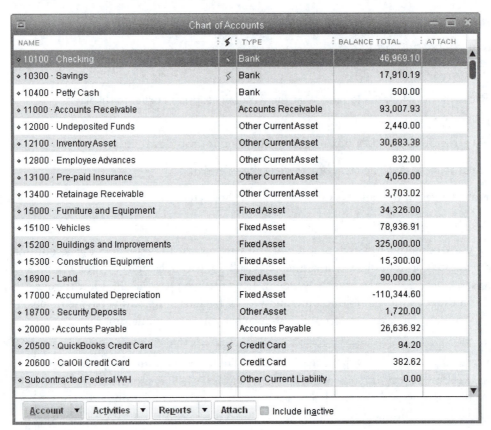

NAME	⚡	TYPE	BALANCE TOTAL	ATTACH
◆ 10100 · Checking	✓	Bank	46,969.10	
◆ 10300 · Savings	⚡	Bank	17,910.19	
◆ 10400 · Petty Cash		Bank	500.00	
◆ 11000 · Accounts Receivable		Accounts Receivable	93,007.93	
◆ 12000 · Undeposited Funds		Other Current Asset	2,440.00	
◆ 12100 · Inventory Asset		Other Current Asset	30,683.38	
◆ 12800 · Employee Advances		Other Current Asset	832.00	
◆ 13100 · Pre-paid Insurance		Other Current Asset	4,050.00	
◆ 13400 · Retainage Receivable		Other Current Asset	3,703.02	
◆ 15000 · Furniture and Equipment		Fixed Asset	34,326.00	
◆ 15100 · Vehicles		Fixed Asset	78,936.91	
◆ 15200 · Buildings and Improvements		Fixed Asset	325,000.00	
◆ 15300 · Construction Equipment		Fixed Asset	15,300.00	
◆ 16900 · Land		Fixed Asset	90,000.00	
◆ 17000 · Accumulated Depreciation		Fixed Asset	-110,344.60	
◆ 18700 · Security Deposits		Other Asset	1,720.00	
◆ 20000 · Accounts Payable		Accounts Payable	26,636.92	
◆ 20500 · QuickBooks Credit Card	⚡	Credit Card	94.20	
◆ 20600 · CalOil Credit Card		Credit Card	382.62	
◆ Subcontracted Federal WH		Other Current Liability	0.00	

Account ▼   Activities ▼   Reports ▼   Attach   ☐ Include inactive

Figure 1-18 The Chart of Accounts

Items

QuickBooks items help you track what you buy and sell. You also create items for other things you add to sales forms, like discounts, shipping charges, and subtotals. If you use QuickBooks sales transactions like invoices and sales receipts, you have to create items. The only way you can fill in an invoice or sales receipt in QuickBooks is by adding items to the transaction. Because every business is different, you can create items for the products and services you sell.

Items link what you buy and sell with the accounts in your chart of accounts. QuickBooks uses those links to automatically create accounting entries to go with the transactions you record. When you create an item, you tell QuickBooks all about it: what the item is, what you pay for it, the price you sell it for, and the accounts you use to track the corresponding income, expense, and so on. For example, in the *Item List* shown in Figure 1-19, the Cabinet Pulls item is linked to the Materials Income account in the Chart of Accounts. Whenever you add that item to an invoice, QuickBooks increases the value in the Materials Income account by the amount of the sale.

Items also make it easy to analyze your business in different ways. You can set up items to track income and expenses to the level of detail you want.

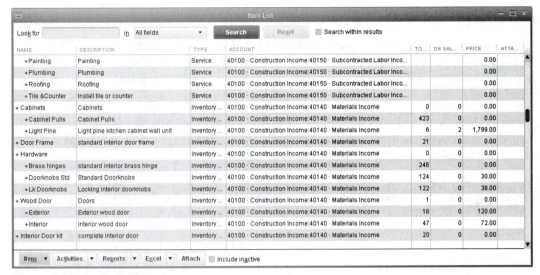

Figure 1-19 The Item List

Computer Practice

1. To open the *Item List*, on the *Home Page*, click *Item & Services* in the *Company* section. Alternatively, on the *Lists* menu, choose *Item List*.

2. To edit the Cabinet Pulls item, double-click it.

3. In the *Edit Item* window (Figure 1-20), click the down arrow in the *Income Account* field. This item is linked to the Materials Income account.

4. Close the *Edit Item* and *Item List* windows.

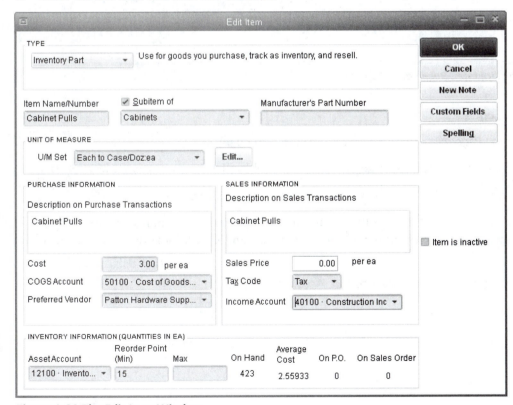

Figure 1-20 The Edit Item Window

Registers

Asset, liability, and equity accounts have registers that work just like the paper checkbook register you use to track the checks you write and deposits you make. When you open the QuickBooks register for an account, you see all the transactions for that account, like the *Accounts Receivable* register shown in Figure 1-21.

This register shows information about customer invoices: the invoice date, the date it's due, the customer name, and the amount. It also shows payments you've received against your invoices and any other transactions that affect the amount customers owe.

Figure 1-21 The Accounts Receivable Register

Computer Practice

1. On the *Home Page*, click *Chart of Accounts* (in the *Company* section).

2. To open the *Accounts Receivable* account register, double-click it in the account list.

3. Close the register window by clicking the X at the top-right corner.

4. In the *Charts of Accounts* list, scroll down to the Income accounts. Double-click the Design Income account. Because this is not a balance sheet account, QuickBooks displays a report (Figure 1-22).

5. Close the report window and the *Chart of Accounts* window.

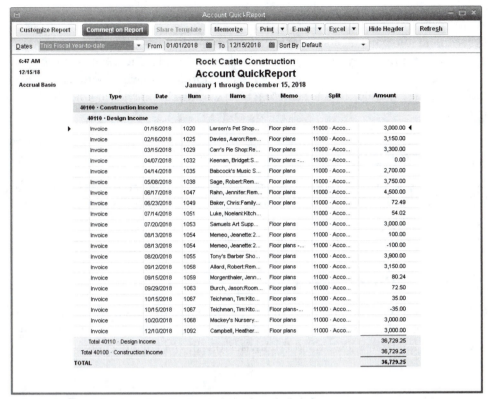

Figure 1-22 QuickReport for the Design Income Account

QuickBooks Help and Support

QuickBooks provides help and support in several ways. QuickBooks Help is available on your computer, but it also connects to the Internet. When you open the *Help* window, QuickBooks displays help topics based on what you did in the program recently. You can also type questions or keywords, and QuickBooks will search for relevant answers within Help and the Intuit Community.

> Note: Intuit Community is Intuit's QuickBooks community message board. You can ask a question, and the program looks for answers from other QuickBooks users. If none of the answers solve your problem, you can post your question to the community. (As you learn more about QuickBooks, you can post *your* answers to other people's questions.)

QuickBooks Help includes explanations of concepts and how to apply QuickBooks to your business situation. It also includes step-by-step instructions for performing tasks.

To access QuickBooks Help, you can use any of the following methods:

- Press the *F1* key on your keyboard.

- From the *Help* menu, choose *QuickBooks Help*.

- In the search box at the top of the left icon bar, type a search value, click the down arrow, choose *Help* in the drop-down list, and then click the magnifying glass icon.

> Tip: You can also use your favorite Internet search engine to look for answers to your questions.

Quick Start Center

The *Quick Start Center* (on the *Help* menu, choose *Quick Start Center*) includes a few of the most commonly used QuickBooks features, so you can get up and running quickly. The *Track money in* section on the left has icons for creating invoices, entering sales receipts, and viewing customers. The *Track money out* section on the right has icons for entering bills, writing checks, viewing the check register, and viewing vendors.

QuickBooks Learning Center

If you like to see how things work, the *QuickBooks Learning Center* offers interactive video tutorials for common business situations, such as adding customers, adding products and services you sell, creating an invoice, entering and paying bills, and so on. If the *Learning Center* doesn't open when you launch QuickBooks, on the *Help* menu, choose *Learning Center Tutorials*.

Certified QuickBooks ProAdvisors

If you want help from an expert, consider hiring a Certified QuickBooks ProAdvisor. These people are independent accountants, bookkeepers, consultants, and trainers who have passed tests demonstrating their proficiency in QuickBooks. To find a Certified ProAdvisor, on the *Help* menu, choose *Find a Local QuickBooks Expert*.

A Brief Introduction to Accounting

You can use QuickBooks even if you don't have an accounting background. However, understanding accounting basics and common business terminology has several advantages: learning QuickBooks will go a lot faster; you'll be more productive working in QuickBooks; your books will be more accurate; and you'll be able to manage your business more effectively.

What Accounting Does

Accounting comprises recording transactions and classifying financial results so you can produce reports that accurately convey an organization's financial state: is the company making or losing money, and by how much? Accounting reports help company management, investors, creditors, and government agencies assess the company's financial health. The key to these assessments is the relationship between assets (what the company owns), liabilities (its debts), and the difference between them (called equity or net worth).

The equation that defines this relationship (called the Accounting Equation) is:

Assets – Liabilities = Equity

> Note: The Balance Sheet report (which you'll learn about in a moment) gets its name from this equation, because assets, liabilities, and equity must remain in balance.

Understanding Accounts

In accounting, you track money with accounts, just like you keep track of your ready cash, savings, and retirement funds in your checking, saving, and IRA accounts at financial institutions. The difference is that accounting uses several types of accounts to track different types of income, expense, assets, and liabilities. The chart of accounts is a list of all the accounts you use to categorize your finances.

Accounts come in two primary categories:

- **Balance sheet accounts,** such as checking, accounts receivable, and fixed asset, get their name because these accounts have balances, like the balance in your personal checking account.

- **Accounts without balances,** such as income and expense accounts, are used to categorize money for reporting purposes, like the reports you might get from your bank showing the interest you earned during the year.

QuickBooks has account types for all the standard account types used in accounting. The following sections provide a quick introduction to the different account types used in accounting and what they represent:

Assets

Asset accounts track what you own and what other people owe you. The following are the asset account types used in accounting:

- **Bank:** Accounts held at a financial institution, such as checking, savings, or money market.

- **Accounts Receivable:** This is the money that your customers owe you, such as open invoices.

- **Other Current Asset:** This type represents assets that you'll use (or convert to cash) within 12 months, such as prepaid expenses or an asset you're planning to sell.

- **Fixed Asset:** These are assets that depreciate, like equipment or buildings.

- **Other Asset:** If an asset doesn't fall into the other current asset or fixed asset category, it's an other asset.

Liabilities

Liabilities are what your company owes to others. The following are the liability account types used in accounting:

- **Accounts Payable:** This represents money you owe, such as what you owe to vendors.

- **Credit Card:** This is simply an account type for your real-world credit card accounts.

- **Other Current Liability:** Money you owe in the next 12 months, such as sales tax.

- **Long Term Liability:** Money you owe after the next 12 months, like mortgage payments.

Equity

As the Accounting Equation shows, equity is the difference between what you own (your assets) and what you owe (your liabilities). In other words, if you sold all your assets today and used that money to settle your liabilities, the leftover money is your equity.

Equity comes from three sources:

- Money invested in the company by its owners

- Net profit from operating the business during the current accounting period

- Retained earnings, or net profits, from earlier periods that haven't been distributed to the owners

Owners can withdraw money from the company, called owners' draws or shareholders' distributions, depending on the type of company. These withdrawals reduce the equity in the company.

Accounts without balances

Income and expense accounts track money you earn or spend over a specific time frame, such as month, quarter, or year. These accounts appear in the Profit and Loss report (also known as an Income Statement). The following are the account types used in accounting that don't have balances:

- **Income:** This type of account tracks revenue you generate from your primary business, such as performing services or selling products.

- **Cost of Goods Sold:** The cost of products and materials originally held in inventory that you have sold. This type of account can also represent other costs related to sales, such as money you pay subcontractors to perform work for your customers.

- **Expense:** Money you spend running your business.

- **Other Income:** Income that comes from sources other than your primary business operations, such as interest income.

- **Other Expense:** Money you pay for things outside of your primary business operations, like interest you pay.

- **Non-posting Account:** QuickBooks non-posting accounts don't have balances and the totals in them don't appear on reports. These accounts come into play for money that you haven't earned or spent yet, such as estimates you've provided to customers or purchase orders you've issued to vendors.

Double-Entry Accounting

Double-entry accounting is the name for tracking where money comes from and where it goes to in every transaction in your company records. Each account in the chart of accounts has transactions that increase its balance and other transactions that decrease its balance. At the same time, in each transaction, money comes from one or more accounts and that money moves into one or more accounts. These two transaction components are called *debit* and *credit*. For example, when you record a bill for services you receive from a vendor, the bill adds a debit to an expense account (which increases its balance) and a credit to the Accounts Payable account (a liability account, so it increases what you owe), as shown in (Figure 1-23). Debits and credits have different effects on different types of accounts, as Table 1-1 shows. Debits and credits aren't inherently bad or good. They simply increase or decrease balances to make double-entry accounting work. With double-entry accounting, the total debits in a transaction must equal the total credits.

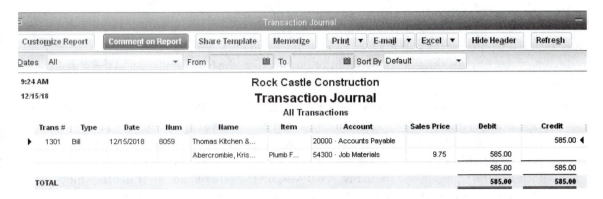

Figure 1-23 Transaction Debits and Credits

> Note: To view a transaction's debits and credits, open the transaction in its transaction window. Then, on the *Reports* menu, choose *Transaction Journal (Figure 1-23)*.

Account Type	Debit	Credit
Asset	Increases balance	Decreases balance
Liability	Decreases balance	Increases balance
Equity	Decreases balance	Increases balance
Income	Decreases balance	Increases balance
Expense	Increases balance	Decreases balance

Table 1-1 Debits and Credits

Cash versus Accrual Accounting

Companies can choose between two methods for tracking income and expenses: *cash basis* and *accrual basis*. In cash basis accounting, income and expenses aren't recognized until cash changes hands. For example, with cash basis accounting, you don't recognize income until you receive a payment, and you don't recognize expenses until you pay bills.

Accrual basis accounting uses a concept known as the *matching principle*, because it matches income with the corresponding expenses. With this method, income and expenses are recognized in the period in which transactions occur, not when money changes hands. For example, you recognize income when you record an invoice, not when you receive payment for the invoice. You recognize expenses when you enter a bill, not when you pay it. Accrual basis accounting provides a more accurate view of profitability because income and its corresponding expenses are associated with the same period.

> Note: IRS regulations prohibit some organizations from using the cash basis method of accounting. Check with your tax accountant to determine whether you should use cash basis or accrual basis accounting.

Financial Reports

Three financial reports are the mainstay for viewing and evaluating company financial performance: the income statement (also known as the Profit & Loss report), the balance sheet, and the statement of cash flows.

- The *income statement*, called a Profit & Loss report in QuickBooks, shows your income and expenses over a period of time. The name, Profit & Loss, is appropriate because this report also shows the difference between income and expenses, called net income, which represents your profit or loss for that period. When net income is positive (income exceeds expenses), it increases the equity in the company. A net loss, on the other hand, decreases the equity. For that reason, income and expense accounts indirectly affect company equity.

- The *balance sheet* represents a snapshot of the account equation: assets minus liabilities equals equity.

- The *statement of cash flows* shows the true amount of cash you have. The statement of cash flows removes noncash transactions, such as depreciation, from the picture. It categorizes cash in three ways: money earned or spent operating the business, investing in the company, or financing (such as debt or selling shares of stock).

Review Questions and Exercises

Select the best answer(s) for each of the following:

1. QuickBooks can help you track:

   a) Job costs

   b) What customers owe

   c) Payroll

   d) Personal finances

   e) All of the above

2. Which of the following statements is true?

   a) A debit decreases a liability account balance.

   b) Equity decreases if liabilities increase.

   c) In a transaction, the total debits must equal the total credits.

   d) A credit increases an asset account balance.

3. The equation that governs accounting is:

   a) Net income = Income - expenses

   b) Assets + Liabilities = Equity

   c) Assets – Liabilities = Equity

   d) Assets = Liabilities – Equity

4. Using cash basic accounting:

   a) Income is not recorded until the customer pays the invoice.

   b) Income and expenses are recognized when transactions are created.

   c) Income is recorded when you create an invoice.

   d) An expense is recorded when you pay a bill.

5. Which methods can you use to open transaction windows?

   a) The menu bar

   b) The Home Page

   c) The icon bar

   d) QuickBooks Centers

   e) All of the above

6. Which features help you view income?

   a) Income Tracker

   b) Company Snapshot

   c) The Customer Center

   d) The Vendor Center

   e) The Insights tab in the Home Page window

Introduction Exercise 1

Restore the sample file, *sample_product-based business 2015 (Portable).QBM.* (Or, if you are using QuickBooks 2014, restore *sample_product-based business 2014 (Portable).QBM.*)

1. Open the *Customer Center* by clicking *Customers* in the icon bar.

   a) What is the name of the first customer listed in the Customers & Jobs list?

   b) What is Robert Allard's total balance?

   c) Click Brian Cook's 2nd story addition job. On the *Transactions* tab in the bottom-right panel, click the *Show* down arrow and choose *All Transactions*. Click the *Date* dropdown list down arrow and choose *All*. How many transactions are there and what types are they?

   d) Close the *Customer Center*.

2. On the *Home Page*, click *Enter Bills*.

   a) At the upper-left corner of the *Enter Bills* window, click the previous button. What is the name of the vendor for the bill that appears?

   b) What is the amount due?

   c) What is the bill for?

   d) Close the *Enter Bills* window.

3. On the *Lists* menu, choose *Chart of Accounts* to display the *Chart of Accounts* window.

   a) What type of account is the Checking Account?

   b) How many other accounts are that same type?

   c) What is the Balance Total for the Accounts Receivable account?

   d) What is the Balance Total for the Design Income account?

   e) Close the *Chart of Accounts* window.

Introduction Exercise 2 (Advanced)

Restore the sample file, *sample_product-based business 2015 (Portable).QBM*. (Or, if you are using QuickBooks 2014, restore *sample_product-based business 2014 (Portable).QBM*.)

1. On the *Home Page*, click the *Customers* button to open the *Customer Center*.

   a) Click the *Transactions* tab on the left side of the window and then choose *Sales Receipts*. How many sales receipts are there for This Fiscal Year?

   b) What is the total amount of those sales receipts?

   c) Click the *Date* down arrow above the transaction table and choose *This Fiscal Quarter*. How many sales receipts are there and what is the total for those?

   d) Close the *Customer Center*.

2. On the *Vendors* menu, choose *Vendor Center* to open the *Vendor Center*.

   a) Double-click C.U. Electric to open the *Edit Vendor* window. What is the main phone number and address?

   b) Close the *Edit Vendor* window.

   c) What is the amount of earliest open bill for Daigle Lighting?

   d) Close the *Vendor Center*.

3. On the *Home Page*, click *Chart of Accounts* icon to open the *Chart of Accounts* window.

   a) What type of account is the Construction Equipment Account?

   b) How many accounts of type Bank are in the *Chart of Accounts*?

   c) How many accounts of type Fixed Asset are in the *Chart of Accounts*?

4. In the *Chart of Accounts* window, double-click the *Checking* account to open the *Checking account register* window.

   a) Who was the payee for the bill payment on 12/11/2018?

   b) What was the amount of the payment?

   c) What was the check number?

   d) Which vendor was paid by the last bill payment in the register?

   e) What is the amount of the last bill payment in the register?

   f) Close the *Checking account register* and *Chart of Accounts* windows.

5. On the *Home Page*, click *Enter Bills*, and then follow these steps:

   a) In the *Pay to the Order of* field, choose *McClain Appliances*.

   b) In the *Amount Due* field, type *80.00*.

   c) What is the city displayed in the *Address* field for McClain Appliances?

   f) Click *Clear*, and then close the *Enter Bills* window.

6. In the icon bar, click *Invoice*. In the *Create Invoices* window, click the *Previous* arrow at the top-left corner of the window.

   a) What is the invoice number?

   b) How many items appear in the invoice table?

   c) Close the *Create Invoices* window.

7. On the *Lists* menu, choose *Chart of Accounts*. In the *Chart of Accounts* window, double-click *Accounts Receivable*.

   a) What is the ending balance in the account?

   b) Who was the customer on the last transaction in the register?

   c) Close the register and the *Chart of Accounts* windows.

8. On the *Home Page*, click *Check Register* (in the *Banking* section).

   a) In the *Use Register* dialog box, choose *10400 – Petty Cash*, and then click *OK*.

   b) What is the ending balance in the register?

   c) Close the *Petty Cash register* window.

9. In the icon bar, click *Income Tracker*.

   a) What is the total for open invoices?

   b) What is the total for unbilled time and expenses?

   c) Click the *Open Invoices* box at the top of the window. Who is the customer for the first invoice in the list?

   d) Close the *Income Tracker* window.

10. Close the company file.

Chapter 2
Managing Expenses

Topics

This chapter covers the following topics:

- The Expenses Workflow
- Setting Up Vendors
- Turning On Class Tracking
- Entering Bills
- Paying for Expenses
- Printing Checks
- Handling Vendor Credits
- Viewing Accounts Payable

This chapter introduces you to tracking and managing company expenses in QuickBooks. It begins with an overview of the expenses workflow, from entering bills to paying them. After that, you'll learn how to set up records in QuickBooks for the vendors you work with. You can pay for expenses right away by writing a check or using a credit card. Alternatively, you can pay later by recording bills you receive and then paying them by their due dates (the money you owe vendors is called *Accounts Payable*). In this chapter, you'll learn how to record typical expense transactions, whether you pay immediately or enter bills and pay them later. This chapter also covers other expense-related tasks, such as tracking job costs and applying vendor credits. It concludes with ways to examine the status of your Accounts Payable.

> Note: Although sales tax agencies are vendors, this chapter doesn't cover paying sales taxes. Instead, Chapter 4 describes the QuickBooks sales tax process from setting up sales codes and items, to collecting sales tax from customers, to remitting sales taxes to the appropriate tax agencies. Similarly, this chapter doesn't cover purchase orders, even though you can use them to record orders for non-inventory items and services. Chapter 8, Inventory, describes working with purchase orders.

> Note: For the computer practice in this chapter, restore the sample file, *sample_product-based business 2015 (Portable).QBM*. (Or, if you are using QuickBooks 2014, restore *sample_product-based business 2014 (Portable).QBM*.)

The Expenses Workflow

QuickBooks offers numerous features for tracking and managing business expenses. In QuickBooks, you create vendor records for the vendors you purchase from in the real world. With your vendors in place, you can record expense transactions to track what you spend in detail. QuickBooks reports, the *Company Snapshot*, and the *Insights* page can help you control expenses and manage vendor relationships.

The *Home Page* window presents the expenses workflow graphically (Figure 2-1):

- **Purchase Order:** Some vendors require purchase orders to process orders. Purchase orders are non-posting transactions; they don't affect balances in your accounts. See Chapter 8, Inventory, to learn about purchase orders.

- **Enter Bills:** If you don't have to pay immediately, click this *Home Page* icon to record a bill in QuickBooks. When you record a bill, QuickBooks debits (increases) expense and credits (increases) Accounts Payable.

- **Pay Bills:** This step helps you pay the vendors you owe. When bills are due, QuickBooks can remind you to pay them. When you pay a bill, QuickBooks debits (decreases) Accounts Payable and credits (decreases) your checking account.

- **Write Checks and Print Checks:** If you pay for expenses right away, you can click the Home Page *Write Checks* icon to record checks you write. If you queue up checks to print in QuickBooks, click the *Print Checks* icon to start printing them. When you write a check, you don't use Accounts Payable. A check debits (increases) an expense account and credits (decreases) your checking account.

- **Enter Credit Card Charges:** Click this icon to record credit card transactions.

- **Check Register:** Click this icon to open the register window for any balance account in your Chart of Accounts, such as a checking, savings, or credit card account.

- **Vendors:** At the top of the *Vendors* panel is the *Vendors* button. Click this button to open the *Vendor Center* (Figure 2-2), where you can view information about your vendors and their transactions. You can add new vendors, record vendor transactions, and perform other vendor-related tasks from this center.

> Note: You can also access these features by choosing *Vendors* on the QuickBooks menu bar. In the *Vendor Center*'s menu bar, click *New Transactions* to access *Enter Bills* and *Pay Bills*.

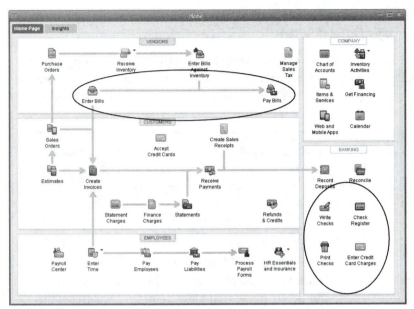

Figure 2-1 The Vendors panel of the Home Page

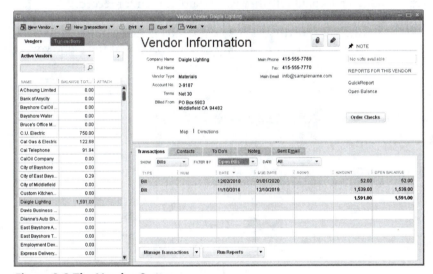

Figure 2-2 The Vendor Center

Setting Up Vendors

Vendors are the people and companies you purchase services and products from: the phone company, your landlord, the office supplies store, subcontractors, and sales tax agencies. Whether you pay for expenses by writing checks, charging on credit, or pay bills, you need vendors in QuickBooks to record those transactions.

Computer Practice

Here are the steps for setting up a vendor:

1. On the *Home Page*, click *Vendors* (or in the icon bar, click *Vendors*).

2. In the *Vendor Center's* menu bar, click *New Vendor*, and then choose *New Vendor*.

   The *New Vendor* window (Figure 2-3) opens.

3. In the *Vendor Name* field, type the vendor's name as you'd like it to appear in your *Vendors List*. For this exercise, type *Out of Sight Disposal Services*.

The *Vendor Name* field is an identifier for the vendor's record, so it can be the company name, a person's name, or a code, such as 31NG4. However, because QuickBooks fills in the *Vendors* list using values from *Vendor Name* fields, it's a good idea to use an easily recognized value, such as a company or person's name.

> Tip: If a vendor is also a customer, you must create both a vendor record and a customer record for that person or company. The names must be different. For example, you could name the vendor in this example *Out of Sight Disposal Services-Vend* and name the customer *Out of Sight Disposal Services-Cust*.

4. Skip the *Opening Balance* field and *As Of* field.

These fields appear when you first create a vendor record. However, filling in these fields is not the best way to record a vendor's open balance. If you do fill them in, QuickBooks records a bill that credits (increases) Accounts Payable and debits (increases) Uncategorized Expense, which means that you don't have detailed information about what you owe the vendor. Instead, define a vendor's open balance by recording each unpaid bill after you set up the vendor record.

5. In the *Address Info* tab's *Company Name* field, type the vendor's company name, if the vendor is an organization. If the vendor is an individual, you can skip this field or repeat the name you typed in the *Vendor Name* field.

6. Fill in the *Full Name* fields with the primary contact's name.

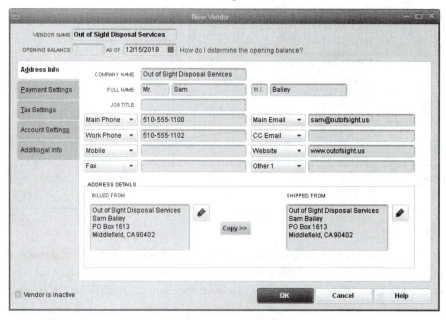

Figure 2-3 New Vendor window's Address Info tab filled in

7. Fill in the phone and email fields with the values shown in Figure 2-3.

8. In the *Billed From* box, add the vendor's address (see Figure 2-3).

9. To copy the address in the *Billed From* field into the *Shipped From* field, click the *Copy>>* button.

10. Click the *Payment Settings* tab (Figure 2-4) to enter payment-related information about this vendor.

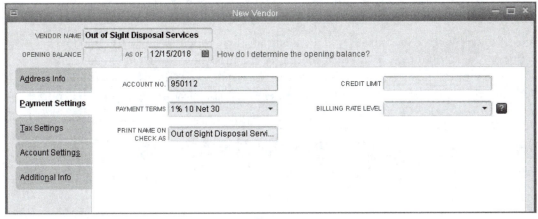

Figure 2-4 New Vendor window's Payment Settings tab filled in

11. In the *Account No.* field, type the account number that the vendor has assigned to your company. In this example, type *950112*.

    QuickBooks prints this field's value in a check's Memo field, so it's an easy way to add your account number to the checks you print to pay vendors.

12. In the *Payment Terms* drop-down list, choose the payments terms that the vendor has extended to your company. In this example, choose *1% 10 Net 30*.

    The QuickBooks *Terms* list contains various payment terms, which can be used for both customers and vendors. These terms can represent the number of days you have to pay or incorporate discounts for early payment. In this example, 1% 10 Net 30 means the bill is due within 30 days, but you receive a 1% discount if you pay within 10 days of the bill date. By filling in this field, you set the default payment terms for this vendor, that is, the terms that QuickBooks fills in automatically for each new bill you record for this vendor. You can override the default terms when you enter a vendor bill by choosing different terms from the *Terms* drop-down list. When you run Accounts Payable reports, QuickBooks takes into account each bill's terms. Chapter 7, Customizing QuickBooks, provides more information on setting up terms.

13. In the *Print Name on Checks As* field, type the vendor's name as you want it to appear on the checks you print.

    This field is helpful when vendors are individuals. You can set up an individual's Vendor Name as *Last Name, First Name*. In this field, you can type the individual's name *First Name Last Name*, so it prints the way names usually appear on checks.

    > Note: In this example, keep the *Credit Limit* field blank. If vendors limit your account balances with them, then fill in this field in their records with the maximum amount you owe. That way, QuickBooks can warn you when a purchase transaction exceeds your credit limit.

14. Click the *Tax Settings* tab (Figure 2-5) to fill in tax-related fields. In the *Vendor Tax ID* field, fill in the vendor's Tax ID, such as a Social Security number for an individual or FEIN (Federal Employer Identification Number) for a company.

QuickBooks prints the value in the *Vendor Tax ID* field on Form 1099-MISC forms that you create at the end of the year. To track the payments you make to a vendor so you can produce a Form 1099-MISC for them, turn on the *Vendor eligible for 1099* checkbox.

> Note: If QuickBooks is in multi-user mode, you must first switch to single-user mode to turn on the 1099 feature. To do that, on the *File* menu, choose *Switch to Single user Mode*. On the *Edit* menu, choose *Preferences*. In the *Preferences* window, click the *Tax: 1099* category on the left. On the *Company Preferences* tab, select the *Yes* option button for *Do you file 1099 MISC forms?*

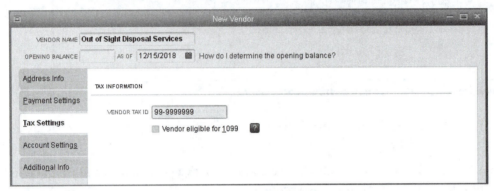

Figure 2-5 New Vendor window's Tax Settings tab filled in

14. Click the *Account Settings* tab (Figure 2-6) to specify default expense accounts you want Quick-Books to include in new transactions for this vendor. In this example, choose account *54500 Subcontractors*.

    If you choose accounts in these fields, QuickBooks automatically adds them to new transactions for this vendor. (You can change them in a bill, if necessary.) See page 42 in the Entering Bills section for another approach to filling in Account fields.

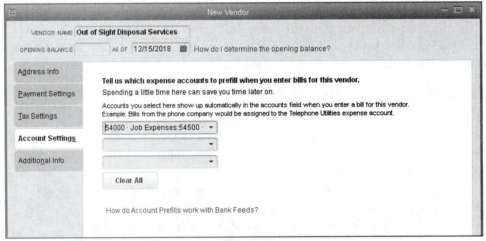

Figure 2-6 New Vendor window's Account Settings tab filled in

15. Click the *Additional Info* tab (Figure 2-7) to associate a vendor type to this vendor in the *Vendor Type* field, in this example, *Subcontractors*.

    The *Vendor Type* list helps you classify your vendors. For example, the sample file has vendor types such as Subcontractors, Utilities, Materials, and Tax agencies. If you choose a vendor type for each vendor you create, you can then run a report to see how much you spend with each vendor type.

16. If you assign custom fields to the *Vendor* list (click the *Define Fields* button at the *Custom Fields* section's bottom right), those fields appear in the *Custom Fields* section. Fill in a value if a custom field applies to this vendor. In this example, leave the custom field blank.

Figure 2-7 New Vendor window's Additional Info tab filled in

> Tip: For more information on setting up and using Custom Fields, see Chapter 7, Customizing QuickBooks.

17. Click *OK* to save the vendor record and close the *New Vendor* window.

Turning On Class Tracking

QuickBooks classes help you classify transactions that cut across multiple accounts in your chart of accounts; multiple customers, jobs, and vendors, or other categories like months. For example, you can use classes to track income and expenses by business unit, profit center, store location, partner, or monthly magazine issue. Class tracking might reduce the need for multiple accounts or subaccounts in your chart of accounts. You can generate reports for each class (without affecting your chart of accounts). So you could generate separate Profit & Loss reports for each partner in a business or each store location in a national chain. The product-based sample file used in this course includes three classes: Remodel, New Construction, and Overhead.

To turn on class tracking, do the following:

1. On the *Edit* menu, choose *Preferences*.

2. In the *Preferences* window, choose the *Accounting* category on the left, and then click the *Company Preferences* tab.

3. Turn on the *Use class tracking* checkbox (see Figure 2-8).

Figure 2-8 Turning on class tracking

4. Turn on the *Prompt to assign classes* checkbox.

    When you turn on this setting, QuickBooks will prompt you to fill in the *Class* field if you try to save a transaction without a class assigned.

5. Click *OK*.

    When you turn on QuickBooks' class-tracking feature, every transaction window includes a *Class* field (see Figure 2-9). For each transaction you record, you choose the class related to the income or expense.

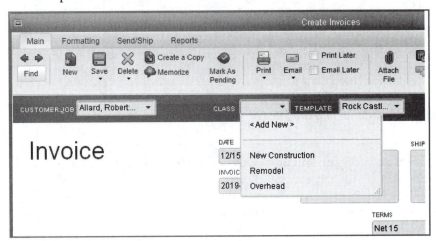

Figure 2-9 Class field in a transaction window

The *Profit & Loss by Class* report shows the income and expenses for each class. In Figure 2-10, the report shows income and expenses for new construction work, remodel work, and company overhead. The *Unclassified* column shows totals for transactions with no assigned class. (In Figure 2-10, the *Unclassified* column contains all zeroes, which is what you want to see. For more information about the *Profit & Loss by Class* report, see Chapter 6, Reports.)

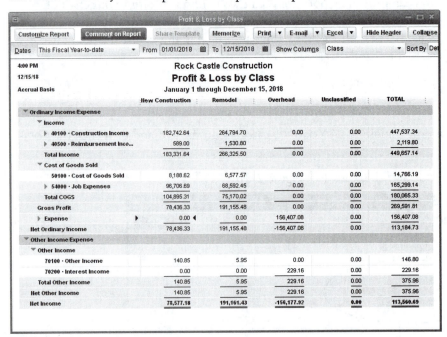

Figure 2-10 The Profit and Loss by Class report

Entering Bills

Entering bills to pay later has a couple of advantages. The most common reason for entering bills instead of paying right away is that it helps your cash flow: you don't pay out money until bills are due (unless you want to use an early payment discount). In addition, you can set aside time to pay bills and print your bill payment checks all at once. If you assign terms to your vendors, as you learned in the previous section, QuickBooks will tell you when bills are due. Using vendor bills is called *managing Accounts Payable* because your unpaid bills represent expense account balances you need to pay.

Computer Practice

To enter a bill, follow these steps:

1. On the *Vendors* menu, choose *Enter Bills*. Or click *Enter Bills* on the *Home Page*.

    Initially, QuickBooks selects the *Bill* option and turns on the *Bill Received* checkbox to indicate that you're creating a bill. You turn off the *Bill Received* checkbox only if you want to record inventory items you've received without an accompanying bill. (See Chapter 8 to learn about recording inventory receipts.) If you want to record a vendor credit, select the *Credit* option instead. (When you do, the *Bill Received* checkbox disappears.)

2. In the *Vendor* field, fill in the vendor's name, in this example, *Cali Copy Right*, and then press Tab.

3. QuickBooks displays the *Vendor Not Found* dialog box, because the vendor doesn't exist in the *Vendor List*. To add the vendor name to the list, click *Quick Add*.

    QuickBooks creates a new vendor record containing just the vendor name. You can edit the record later to add more information.

4. In the *Date* field, click the calendar icon, and then choose the date on the bill you received, in this example, *1/21/2019*.

5. In the *Amount Due* field, type the total on the bill you received, in this example, *450*.

6. Click the *Bill Due* field.

    Initially, QuickBooks fills in the *Bill Due* field with a date ten days later than the date in the *Date* field. You can change the date in the *Bill Due* field to match the due date on the bill you received. If the vendor record includes payment terms, QuickBooks uses those terms to calculate the bill's due date. For example, in the *Terms* field, choose *Net 30*. QuickBooks changes the *Bill Due* field to 2/20/2019. (When you save the bill, QuickBooks will ask you if you want to save the new Terms to the vendor's record.)

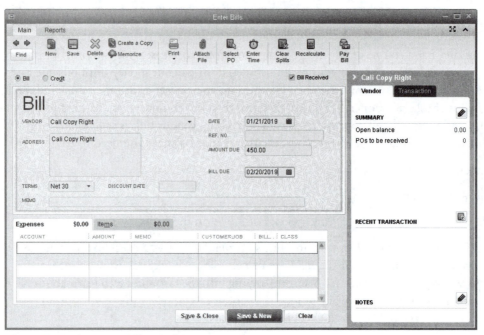

Figure 2-11 The Enter Bills window

7. On the *Expenses* tab, click the first *Account* cell. In the drop-down list, choose the expense account associated with the bill, such as *Printing and Reproduction*.

    If you click the *Account* cell's down arrow to display the drop-down list and then begin to type the account name or number, such as *Pri*, QuickFill completes the entry for you, and fills in *Printing and Reproduction*.

    > Tip: You can set a preference so QuickBooks automatically recalls your previous transactions (bills, checks, or credit card charges), filling in the accounts and values you used in the last transaction for a name. To activate this behavior, on the *Edit* menu, choose *Preferences*. In the *Preferences* window, choose *General* in the category list on the left. Turn on the *Automatically recall last transaction for this name* option.

8. Press Tab to move to the *Amount* cell.

9. Type *375* to change the amount from 450 to 375.

    QuickBooks automatically fills in the first *Amount* cell with the bill's total amount. If the bill applies to only one account, you can skip the *Amount* cell. In this example, the bill applies to two different accounts, *Printing and Reproduction* and *Postage*. The first line in the table specifies the expense for the first account, so you edit the value to reflect the amount associated with that account.

10. If the expense is associated with a customer or job, in the *Customer:Job* cell, choose that customer or job (in this example, *Babcock's Music Shop:Remodel*).

    QuickBooks automatically turns on the *Billable* checkbox to flag the expense as billable to the customer or job you selected. When you track billable expenses, you can easily add those expenses to the invoices you create, as described on page 271. And if you track billable expenses for jobs, the *Profit & Loss by Job* report (see page 171) displays income and expenses for each job.

11. If you use classes, in the *Class* cell, choose the class associated with this expense, in this example, *Remodel*.

12. Click the *Account* cell in the next row, choose the next account from the drop-down list, in this example, *Postage*, and then press Tab.

    QuickBooks automatically assigns the remainder of the bill amount ($75.00) to Postage.

13. If you use classes, in the *Class* cell, choose the class associated with this expense, such as *Overhead*.

    Figure 2-12 shows what the bill should look like.

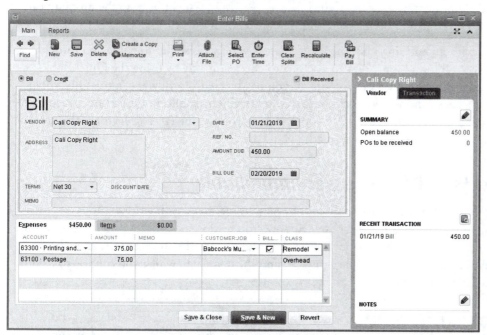

Figure 2-12 The Enter Bills window with a completed bill

14. Click *Save & Close* to record the bill.

    When you record the bill, QuickBooks credits (increases) the Accounts Payable account, because you owe the vendor money. It debits (increases) the expense accounts associated with the bill to show what you spent the money on.

15. If the *Information Changed* dialog box appears (in this example, the vendor's terms changed) and you want to save those changes to the vendor's record, click *Yes*. To use the changed values only in this bill, click *No*.

See the section, Paying Bills, to learn how to pay the bills you enter in QuickBooks.

Attaching Documents to Transactions

In QuickBooks, you can attach electronic copies of documents, such as scanned copies of bills or warranties, to transactions, such as bills or invoices. You can attach files from your computer, files that you scan, or files you store in QuickBooks' *Doc Center*. When you attach files to transactions, QuickBooks stores these files on your computer in a special folder structure. To attach a file to a transaction, click the *Attach File* button in a transaction window's ribbon.

Paying for Expenses

You can pay vendors in different ways and QuickBooks has features to help you with each one. You might set aside the bills that arrive each day without entering bills in QuickBooks. Then, at the end of the day, you can record several checks in QuickBooks, print them, and put them in the mail to your vendors. Or you might write a handwritten check to hand to the person who plows your parking lot. On the other hand, you might enter most of the bills you receive in QuickBooks so the program can notify you about early payment discounts and bills that are coming due.

If you write checks without entering bills, the *Write Checks* window is set up to guide you through entering all your payment information. You can also record checks quickly by using the QuickBooks *account register* window for your checking account. If you pay by credit card, you can use QuickBooks' *Enter Credit Card Charges* window to record those payments. Entering bills in QuickBooks records the details about what you owe to vendors. To pay your vendors, you use the *Pay Bills* feature. This section describes paying vendors using each of these methods.

Writing Checks to Pay Expenses Immediately

The *Write Checks* window makes it easy to fill in information for checks you write without corresponding bills entered in QuickBooks. The window's top section looks like a paper check, so you can fill it in without much help. The bottom half of the window includes the *Expenses* tab, which makes it easy to allocate a check to multiple accounts, and the *Items* tab, which you can use to record items (see page 212) you purchase.

> Note: Do not use the *Write Checks* window if you are paying sales tax, payroll taxes and liabilities, or bills that you entered previously. Instead, use the *Pay Sales Tax* window (on the *Vendors* menu, choose *Sales Tax*, and then choose *Pay Sales Tax* on the submenu) for a sales tax payment, *Pay Liabilities* (on the *Employees* menu, choose *Payroll Taxes & Liabilities*, and then choose *Pay Scheduled Liabilities* on the submenu) for payroll taxes, or the *Pay Bills* window (on the *Vendors* menu, choose *Pay Bills*) for paying Accounts Payable bills.

Computer Practice

To write a check, follow these steps:

1. To display the *Write Checks* window, in the *Home Page*'s *Banking* section, click *Write Checks* (or press Ctrl+W).

   The *Bank Account* field represents the account you write this check from. In this example, the account is *10100 Checking*. If you have more than one checking account and want to write a check from another account, choose it in the drop-down list.

2. QuickBooks fills in the *No.* field with the next check number in your check numbering sequence. If you're recording a handwritten check and the check number is correct, you can skip this field. If you want to print the check, in the *Write Checks* window's ribbon, turn on the *Print Later* checkbox.

   If you turn on the *Print Later* checkbox, QuickBooks replaces the check number value with the words *To Print*. When you print the checks queued up to print, QuickBooks assigns the check numbers.

3. The *Date* field is initially set to the current date. To change the date, click the calendar icon, and then choose the check date, in this example, *1/28/2019*.

4. In the *Pay to the Order of* field, click the down arrow and choose the payee in the drop-down list, in this example, *CalOil Company*.

   QuickBooks fills in the name and address if you entered them in the payee's record. (The payee can be a vendor, customer, employee, or name from the Other Names list.)

5. In the *$* field, type the check amount, in this example, *289.76*.

   > Tip: The AutoRecall feature fills in new transactions using accounts, amounts, classes, and so on from the previous transaction for a payee. This feature is a great shortcut when you have recurring payments that use the same accounts and amounts. To activate this behavior, on the *Edit* menu, choose *Preferences*. In the *Preferences* window, choose *General* in the category list on the left. Turn on the *Automatically recall last transaction for this name* option.

6. Click the first *Account* cell on the *Expenses* tab, and then choose the account associated with the check from the drop-down list, in this example, *65110 Gas and Electric*.

7. Because this check applies to only one account, leave the *Amount* value that QuickBooks filled in.

8. If you use classes, in the *Class* cell, choose the class associated with the check, in this example, *Overhead*.

9. In the *Memo* field in the top half of the window, type a note about the check, such as *December gas and electric*.

   If the check applies to more than one account, you can type notes in the *Memo* cells in each row of the *Expenses* tab.

10. The *Write Checks* window should look like the one in Figure 2-13. Click *Save & Close*.

    QuickBooks places the check in the queue of checks waiting to print. See page 56 to learn how to print checks.

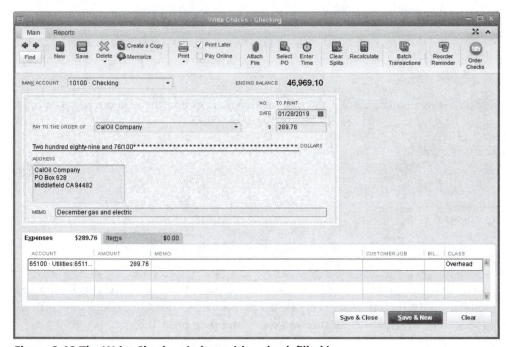

Figure 2-13 The Write Checks window with a check filled in

To view the check that you just recorded in the checking account register, do the following:

1. On the *Banking* menu, choose *Use Register*.

2. In the *Use Register* dialog box, you can choose the bank account you want to open. In this example, keep the *Select Account* field set to *10100 Checking*.

3. Click *OK* to open the *Checking account register* window.

4. Figure 2-14 shows the check to CalOil Company. The words *To Print* in the *Number* cell indicate that the check is in the queue to print later.

5. Click the X at the window's top right to close it.

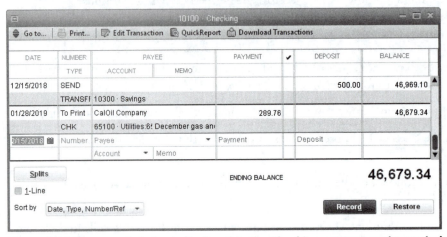

Figure 2-14 The recorded check displayed in the Checking account register window

Recording a Check in the Register Window

Recording checks in a QuickBooks bank account register is quick and easy. Here are the steps to recording a check in a register window:

Computer Practice

1. On the *Banking* menu, choose *Use Register* (or click *Check Register* in the *Home Page*'s *Banking* section).

2. In the *Use Register* dialog box (Figure 2-15), click the down arrow and then choose the account you want to open. In this example, keep the entry, *Checking*. Click *OK*.

Figure 2-15 The Use Register dialog box

3. In the register window, QuickBooks automatically selects the text in the first blank row's *Date* cell. Type the date for the check, in this example, *2/4/2019*.

4. Press Tab to move to the *Number* field. QuickBooks automatically fills in the next check number, as shown in Figure 2-16. In this example, keep the check number *491*. If QuickBooks doesn't fill in the correct check number, type the number you want, and then press Tab.

When you Tab into the *Number* field, the program automatically selects the text in the cell, so you can replace it by starting to type.

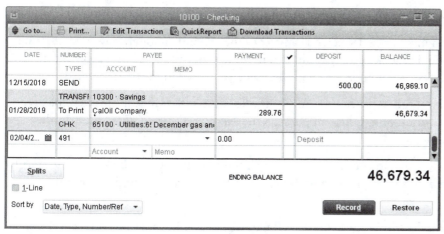

Figure 2-16 Recording a check in the register window

5.   In the *Payee* field, type *Bayshore Office Supply*, and then press Tab.

If this payee isn't in a QuickBooks name list (like a customer, vendor, or employee), the *Name Not Found* dialog box appears (see Figure 2-17).

Figure 2-17 The Name Not Found dialog box

6.   To add the payee to a name list, click *Quick Add*.

7.   In the *Select Name Type* dialog box (Figure 2-18), select the option button for the name list to which you want to add the payee (Vendor, Customer, Employee, or Other). In this example, keep the *Vendor* option selected. Click *OK*.

QuickBooks adds the name to the list you selected. You can edit the record whenever you want to add more information.

Figure 2-18 The Select Name Type dialog box

8.   In the *Payment* field, type *120.95*, and then press Tab.

QuickBooks fills in the Type cell with the text *CHK* to indicate that the transaction is a check.

9.   In the *Account* field, type *Of*. QuickBooks finds the list entries that match the letters you've type so far. In this example, it selects Office Supplies.

10. If you want to allocate the check to multiple accounts, click the *Splits* button.

    A table appears, shown in Figure 2-19, so you can record the account, amount, class, and other values for each account. QuickBooks automatically fills in the account you filled in before you clicked the *Split* button and fills in the *Amount* cell with the value you typed in the *Payment* field.

11. In the first row's *Amount* cell, type the amount for the account in that row, in this example, type *105.95* to allocate that amount to office supplies. In the *Memo* cell, type *Office Chair*. In the *Class* cell, choose *Overhead*.

12. To allocate some of the check to another account, click the second row's *Account* cell, and start to type the account name, in this example, type *Pri* to select Printing and Reproduction. Press Tab to move to the *Amount* cell.

13. QuickBooks automatically fills in the *Amount* cell with the remaining amount from the check total. If that value is correct, press Tab. Otherwise, type the correct value in the cell. Fill in the rest of the cells. In this example, type *Color copies* in the *Memo* cell and choose *Overhead* in the *Class* cell.

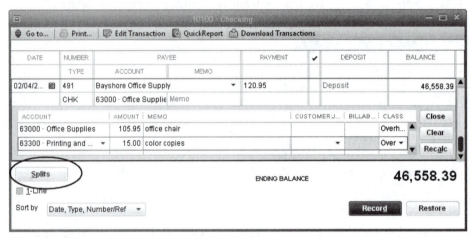

Figure 2-19 The Split panel in a register window

14. Click *Record*.

    QuickBooks saves the check and updates the checking account balance, as shown in Figure 2-20.

    Similar to the paper check register you might use with your personal checking account, a Quick-Books register window lists every transaction that affects the account's balance. For example, in a checking account register window, you can see checks you've recorded, deposits, withdrawals, bank charges, and interest paid (if the account pays interest). To the right of each transaction line, QuickBooks displays the account's running balance. The ending balance appears below the right end of the register window's table.

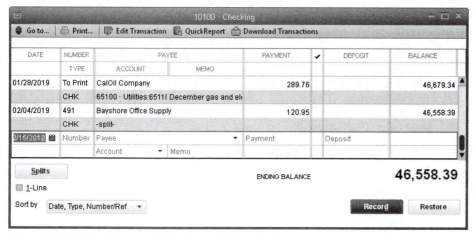

Figure 2-20 A check recorded in the register window

15. Click the X at the window's top right to close the Checking account register window.

Paying with a Credit Card

Credit cards are a convenient way to pay for many expenses, such as travel or things you purchase online. The best way to track credit card charges and payments is to set up a credit card account in QuickBooks for each card you have. When you set up a credit card account in QuickBooks, you can then record credit card charges using the *Enter Credit Card Charges* window. Later, when you receive your credit card bill, you can record the bill using the *Enter Bills* window (see page 41 for how to enter a bill) and pay the bill (see page 50) like any other bill you receive.

> Note: Another advantage to setting up a credit card account is that you can reconcile the account to the statement you receive from the credit card company. See Chapter 4, Working with Bank Accounts, to learn about reconciling bank accounts and credit card accounts.

Entering Credit Card Charges

Computer Practice

To enter a credit card charge, follow these steps:

1. On the *Banking* menu, choose *Enter Credit Card Charges* or, in the *Home Page's Banking* section, click *Enter Credit Card Charges*.

   The *Credit Card* field represents the credit card account you're charging to. In this example, the account is *QuickBooks Credit Card*. If you have more than one credit card account and want to record a charge to another account, choose it in the drop-down list.

2. In this example, QuickBooks automatically selects the *Purchase/Charge* option, which is what you want to record a credit card charge. If the *Refund/Credit* option is selected instead, be sure to select the *Purchase/Charge* option.

3. In the *Purchased From* field, click the down arrow and choose the payee in the drop-down list, in this example, *East Bayshore Tool & Supply*.

4. In the *Date* field, type the date you made the charge (or click the calendar icon, and then choose the check date), in this example, *1/30/2019*.

5. If you want to record a reference number for the transaction, type it in the *Ref No.* field. In this example, leave this field blank.

6. In the *Amount* field, type the charge amount, in this example, *542.66*.

The AutoRecall feature, described on page 42, fills in new credit card charges with accounts, amounts, classes, and other values from the previous transaction for the *Purchased From* name.

7. Fill in the first row of the *Expenses* tab as shown in Figure 2-21.

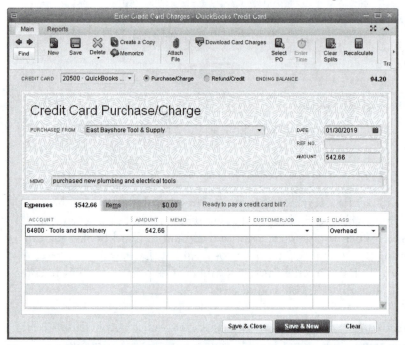

Figure 2-21 The Enter Credit Card Charges window with a charge filled in

Paying Bills You Recorded in QuickBooks

When you record bills in QuickBooks, the program stores them in your Accounts Payable account, which increases its balance (that is, the amount you owe to vendors). But the program also keeps track of when bills are due and whether you can earn a discount for paying early. This section explains how to see the bills you owe and then how to pay them.

Viewing Unpaid Bills

The *Unpaid Bills Detail* report (Figure 2-22) displays a list of all your unpaid bills. You can specify the cutoff date for the report in order to see bills that are due before that date. To generate this report, follow these steps:

1. On the *Reports* menu, choose *Vendors & Payables*, and then choose *Unpaid Bills Detail*.

2. The *Dates* box is initially set to *Today*. To choose a different date, you can choose a date range in the *Dates* drop-down list, or type a date in the second *Dates* box.

If a bill is overdue, the *Aging* column displays the number of days that the bill is past due.

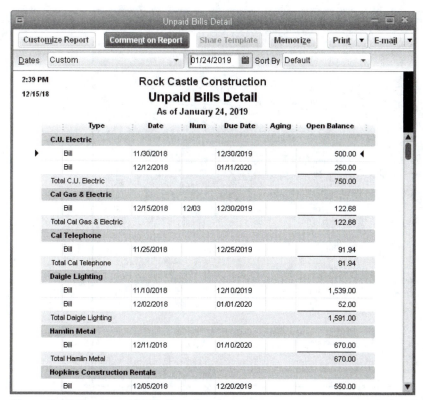

Figure 2-22 The Unpaid Bills Detail report

Note: The *A/P Aging Summary* report (also available on the *Vendors & Payables* sub-menu) summarizes the age of your unpaid bills. This report displays how much you owe to each vendor and also breaks that total down to what you owe for the current billing period and for previous billing periods.

Paying Bills

Computer Practice

Here are the steps for paying bills in QuickBooks:

1. On the *Vendors* menu, choose *Pay Bills* or, on the *Home Page*, click *Pay Bills*.

2. In the *Pay Bills* window, select the *Due on or before* option and then type the cutoff date you want, in this example, type *1/31/2020*.

   QuickBooks filters the unpaid bills to show only the ones due before the date you entered. (You can't filter the list to show only bills that still qualify for an early payment discount.)

3. In this example, the bills are sorted by vendor, so you can see multiple bills from the same vendor, as shown in Figure 2-23.

   To look for bills with an early discount, in the *Sort By* drop-down list, choose *Discount Date*. You can also filter the list to show only the bills from one vendor. To do that, in the *Filter By* drop-down list, choose the vendor you want.

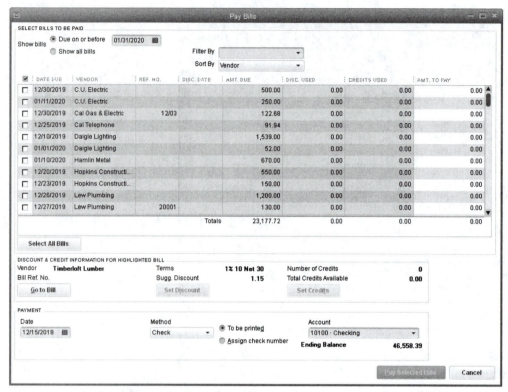

Figure 2-23 The Pay Bills window

4. To choose the bills you want to pay, turn on each bill's checkmark cell. To pay all the bills in the table, click the *Select All Bills* button below the table. Click *Select All Bills* for this example.

   If you want to view a bill, click its row in the *Pay Bills* table, and then click the *Go To Bill* button.

   You can make a partial payment on a bill. To do that, in the bill's *Amt To Pay* cell, type the amount that you want to pay.

5. In the *Payment* section's *Date* box, fill in the date that you want to pay the bills, in this example, *12/15/2018*.

6. In the *Method* drop-down list, choose the payment method you want to use, in this example, keep the *Check* method selected.

7. To set a discount on a bill, click the bill in the table. The *Discount & Credit Information for Highlighted Bill* section displays the bill's terms and suggested discount (Figure 2-23). (If you have a credit available, this section displays that, too.)

8. Click *Set Discount*.

   QuickBooks automatically calculates the discount based on the bill's terms. In this example (Figure 2-24), the terms are 1% 10 Net 30, so QuickBooks calculates a 10% early discount.

9. In the *Discount Account* field, choose the account you want to use to track the discount, in this example, *54599 Less Discounts Taken*.

10. In the *Discount Class* field, choose a class to allocate the discount to that class, in this example, *Remodel*. (Choose the same class that was assigned to the original bill.)

11. Click *Done* to close the dialog box and return to the *Pay Bills* window.

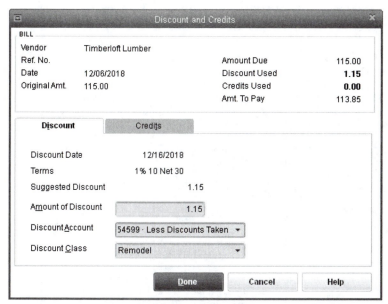

Figure 2-24 The Discount and Credits window

> Note: You can apply available bill credits in the *Discount and Credits* dialog box. To do that, click the *Credits* tab, and then select the credits that you want to apply.

12. Keep the *To be printed* option selected so QuickBooks adds all the bill payment checks to a queue to print later.

Before you click *Pay Selected Bills*, look at the *Ending Balance* value at the window's bottom right. This number tells you how much money will remain in your checking account after you pay all the selected bills.

Figure 2-25 displays the *Pay Bills* window with the discount applied and all the bill payment settings in place.

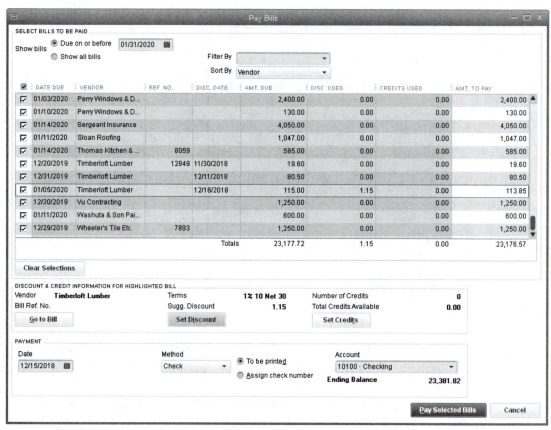

Figure 2-25 The Pay Bills window with bills set up to pay

13. Click *Pay Selected Bills*.

QuickBooks opens the *Payment Summary* dialog box, as shown in Figure 2-26.

Figure 2-26 The Payment Summary dialog box

14. Click *Done* to close the dialog box.

> Note: If you select more than one bill for the same vendor, QuickBooks creates a single bill payment for all the bills to that vendor.

When you pay bills by check, QuickBooks records the bill payments in your Checking account register (Figure 2-27). These bill payments reduce the balance in your Checking account and also reduce the balance in your Accounts Payable account (see Figure 2-28).

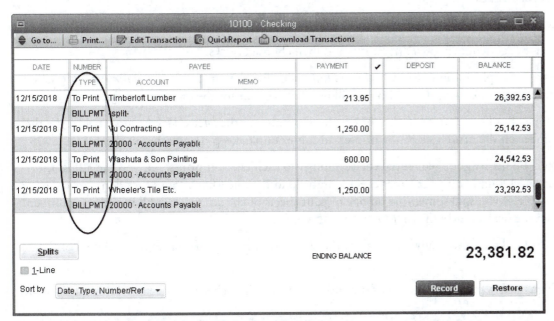

Figure 2-27 Bill payments in the Checking account register

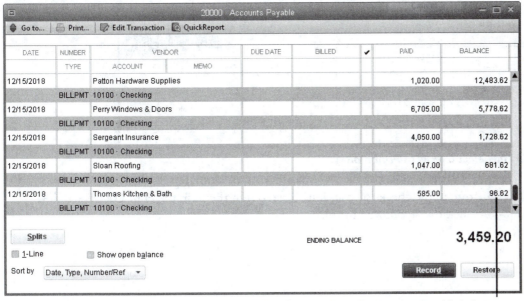

Bill payments reduce the Accounts Payable balance

Figure 2-28 The Accounts Payable register

Printing Checks

Instead of printing checks one by one, you can tell QuickBooks to queue up the checks you record and the bill payments you set up to pay by check, and then print them in one big batch. (As you learned in the previous sections, you queue up checks to print by turning on the *Print Later* checkbox in the *Write Checks* window or by selecting the *To be Printed* option in the *Pay Bills* window.)

Computer Practice

Here are the steps for printing queued up checks and bill payments:

1. On the *File* menu, choose *Print Forms,* and then choose *Checks*.

2. In this example, in the *Select Checks to Print* dialog box (Figure 2-29), the *Bank Account* field is already set to *Checking*. QuickBooks will use that account for the checks it produces.

3. If QuickBooks doesn't fill in the correct check number in the *First Check Number* field, type the number on the first check in the printer. In this example, keep the number in this field.

   QuickBooks assigns a sequential check number to each check it prints, but you can adjust the first check number if your paper check number and the one QuickBooks uses don't agree. For example, if you spill something on one of your sheets of checks, you can fill in the first number from the next sheet in the *First Check Number* field.

4. QuickBooks automatically selects all of the checks for printing. If you want to print all of them, click *OK*.

   If you don't want to print some of the checks, turn off their checkmark cells before you click *OK*.

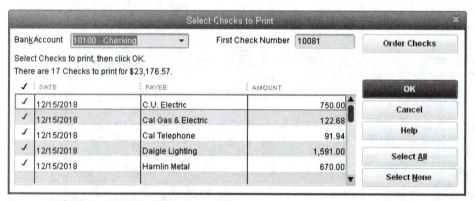

Figure 2-29 The Select Checks to Print dialog box

5. To add a signature to the checks so you don't have to sign them, in the *Print Checks* window (Figure 2-30), click the *Signature* button.

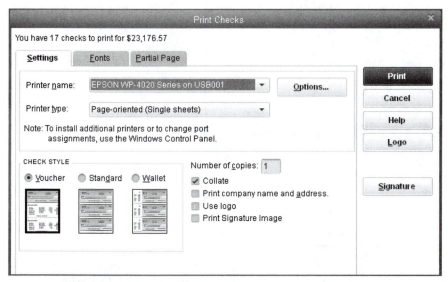

Figure 2-30 The Select Checks to Print dialog box

6. In the *Signature* window, click the *File* button to upload the graphic file of the signature you want to use.

7. In the *Open File* window, navigate to your exercise files folder, and select *signature.png*. Click *Open*.

8. If a message box appears, click *OK*.

    QuickBooks copies the graphic file into a new folder named *<company file>– Images*, where <company file> is the name of the company file you're working on. The *Signature* dialog box displays an image of the uploaded signature file (Figure 2-31). Click *OK*.

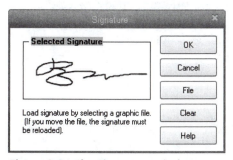

Figure 2-31 The Signature window

> Note: Make sure you put the sheets of checks into the printer the right way. For example, you might need to put the sheets in with the top of the page first, print side down. Print one sheet as an experiment and then tape a note to the printer that tells you how to feed in sheets.

9. After you're sure the printer settings in the *Print Checks* window are what you want, click *Print*.

10. After QuickBooks prints the checks, the *Print Checks – Confirmation* dialog box (Figure 2-32) appears.

    If some of the checks didn't print correctly, you can select checks to reprint. However, accounting best practices recommend voiding each damaged check and recording new checks instead. The next section describes how to void checks.

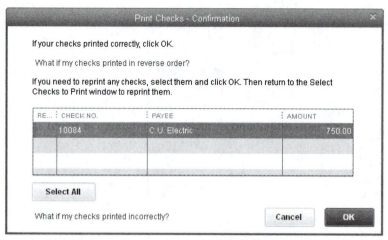

Figure 2-32 The Print Checks – Confirmation window

> Tip: If you pay multiple vendor bills with a single check, you can print a Bill Payment Stub to show which bills the check covers. To do that, on the *File* menu, choose *Print Forms*, and then choose *Bill Payment Stubs* on the submenu.

Voiding Checks

You can void checks in QuickBooks, so you have a record of them even though they're voided. That way, your checking account register won't show gaps in your check number sequence.

> Note: If you want to look for missing checks in your checking account register, run the *Missing Checks* report. (On the *Reports* menu, choose *Banking*, and then choose *Missing Checks* on the submenu.) The report inserts a line ***Missing numbers here*** wherever there is a gap in your check number sequence.

Computer Practice

To void a check, follow these steps:

1. Open the *Checking account register* window (on the *Home Page*, click *Check Register*, and then click *OK* in the *Use Register* dialog box).

2. At the register window's top left, click *Go to*. In the *Which Field* box, choose *Number/Ref.* In the *Search For* field, type *501*, and then click *Back*.

    The entry for bill payment 501 is outlined in the register.

3. Right-click the bill payment transaction and then choose *Void Bill Pmt-Check* on the shortcut menu (see Figure 2-33). Alternatively, you can select the transaction, and then, on the *Edit* menu, choose *Void Bill Pmt – Check*.

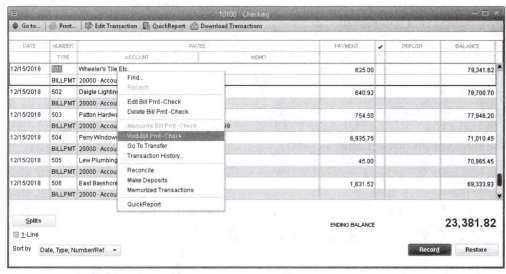

Figure 2-33 Voiding a bill payment

4. Click *Record* to save the voided transaction.

    In this example, you're voiding a bill payment, so QuickBooks displays a warning that you used this check to pay some bills (Figure 2-34). Voiding the bill payment means that the bill will become payable again.

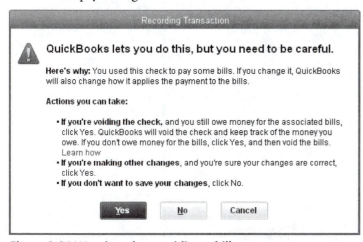

Figure 2-34 Warning about voiding a bill payment

5. To void the bill payment and make the bill payable again, click *Yes*.

    When you void a check, QuickBooks does several things (all shown in Figure 2-35). It changes the *Payment* amount to 0.00, adds a checkmark to the *Cleared* cell to indicate that the check is cleared, and fills in the *Memo* field with the word VOID.

Figure 2-35 Voided bill payment

Now that the bill payment has been voided, you need to repay the bill. To do that, see the section, Pay Bills, and repeat those steps.

Handling Vendor Credits

When you receive a credit from a vendor, you record it in the *Enter Bills* window as a credit. Then you can apply it to one of your unpaid bills from that vendor.

> Tip: You can use a bill credit instead of the *Discount* window to record some vendor credits. That way, you can record reference numbers, memos, credited items, and allocation to multiple accounts or customer or jobs.

Computer Practice

Before creating a bill credit, enter a bill that you can apply the credit to. Use the values in Figure 2-36.

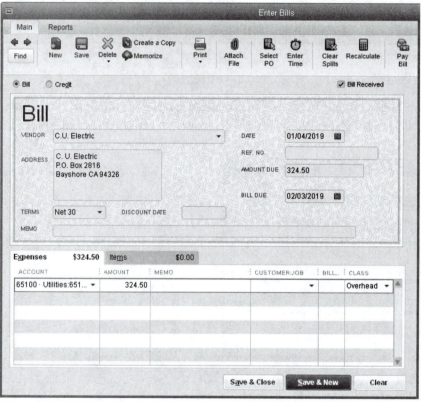

Figure 2-36 Bill from C. U. Electric

To record a vendor credit, follow these steps:

1. On the *Home Page*, click *Enter Bills*.

2. In the *Enter Bills* window, select the *Credit* option.

   The heading in the window changes to *Credit*.

3. In the *Vendor* drop-down list, choose the vendor who issued you a credit. In this example, choose *C.U. Electric*.

4. In the *Date* field, choose the date that the credit was issued, in this example, *1/15/2019*.

5. In the *Credit Amount* field, type the credit amount (*100,* in this example).

6. On the tabs at the bottom of the window, fill in the information about the credit you received.

   In this example (Figure 2-37), on the *Expenses* tab, QuickBooks automatically selects the Gas & Electric account based on the bill you recorded and fills in the *Amount* cell with 100.00 based on what you typed in the *Credit Amount* field.

7. Click *Save & Close* to record the credit.

   Behind the scenes, a bill credit debits (decreases) the Accounts Payable account and credits (decreases) the account you selected on the *Expenses* tab.

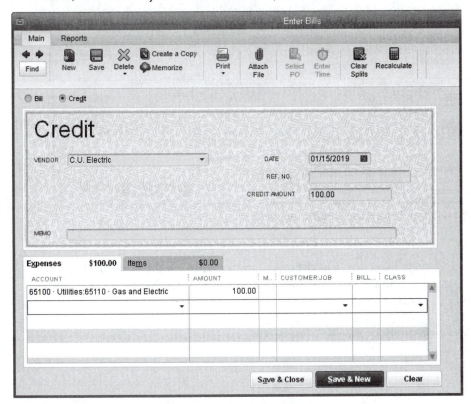

Figure 2-37 Creating a bill credit in the Enter Bills window

Now that the vendor credit exists, follow these steps to apply it to a bill:

1. On the *Home Page*, click *Pay Bills*.

2. In the *Due on or before* field, choose the bill cutoff date you want, for this example, *2/10/2019*.

3. Turn on the checkmark cell for the unpaid bill for *C.U. Electric.*

   When you select a vendor's bill in the table, QuickBooks displays the total amount of credits for the vendor to the right of the *Total Credits Available* heading.

4. In the *Payment Date* field, choose the date you want to apply the credit, in this example, *2/4/2019*.

   Figure 2-38 displays the *Pay Bills* window with these entries.

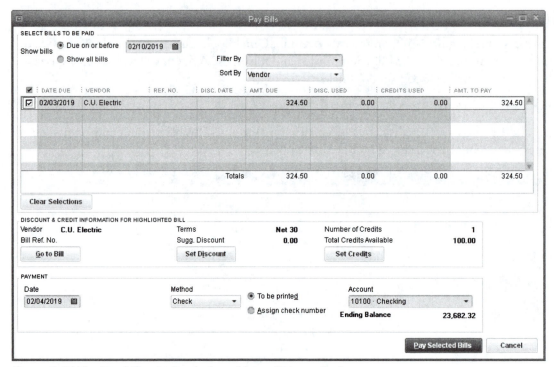

Figure 2-38 The Pay Bills window before the credit is applied

5. Click *Set Credits*.

    In the *Discount and Credits* dialog box, QuickBooks automatically selects the available credits (Figure 2-39). To select different credits or remove a credit, turn off its checkmark cell. You can also edit the value in the *Amt To Use* cell.

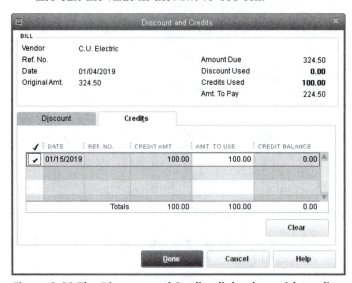

Figure 2-39 The Discount and Credits dialog box with credit applied

6. Click *Done*.

    Figure 2-40 shows the credit applied to the bill so that the *Amt To Pay* value is decreased by the amount of the credit.

Figure 2-40 The Discount and Credits dialog box with credit applied

7. If you want to apply the credit without paying the bill, change the *Amt. To Pay* cell to zero and then click *Pay Selected Bills*. Otherwise, click *Pay Selected Bills* to pay the bill as described earlier in this chapter.

Viewing Accounts Payable

You can track how much you owe and the business you've done with vendors with several QuickBooks reports. Chapter 6, Reports, provides more information on generating reports.

Vendor Balance Reports

The *Vendor Balance Summary* report (Figure 2-41) shows how much you owe to each vendor as of the report date you select. If you want to examine each accounts payable transaction (bills and bill payments), use the *Vendor Balance Detail* report instead. To run these reports, on the *Reports* menu, choose *Vendors & Payables*, and then choose either *Vendor Balance Summary* or *Vendor Balance Detail*.

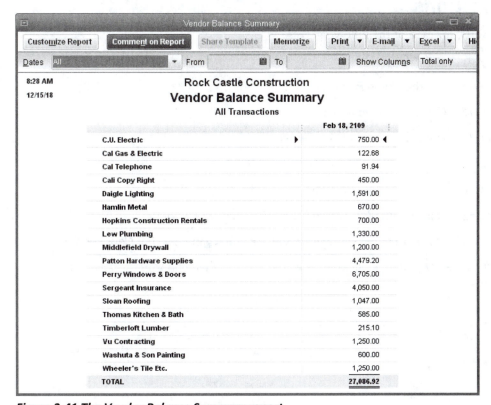

Figure 2-41 The Vendor Balance Summary report

Transaction List by Vendor Report

For a more complete look at vendor transactions than what the *Vendor Balance Detail* report provides, run the *Transaction List by Vendor* report (Figure 2-42). This report shows all transactions for each vendor including checks, credit card charges, and credit accounts payable transactions (bills and bill payments). To run this report, on the *Reports* menu, choose *Vendors & Payables*, and then choose *Transaction List by Vendor*.

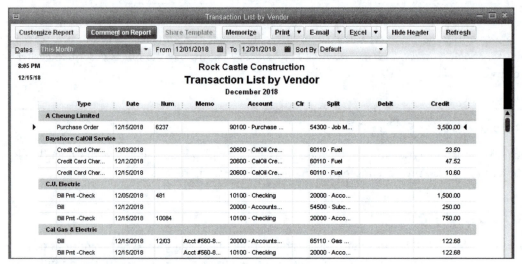

Figure 2-42 The Transaction List by Vendor report

Review Questions

Select the best answer(s) for each of the following:

1. You can display the *Vendor Center* by:

    a) Clicking *Vendors* on the *Home Page*.

    b) Clicking *Vendor Center* in the icon bar.

    c) On the *Vendor* menu, choosing *Vendor Center*.

    d) All of the above.

2. You can add a vendor in the *Vendor Center* by:

    a) Right-clicking within the *Vendors* tab and then choosing *New Vendor*.

    b) In the *Vendor Center* icon bar, clicking *New Vendor*, and then choosing *New Vendor*.

    c) In the *Vendor Center* icon bar, clicking *New Vendor*, and then choosing *Add Multiple Vendors*.

    d) Pressing Ctrl+N.

    e) All of the above.

3. You can pay vendors by:

   a) Recording a transaction in the check register.

   b) Using *Write Checks* to record and print a check without using Accounts Payable.

   c) Using *Enter Bills* to record a transaction using Accounts Payable and then using *Pay Bills* to pay open bills.

   d) All of the above.

4. Which statement is true?

   a) When you pay a bill, QuickBooks records the payment in a bank account (or credit card account) and the Accounts Payable Account.

   b) Bill payments increase the balance in your bank account and Accounts Payable account.

   c) You apply discounts when you enter a bill.

   d) You must use items to fill out a bill.

5. Which QuickBooks feature should you use to categorize income and expenses that span different customers, vendors, accounts, and time periods?

   a) Jobs

   b) Class tracking

   c) Customer types

   d) Vendor types

   e) Job types

Managing Expenses Exercise 1

Restore the sample file, *sample_product-based business 2015 (Portable).QBM*. (Or, if you are using QuickBooks 2014, restore *sample_product-based business 2014 (Portable).QBM*.)

1. Is class tracking turned on in the sample file? If not, turn it on.

2. Create a new vendor using the data in the following table. If the table doesn't contain data for a field in the *New Vendor* window, leave the field blank.

Table 2-1 Use this data to create a vendor

Field Name	Data
Vendor Name	Rustic Roofing
Company Name	Rustic Roofing
Mr./Ms./...	Mr.
First Name	Russ
Last Name	Cedar
Main Phone	510-555-1111
Main Email	russ@rusticroofing.us
Name	Rustic Roofing
Address	Russ Cedar, 125 Cedar Lane. Monterey, CA 93942
Account #	1234-1
Terms	Net 30
Print on Check as	Rustic Roofing
Tax ID	999-99-0000
Check Box	Vendor eligible for 1099
Account Prefill	Subcontractors
Vendor Type	Subcontractor
County	Monterey

3. Print a vendor contact list. (On the *Reports* menu, choose *Vendors & Payables*, and then choose *Vendor Contact List* on the submenu.)

4. Record check number *10080* in the Checking account register.

    Set the date to *1/4/2019*. Use *Quick Add* to add the vendor, *Tough Tools*.

    Set the check amount to *$800*. Split the amount of the check to assign *$600* to *Tools and Machinery* for *Remodel* and *$200* to *Tools and Machinery* for *Overhead*.

5. Enter bill number *84-6542*.

    Set the date to *1/5/2019* and choose *Gallion Masonry*.

    Set the check amount to *$500*, Terms equal to *Net 30*, and choose the *Tools and Machinery* account. Allocate the expense to *New Construction*.

6. Print a report of all unpaid bills. (Create and print an *Unpaid Bills Detail* report dated *01/31/2019*.)

7. Pay all of the bills due on or before *02/28/2019*.

   Pay the bills from the Checking account and set the check date to *2/28/2019*.

Managing Expenses Exercise 2 (Advanced)

Restore the sample file, *sample_product-based business 2015 (Portable).QBM*. (Or, if you are using QuickBooks 2014, restore *sample_product-based business 2014 (Portable).QBM*.)

1. Is class tracking turned on in the sample file? If not, turn it on.

2. Create a new vendor using the data in the following table. If the table doesn't contain data for a field in the *New Vendor* window, leave the field blank.

Table 2-2 Use this data to create a vendor

Field Name	Data
Vendor Name	All About Stone
Company Name	All About Stone
Mr./Ms./...	Ms.
First Name	Janet
Last Name	Smith
Main Phone	510-555-4200
Main Email	janet@allaboutstone.us
Name	All About Stone
Address	Janet Smith 12 Main St Santa Barbara, CA 93101
Account #	9104
Terms	Net 15
Print on Check as	All About Stone
Tax ID	111-22-1111
Check Box	Vendor eligible for 1099
Account Prefill	Job Materials
Vendor Type	Materials
County	Santa Barbara

3. Print a vendor contact list. (On the *Reports* menu, choose *Vendors & Payables*, and then choose *Vendor Contact List* on the submenu.)

4. Enter check number *10080* in the Checking account register on *01/15/2019*.

   Choose *Zeng Building Supplies* as the vendor. Set the amount to *$700*. Split the expense to *$350.00* for *Office Supplies* allocated to *Overhead* and *$350.00* for *Tools and Machinery* allocated to *Remodel*.

5. In the *Write Checks* window, write a check to print later.

   Record a check to *Cal Telephone* dated *01/16/2019* for *$297.50* for *Telephone* allocated to *Overhead*. Don't print the check.

6. Enter a credit card charge on the *QuickBooks credit card* on *1/16/2019*.

   Use *Quick Add* to add the vendor, *Super Supplies*. Fill in a reference number: *1234*. The charge was for *$125.69* for *office supplies* allocated to *Overhead*.

7. Enter bill number *2204* from *Kershaw Computer Services* dated *01/22/2019*.

   Set the bill amount to *$600.00* and choose *Net 30* for Terms. Choose the *Computer Repairs* account and allocate the entire amount to *Overhead*.

8. Enter bill number *4215* from *Gallion Masonry* dated *01/22/2019*.

   Set the bill amount to *$3,500* and choose *Net 15* Terms.

   The bill is for the *Mark Bauman Home Remodel* job. Choose the *Subcontractors* Cost of Goods Sold account. Link the cost to the appropriate job and class.

9. Print a report to look at unpaid bills.

   Create and print an *Unpaid Bills Detail* report dated *1/31/2019*.

10. Pay all of the bills due on or before *1/31/2019* from the Checking account.

    Record the payments on *02/1/2019* and set the checks up to be printed.

11. Print the checks you recorded with a *Print Later* setting. Print them on blank paper and start the check numbers at *517*.

12. Enter bill number *14956* from *Daigle Lighting* on *01/25/2019*.

    Set the Terms to *Net 30* and the amount to *$1792.33*. Choose the *Job Materials* Cost of Goods Sold and assign it to the *Heather Campbell remodel* job. Allocate the cost to the correct class.

13. Enter a bill credit on *01/30/2019* for *$500.00* from *Daigle Lightning*.

    Enter reference number *Credit115*. Choose the *Job Materials* Cost of Goods Sold and assign it to the *Heather Campbell remodel* job. Allocate the cost to the correct class.

14. Apply the credit to bill number *14956*.

15. Pay the remainder of the bill on *2/1/2019* using a handwritten check.

16. Generate a *Vendor Balance Summary* report for *All* transactions.

Chapter 3

Sales and Income

Topics

This chapter covers the following topics:

- The Sales and Income Workflow
- Setting Up Customers and Jobs
- Recording Sales Transactions
- Receiving Payments from Customers
- Making Bank Deposits
- Using Income Tracker

This chapter begins by explaining the difference between sales receipts and invoices and explains when to use each one. You'll also learn the workflow for sales and income transactions from the initial sale until you deposit money into your bank account.

In this chapter, you'll learn how to set up customer and job records in QuickBooks for each of the customers and jobs you have in real life. After that, the chapter steps through creating sales receipts and invoices to record the details of each sale. Then, you learn how to record in QuickBooks the payments you receive from customers. The last step is recording deposits into your bank account. You'll also learn about *Income Tracker*, one of QuickBooks' features that helps you see the status of sales transactions and perform the next steps in the sales and income process.

> Note: For the computer practice in this chapter, restore the sample file, *sample_product-based business 2015 (Portable).QBM.* (Or, if you are using QuickBooks 2014, restore *sample_product-based business 2014 (Portable).QBM.*)

The Sales and Income Workflow

Similar to your choices when you pay for company expenses, customers can pay what they owe you right away (called *cash sales*) or later (called *credit sales*). Here's how each type of customer sale works:

- **Cash sale:** This is the name for a sales transaction in which a customer pays you at the time of sale (or service) with cash, a check, or a credit card, and you receive your money right away. For cash sales, you record a sales receipt in QuickBooks to document what you sold and the amount you received. If you use the *Undeposited Funds* account (a special *Other Current Asset* account that stores payments and other deposits you receive until you deposit them in the bank), a sales receipt debits (increases) the *Undeposited Funds* account and credits (increases) the income account for the sale. If funds are deposited directly into an account (such as with a PayPal account), a sales receipt takes care of recording the deposit in Quick-

Books. In that case, it debits (increases) your bank account balance and credits (increases) the income account for the sale.

> Note: "Paying with a credit card" contains the word "credit," but this type of customer payment is a cash sale to you, because you receive your payment immediately (that is, as soon as the credit card company processes the payment).

- **Credit sale:** The process you follow with credit sales is a little different. Often, you start by recording an invoice that documents what the customer purchased and how much they owe you. Later, when the customer sends a payment, you record that payment in QuickBooks and apply it to the customer's corresponding open invoice. Finally, you record the deposit of the payment into your bank account. The *Home Page* window shows the sales and income workflow (circled) (Figure 3-1).

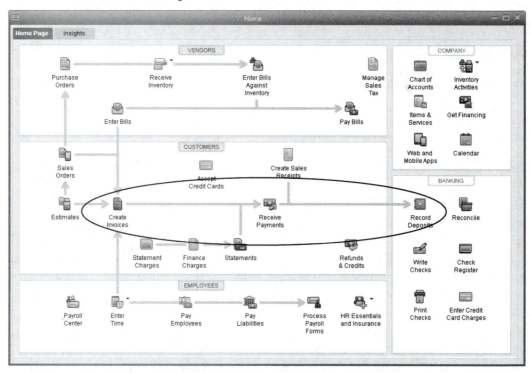

Figure 3-1 The Sales and Income Workflow on the Home Page

Table 3-1 summarizes the accounting for a credit sale from the time you record an invoice until you deposit the customer's payment in the bank. Here is an explanation of the debits and credits for a credit sale:

1. When you create an invoice, QuickBooks debits (increases) Accounts Receivable because the customer owes you more money and credits (increases) the appropriate income account because you've earned income from the sale.

2. When you receive payment for the invoice from your customer, you record the payment with the *Receive Payments* feature. When you do that, QuickBooks credits (increases) the Undeposited Funds account, because you have a payment waiting to be deposited, and credits (decreases) the Accounts Receivable account, because the customer no longer owes you that money.

3. Finally, when you deposit the payment to your bank account (and record the deposit with QuickBooks' *Make Deposits* feature), QuickBooks debits (increases) your bank account because the deposit increases your bank balance and credits (decreases) the Undeposited Funds account because the deposit is now in the bank account.

Table 3-1 Behind the scenes accounting for a credit sale

Transaction	Debit	Credit
Invoice	Accounts Receivable	Income account
Receive payment	Undeposited Funds	Accounts Receivable
Deposit money in bank	Bank account	Undeposited Funds

Note: QuickBooks' sales receipts and invoices also handle the accounting for sales tax and inventory items. For example, if these sales forms include taxable items, the transaction credits (increases) the sales tax liability account for the sales tax the customer paid. If the sales form includes inventory items, it credits (decreases) the Inventory Asset account to reflect the sale of inventory and debits (increases) the appropriate Cost of Goods Sold account to show the cost of what you sold.

Optional Steps in the Sales and Income Process

There are two other types of sales transactions that you might record in QuickBooks: estimates and sales orders. Both of these transaction types are non-posting, which means that they don't affect the balances in your financial accounts. Here is a description of each of these additional sales transactions:

- **Estimate:** Customers sometimes ask for estimates or bids to help them decide whether to purchase goods and services or to give you approval to start a job. In that case, you can create an estimate in QuickBooks that shows what you're going to provide to the customer and how much you'll charge. No money changes hands when you create an estimate, which is why an estimate is a non-posting transaction. Later, if a customer approves your estimate, you can turn it into an invoice. In addition, QuickBooks includes reports that help you compare your estimates to your actual income and costs.

- **Sales order:** A sales order documents goods that a customer orders that you haven't yet invoiced. For example, if a customer orders items that you don't have in stock, you can create a sales order to record the pending sale. (Sales orders are available only in QuickBooks Premier and Enterprise editions.) Then when the items are in stock, you can turn the sales order into an invoice. In that respect, a sales order is similar to an estimate: it tracks a future sale and doesn't post any values to your accounts.

Setting Up Customers and Jobs

For each customer, you create a record in the *Customer:Job* list (which appears as the *Customers & Jobs* list in the *Customer Center*). If you perform multiple jobs for the same customer, you can create jobs associated with that customer in QuickBooks. This section describes how to create customers and jobs.

Creating a Customer

This section describes how to create a customer record in QuickBooks.

Computer Practice

To add a customer, follow these steps:

1. On the *Home Page*, click *Customers* (or, in the icon bar, click *Customers*).

   The *Customer Center* opens.

2. In the center's toolbar, choose *New Customer & Job*, and then choose *New Customer* on the drop-down menu.

3. In the *Customer Name* field, fill in the customer's name as you want it to appear in your *Customers & Jobs* list. In this example, type *Marsh, Joe*.

   The *Customer Name* field is like an identifier: it appears in the *Customers & Jobs* list and in customer and job drop-down lists. For that reason, you should use names that make it easy to find the customer you want, for example, a format like <last name>, <first name> for individuals.

   > Note: The *Opening Balance* field represents the balance that the customer owes you as of a specific date (for example, the day that you create the record or the date that you start using QuickBooks for your company finances). However, you should leave this field blank when you create a customer. The best way to define a customer's balance is by recording all the customer's open invoices. That way, you can see the details of your sales to the customer and use the *Receive Payments* feature to close the invoices when the customer pays you.

4. Because this customer is an individual, do not fill in the *Company Name* field. If the customer is a company, fill in the *Company Name* field with the company name as you want to see it on sales forms like sales receipts or invoices.

5. Fill in the other fields on the *Address Info* tab using the data in Table 3-2.

Table 3-2 Customer data

Field Name	Data
Customer Name	Marsh, Joe
Mr./Ms.	Mr.
First Name	Joe
Last Name	Marsh
Main Phone	415-555-0001
Main Email	jmarsh@jmarsh.us
Invoice/Bill To Address	Mr. Joe Marsh, 14 Vista Ave. Monterey, CA 93942
Ship To	Same as Invoice/Bill To Address

6. To copy the address in the *Invoice/Bill To* box to the *Ship To* box, click the *Copy* button (circled in Figure 3-2), and then click *OK* in the *Add Shipping Address Information* window.

You can define more than one *Ship To* address, for example, to ship to several store locations. To create another *Ship To* address, click the + button (circled in Figure 3-2) to the right of the *Ship To* address box and then fill in the fields in the *Add Shipping Address Information* dialog box.

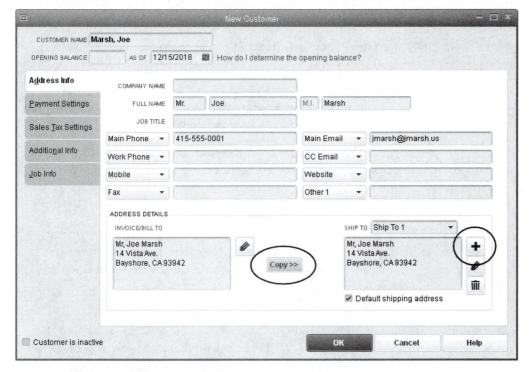

Figure 3-2 The Address Info tab filled in

7. Click the *Payment Settings* tab to fill in details about how the customer pays.

8. If you assign account numbers to your customers, fill in the *Account No.* field with the customer's account number. In this example, type *2672*.

9. In the *Credit Limit* field, fill in the amount of credit you're going to extend to the customer, in this example, *$30,000*.

    When you fill in the *Credit Limit* field with a value, QuickBooks will warn you when you record an invoice that increases the customer's balance beyond this credit limit. Although you receive a warning about the exceeded credit limit, you can still save the invoice.

10. In the *Terms* drop-down list, choose the payment terms you've offered this customer. In this example, choose *Net 30*.

    As you learned in Chapter 2, the *Terms* list includes payment terms that you can apply to both vendors and customers. QuickBooks uses these terms to calculate vendor bill and customer invoice due dates. If you assign terms, such as 1% 10 Net 30 to a customer or invoice, the program can determine whether a customer qualifies for an early payment discount and calculate that discount.

11. In the *Price Level* drop-down list, choose *Commercial*.

    Price levels represent discounts or markups that you apply to transactions. If you assign a price level to a customer, QuickBooks applies that price level to every transaction for that customer. For example, Joe Marsh is a commercial customer, so he gets the contractors' discount (10% in the sample file) on all his purchases. See page 220 for more information about setting up and using price levels.

12. If the customer has a preferred method for receiving information, choose it in the *Preferred Delivery Method* field. In this example, choose *E-mail*.

    When you create an invoice for a customer with Email as the preferred delivery method, QuickBooks automatically turns on the *E-mail Later* checkbox in the *Create Invoices* window.

13. In the *Preferred Payment Method* field, choose the form of payment that the customer uses most often, in this example, *Visa*.

    This drop-down list includes common payment methods, such as Cash, Check, Visa, and American Express. When you set this preferred method, QuickBooks automatically chooses this payment method when you select this customer in the *Receive Payments* window.

14. If you choose a credit card in the *Preferred Payment Method* field, then fill in the customer's credit card information in the *Credit Card Information* fields. (Use the values in Figure 3-3 to complete this section.)

    You can enter only one credit card number for each customer.

> Note: If you store customer credit card numbers in QuickBooks, turn on the *Customer Credit Card Protection* feature so QuickBooks can help you comply with credit card industry security requirements. To enable this feature, on the *Company* menu, choose *Customer Credit Card Protection*, and then click *Enable Protection*.
>
> In addition, if more than one person works in QuickBooks, set up a separate user name and password for each person. That way, you can specify the privileges that each user has, for example, to turn off access to *Sensitive Accounting Activities* to prevent a user from seeing customers' credit card information.

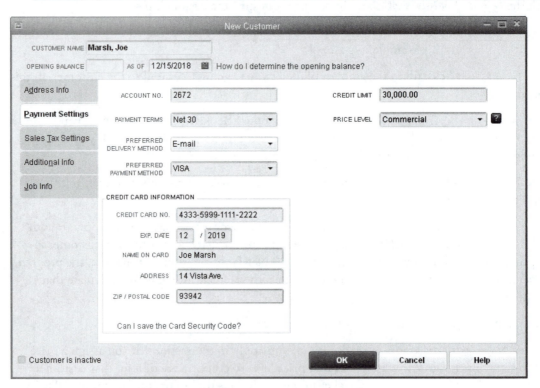

Figure 3-3 The Payment Settings tab filled in

15. Click the *Sales Tax Settings* tab to specify the customer's sales tax status.

16. In the *Tax Code* drop-down list, choose *Tax* if the customer pays sales tax. If the customer is exempt from paying sales tax, choose *Non*.

17. In the *Tax Item* field, choose the sales tax item that applies to the customer, in this example, *East Bayshore*.

    In most states, the sales tax is based on where goods are delivered, for example, the county, city, or other tax location that corresponds to the *Ship To* address you filled in on the *Address Info* tab. Figure 3-4 shows the *Sales Tax Settings* tab filled in.

    > Note: To learn how to set up tax codes and tax items, see page 124.

18. Leave the *Resale No.* field blank.

    You fill in this field only if the customer is a reseller. Resellers don't pay sales tax, because it's *their* customers who pay the sales tax.

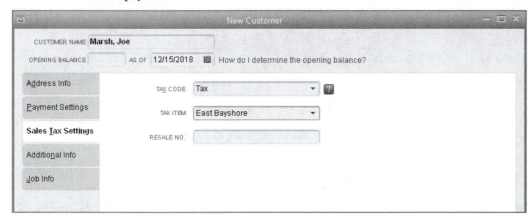

Figure 3-4 The Sales Tax Settings tab filled in

19. Click the *Additional Info* tab.

20. In the *Customer Type* drop-down list, choose the type that corresponds to the customer, in this example, *Commercial*.

    You can use customer types to categorize your customers, for example, to evaluate the profitability of commercial versus residential customers. By applying customer types to customers, you can create reports by customer type or send messages to all customers of a specific type.

21. In the *Rep* drop-down list, choose the sales rep for the customer. For this example, leave the field blank.

    You can assign employees or vendors to the *Rep* list (on the *Lists* menu, choose *Customer & Vendor Profile Lists*, and then choose *Sales Rep List*). If someone in your company is the primary representative for this customer, choose that person's name in the list. You can use the *Sales by Rep* report to view sales rep performance.

22. If you create custom fields and assign them to the *Customer:Job* list, type in their values. In this case, type *19012* in the *Contract #* field, *5/10/1970* in the *B-Day field*, and *Ethel* in the *Spouse's Name* field.

See page 224 to learn how to set up custom fields.

Figure 3-5 shows the *Additional Info* tab filled in.

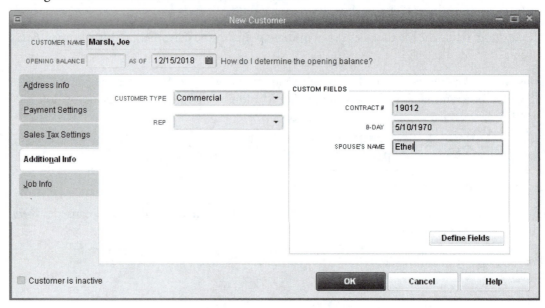

Figure 3-5 The Additional Info tab filled in

23. Click *OK* to save the customer record and close the *New Customer* window.

24. To close the *Customer Center*, click the X at the window's top right.

Setting Up Jobs for Job Costing

If you perform multiple jobs for the same customer (which is typical in construction, for example), you can create job records in QuickBooks to track each job separately (called job costing). That way, you can generate reports that show the income, expenses, and profitability for each job.

The *New Customer* window includes a *Job Info* tab, but that isn't how you create a job for a customer. To create a job record for an existing customer in QuickBooks, follow these steps:

1. On the *Home Page*, click *Customers* to open the *Customer Center*.

2. On the *Customers & Jobs* tab, right-click the customer who has hired you for a new job, and then choose *Add Job* on the shortcut menu. (Or select the customer in the *Customers & Jobs* tab, in the center's toolbar, choose *New Customer & Job*, and then choose *Add Job* on the drop-down menu.) In this example, right-click *Balak, Mike* and choose *Add Job*.

   The *New Job* window opens with information from the customer record already filled in, as shown in Figure 3-6. The fields in the *New Job* window are almost identical to the ones in the *New Customer* window (see Figure 3-2).

Figure 3-6 The New Job window

3. In the *Job Name* field, type the job name, in this example, *Finish Basement*.

4. If the job uses different values than the customer to which is belongs, fill in the *New Job* window's fields with the values that are different. If the job values are the same as those in the customer's record, you can skip those fields.

5. After you fill in the job fields, click *OK* to save the job record and close the *New Job* window.

    The job name is indented from the customer's name, as shown in Figure 3-7.

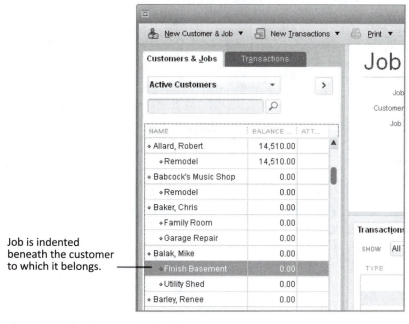

Job is indented
beneath the customer
to which it belongs.

Figure 3-7 The Customer & Job List

Recording Sales Transactions

After you set up customer and job records in QuickBooks to go with your real-world customers and job, you're ready to record sales transactions. This section describes the steps for creating sales receipts for cash sales and invoices for credit sales.

Creating a Sales Receipt

When customers pay at the time of the sale or service, whether they pay with cash, check, debit card, or credit card, you record a sales receipt in QuickBooks.

Computer Practice

Here are the steps:

1. On the *Home Page*, click *Create Sales Receipts*. Or on the *Customers* menu, choose *Enter Sales Receipts*.

2. In the *Enter Sales Receipts* window, in the *Customer:Job* drop-down list, choose the customer or job for the sale (Figure 3-8). In this example, choose the *Garage Repair* job for *Baker, Chris*.

   QuickBooks fills in information from the job record, such as the address, tax code, and tax item. In addition, the *History* pane on the right side of the window displays summary information about the customer (or job), such as the open balance, and recent transactions, as shown in Figure 3-9. Many QuickBooks transaction windows include a *History* pane.

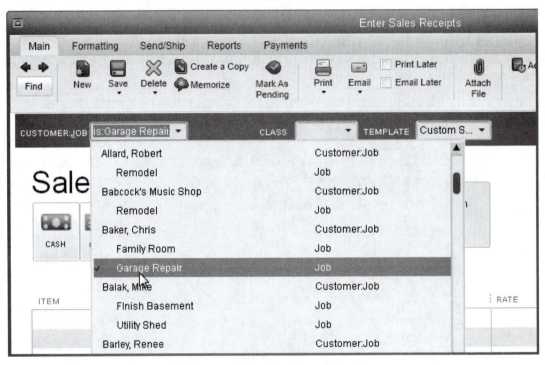

Figure 3-8 Choose the customer or job in the Customer:Job list

> Tip: You can quickly create a new customer or job in the *Enter Sales Receipt* window. In the *Customer: Job* field, type the customer name and then press Tab. (To create a new job, type the customer name, followed by a colon, and then the job name.) When the *Customer:Job Not Found* warning appears, click *Quick Add* to add the new customer or job to the *Customer:Job List*. If you choose this option, you can fill in more details later by editing the customer or job record.
>
> This *Quick Add* shortcut works in all QuickBooks' lists. If the name you type doesn't exist in QuickBooks, the *<name> Not Found* dialog box appears. You can click *Quick Add* to add the entry without any additional information or click *Set Up* to open the corresponding *New* dialog box to fill in the record's details. If you don't want to create a new record, click *Cancel*.

3. In the *Class* field, choose the class associated with the sale, in this example, *Remodel*. (See page 39 to learn more about classes.)

4. If you want to use a specific template, choose it in the *Template* drop-down list. In this example, leave *Custom Sales Receipt* selected. (See page 225 to learn about customizing form templates.)

5. In the *Date* field, choose the sale date, in this example, *1/21/2019*.

> Tip: You can use shortcut keys to choose a different date. For example, if the date is a few days away from the date that QuickBooks enters, press the + key one or more times to move the date one or more days forward or press the – key to move it backward. You can also type "t" to choose today's date. You can also move the date one period forward or backward. For example, type "m" or "y" to move one month or year into the future. Type "h" or "r" to move one month or year into the past. (These shortcuts are easy to remember once you realize that "m" and "h" are the first and last letters of the word "month" and "y" and "r" are the first and last letters of the word "year."

6. In the *Sale No.* field, type the sales receipt number, in this example, *2019-100*.

   QuickBooks automatically increments the number you typed in this field in the previous transaction. If the number is correct, you can skip this field.

7. Click the button that corresponds to the payment method that the customer used, in this example, *Check*. Fill in the *Check No.* field with the customer's check number (*2491* here).

   Leave the *Check No.* field blank if the payment method is cash or a credit card.

8. In the first *Item* drop-down list, choose the item you sold, in this example, *Appliance*. In the *Description* cell, type the description if QuickBooks doesn't fill in the description you want. In this example, type *"Garage Door Opener."*

   When you choose an item, QuickBooks fills in the *Description*, *Rate*, and *Tax* cells with the values from the item record. In this example, Appliance is a generic item, so the item record doesn't include a description.

9. In the *Qty* (quantity) cell, type the quantity purchased, in this example, *1*.

> Note: If you use QuickBooks Premier or Enterprise, the *Custom Sales Receipt* includes a column, *U/M*, which stands for unit of measure and represents the units for the selected item, such as linear feet or gallons. Leave this cell blank in this example.

10. In the *Rate* cell, if necessary, type the price you charge for the item, *300,* in this example. You can type a value in the *Rate* cell if the rate from the item record isn't the value you want.

   QuickBooks calculates the *Amount* cell by multiplying the value in the *Qty* cell by the value in the *Rate* cell.

11. Fill in the second row of the table with the values shown in Figure 3-9.

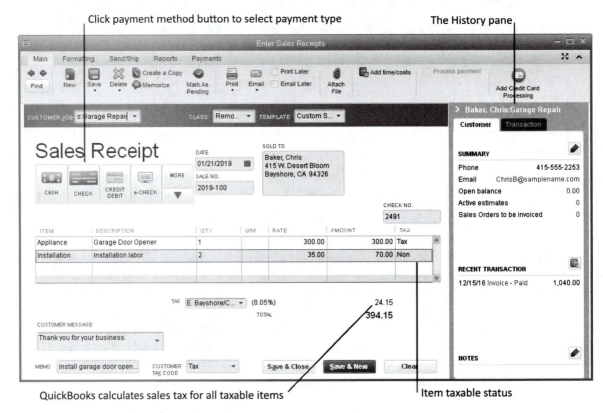

Click payment method button to select payment type   The History pane

QuickBooks calculates sales tax for all taxable items   Item taxable status

Figure 3-9 A filled in sales receipt transaction

12. If necessary, choose the tax item in the *Tax* drop-down list. In this example, choose *E. Bayshore/ County.*

   QuickBooks uses this tax item to calculate the sales tax for all taxable items on the sales receipt. In this example, it calculates sales tax on the garage door opener, which is taxable, but doesn't add any sales tax for the non-taxable installation service. (The rightmost column in the table shows the taxable status of each item, as shown in Figure 3-9.)

13. In the *Customer Message* drop-down list, choose a message to include on the sales receipt, *Thank you for your business,* in this example.

   The messages that appear in this drop-down list come from the *Customer Message List* (on the *Lists* menu, choose *Customer & Vendor Profile Lists*, and then choose *Customer Message List*).

14. In the *Memo* field, type a memo about the sale, in this example, *install garage door opener.*

15. To save the sales receipt and close the *Enter Sales Receipt* window, click *Save & Close.*

16. In this example, you changed the class and tax item, so QuickBooks displays the *Information Changed* message box. To apply these changes to the customer or job record, click *Yes*.

If the values you changed apply only to this sales receipt, click *No* instead.

Figure 3-10 The Information Changed message box

> Note: The *Enter Sales Receipt* window in the previous example didn't include a field to select a bank account for the deposit. That's because QuickBooks puts the payment in an account called Undeposited Funds until you're ready to deposit it. To learn how the Undeposited Funds account works, see the section, Using the Undeposited Funds Account on page 87.

Creating an Invoice

You use invoices to record credit sales, that is, sales in which the customer doesn't pay you at the time of the sale. For that reason, the *Create Invoices* window is a little different than the *Enter Sales Receipt* window, as this section explains. Behind the scenes, when you create an invoice in QuickBooks, the program increases the Accounts Receivable account to reflect the money that the customer owes you.

Computer Practice

To create an invoice, follow these steps:

1. To create an invoice for an existing customer, in the *Customer Center*, select the customer or job name. In the center's toolbar, choose *New Transactions*, and then choose *Invoices* from the drop-down menu. In this example, choose the *Room Addition* job for *Jason Burch*.

   Alternatively, on the *Home Page* or on the *Customers* menu, click *Create Invoices*. Then, in the *Customer:Job* drop-down list, choose the customer or job.

   > Note: Once you select the customer or job in the *Customer:Job* field, QuickBooks fills in other fields with values from the customer's or job's record, as shown in Figure 3-11. If you want to make any changes to that information, such as the *Bill To* address, edit the values in those fields.
   >
   > The *History* pane on the window's right displays recent transactions, such as the invoice dated 11/25/2018. If you want more room in the window for the invoice item table, click the right arrow at the top of the *History* pane to collapse it.

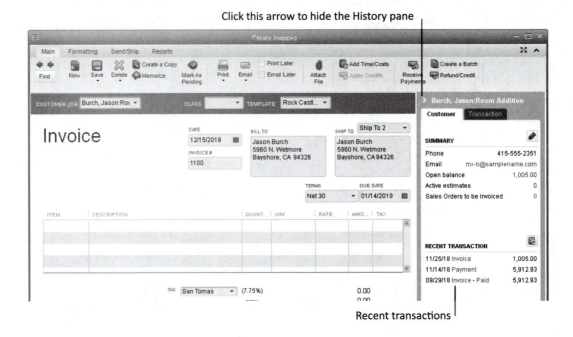

Figure 3-11 The Create Invoices window

2. In the *Class* field, choose the class associated with the sale, in this example, *Remodel*. (See page 39 to learn more about classes.)

3. If you want to use a specific template, choose it in the *Template* drop-down list. In this example, leave Rock Castle Invoice template selected. (See page 225 to learn about customizing form templates.)

4. In the *Date* field, choose the invoice date, in this example, *1/22/2019*.

5. In the *Invoice #* field, type the invoice number, in this example, *2019-1*.

   When you type a value in the *Invoice #* field, QuickBooks automatically increments the number when you create your *next* invoice, for example, to 2019-2. If the number you want is already filled in, skip this field.

6. In the *Terms* field, choose the terms for the customer. In this example, choose *1% 10 Net 30*.

   The *Terms* field is one of the differences between the *Create Invoices* window and the *Enter Sales Receipts* window. Because the customer doesn't pay right away, QuickBooks uses the *Terms* field to determine the invoice due date and the invoice's *Aging* value (how many days the invoice is past due if it's late). See page 218 for more information about the *Terms* list.

   > Note: The Rock Castle Invoice Template doesn't contain the *P.O. Number* field. If your customers use PO numbers, choose the Intuit Product Invoice template, instead. Then you can fill in the *P.O. Number* field with the value from the customer's purchase order.

7. In the first *Item* drop-down list, type the name of the item you sold, in this example, *Counter*.

   As you type the item's name, QuickBooks selects the first item in the list that matches the letters you've typed so far. For example, when you type "c," the program selects Cabinets. Then when you type "o," the selection changes to Concrete Slab. After you type "cou," QuickBooks selects Counter and you can press Tab to move to the *Description* cell.

8. Because the rest of the row's cells are filled in with the values from the item record, click the second *Item* cell, click the down arrow, and then choose *Installation*. In the *Quantity* cell, type *5*.

> Note: Figure 3-12 includes the column, *U/M*, which stands for unit of measure and represents the units for the selected item, such as linear feet or gallons. You can leave this cell blank in this example.

9. If necessary, choose the tax item in the *Tax* drop-down list. In this example, choose *East Bayshore*.

   QuickBooks uses this tax item to calculate the sales for all taxable items on the invoice. In this example, it calculates sales tax on the counter top, which is taxable, but doesn't add any sales tax for the non-taxable installation service. (The rightmost column in the table shows the taxable status of each item, as shown in Figure 3-12.)

10. In the *Memo* field, type a memo about the invoice, in this example, *purchase and installation for customer countertop.*

> Tip: If you send statements to your customers and don't include line item detail in those statements, QuickBooks displays the value from invoices' *Memo* fields on the statements along with the invoice numbers and dates. For that reason, it's a good idea to summarize the invoice by adding an entry in the *Memo* field.

11. If you want to print the invoice later, turn on the *Print Later* checkbox at the top of the window. (See page 56 to learn more about printing invoices.)

12. Figure 3-12 shows what the invoice should look like. To save the invoice and close the window, click *Save & Close*.

   If the *Information Changed* message box appears, which it does because you changed some values in this example, click *Yes*.

Turn on this checkbox to flag the invoice to print later

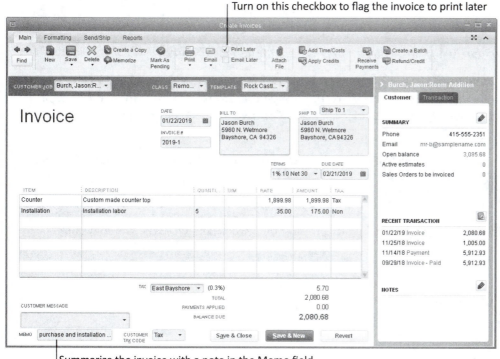

Summarize the invoice with a note in the Memo field

Figure 3-12 A filled in invoice transaction

Creating an Invoice with Calculated Items

QuickBooks includes items that perform calculations on an invoice's line items, such as the *Subtotal* item and *Other Charge* items. For example, if you charge shipping as a percentage of the product prices, you can subtotal all the products on the invoice and then apply an other charge item to calculate shipping. If you want to calculate the discount on sale items, you can subtotal those items and then apply an item to calculate the discount.

Computer Practice

Here are the steps to create an invoice with calculated items:

1. In the *Customer Center*, select the customer or job name. In this example, choose the *Repairs* job for *Renee Barley*. On the center's toolbar, choose *New Transactions*, and then choose *Invoices*.

2. In the *Create Invoices* window, in the *Class field*, choose *Remodel*.

3. In the *Date* field, choose the invoice date, in this example, *1/23/2019*.

4. QuickBooks fills in the *Invoice #* field with 2019-2. Keep that value.

5. Fill in the first two lines of the invoice table with the following items:

    2 Wood Door:Exterior ($120.00 apiece)

    2 Hardware: Doorknobs Std ($30.00 apiece)

6. To subtotal the products on the invoice, click the first blank *Item* cell and then start to type *Subtotal*. As soon as QuickBooks selects *Subtotal* in the list, press Tab.

    QuickBooks calculates the subtotal of the first two lines in the table ($300.00, in this example) and puts the result in the *Amount* cell.

7. To calculate delivery charges, click the *Item* cell below the Subtotal row, type *Shipping*, and then press the Tab key.

8. In the *Item Not Found* message box, click *Yes*.

9. In the *New Item* dialog box, choose *Other Charge* in the *Type* drop-down list.

10. In the *Description* field, type *Shipping as a percentage of sales*. In the *Amount or %* field, type *10%*. Keep the *Tax Code* field set to *Tax*. In the *Account* drop-down list, choose the Cost of Goods Sold account *Freight & Delivery*. Click *OK* to save the item and close the *New Item* dialog box.

    The Shipping item multiplies the subtotal on the previous line by 10% to calculate a shipping charge of $30.

11. In the *Memo* field, fill in a memo about the invoice, in this example, *Calculated Shipping*.

12. Figure 3-13 displays the filled in invoice. To save the invoice and close the window, click *Save & Close*.

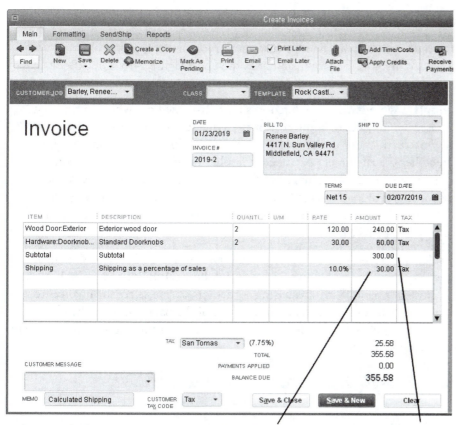

Shipping calculated as a percentage of product subtotal

Subtotal of previous item lines

Figure 3-13 Invoice with calculated shipping

Payment Preferences

Now that you've recorded sales transactions, you're almost ready to receive customer payments. Before you do that, it's a good idea to set QuickBooks' preferences that control how the program applies customer payments you receive. Your work in QuickBooks will flow more smoothly if you set these preferences to match how you prefer to work and how your bank records deposits. To access these preferences, on the *Edit* menu, choose *Preferences*. In the *Preferences* dialog box, choose the *Payments* category, and then click the *Company Preferences* tab (see Figure 3-14). This section describes the preferences you can set for receiving payments and when to use each one.

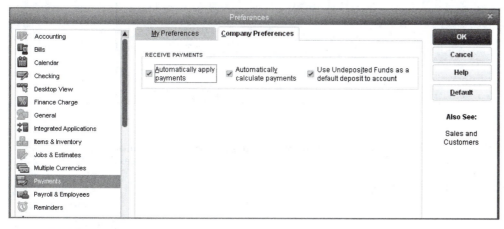

Figure 3-14 Payment preferences

Preferences for Applying Payments

In the *Receive Payments* window, when you choose a customer or job name, QuickBooks automatically displays the open invoices for that customer as shown in Figure 3-15. QuickBooks has two settings that determine how the program applies payments to open invoices:

- **Automatically apply payments.** This preference is initially turned on, which means that QuickBooks chooses the invoices to apply customer payments to in the *Receive Payments* window (which you'll learn about in the next section). If QuickBooks finds an open invoice whose amount matches the customer's payment, it applies the payment to that invoice. However, if a customer's payment *doesn't* match any of its open invoice amounts, QuickBooks applies the payment to the oldest invoices first, which might not be what you want. If customers often make partial payments, you can turn this preference off. That way, *you* choose the invoices to apply payments to.

- **Automatically calculate payments.** This preference is also turned on initially. When you receive a customer payment, in the *Receive Payments* window's *Amount* box, you fill in the amount that the customer paid. With this setting turned on, as you select the invoices to apply the payment to, QuickBooks calculates how much of the payment to apply. If you turn this setting off, you must select the invoices to apply payments to and type the payment amount you want to apply to each invoice.

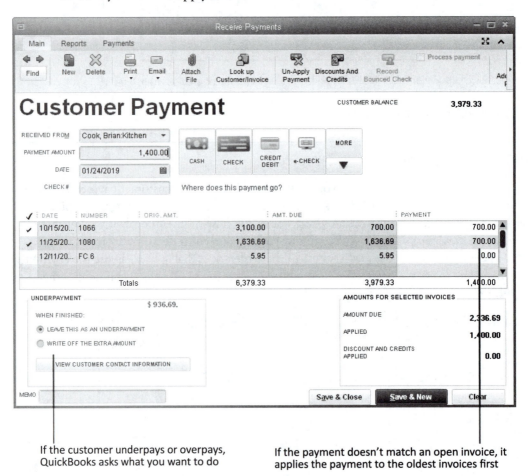

If the customer underpays or overpays, QuickBooks asks what you want to do

If the payment doesn't match an open invoice, it applies the payment to the oldest invoices first

Figure 3-15 Open invoices in the Receive Payments window

Using the Undeposited Funds Account

As mentioned in the previous sections, QuickBooks is initially set up to store payments you receive in the Undeposited Funds account (see Figure 3-14). This setting works well when you receive cash or checks and wait until you have a day's worth of cash payments or several checks to deposit them in the bank. With this setting turned on, you don't see the *Deposit To* field in the *Enter Sales Receipts* window or *Receive Payments* window. In that case, when you're ready to deposit a batch of payments, you use the *Make Deposits* window to select the payments to deposit (see page 96).

> Note: When you store payments in the Undeposited Funds account for a sales receipt payment, QuickBooks debits (increases) the Undeposited Funds account and credits (increases) the appropriate income account. For an invoice payment, QuickBooks debits (increases) the Undeposited Funds account and credits (decreases) the Accounts Receivable account.

If a financial institution records your payments individually, such as credit card payments, you want to record those payments individually in QuickBooks as well. In that case, turn off the *Use Undeposited Funds as a default deposit to account* preference. That way, the *Enter Sales Receipts* window and *Receive Payments* window display the *Deposit To* field (see Figure 3-16). In that field, choose a bank account to deposit the payment immediately or Undeposited Funds to hold it to deposit later.

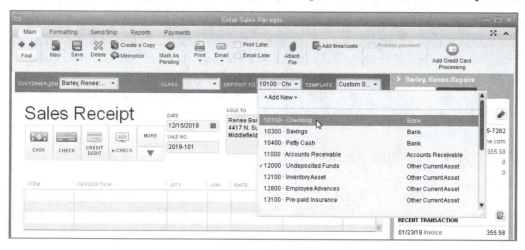

Figure 3-16 The Deposit To field

Viewing Open Invoices

The *Open Invoices* report in QuickBooks lists invoices that are open and their age (that is, how many days they're past due if they're late).

Computer Practice

To run this report, follow these steps:

1. On the *Reports* menu, choose *Customers & Receivables,* and then choose *Open Invoices.*

2. The *Date* field is automatically set to Today. Choose a different date if you want to, in this example, *1/31/2019.*

    Figure 3-17 displays the *Open Invoices* report.

3. To close the report, click the X at the window's top right.

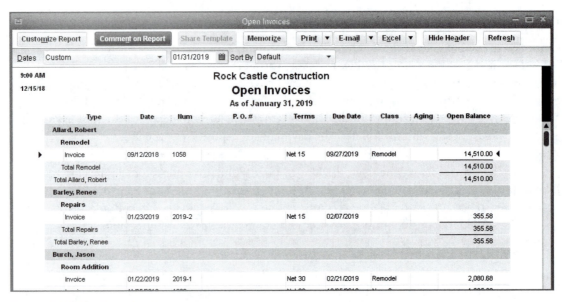

Figure 3-17 The Open Invoices report

Receiving Payments from Customers

As you learned earlier in this chapter, when you record a sales receipt in QuickBooks, the program also records the payment because the sale and payment occur at the same time. (Depending on the payment setting you choose [page 86], QuickBooks deposits the payment in the Undeposited Funds account or the bank account you select.) However, when you record an invoice, the customer doesn't pay right away. In that case, when the customer sends you a payment, you record it in the *Receive Payments* window. This section describes how to receive payments for invoices in QuickBooks.

Receiving Payments by Check

Computer Practice

To record payments that your customers pay by check and apply them to the appropriate invoices, do the following:

1. On the *Home Page*, click *Receive Payments* to open the *Receive Payments* window.

2. In the *Received From* field, choose the customer or job that the payment is associated with. In this example, choose the *Kitchen* job for *Brian Cook*.

   You can also receive a payment from the *Customer Center*. On the *Customers & Jobs* tab, select the customer or job. Then, in the window's toolbar, choose *New Transactions*, and then choose *Receive Payments* on the drop-down menu.

   When you choose a customer or job, QuickBooks fills in the table with the open invoices for that customer or job. Figure 3-18 lists three open invoices for this job. (Invoice number FC 6 represents a finance charge invoice, because the customer's invoices are overdue.)

2. In the *Payment Amount* field, type the amount of the payment, in this example, *700.00*.

   After you fill in the *Payment Amount* field and click another field, QuickBooks automatically applies the payment to invoices. (See page 86 to learn about the payment preferences you can use.) In this example, the payment amount matches the amount of the oldest invoice, so the program turns on that invoice's checkmark and fills in the *Payment* cell with the payment amount.

3. In the *Date* field, choose the date that you received the payment, in this example, *1/21/2019*.

4. Click the *Check* payment button to indicate that the customer paid by check. Type the check number in the *Check #* field (*7721,* in this example).

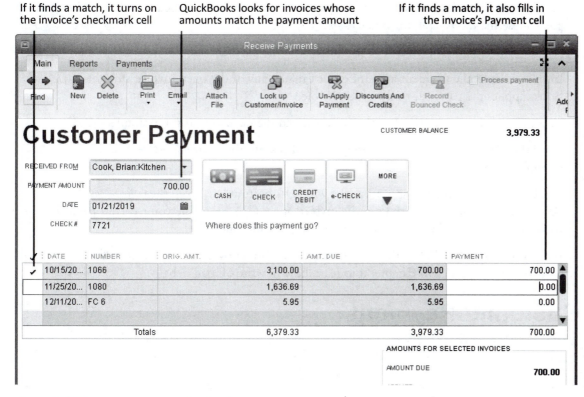

Figure 3-18 Receive a payment by check

5. Verify that QuickBooks selected the correct invoice and applied the correct amount to that invoice. In this example, it selected invoice 1066 and applied $700.00 to it.

   If QuickBooks doesn't find a matching invoice, it applies the payment to the oldest invoice first. If there is money left over, it applies it to the next oldest invoice, and so on, until the payment is completely applied.

   If the program doesn't select the correct invoice or doesn't apply the correct amount, you can turn off the checkmark cell that QuickBooks turned on and click a different checkmark cell to select that invoice. You can also edit the amount in an invoice's *Payment* cell to change the amount applied.

6. In the *Memo* cell, type a note such as *Payment Received for invoice 1066.*

   Filling in the *Memo* cell is helpful when you send customer statements, because QuickBooks statements display the *Memo* field along with the check number and date.

7. To save the received payment, click *Save & Close.*

Recording Partial Payments

Recording a partial payment is almost identical to recording a payment that covers an invoice in full. You might have to select the invoice to apply the payment to, because QuickBooks won't be able to match the payment amount to the invoice amount. In addition, QuickBooks asks you how you want to handle the underpayment.

Computer Practice

To record a partial payment, follow these steps:

1. On the *Home Page*, click *Receive Payments* to open the *Receive Payments* window. In the *Received From* field, choose the customer or job that the payment is associated with. In this example, choose the *Kitchen* job for *Brian Cook*.

2. In the *Payment Amount* field, type the amount of the payment, in this example, *1,000.00*.

    In this example, the payment amount doesn't match any of the open invoice amounts, so Quick-Books applies the payment to the oldest invoice.

3. In the *Date* field, choose the date that you received the payment, in this example, *1/25/2019*.

4. Click the *Check* payment button and type the check number in the *Check #* field (*7732*, in this example).

5. The *Underpayment* section appears at the window's bottom left. Keep the *Leave This As An Underpayment* option selected to keep the invoice open. (The next time you receive a payment from this customer, QuickBooks shows the remaining amount due.)

    If you don't expect to receive the rest of what the customer owes, you can write off the remaining amount. (See page 115 in Chapter 4 to learn how to write off bad debt.)

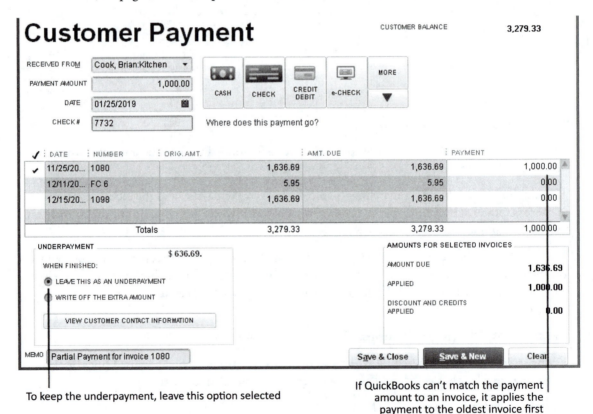

To keep the underpayment, leave this option selected

If QuickBooks can't match the payment amount to an invoice, it applies the payment to the oldest invoice first

Figure 3-19 Receive a payment by check

6. In the *Memo* cell, type a note such as *Partial Payment for invoice 1080*.

7. To save the received payment, click *Save & Close*.

Receiving Payments by Credit Card

Computer Practice

Here are the steps for recording a payment made by credit card:

1. In the *Customer Center's Customers & Jobs* list, right-click the *Repairs* job for *Barley, Renee* (which you recorded earlier in this chapter), and then choose *Receive Payments* on the shortcut menu.

2. In the *Payment Amount* field, type the amount *(355.58)*. In the *Date* field, type the payment date *(1/24/2019)*.

3. Click the *Credit Debit* button to indicate that the payment was made by credit card.

    The *Enter Card Information* dialog box (Figure 3-20) opens so you can enter the credit card information. (If you fill in credit card information on the *Payment Settings* tab in the customer's record, as described on page 73, QuickBooks fills in these fields automatically.)

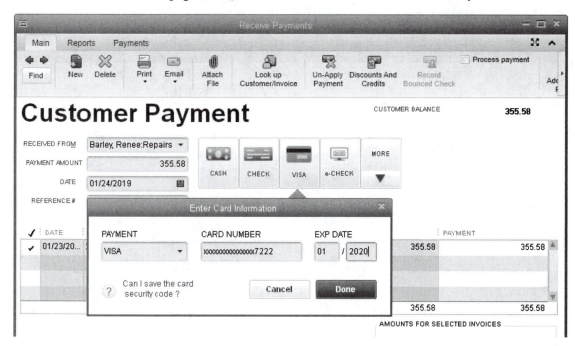

Figure 3-20 Receive a payment by credit card

4. Fill in the credit card information as shown in Figure 3-20. Click *Done*.

    QuickBooks replaces the first 12 numbers in the credit card number with x's for security.

5. Leave the *Reference #* field blank.

6. Click *Save & Close*.

Recording Customer Discounts

If customers pay early to take advantage of the early payment discounts you offer, the payments they send won't match the amounts on their invoices. However, when you record a payment from a customer who has terms like 1% 10 Net 30 (see page 219), QuickBooks recognizes whether the customer qualifies for a discount and notifies you that a discount is available.

Computer Practice

To record a payment that includes an early payment discount, follow these steps:

1. In the *Customer Center's Customers & Jobs* list, select the *Room Addition* job for *Burch, Jason* (which you recorded earlier in this chapter). In the center's toolbar, choose *New Transctions*, and then choose *Receive Payments* on the submenu.

2. Click the *Credit Debit* button to indicate that the payment was made by credit card. Use Visa *1234-5678-9012-3456* and expiration date *05/2019*.

3. In the *Payment Amount* field, type the payment amount, in this example, *$2,059.87*. In the *Date* field, choose the payment date (*1/24/2019*).

    Because this customer has two open invoices and the payment amount doesn't match either one, QuickBooks applies the payment starting with the oldest invoice first, as shown in Figure 3-21. Because of the early payment discount, the *Underpayment* section appears, displaying the amount of underpayment. However, QuickBooks also displays a message about an available discount

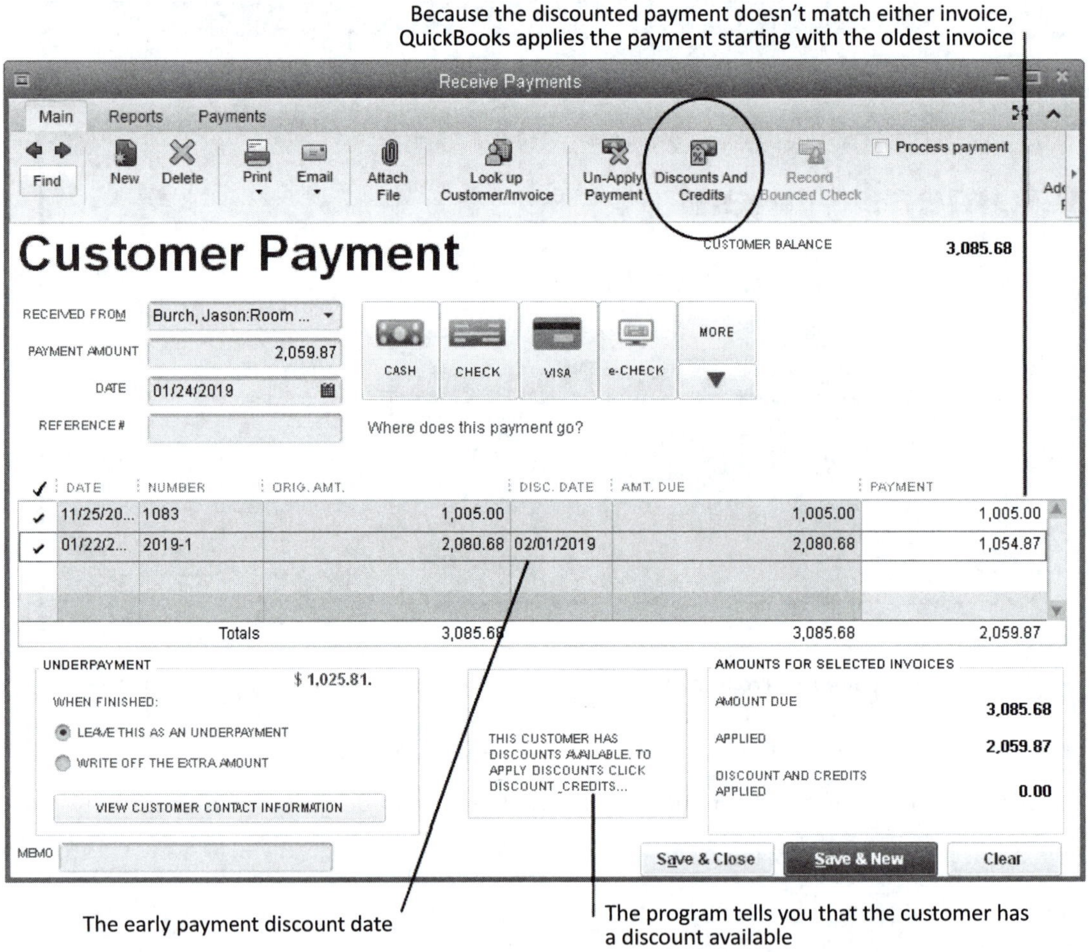

Figure 3-21 A payment that includes a discount

4. In this example, turn off invoice 1083's checkmark cell to remove the value from its *Payment* cell. Click invoice 2019-1's checkmark cell twice to turn it off and then back on, so that QuickBooks applies the full payment amount to the invoice.

    Figure 3-22 shows the payment applied to the correct invoice.

Underpayment section shows the amount of underpayment

Figure 3-22 Payment applied to the correct invoice

5. To apply the available discount to the invoice, click *Discounts And Credits* (circled in Figure 3-21) at the top of the *Receive Payments* window.

   The *Discount and Credits* dialog box opens (Figure 3-23). QuickBooks calculates the suggested discount and fills in the *Amount of Discount* field. You can edit the value if you wish.

6. If necessary, choose the account that you want to use to post the discount. In this example, keep the *Less Discounts Given* account.

   QuickBooks automatically applies the discount to the invoice. In Figure 3-23, the *Discount Used* value shows the discount amount applied. In addition, the *Balance Due* value equals the payment that the customer sent, which confirms that he used the early payment discount.

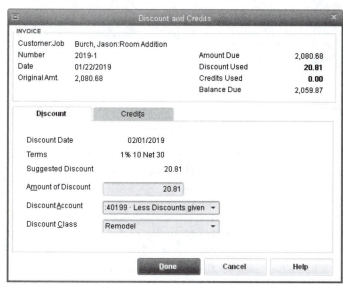

Figure 3-23 Discount applied to the invoice

> Note: If the payment amount doesn't match the discounted amount, you can edit the value in the *Amount of Discount* field so the payment and balance due match. However, if the payment amount is significantly different than the discounted amount, you can apply the payment as it is and then either send the customer a refund or a statement showing how much they still owe.

7. If you use classes, choose the class for the discount, in this example, *Remodel*.

8. Click *Done* to close the dialog box and return to the *Receive Payments* window.

   The *Receive Payments* window shows the discount applied (Figure 3-24).

9. When your screen matches Figure 3-24, click *Save & Close*.

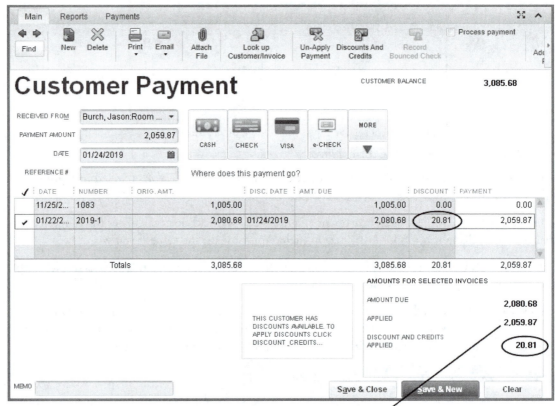

Figure 3-24 Discount applied to the invoice

Making Bank Deposits

When you record customer payments in the *Enter Sales Receipt* window or *Receive Payments* window, by default, QuickBooks posts these payments to the *Undeposited Funds* account (page 87). When you're ready to deposit those payments, you record a deposit transaction in QuickBooks.

If customers use different payment methods, you need to record your deposits in QuickBooks to match the deposits that your bank posts to your account. For example, when you deposit cash and checks, the bank might post a single deposit transaction for the total amount. However, customer credit card payments might post individually and include a deduction for the credit card fee. This section explains how to record both of these types of deposits.

Depositing Cash and Checks

Computer Practice

To record a deposit for cash and checks, follow these steps:

1. On the *Home Page*, click *Record Deposits* (or, on the *Banking* menu, choose *Make Deposits*).

    The *Payments to Deposit* window opens and lists the payments stored in the *Undeposited Funds* account.

2   In the *View payment method type* drop-down list, choose *Cash and Check*.

    QuickBooks filters the payment list to show only payments made by cash or check (Figure 3-25).

3. Click the *Select All* button below the table to select all the cash and check payments.

    As shown in Figure 3-25, when you click *Select All*, QuickBooks selects all the payments in the table (indicated by the checkmarks). It also grays out the *Select All* button and activates the *Select None* button.

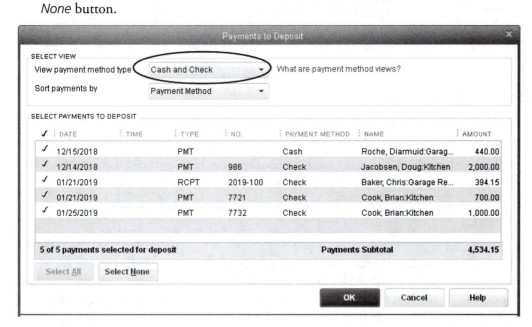

Figure 3-25 Cash and check payments

4. Click *OK*.

    The *Make Deposits* window (Figure 3-26) opens and lists all the payments you selected.

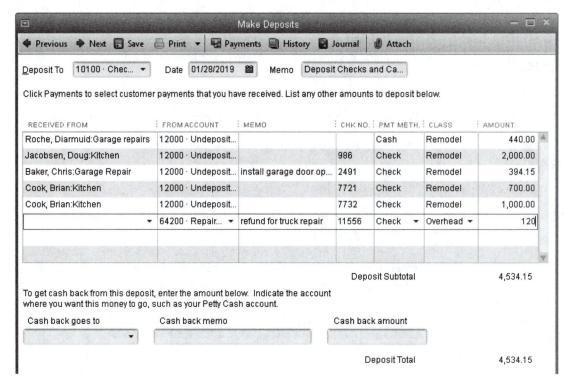

Figure 3-26 Cash and check payments

5. In the *Deposit To* field, make sure that the correct bank account is selected, in this example, *Checking*.

6. In the *Date* field, choose the date you're going to deposit the money, in this example, *1/28/2019*. In the *Memo* field, type a note about the deposit, such as *Deposit Checks and Cash*.

   The *Deposit Subtotal* (below the table's *Amount* column) shows the amount of the selected payments.

   > Note: If you want to hold cash back from the deposit, for example, to fill your petty cash drawer, fill in the fields below the table. In the *Cash back goes to* field, choose the account for the money, such as Petty Cash. In the *Cash back memo* field, type a note about why you're holding cash back. In the *Cash back amount* field, type the amount you are deducting from the deposit. (In this example, do not hold any cash back.)

7. You can deposit additional checks right in the *Make Deposits* window. For example, to add a vendor's refund check to the deposit, fill in the cells in the first blank line in the table, as shown in Figure 3-26.

8. If you want to print a deposit slip, in the *Make Deposits* window's toolbar, click *Print*.

   Typically, you would load preprinted deposit slips into your printer before printing a deposit slip. In this example, you can print to blank paper.

9. In the *Print Deposit* dialog box, select the *Deposit slip and deposit summary* option, and then click *OK*.

   In the *Print Deposit Slips* dialog box, make sure that the correct printer appears in the *Printer name* field.

10. Click *Print*. Figure 3-27 shows the deposit slip and deposit summary that QuickBooks prints.

11. Click *Save & Close* to save the deposit.

	440.00		
	2,000.00		
	394.15		
	700.00		
	1,000.00		
1/28/2019	120.00		4,654.15
		06	$4,654.15

Deposit Summary

12/15/2018

Summary of Deposits to 10100 · Checking on 01/28/2019

Chk No.	PmtMethod	Rcd From	Memo	Amount
	Cash	Roche, Diarmuid:Garage repairs		440.00
986	Check	Jacobsen, Doug:Kitchen		2,000.00
2491	Check	Baker, Chris:Garage Repair	install garage door opener system	394.15
7721	Check	Cook, Brian:Kitchen		700.00
7732	Check	Cook, Brian:Kitchen		1,000.00
11556	Check		refund for truck repair	120.00
			Deposit Subtotal:	4,654.15
			Less Cash Back:	
			Deposit Total:	4,654.15

Figure 3-27 Printed deposit slip and summary

Depositing Credit Card Payments

Because your bank posts customer credit card payments separately from the cash and checks you deposit, it's best to deposit credit card payments in a separate pass through the *Make Deposits* window. That way, it will be easier to reconcile your bank account when you receive your bank statement, because the deposits in QuickBooks will match the deposits on your statement.

Computer Practice

To record customer credit card payments, follow these steps:

1. On the *Home Page*, click *Record Deposits* (or, on the *Banking* menu, choose *Make Deposits*).

2   In the *View payment method type* drop-down list, choose *MasterCard, Visa, Discover*.

    QuickBooks filters the payment list to show only payments made by these credit card types, as shown in Figure 3-28. In Figure 3-28, you can see the two Visa payments you recorded earlier in this chapter.

3. Click the *Select All* button below the table to select all the credit card payments listed in the table.

    Be sure to deposit credit card payments in the same way that your bank posts those deposits. If your bank deposits all your credit card payments in a lump sum, click *Select All*. If credit card payments are posted individually, then select one credit card payment and deposit it before recording the next deposit.

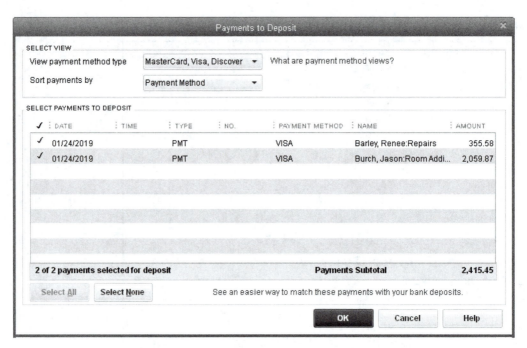

Figure 3-28 Credit card payments selected to deposit

4. Click *OK*.

    The *Make Deposits* window opens and lists all the credit card payments you selected.

5. In the *Deposit To* field, make sure that the correct bank account is selected, in this example, *Checking*.

6. In the *Date* field, choose the date you're going to deposit the money, in this example, *1/29/2019*. In the *Memo* field, type a note about the deposit, such as *Visa deposit with bank card fees*.

7. If your bank deducts its fee for processing credit card payments from the deposit, you can record that fee in the *Make Deposits* window. In the first blank *From Account* cell, choose the expense account you use for bank fees, in this example, *Bank Service Charges*.

8. In the *Memo* field, type a note, such as *Fees for credit card payments*. In the *Pmt Meth.* cell, choose the credit card associated with the fees, *Visa*, in this example. Assign the appropriate class, such as *Overhead*.

9. You can calculate the bank service charge right in the *Make Deposits* window.

    Click the *Amount* cell in the bank service charge row. Type the deposit subtotal as a negative number (because the bank service charge reduces the amount of the deposit). In this example, type *-2415.45*. Then, press the * key on your numeric keypad (or Shift+8). Then, type the service charge percentage, in this example, *.02*. QuickBooks displays a popup box that looks like an adding machine tape, as shown in Figure 3-29. When you click another cell, the program fills in the fee (in this example, -48.31), as shown in Figure 3-30. The bank service charge reduces the deposit amount.

10. To save the deposit, click *Save & Close*.

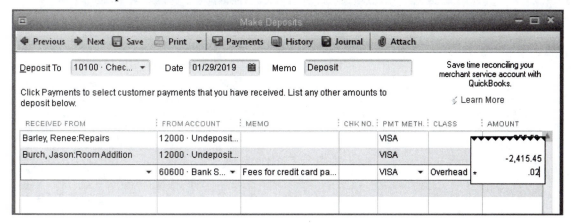

Figure 3-29 Calculating a bank service charge

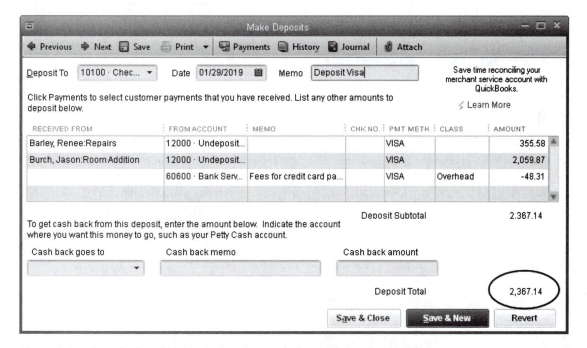

Figure 3-30 The calculated bank service charge deducted from the deposit

The deposits you make appear in your bank account register. To view the checking account register for these deposits, on the *Home Page*, click *Check Register* in the *Banking* section. In the *Use Register* dialog box, choose the bank account you want to look at, and then click *OK*. In this example, Checking is already selected. Figure 3-31 shows the cash and check, and credit card deposits in the Checking account register.

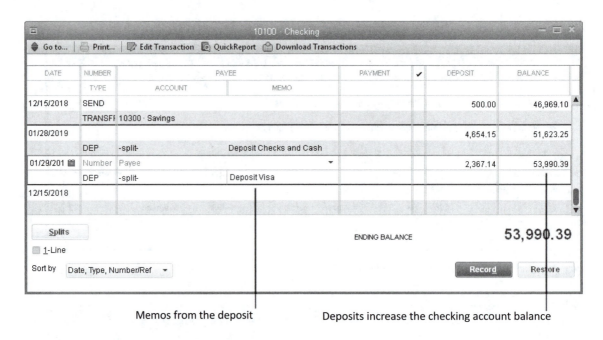

Memos from the deposit   Deposits increase the checking account balance

Figure 3-31 Deposits in the bank account register

Using Income Tracker

Income Tracker (Figure 3-32) provides a quick and easy way to view the status of your sales transactions. You can see how much is unbilled, unpaid, and overdue. It also shows the amount that customers have paid in the past 30 days. You can also launch income-related tasks, such as receiving payments, from this window. *Income Tracker* was introduced in QuickBooks 2014. QuickBooks 2015 adds a few enhancements. This section provides an overview of what you can do with *Income Tracker*.

Apply filters to the transactions in the table   Or click a bar to see the transactions that make up that amount   Choose an action for a transaction

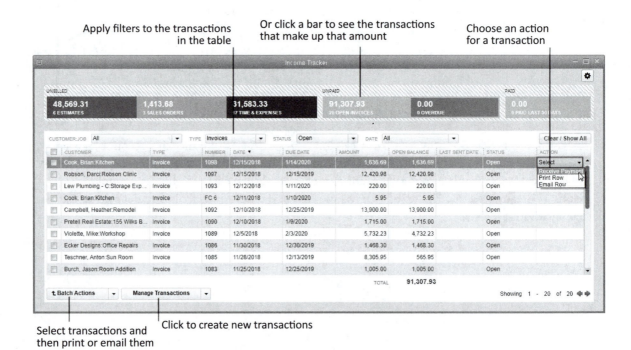

Select transactions and then print or email them   Click to create new transactions

Figure 3-32 The Income Tracker window

Computer Practice

Here is a brief example of using *Income Tracker* to process sales transactions:

1. To open the *Income Tracker* window, on the icon bar, choose *Income Tracker* (or, on the *Customers* menu, choose *Income Tracker*).

2. Review the colored bars above the table to see totals for unbilled sales, unpaid sales, and payments received in the past 30 days.

    Unbilled sales appear in blue bars on the left. The *Open Invoices* bar is orange. The *Overdue Invoices* bar is red.

    > Note: QuickBooks 2015 added the *Time & Expenses* bar so you can check the unbilled time and expenses total. You can also choose which unbilled bars to include. To do that, click the *Settings* icon (which looks like a gear) at the top right of the *Income Tracker* window. Then, turn checkboxes on or off to display or hide *Estimates, Sales Orders,* and *Time & Expenses.*

3. To view the transactions that make up the total in a colored bar, click the bar, in this example, *Open Invoices.*

    QuickBooks filters the table to include only the transactions that contribute to the total in the selected colored bar. Notice that the *Type* field below the bars changes to *Invoices* and the *Status* field changes to *Open.*

4. To launch an action, click the *Action* cell for a transaction, in this example, the first open invoice in the table. Then choose *Receive Payment* (Figure 3-33) to open the *Receive Payments* window with the customer, job, and invoice already selected. Close the *Receive Payments* window without recording the payment.

5. To print or email copies of sales transactions, turn on the first three checkboxes on the left side of the window. Click the *Batch Actions* down arrow, and then choose *Invoices* to print the selected invoices.

6. To filter the transactions using the fields below the colored bars, click the field's down arrow and then choose the filter you want. In this example, click the *Type* down arrow and choose *Time & Expenses* (or, in QuickBooks 2014, *Estimates*). In the *Status* drop-down list, choose *Open.* In the *Date* drop-down list, choose *This Fiscal Year.*

7. To sort the transactions in the table, click a column heading, in this example, click *Amount.*

8. To create new customer transactions, click the *Manage Transactions* down arrow and then choose the type of transactions you want to create.

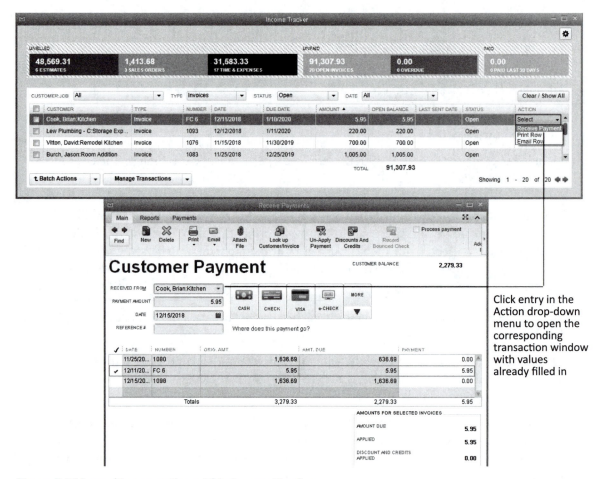

Click entry in the
Action drop-down
menu to open the
corresponding
transaction window
with values
already filled in

Figure 3-33 Launching an action within Income Tracker

Review Questions

Select the best answer(s) for each of the following:

1. Which sales form(s) should you use if a customer doesn't pay its balance in full?

    a) Invoice

    b) Sales receipt

    c) Statement

    d) All of the above

2. What does the *Customer Name* field do?

    a) It is an identifier that appears in the *Customer & Jobs* list.

    b) It appears in the *Bill To* field in an invoice.

    c) It is the customer's legal company name.

    d) It does the same things as the *Company Name* field.

3. Which statement(s) is true?

    a) Invoices decrease the Accounts Receivable balance.

    b) Sales receipts can handle payments in full at the time of a sale.

    c) Sales Receipts increase the Accounts Receivable balance.

    d) Sales receipts can't handle sales tax.

4. Settings such as *Terms* in a customer's record:

    a) Can be changed in a sales form, but not in the customer record.

    b) Are filled in automatically when you create a sales receipt or invoice.

    c) Can be changed in a sales form and updated in the customer record.

    d) Appear at the top of the appropriate drop-down lists when you display that list in a sales form.

5. A customer sent a check as payment for an invoice. What should you do to record this payment?

    a) On the *Home Page*, click *Invoice* to open the invoice, and then add a *Payment* item to the invoice, and save the transaction.

    b) Create a credit memo with the payment and then apply the credit to the invoice.

    c) On the *Home Page*, click *Receive Payments* to receive the payment.

    d) On the *Home Page*, click *Record Deposits* to deposit the payment.

Sales and Income Exercise 1

Restore the sample file, *sample_product-based business 2015 (Portable).QBM.* (Or, if you are using QuickBooks 2014, restore *sample_product-based business 2014 (Portable).QBM.*)

1. Create a sales receipt using data from the following table. You can use *Quick Add* to create the customer. Save changes to lists to the customer record.

Field Name	Data
Customer Name	Walters, John
Company Name	
Class	Remodel
Date	1/21/2019
Sale No.	2019-1
Sold To	John Walters 993 Main St. Middlefield, CA 94482
Check No.	2234
Payment Methods	Check
Item	Standard Door Knobs quantity 2
Sales Tax Item	San Domingo
Customer Tax Code	Tax
Memo	Honey-do project

2. Record an invoice using data from the following table. Print the invoice on blank paper. Save changes to lists to the customer record.

Field Name	Data
Customer Name	Johnson, Berilyn
Company Name	
Class	New Construction
Custom Template	Rock Castle Invoice
Date	1/23/2019
Invoice No.	2019-101
Bill To	Berilyn Johnson 2 Moss Lane Bayshore, CA 94326
Terms	Net 30
Item	Blueprints, Quantity 4, $95 per hour
Item	Floor Plans, Quantity 8, $95 per hour
Item	Appliance, Quantity 1, Amount $425.00
Sales Tax Item	San Tomas
Customer Tax Code	Tax
Memo	She bought a dishwasher for her second home

4. Record a payment dated *2/15/2019* for the full amount of *Berilyn Johnson's* invoice (check number *3195*) and apply it to invoice *2019-101*.

5. Deposit all transactions from the *Undeposited Funds* account into the *Checking* account on *2/18/2019*. Print the *Deposit Slip* and the *Deposit Summary* report on blank paper.

Sales and Income Exercise 2 (Advanced)

Restore the sample file, *sample_product-based business 2015 (Portable).QBM*. (Or, if you are using QuickBooks 2014, restore *sample_product-based business 2014 (Portable).QBM*.)

1. Create a sales receipt using data from the following table. You can use *Quick Add* or the *New Customer* window to create the customer. Save changes to lists to the customer record.

Field Name	Data
Customer Name	Swann, Laura
Company Name	
Class	Remodel
Date	1/23/2019
Sale No.	2019-1
Sold To	Laura Swann 4540 E. 1st Ave. Millbrae, CA 94030
Check No.	1012
Payment Methods	Check
Item	Decking Lumber, Quantity 12, Rate $8
Item	Interior Doors, Quantity 2
Sales Tax Item	San Tomas
Customer Tax Code	Tax
Memo	Materials for change order

2. Record an invoice using data from the following table. Print the invoice on blank paper. Save changes to lists to the customer record.

Field Name	Data
Customer Name	Abrams, RM
Company Name	RM Abrams Construction
Class	New Construction
Job	7200 Tow Rd. Building
Custom Template	Rock Castle Invoice
Date	1/30/2019
Invoice No.	2019-101
Bill To	RM Abrams Construction 8332 Monterey Blvd. San Mateo, CA 90402
Terms	Net 30
Item	Lumber Rough, Amount $6,000
Item	Doors Exterior, Quantity 15
Sales Tax Item	San Domingo
Customer Tax Code	Tax
Memo	Call when materials are in. He will pick up.

3. Record another invoice using data from the following table. Print the invoice on blank paper. Save changes to lists to the customer record.

Field Name	Data
Customer Name	Barstow, Joan
Company Name	
Class	Remodel
Date	1/31/2019
Invoice No.	2019-102
Bill To	Joan Barstow 525 156th Ave. Apt. H East Bayshore, CA 94326
Terms	2% 10 Net 30
Item	Repairs, Quantity 2
Item	Appliance, Total $250
Sales Tax Item	E. Bayshore/County
Customer Tax Code	Tax
Memo	Fix stove

4. Record a payment dated *2/20/2019* for the full amount of *Joan Barstow's* invoice (paid with *Visa #4300-1111-2222-3333*, expiration *7/2020)* and apply it to invoice *2019-102*.

5. Record a check payment from *RM Abrams Construction* (number *11321*) dated *2/21/2019* for *$5,000* and apply it to invoice *2019-101*.

6. Deposit all transactions from the Undeposited Funds account into the Checking account on *2/25/2019*.

    a. Deposit cash and check payments together. Memo: *Deposit checks*. Print the *Deposit Slip* and the *Deposit Summary* report on blank paper.

    b. Deposit the Visa payment separately. Memo: *deposit Visa*.

    c. Record a *2% bankcard fee* on the credit card deposit. (Use *QuickMath* in the *Amount* cell to calculate the fee.) Use *Account 60600 Bank Service Charges*, Payment Method – *Visa*, Memo – *2% bankcard fee*. (The amount should be negative.) Print *Deposit Summary Only* on blank paper.

Chapter 4

More Customer Transactions and Reports

Topics

This chapter covers the following topics:

- Recording Customer Returns and Credits

- Writing Off Bad Debt

- Creating Customer Statements

- Working with Sales Tax

- Creating Sales Reports

Now that you've learned how the sales and income process works and recorded customer sales receipts and invoices, it's time to look at a few additional customer transactions. In this chapter, you'll learn how to handle customer returns and credits. And, if a customer goes out of business or isn't going to pay for any other reason, you have to write off the money they owe you, which is called writing off bad debt.

In the previous chapter, you learned how to apply sales tax codes and sales tax items to customers. That chapter demonstrated how QuickBooks calculates sales taxes based on the sales tax codes and sales tax items applied in sales forms. This chapter takes a few steps back and shows how to set up sales tax codes and items. Then you'll learn how to remit sales taxes you collected to the appropriate sales tax authorities.

This chapter also describes how to create customer statements to summarize your customers' activity and how much they owe. Finally, you'll learn how to use several QuickBooks reports to analyze sales.

> Note: For the computer practice in this chapter, restore the sample file, sample_product-based business 2015 (Portable).QBM. Or, if you are using QuickBooks 2014, restore sample_product-based business 2014 (Portable).QBM.

Recording Customer Returns and Credits

Sometimes, you need to give money back to customers, for example, when they return merchandise, cancel an order that they've already paid for, or contact you about an overcharge on an invoice. You can handle these situations in two ways:

- **Issue a credit against the customer's balance:** When you issue a credit, you can apply that credit to one of the customer's open invoices to reduce the amount owed. Or you can keep the credit to apply to the customer's next invoice.

- **Issue a refund:** When you issue a refund, you either write a check or record a credit to the customer's credit card.

Regardless which approach you choose, you create a *credit memo*, a sales form that reduces the amount a customer owes to your company. A credit memo documents the return or credit. Then you can apply that credit memo to one or more invoices or use it to issue a refund to the customer.

> Note: Because customers owe you less money, credit memos credit (decrease) the Accounts Receivable account and debit (decrease) income. (They also decrease *Sales Tax Payable* if any items returned were taxable.)

Creating a Credit Memo

A credit memo includes the details of the products or services returned or credited. The easiest way to create a credit memo is from an existing invoice.

> Note: You can create a credit memo from scratch by clicking the *Refunds & Credits* icon on the *Home Page*. If you do that, you have to fill in the entire form.

Computer Practice

Creating a credit memo from an invoice saves several steps, because QuickBooks copies the invoice's details into the credit memo:

1. Open the *Customer Center* by clicking *Customers* on the *Home Page* or in the left icon bar.

2. On the *Customers & Jobs* tab, select the customer or job, in this example, the *Remodel* job for *Robert Allard*.

3. On the *Transactions* tab on the right, double click invoice *#1058* to open it in the *Create Invoices* window (Figure 4-1).

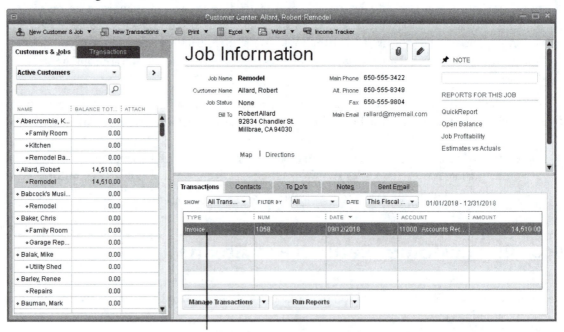

Double-click an invoice to open it in the Create Invoices window

Figure 4-1 Opening an Invoice in the Customer Center

4. At the top of the *Create Invoices* window, click *Refund/Credit*, circled in Figure 4-2.

   The *Create Credit Memos/Refunds* window opens. In this example, the credit memo fields are filled in with information from the original invoice.

   The *Create Credit Memos/Refunds* window looks almost identical to the *Create Invoices* window. However, it does the opposite of what the *Create Invoices* window does. An invoice charges customers for products and services they purchase. A credit memo credits customers for products and services they return (or for credits or discounts they request).

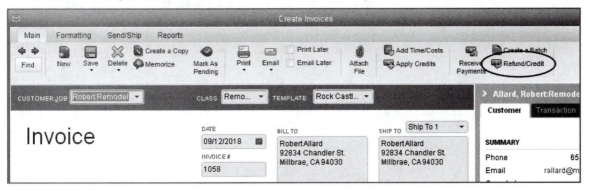

Figure 4-2 The Refund/Credit button in the Create Invoices window

5. In the *Date* field, choose the date for the credit, in this example, *1/21/2019*.

6. In the *Credit No.* field, type a number that indicates the invoice being credited, in this example, *1058C.*

   Including the invoice number for the credited invoice followed by the letter "C" makes it easy to identify the invoice to which the credit memo applies when it appears on statements and customer reports.

7. Delete line items if you aren't crediting them. In this example, select the first line of the table and then press Ctrl+Delete to delete the *Floor Plans* line. Also delete the *Installation* line.

8. In the *Labor* item's line, change the *Qty* cell to *12* to credit the job for 12 hours of labor. In the *Removal* item's line, change the *Qty* cell to *5* to credit the job for 5 hours of removal work.

   Although the numbers you enter are positive, the credit memo reduces the amount owed (that is, it reduces the customer's balance in the Accounts Receivable account.)

9. In the *Memo* field, type a note about the credit, such as *Refund for change order 12.*

10. When your credit memo matches the one shown in Figure 4-3, click *Save & Close.*

    After you save the credit memo, QuickBooks opens the *Available Credits* dialog box (Figure 4-4) with three options for handling the customer's credit. If the customer plans to purchase from you in the near future, you can select the *Retain as an available credit* option to save the credit to the customer's account. Later when you create an invoice for the customer, you can apply this credit to it as described in the next section. Issuing a refund is explained on page 114.

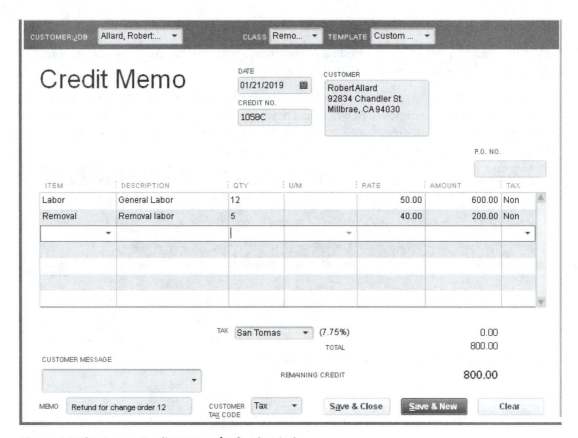

Figure 4-3 The Create Credit Memos/Refunds window

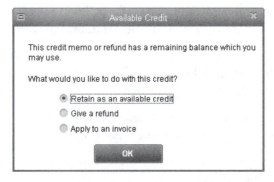

Figure 4-4 The Available Credit dialog box

Applying a Credit Memo to an Invoice

Computer Practice

In this section, you apply the credit that you created in the previous section to an existing invoice.

1. When you save a credit memo, the *Available Credit* dialog box (see Figure 4-4) appears. If the customer has an existing open invoice, you can apply the credit to that invoice by choosing the *Apply to an invoice* option.

> Tip: If the customer doesn't have an open invoice to apply the credit to, simply keep the *Retain as an available credit* option selected, and then click *OK*. Later, when you create another invoice for this customer, you can apply the credit to that invoice in the *Create Invoices* window by clicking *Apply Credits*.

2. In the *Apply Credit to Invoices* dialog box that opens (Figure 4-5), turn on the checkmark cell for the invoice you want to apply the credit to.

3. Click *Done*.

   QuickBooks opens the *Create Invoices* window to the invoice you selected and applies the credit to that invoice, reducing its balance, as shown in Figure 4-6.

4. Click *Save & Close* to save the invoice with the credit applied.

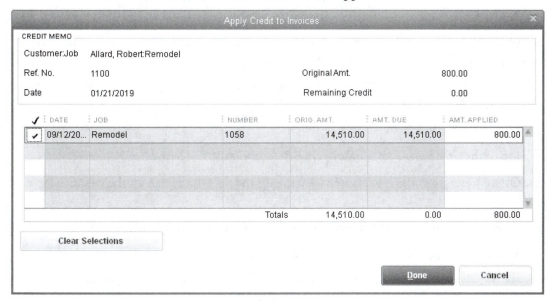

Figure 4-5 The Apply Credit to Invoices dialog box

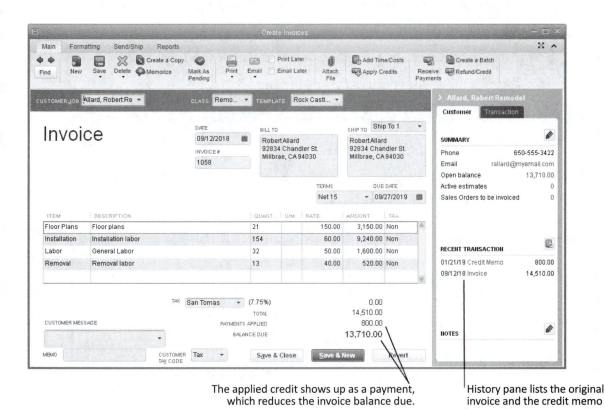

The applied credit shows up as a payment, which reduces the invoice balance due.

History pane lists the original invoice and the credit memo

Figure 4-6 The Applied Credit reduces the invoice's Balance Due

Issuing a Refund

You may need to issue a refund rather than a credit, for example, when the customer doesn't plan to purchase from you again. When you issue a refund, you typically use the same payment method as the customer. For example, if the customer paid with a check, you issue a refund check; if the customer paid by credit card, you issue the refund to that credit card.

Computer Practice

Here are the steps for creating a credit memo and using it to issue a refund:

1. In the *Customer Center* on the *Customers & Jobs* tab, select the customer or job for the credit, in this example, the *Room Addition* job for *Jason Burch*.

2. On the *Transactions* tab at the *Center's* bottom right, double-click the invoice you want to credit, in this example, invoice 1083.

    The *Create Invoices* window opens to that invoice.

3. At the top of the *Create Invoices* window, click *Refund/Credit*.

4. In the *Create Credit Memos/Refunds* window, change the date to the date of the credit, in this example, *01/28/2019*.

5. Change the *Credit No.* to reflect the associated invoice number, in this example, *1083C*.

6. In this example, leave the table as it is to refund the entire invoice.

    If you are crediting only a portion of the invoice, modify the quantities, items, or amounts as needed.

7. In the *Memo* field, type a note about the credit, such as *Work cancelled due to weather*.

8. Click *Save & Close*.

9. In the *Available Credit* dialog box, select the *Give a refund* option and click *OK*.

    The *Issue a Refund* dialog box opens, as shown in Figure 4-7.

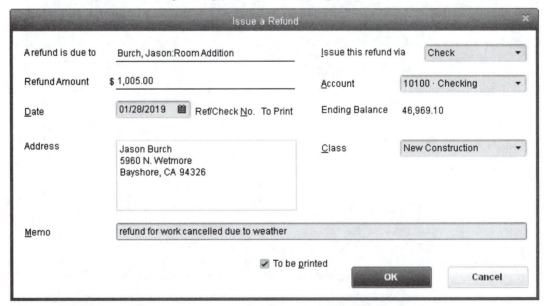

Figure 4-7 The Issue a Refund dialog box

10. In the *Issue this refund via* field, choose the method you want to use to refund the customer's money. In this example, choose *Check* to issue a refund check.

   If the customer paid with a credit card, choose the credit card type the customer used.

11. If necessary, change the date, in this example, *1/28/2019*. Type a note about the refund in the *Memo* field, as shown in Figure 4-7.

12. Click *OK*.

   QuickBooks records the refund check in the checking account (and in this example, sets it up to print later). It also flags the credit memo as refunded.

13. To view the credit memo, in the *Customer Center* on the *Transactions* tab on the left, choose *Credit Memos*. Then, double-click the credit memo, *1083C* in this example.

   A checkmark and the word Refunded appear below the *Credit Memo* heading, as shown in Figure 4-8.

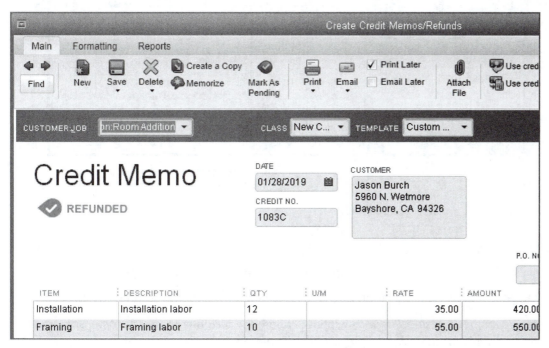

Figure 4-8 A Credit Memo that has been refunded

14. Close the *Create Credit Memos/Refunds* and *Create Invoices* windows.

   The refund check is queued up to print the next time you print checks (page 56).

Writing Off Bad Debt

If you realize that you aren't going to collect on an invoice you sent to a customer, you need to perform a bookkeeping task called *writing off bad debt*. To write off bad debt properly from an accounting perspective, you first credit the customer's balance for the amount of the bad debt. (This amount is posted to an expense account specifically for bad debt.) Then, you reverse the sale to remove the income (and sales tax if items were taxable) from your records by applying the bad debt credit memo to the customer's open invoice. This section describes the entire process.

> Note: The sample file includes an *Other Expense* account called Bad Debt and an *Other Charge* item called Bad Debt, as you can see in Figure 4-9. You'll learn more about accounts in Chapter 12 and more about items in Chapter 7.

Bad debt is assigned to an expense account

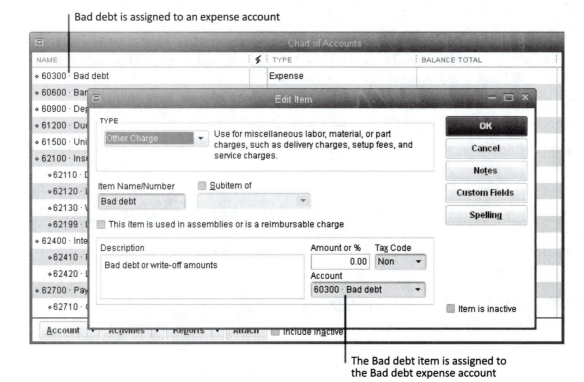

Figure 4-9 An Account and Item for bad debt

The Bad debt item is assigned to the Bad debt expense account

Computer Practice

To record a credit memo for bad debt and apply it to an invoice, follow these steps:

1. On the *Home Page*, click the *Refunds & Credits* icon in the *Customers* section.

2. In the *Create Credit Memos/Refunds* window, choose the customer in the *Customer:Job* drop-down list, in this example, *Ecker Designs' Office Repair* job.

3. Set the *Class* field to *Remodel*. Change the date to *1/25/2019*. Type *1086C* in the *Credit No.* field, and type a note, *Write off bad debt*, in the *Memo* field.

4. To view the invoice that you're writing off, click its link in the *History* pane, shown in Figure 4-10.

    The invoice appears in the *Create Invoices* window. In this example, the invoice you're writing off covers $477 of non-taxable items and $920 of taxable items, so you need two bad debt lines in the credit memo.

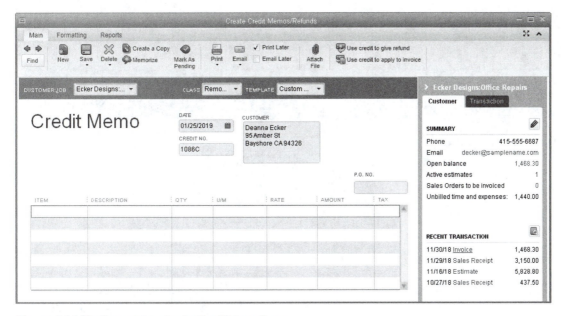

Figure 4-10 Finding an Invoice in the History Pane

5. Close the *Create Invoices* window and return to the *Create Credit Memos/Refunds* window.

6. In the first line's *Item* cell, choose *Bad Debt,* and then press Tab.

   A *Warning* dialog box appears telling you that the item is associated with an expense account. Click *OK.* (QuickBooks displays this message because invoices and credit memos typically affect income accounts, not expense accounts. For bad debt, affecting an expense account is exactly what you want to do.)

7. In the *Tax* cell in the first row, choose *Non* and fill in that row's *Amount* cell with the non-taxable amount from the invoice, in this example, *$477.*

8. In the second row's *Item* cell, choose *Bad Debt* (you can type "bad" and then press Tab when QuickBooks selects the item name in the drop-down list). Click *OK* to dismiss the warning dialog box.

9. In the second row's *Tax* cell, choose *Tax.* In the row's *Amount* cell, type the taxable amount from the invoice, in this example, *$920.*

   When you click away from the *Amount* cell, QuickBooks calculates the sales tax that was due on the taxable items. The credit memo reduces your sales tax liability by that amount.

10. When the credit memo looks like the one in Figure 4-11, click *Save & Close.*

    The *Bad Debt* item on a credit memo credits (decreases) your Accounts Receivable account and debits (increases) your Bad Debt expense account.

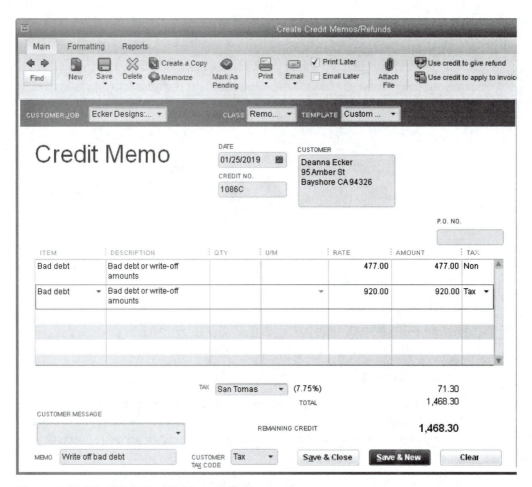

Figure 4-11 A Bad Debt Credit Memo filled in

11. When the *Available Credit* dialog box appears, select the *Apply to an invoice* option and click *OK*.

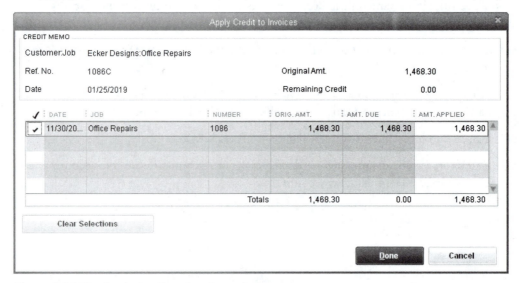

Figure 4-12 The Apply Credit to Invoices window

12. In the *Apply Credit to Invoices* dialog box, turn on the checkmark for the invoice or invoices that the customer isn't going to pay, and then click *Done*.

If you open the invoice in the *Create Invoices* window, you'll see that the *Balance Due* is zero.

Creating Customer Statements

Statements summarize customers' accounts receivable activity for a period of time (usually a month). You can use them to add up all the charges for a period, such as a lawyer's time or cable TV charges. Statements are also a great way to show the invoices you've sent, the payments the customers have made, and their remaining balances. This section describes how to create customer statements.

Computer Practice

To generate statements for customers, follow these steps:

1. On the *Home Page* click the *Statements* icon, or choose *Create Statements* from the *Customers* menu.

   The *Create Statements* window, shown in Figure 4-13, opens.

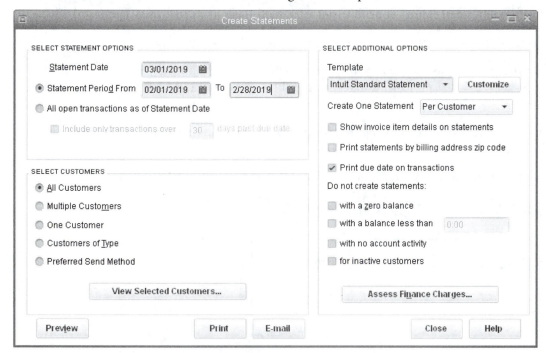

Figure 4-13 The Create Statements window

2. In the *Statement Date* field, choose the date that you want to appear on the statement, in this example, *3/1/2019.*

3. In the *Statement Period From* and *To* fields, choose the beginning and ending dates for the statement, in this example, use *2/1/2019* to *2/28/2019.*

   The *Statement Period* dates determine which accounts receivable transactions appear on the *Statement*. If you want to include all open transactions on customer statements, select the *All open transactions as of Statement Date* option instead.

4. In the *Select Customers* section, keep the *All Customers* option selected.

   The *Select Customers* options let you specify the customers for which you want to generate statements. For example, if you noticed an error on one customer's statement, you can recreate only that statement by selecting the *One Customer* option and then choosing the customer in the field that appears.

> Tip: If you print statements for some customers and email statements to others, you can create batches of statements for each group. To do that, first be sure to fill in the *Preferred Delivery Method* field in each customer's record (page 74). In the *Create Statements* window, select the *Preferred Send Method* option. In the box that appears, select the send method, such as Email. Then, in step 8, click the corresponding send button, *Print* or *Email*.

5. In the *Create One Statement* drop-down list on the window's right, keep *Per Customer* selected.

    This setting creates one statement for each customer regardless of the number of jobs you perform for each one.

> Note: If you want to include the details from every invoice on statements, turn on the *Show invoice item details on statements* checkbox.

6. In the *Do not create statements* section, turn on the *with a zero balance* checkbox.

    When you turn on this checkbox, QuickBooks generates statements only if customers have an open balance. If you want to send statements to show that customers have a zero balance, then turn off this checkbox.

7. To make sure that you're generating the statements you want and they look the way you want them to, click *Preview* at the window's bottom left.

8. If the statements are correct, then click *Print* or *Email* to print or email the statements.

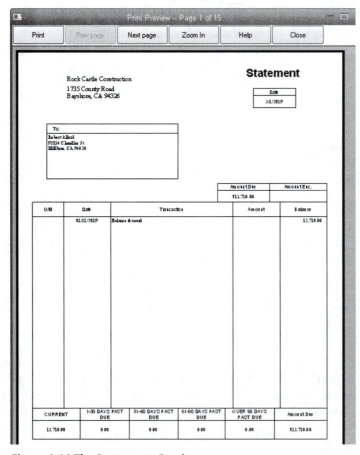

Figure 4-14 The Statements Preview

Working with Sales Tax

Depending on where your customers are located and what you sell, you might have to collect sales tax when you create customer invoices and sales receipts. Sales taxes have a lot of variables. Some products and services are taxable, whereas others aren't. Some customers must pay sales tax, while others don't have to. When you sell to customers in some places, you have to collect several types of sales tax, such as state, county, city, and special sales taxes. You might remit several types of sales taxes to the same tax authority, or you might send each sales tax to a different one. QuickBooks sales tax features can help you handle all these situations. This section describes the setup you need to do.

After QuickBooks sales tax setup is complete, the program calculates sales taxes on invoices and sales receipts you create, which is described in Chapter 3. The payments your customers make might include sales tax, which you need to send to the appropriate tax authorities. In this section, you'll learn how to do that.

How QuickBooks Calculates Sales Tax

In QuickBooks, sales tax codes and sales tax items are the basis for the program's sales tax calculations:

- **Sales tax codes** do two things. First, they flag items you sell and customers as taxable or non-taxable, which is why QuickBooks comes with two sales tax codes: Tax and Non. However, you can create additional sales tax codes to categorize sales by the reason they're taxable or non-taxable, such as sales you make to resellers, who don't pay sales tax on the items they resell. These additional sales tax codes are helpful if tax authorities require documentation about your taxable and non-taxable sales.

- **Sales Tax items**, on the other hand, provide the details about the sales taxes you need to collect. For example, sales tax items specify the sales tax rate and the tax authority you remit the tax to.

When you create a customer record, you assign a sales tax code *and* a sales tax item to that customer (see page 75). The sales tax code specifies whether the customer must pay sales tax. And the sales tax item tells the program which sales tax the customer pays, its rate, and which tax authority receives that tax.

When you set up items for the things you sell, you assign a sales tax code to them (page 216) to specify whether they're taxable and non-taxable.

Here's how QuickBooks uses these sales tax codes and sales tax items to calculate sales tax on a sales receipt or invoice:

1. When you choose a customer in a sales form's *Customer:Job* drop-down list, QuickBooks automatically fills in the sales tax code and sales tax item from the customer's record, as shown in Figure 4-15.

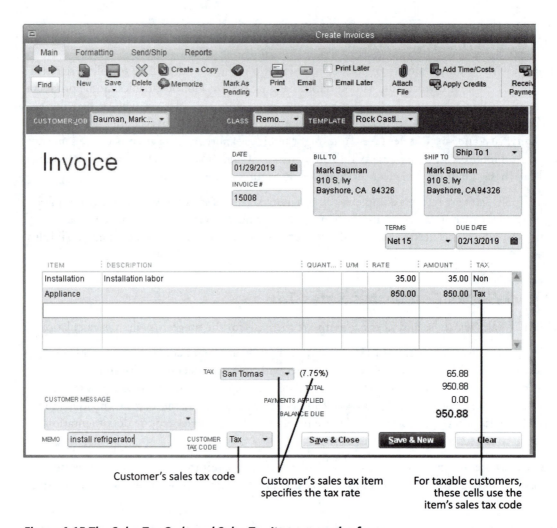

Customer's sales tax code

Customer's sales tax item specifies the tax rate

For taxable customers, these cells use the item's sales tax code

Figure 4-15 The Sales Tax Code and Sales Tax Item on a sales form

2. When you add an item to the sales form's table, the sales tax code that QuickBooks fills in depends on the customer's and the item's sales tax codes.

   If the customer is taxable, QuickBooks fills in the item's sales tax code (Figure 4-15): Tax if the item is taxable and Non if the item is non-taxable.

   If the customer is non-taxable, QuickBooks sets the *Tax* cell to Non regardless of the item's sales tax code.

3. To calculate the sales tax due on a sales form, QuickBooks applies the customer's sales tax rate to all the taxable items on the form.

   Behind the scenes, QuickBooks credits (increases) the *Sales Tax Payable* account by the calculated sales tax. In addition, the *Sales Tax Liability* report tracks how much you must remit to each tax agency.

> Note: You can change the sales tax item and sales tax codes that QuickBooks fills in. To change the sales tax item, click the *Tax* field's down arrow, and then choose the sales tax item you want to apply (for example, if the customer recently moved). To change a sales tax code, click the appropriate *Tax* cell in the table or the *Customer Tax Code* drop-down list, and then choose a different code.

Turning on QuickBooks Sales Tax

Before you can set up sales tax codes and items, you must first turn on the sales tax feature and choose the appropriate sales tax preferences.

1. To turn on sales tax in QuickBooks, on the *Home Page*, click the *Manage Sales Tax* icon or, on the *Vendors* menu, choose *Sales Tax*, and then choose *Manage Sales Tax* on the submenu.

2. In the *Manage Sales Tax* window, click *Sales Tax Preferences*, shown in Figure 4-16.

    The *Preferences* dialog box opens to the *Sales Tax* category and its *Company Preferences* tab (Figure 4-17).

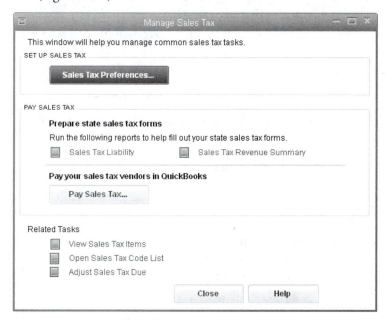

Figure 4-16 The Manage Sales Tax window

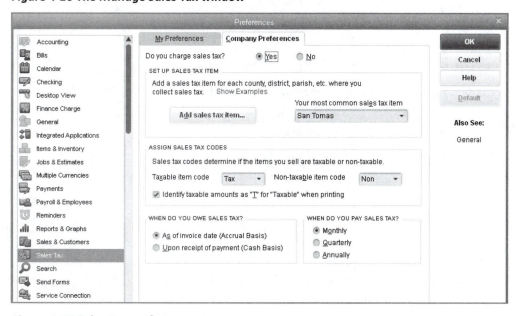

Figure 4-17 Sales Tax preferences

3. In this example, keep the *Yes* option selected in the *Do you charge sales tax?* section.

4. In this example, the *Your most common sales tax item* field contains the San Tomas sales tax item. Keep this value.

When you first turn on sales tax in QuickBooks, you won't have any sales tax items and thus can't choose a most common sales tax item. In that case, click the *Add sales tax item* button to open the *New Item* dialog box. (QuickBooks automatically selects the *Sales Tax Item* type.)

> Note: When you choose a sales tax item in the *Your most common sales tax item* field, QuickBooks automatically assigns that item to new customers you create. It also uses that item on sales receipts and invoices if the customer you choose doesn't have a sales tax item assigned.

5. QuickBooks fills in the *Taxable item code* field with *Tax* and the *Non-taxable item code* field with *Non*. In this example, keep these settings.

If you want to use different sales tax codes for either of these settings, you can create additional sales tax codes (described in the next section), and then choose them in these drop-down lists.

6. In the *When do you owe sales tax?* section and *When do you pay sales tax?* section, select the options based on the schedules that your tax authorities set for your company.

7. Click *OK* to save your changes and close the *Preferences* window.

Creating a Sales Tax Code

If you need to track sales to customers who are exempt from paying sales tax, you can create sales tax codes for each type of exemption. For example, if contractors purchase goods to resell to their customers, they don't pay sales tax. In that case, you might create a sales tax code to track those sales, for example, RSL for reseller.

Computer Practice

Here are the steps to creating a sales tax code:

1. On the *Lists* menu, choose *Sales Tax Code List*.

The *Sales Tax Code List* window opens (see Figure 4-18).

2. Click *Sales Tax Code* at the bottom of the window and then choose *New Sales Tax Code*.

Figure 4-18 The Sales Tax Code List window

3. In the *New Sales Tax Code* dialog box, fill in the information shown in Figure 4-19.

4. Click *OK* to save the sales tax code. Close the *Sales Tax Code List* window.

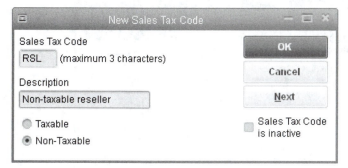

Figure 4-19 The New Sales Tax Code window

After you create a new sales tax code, you can assign it to customers who fit that sales tax category. To change a customer's sales tax code, open the *Customer Center*, and then double-click the customer's name in the *Customers & Jobs* list. (In this example, choose *Lamb, Brad*) In the *Edit Customer* window, click the *Sales Tax Settings* tab, and then choose the sales tax code in the *Tax Code* drop-down list, as shown in Figure 4-20. (Chapter 3 describes how to choose settings in a customer record.)

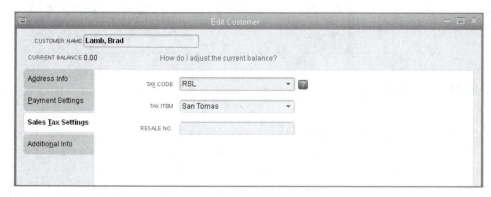

Figure 4-20 Assigning a Sales Tax Code to a customer

Creating a Sales Tax Item

Sales tax items specify the tax rate and the tax authority that levies the tax. For example, you might sell products to customers who live in a part of California that charges only state sales tax. In that case, you need a QuickBooks *Sales Tax Item* for California state sales tax. In most cases, however, more than one sales tax applies to the taxable items you sell, such as state, county, and city sales taxes. In that case, you can create a *Sales Tax Group* to collect all the sales taxes that apply. This section explains how to create each type of sales tax item.

Computer Practice

To create a sales tax item, follow these steps:

1. On the *Lists* menu, choose *Item List* (or, on the *Home Page*, click the *Items & Services* icon).

2. To open the *New Item* window (Figure 4-21), click the *Item* button at the bottom of the window, and then choose *New*. (Or simply press Ctrl+N.)

3. In the *Type* field's drop-down list, choose *Sales Tax Item*.

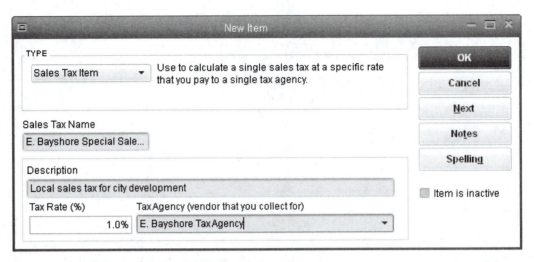

Figure 4-21 The New Item Window for a Sales Tax Item

4. Fill in the fields, as shown in Figure 4-21.

5. Click *OK* to save the sales tax item.

    In this example, the *Vendor Not Found* message box warns that E. Bayshore Tax Agency doesn't exist. Click *Quick Add* to create a vendor record for the tax agency. Click *OK* to close the *New Item* window.

Creating a Sales Tax Group

A *Sales Tax Group* item represents the total tax rate for several *Sales Tax* items. Because you can assign only one sales tax item to a customer, a *Sales Tax Group* is the solution when a customer must pay a combination of sales taxes: state, county, city, and so on. With a *Sales Tax Group*, sales forms show the total tax levied on the sale, but QuickBooks tracks the amount of sales tax owed to each tax authority.

Computer Practice

To create a sales tax group, follow these steps:

1. In the *Item List* window, right-click the window and choose *New* on the shortcut menu (or press Ctrl+N).

2. In the *Type* field, choose *Sales Tax Group*.

3. In the *Group Name/Number* field, type a name for the sales tax group, in this example, *E. Bayshore Combo Tax.*

4. In the *Description* field, fill in a description, in this example, *E. Bayshore County/City/Special.*

5. In the first *Tax Item* cell's drop-down list, choose *E. Bayshore* to include the city tax.

6. In the second *Tax Item* cell's drop-down list, choose *San Tomas* to include the county tax.

7. In the third *Tax Item* cell's drop-down list, choose *E. Bayshore Special* to include E. Bayshore's special local tax.

    As you add all sales tax items to the group, the *Group Rate* below the table displays the total tax, in this example, 9.05%, as shown in Figure 4-22.

8. Click *OK* to save the sales tax group.

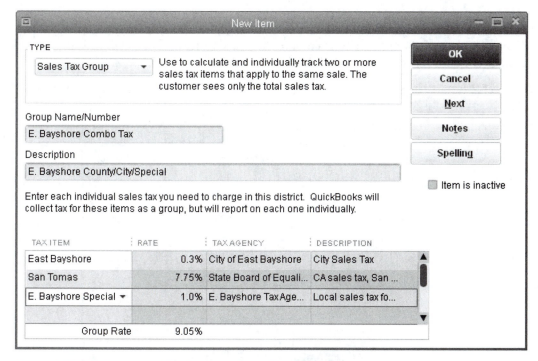

Figure 4-22 The New Item Window for a Sales Tax Group

QuickBooks adds the *Bayshore Group* to the *Item* list.

Paying Sales Tax

You have to fill out forms for tax authorities that report the sales tax you've collected and how much you are sending to them. QuickBooks has a built-in report that provides the information you need to fill out these forms.

The *Sales Tax Liability* report shows the taxable and non-taxable sales you've made and the sales taxes you've collected, subtotaled by each tax authority. On the *Reports* menu, choose *Vendors & Payables*, and then choose *Sales Tax Liability*. (Or, if the *Manage Sales Tax* window is open, click the *Sales Tax Liability* button.) QuickBooks automatically sets the report's dates to match the frequency preference you selected when you set up sales tax (page 124).

After you prepare your sales tax forms, you also have to remit the sales taxes you collected to each tax authority.

> Caution: You don't use QuickBooks' *Enter Bills* or *Write Check* windows to pay sales taxes. The program's *Pay Sales Tax* feature handles remitting sales taxes to tax authorities and tracking what you owe the next time you need to remit taxes.

Computer Practice

Here are the steps to remitting sales taxes:

1. On the *Vendors* menu, choose *Sales Tax,* and then choose *Pay Sales Tax* (or in the *Manage Sales Tax* window, click *Pay Sales Tax*).

   The *Pay Sales Tax* dialog box opens (Figure 4-23.)

2. If necessary, in the *Pay From Account* drop-down list, choose the account you want to use to make your sales tax payments.

---

3. In the *Check Date* field, type the payment date, in this example, *3/15/2019*.

4. In the *Show sales tax due through* field, make sure that the date QuickBooks fills in is the last day of the current sales tax reporting period. In this example, choose *2/28/2019*.

5. If necessary, change the value in the *Starting Check No.* field. In this example, keep the number set to 491.

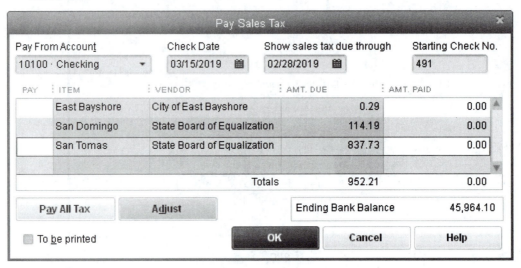

Figure 4-23 The Pay Sales Tax window

> Note: You may need to adjust the sales tax payments you make, for example, to apply a discount for timely payment or add interest and penalties. In that case, click the *Adjust* button to open the *Sales Tax Adjustment* dialog box.

6. In the *Pay* column, click cells to select the payments you want to make. (Or, to pay all the taxes, click *Pay All Tax*.)

   QuickBooks puts a checkmark in the *Pay* cell for selected payments and adds the amount of the payment in the *Amt. Paid* cell.

7. To print the sales tax payment checks, turn on the *To be printed* checkbox, and then click *OK*. (See page 56 for how to print checks.)

   QuickBooks creates a special type of check called a *Sales Tax Payment* for the sales tax due to each sales tax authority. (You'll see the code TAXPMT in the *Type* cell in the checking account register.)

Generating Sales Reports

QuickBooks contains several built-in reports that help you analyze your company's sales and accounts receivable. This section introduces a few of these reports.

- **A/R Aging Summary:** This report (Figure 4-24) shows how much your customers owe you and how old your receivables are (current, less than 30 days old, 31 to 60 days old, 61 to 90 days old, and more than 90 days old). To run this report, on the *Reports* menu, choose *Customers & Receivables*, and then choose *A/R Aging Summary*.

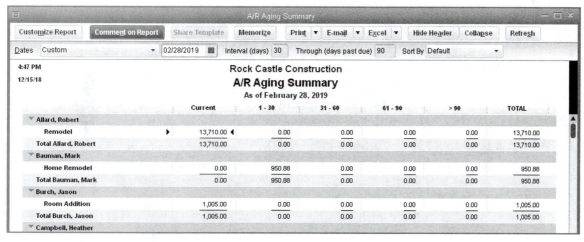

Figure 4-24 The A/R Aging Report

- **Customer Balance Summary:** This report (Figure 4-25) shows each customer's and job's balance. This balance information appears on the *Customer Center's Customers & Jobs* tab, but you can't print the balances from that tab. To run this report, on the *Reports* menu, choose *Customers & Receivables,* and then choose *Customer Balance Summary.*

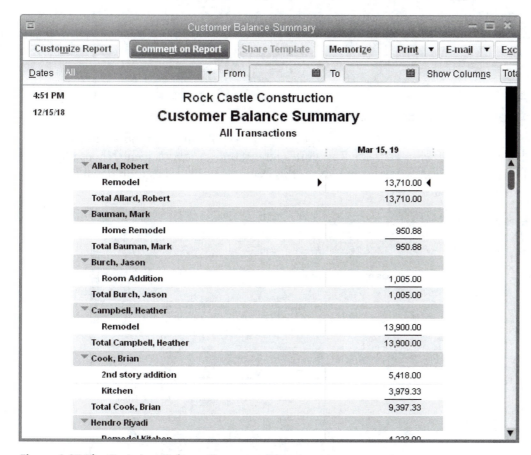

Figure 4-25 The Customer Balance Summary Report

- **Sales by Customer Summary Report:** This report (Figure 4-26) summarizes the sales you've made to each customer and job. To run this report, on the *Reports* menu, choose *Sales,* and then choose *Sales by Customer Summary.* In this example, in the *Dates* drop-down list, choose *This Fiscal Year.*

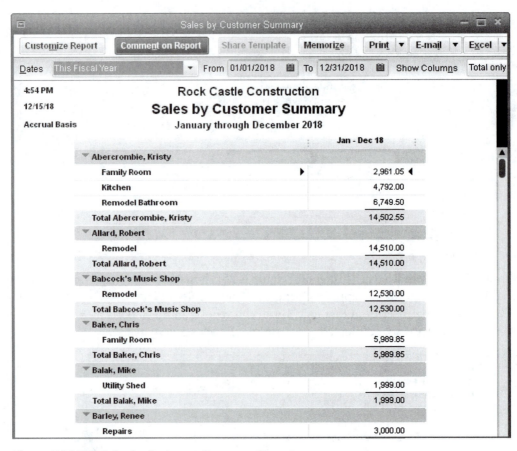

Figure 4-26 The Sales by Customer Summary Report

- **Sales by Item Summary Report:** This report (Figure 4-27) summarizes how much you've sold of each item in your *Item List*. To run this report, on the *Reports* menu, choose *Sales*, and then choose *Sales by Item Summary*. In this example, in the *Dates* drop-down list, choose This Fiscal Year.

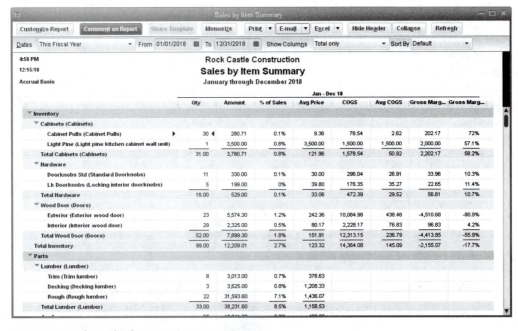

Figure 4-27 The Sales by Item Summary Report

Review Questions

Select the best answer(s) for each of the following:

1. Which sales form(s) should you use if a customer doesn't pay its balance in full?

   a) Invoice

   b) Sales receipt

   c) Statement

   d) All of the above

2. You create a credit memo to:

   a) Request a payment from a customer

   b) Issue a credit to a customer's account

   c) Issue a refund to a customer

   d) None of the above

3. Which method should you use to write off bad debt?

   a) Create an item and account for bad debt and use them to create a credit memo that you can apply to the past due invoice.

   b) Void the past due invoice.

   c) Create a credit memo for the bad debt amount and add it to a statement for the customer.

   d) Any of the above.

4. Which method should you use to set up QuickBooks to calculate state and county sales tax that are paid to two different tax authorities?

   a) Create a sales tax code group for state and county sales tax and apply it to the customers in that county.

   b) Create a sales tax group for state and county sales tax and apply it to the customers in that county.

   c) Create a sales tax item that includes state and county sales tax and apply it to the customers in that county.

   d) Create one sales tax item for state sales tax and another sales tax item for county sales tax, and then apply both items to the customers in that county.

5. Which fields should you fill in on transactions so that transactions on customer statements are easy to identify?

    a) The transaction's number field.

    b) The *Date* field

    c) The *Class* field

    d) The *Memo* field.

More Customer Transactions and Reports Exercise 1

Restore the sample file, sample_product-based business 2015 (Portable).QBM. (Or, if you are using QuickBooks 2014, restore sample_product-based business 2014 (Portable).QBM.)

1. Create an invoice (number *18001*) to *Bauman, Mark's Home Remodel* job, dated *1/20/2019*. Assign it to the *Remodel* class. The customer purchased *40* boards of *trim lumber* (rate of *$5* per board). Apply the *East Bayshore* tax item. Use the class and tax item for all transactions for this job. Print the invoice.

2. Mark Bauman is returning *5* boards of *decking lumber*. Create a credit memo (number *1201-C1*) dated *2/15/2019*. Credit the job for the *5* returned boards (*$5* per board). Apply the credit to the open invoice. Print the credit memo.

3. Print *Sales by Customer Summary* report for *January 2019*.

4. Print *Sales by Item Summary* report for *January 2019*.

5. Create and print customer statements for the period of *1/1/2019* through *1/31/2019*. Print *Statements* for all *residential* customers who have a *balance due*.

More Customer Transactions and Reports Exercise 2 (Advanced)

Restore the sample file, sample_product-based business 2015 (Portable).QBM. (Or, if you are using QuickBooks 2014, restore sample_product-based business 2014 (Portable).QBM.)

1. Create invoice number *18001* dated *1/17/2019* to *Easley, Paula garage* job. Use the *New Construction* class. Apply *2% 10 Net 30* terms only to this invoice. This invoice covers *4* hours of *Removal* service and *8* hours of *Installation* service. Print the invoice.

2. On *1/21/2019*, receive payment by check for the *Easley, Paula garage* job invoice. She paid in full by check *#3633*. She took a *2% early payment discount* of *$8.40*. Use the *Less Discounts Given* account and the *New Construction* class.

3. Create invoice number *18002* dated *1/17/2019* to *Davies, Aaron Remodel* job. Use the appropriate class. Apply *Net 30* terms and use those terms for all future transactions. This invoice is for *one custom made counter top*. Use the *E. Bayshore/County* tax item. Print the invoice.

4. On *2/7/2019*, Mr. Davies called to pay using his credit card. He provided his *Visa* number: *1111-2222-3333-4444* with Expiration *05/2019*. He paid *$2,052.93*.

5. Create invoice number *18003* dated *1/18/2019* to *Vitton, David Remodel* job. Use the appropriate class. This invoice is for appliances: *refrigerator, dishwasher, and stove*. Add the appliances to the *Description*. The amount is *$2,850*. Use the *San Tomas* tax item. Print the invoice.

6. On *2/8/2019*, you received check *#1924* from Mr. Vitton for *$1,000.00* as payment for invoice *18003*. Record that payment and keep it as an underpayment.

7. On *2/7/2019*, Paula Easley requested a refund for *2* hours of installation. Create credit memo number *18001 – C1* and issue a refund check dated *1/7/2019*.

8. On *2/10/2019*, create a credit memo (*1086-C1*) to write off invoice *1086* to *Ecker Designs Office Repairs* job. Use the *Remodel* class. Add the *Bad Debt* item to the credit memo. The invoice includes *$477* of nontaxable items, so record the first *Bad Debt* as nontaxable. Add the *Bad Debt* item to the second row, set the amount to *$920*, and make it taxable. The entire write-off is $1,468.30. Apply the credit memo to the open invoice.

9. Create invoice number *18004* dated *1/18/2019* to *Castillo, Eloisa's utility Room* job. Use the *New Construction* class. This invoice is for *4 interior doors* and *4 locking door knobs*. Use the *East Bayshore* tax item. Print the invoice.

10. Eloisa Castillo is returning *2 doors* and *2 doorknobs*. On *2/16/2019*, create credit memo number *18004-C1* to record the return. *Subtotal* the items being returned. Create an *Other Charge* item called *Restocking Fee* assigned to the *Materials Income* account to hold back a *15%* restocking fee and add it to the credit memo. Keep the credit.

11. On ~~2/7/2019~~ 2/28/2019, deposit all the checks you received in ~~December 2018~~ Jan & Feb 2019. The total deposit amount is ~~$3,851.60~~. Print the *Deposit Slip* and *Deposit Summary*.

1411

12. Deposit all *VISA* payments on *2/8/2019*. Record a *2% bank card fee* to *Bank of Anycity* assigned to the Bank Service Charges expense account. The total deposit amount is *$2,011.87*. Print the *Deposit Summary Only*.

13. Print *Sales by Customer Summary* report for *January 2019*.

14. Print *Sales by Item Summary* report for *January 2019*.

15. Generate and preview statements for customers with open balances for the dates *February 1, 2019* through *February 28, 2019*. Which customers will receive statements and what are their open balances?

$$89960 - 3270 = 56690$$
$$4360 - 1090 = 3270$$

Chapter 5

Bank Reconciliation and Bank Transactions

Topics

This chapter covers the following topics:

- Reconciling Bank Accounts

- Resolving Bank Reconciliation Errors

- Transferring Money between Accounts

- Handling Bounced Checks

- Bank Feeds

Just as you do with your personal checking account, you need to *reconcile* your business bank accounts to your bank statements each month to make sure that your QuickBooks records and your bank's records match. If they don't, you need to track down the source of the discrepancy and fix it. This chapter explains how to reconcile QuickBooks bank and credit card accounts to the statements you receive from your bank or credit card company. You'll also learn how to find discrepancies and fix them, whether the mistake is yours or one your bank made.

In this chapter, you'll learn how to handle transfers between accounts and bounced checks—whether it's your check that bounces or one from a customer. This chapter also provides a brief introduction to *Bank Feeds*, the QuickBooks feature that helps you process online transactions, such as online bill payments, and download transactions from your bank (or other financial institutions) into your QuickBooks company file.

> Note: For the computer work in this chapter, restore Ch05_reconcile_forchapter 2015 (Portable).QBM if you are using QuickBooks 2015. If you run QuickBooks 2014, restore Ch05_reconcile_forchapter 2014 (Portable).QBM.

Reconciling Bank Accounts

When you keep your bank records in QuickBooks, reconciliation discrepancies occur less often because the program doesn't make math mistakes. However, problems still can arise—transactions might be missing in your company file or the numbers you recorded don't match the ones from the bank. By reconciling your QuickBooks records to those of your financial institutions, you can correct errors quickly (and prevent bounced checks charges because your balance wasn't as high as you thought it was) and make sure your records are accurate. This section describes how to reconcile checking accounts and credit card accounts. (The procedures described in this section apply as well to savings and money market fund accounts.)

The statements you receive from your bank or credit card company show all the activity in your account since the previous statement (as you can see in the sample bank statement shown in Figure 5-1):

- The opening balance for your bank account (which is the ending account balance from your previous statement)

- The ending balance for your bank account as of the statement's closing date

- The amount of interest you received during this statement period, if any

- Any service charges assessed by the bank during this statement period

- Checks that cleared the bank during this statement period

- Deposits you made that cleared during this statement period

Figure 5-1 A sample bank statement

- Any other transactions that occurred, such as automatic payments, ATM withdrawals, and so on

Reconciling an account is a two-step process and, as you'll see shortly, QuickBooks has a window for each step. First, you choose the account you want to reconcile and enter the key statement information: the ending balance from your bank statement, and service charges and interest earned during the statement period. Then you reconcile your QuickBooks account to your statement.

Tip: If you don't reconcile your accounts for several months, don't try to reconcile them all at once to catch up. Instead, repeat the reconciliation process for each statement in chronological order.

Reconciling a Checking Account

This section describes how you reconcile a checking account in QuickBooks.

Computer Practice

Here are the steps to reconciling a checking account, using the statement in Figure 5-1 as an example:

1. In QuickBooks, review your checking account to make sure that you've recorded all the bills you paid, checks you wrote, transfers, deposits, debit card transactions, automatic payments and charges, and bank fees.

    Although you can create and edit transactions in the middle of a reconciliation, it's best to enter all your transactions before you reconcile.

2. On the *Banking* menu, choose *Reconcile*.

    The *Begin Reconciliation* window opens.

3. In the *Account* field, choose your checking account, if necessary. In this example, choose *Checking*, if it isn't already selected, as shown in Figure 5-2.

    QuickBooks automatically fills in the *Statement Date* field with a statement date one month after your previous reconciliation date. In this example, the checking account was previously reconciled on October 31, 2018, so the program fills in *11/30/2018*. (Keep this date for this exercise.) However, if the closing date on your checking account statement shows a different date, edit the value here to match the date on your statement.

    QuickBooks also automatically fills in the *Beginning Balance* field with the ending balance from your previous reconciliation. The program calculates the value that it puts in the *Beginning Balance* field by totaling all the reconciled transactions in the account. If you void, delete, or change the amount of a previously reconciled transaction, the *Beginning Balance* field won't match your statement. If that's the case, see the section, Resolving Bank Reconciliation Errors, starting on page 146, to learn how to solve that problem.

Figure 5-2 The Begin Reconciliation window

4. In the *Ending Balance* field, type the ending balance from your statement, in this example, *49668.89*.

> Tip: If you use *Bank Feeds* (page 154), you've probably downloaded any service charge and interest transactions. Or you may have manually recorded those transactions before you started the reconciliation. In either case, skip steps 5 through 7 or you'll end up with duplicate transactions.

5. In the *Service Charge* field, type the service charge that your bank assessed, if any. In this example, type *10.00*.

6. If necessary, fill in the *Date*, *Account*, and *Class* fields. In this example, the date, account, and class are already filled in correctly.

    QuickBooks automatically fills in the *Date* box to the right of the *Service Charge* box with a date one month later than the last service charge date. If the date the program fills in differs from the date your bank recorded the transaction, choose the correct date in this field. In the *Account* box, choose the account you use for bank service charges. And if you use classes, choose the correct class. Once you fill in an account and class the first time, QuickBooks automatically uses those values for subsequent reconciliations (unless you change them).

7. If the account pays interest, fill in that amount in the *Interest Earned* field (in this example, type *137.50*). If necessary, fill in the *Date*, *Amount*, and *Class* fields.

    Figure 5-3 shows the *Begin Reconciliation* window filled in.

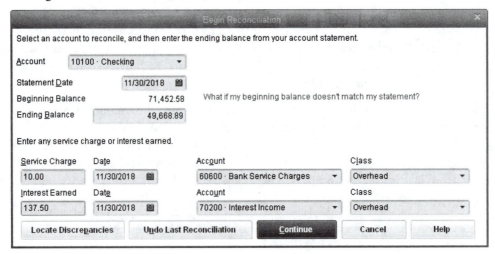

Figure 5-3 The Begin Reconciliation window

8. Click *Continue*.

    The *Reconcile-[bank account name]* window opens. This is where the second step of the reconciliation takes place.

9. At the window's top right, turn on the *Hide transactions after the statement's end date* checkbox (Figure 5-4).

    That way, QuickBooks removes transactions dated after the statement date from the tables so you can focus on only the transactions that may have cleared at your bank.

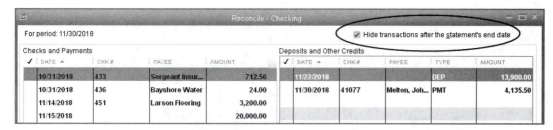

Figure 5-4 Turn on the Hide transactions after the statement's end date check box

10. In the *Deposits and Other Credits* table on the window's right, turn on the checkmark cells for the entries that match deposits or other credits from your bank statement. In this example, both entries match entries on the sample bank statement.

    You can click anywhere in a table line to turn on that transaction's checkmark cell. Click the line again to toggle it back off. QuickBooks displays a checkmark in the cell to indicate that you marked it.

    > Tip: If you need to correct a transaction, for example, to change its amount, select the transaction in the table, and then click *Go To*. QuickBooks opens the corresponding transaction window to that transaction. After you edit and save the transaction, the program takes you back to the *Reconcile* window so you can continue the reconciliation.
    >
    > This technique also works if you've stopped payment on a check and want to void it. After you click *Go To* to open the *Write Checks* window, right-click the window, and then choose *Void Check* on the shortcut menu. Click *Save & Close* to return to the *Reconcile* window.

11. In the *Checks and Payments* table on the window's left, turn on the checkmark cell for each entry that matches a check or other withdrawal from your bank statement. In this example, you can click *Mark All* to select all transactions.

    In this example, the bank statement shows a transfer to savings in an *Other Withdrawals* section. In the *Reconcile* window, that transfer appears in the *Checks and Payments* table. If you transferred money into your checking account from savings, that transfer would appear in the *Deposits and Other Credits* table.

    As shown in Figure 5-4, QuickBooks totals the entries you marked in each table and displays those totals in the *Items you have marked cleared* section at the bottom of the window. In addition, you can see the grand total for the reconciliation to the right of the *Cleared Balance* label on the window's right. When the *Difference* value is equal to 0.00, the reconciliation is complete.

Click anywhere in a row to mark
or unmark a transaction

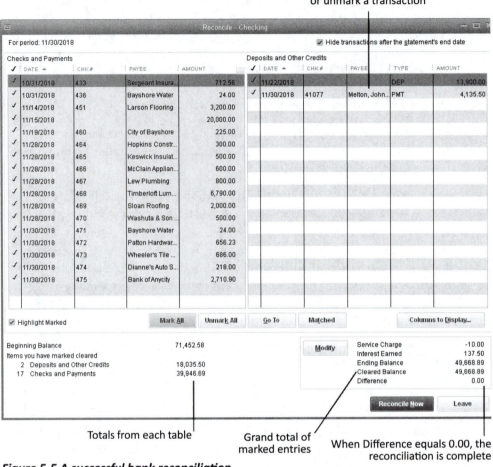

Totals from each table

Grand total of
marked entries

When Difference equals 0.00, the
reconciliation is complete

Figure 5-5 A successful bank reconciliation

> Tip: QuickBooks initially sorts the tables by date. You can change the sort order in the *Reconcile* window by clicking the column heading that you want to sort by. For example, to sort by check number, click the *Chk #* heading. You can also choose the columns to display in the tables by clicking the *Columns to Display* button at the table's lower right.

12. When the *Difference* field equals 0.0, click *Reconcile Now*.

    If the *Difference* field doesn't equal 0.0, don't click *Reconcile Now*. Instead, track down the error, such as an item you forgot to mark, one you marked erroneously, or a transaction with an incorrect amount. See page 146 to learn how to resolve reconciliation errors. If you don't have time to track down an error, click the *Leave* button. QuickBooks saves the work you've done so far, so you can continue the reconciliation later.

> Note: If you click *Reconcile Now* when the *Difference* field is not equal to 0.0, Quick-Books creates an adjustment transaction in your bank account to make up the difference (and posts it to the *Reconciliation Discrepancies* account). Although this entry makes your reconciliation balance, it results in either an over- or under-statement of your company's net income.

13. In the *Select Reconciliation Report* dialog box that opens (Figure 5-6), click *Display* to run both a summary and detail reconciliation report (shown in Figure 5-7). In the *Reconciliation Report* message box that appears, click *OK*.

14. After you view the reports (and, if you want to keep copies, print them or save them as PDF files), close the report windows.

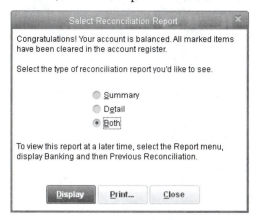

Figure 5-6 Select reconciliation reports to run

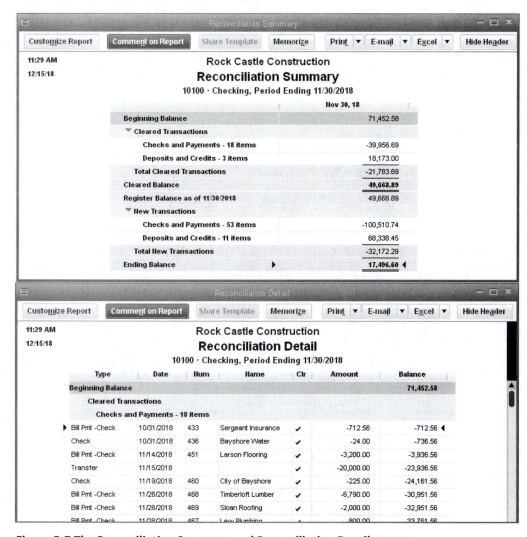

Figure 5-7 The Reconciliation Summary and Reconciliation Detail reports

Running Bank Reconciliation Reports

When you complete a bank reconciliation, QuickBooks gives you the opportunity to run bank reconciliation reports for that reconciliation. But you can also run those reports at any time. If you use QuickBooks Pro, you can run *Bank Reconciliation* reports only for the most recent reconciliation. If you use QuickBooks Premier or Enterprise, you can choose the statement for which you want to run reports.

Computer Practice

Here are the steps to running bank reconciliation reports:

1. To run reconciliation reports at any time, on the *Reports* menu, choose *Banking*, and then choose *Previous Reconciliation* on the submenu.

    The *Select Previous Reconciliation Report* window opens (Figure 5-8).

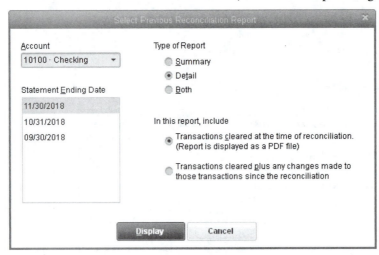

Figure 5-8 The Select Previous Reconciliation Report window

2. In the *Account* field, choose the account you want to run reconciliation reports for. In this example, *Checking* is already selected.

3. Choose the statement ending date for the reports you want to run. In this example, *11/30/2018* is already selected.

    QuickBooks automatically selects the statement date for your most recent bank reconciliation. To select a different date, click it.

4. If necessary, in the *Type of Report* section, select the *Detail* option.

    You can also choose *Summary* or *Both* if you want to run the *Reconciliation Summary* report or both reports, respectively.

5. Make sure that the *Transactions cleared at the time of reconciliation* option is selected.

    When you select this option, QuickBooks displays the report as a PDF file, shown in Figure 5-9. This report doesn't include any changes you may have made to reconciled transactions. If you select the *Transactions cleared plus any changes made to those transactions since the reconciliation* option instead, the program runs the *Reconciliation Detail* report in QuickBooks.

6. Click *Display*.

7. Close the *Reconciliation Detail* report window.

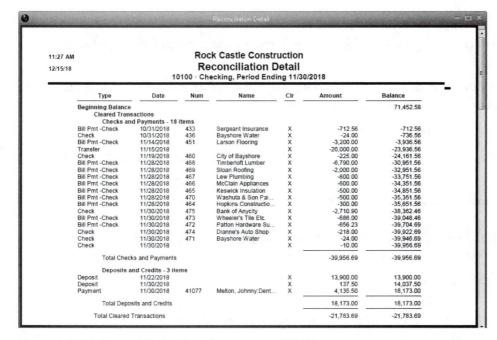

Figure 5-9 The Reconciliation Detail report as a PDF file

Reconciling a Credit Card Account and Paying the Bill

Reconciling a credit card account is almost identical to reconciling a checking account. During reconciliation, the windows you see may have different labels. When you finish the reconciliation, QuickBooks gives you the opportunity to pay your credit card bill. This section shows you how to perform both parts of the credit card reconciliation process using the statement in Figure 5-10 as an example.

Credit Card Statement			
Statement Date	12/31/2018		
Previous Balance as of	11/30/2018		$25.00
New charges/fees		+	$252.90
Payments/refunds		-	$0.00
Ending Balance as of	12/31/2018		**$277.90**

Transactions

Ref. No.	Date	Description	Debits	Credits & Payments
111902	12/6/2018	Bayshore CalOil Service	$247.23	
245612	12/30/2018	Finance Charge	$5.67	
			$252.90	$0.00

Figure 5-10 A sample credit card statement

Computer Practice

Here are the steps to reconciling a credit card account, using the statement in Figure 5-10 as an example:

1. As you do for a checking account reconciliation, review your credit card account in QuickBooks to make sure that you've recorded all your charges.

2. On the *Banking* menu, choose *Reconcile*.

3. In the *Begin Reconciliation* window's *Account* field, choose your credit card account. In this example, choose *QuickBooks Credit Card*.

4. Fill in the information from your statement, as shown in Figure 5-11.

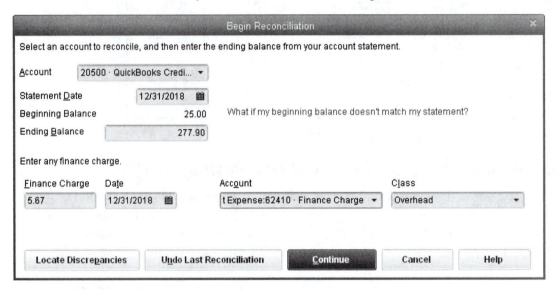

Figure 5-11 The Begin Reconciliation window for a credit card reconciliation

5. Click *Continue*.

6. At the *Reconcile Credit Card* window's top right, turn on the *Hide transactions after the statement's end date* checkbox.

7. In the *Payments and Credits* table on the window's right, turn on the checkmark cells for each entry that matches a payment or other credit from your credit card statement. In this example, neither transaction appears on the credit card statement.

8. In the *Charges and Cash Advances* table on the window's left, turn on the checkmark cells for each entry that matches a charge or cash advance from your credit card statement. In this example, click the *Bayshore CalOil* charge.

   Figure 5-12 shows the reconciled credit card account. As with a checking account reconciliation, the *Difference* value for a credit card reconciliation is equal to 0.00 when the reconciliation is complete.

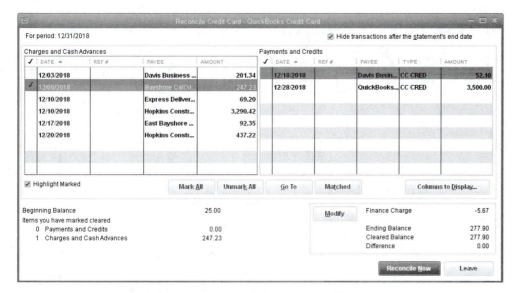

Figure 5-12 A successful credit card reconciliation

9. When the *Difference* field equals 0.0, click *Reconcile Now*.

Unlike a checking account reconciliation, a credit card reconciliation has additional steps, because you have to pay your credit card bill. When you click *Reconcile Now*, the *Make Payment* dialog box opens (Figure 5-13).

Figure 5-13 The Make Payment window

10. In the *Make Payment* dialog box, select the *Enter a bill for payment later* option, and then click *OK*.

The *Enter Bills* window and the *Select Reconciliation* window both open.

11. In the *Select Reconciliation* window, you would normally click *Display* to view the reconciliation reports. In this example, click *Close*.

12. In the *Enter Bills* window, fill in the fields for the bill as shown in Figure 5-14. After you fill in the fields, click *Save & Close*.

When you record the transaction, QuickBooks debits (reduces) the balance in the credit card liability account and credits (increases) the balance in your *Accounts Payable* account. In addition, this bill will appear in the *Pay Bills* window the next time you open it.

If you use classes, you don't have to assign a class to the credit card bill, because it doesn't post to an income or expense account.

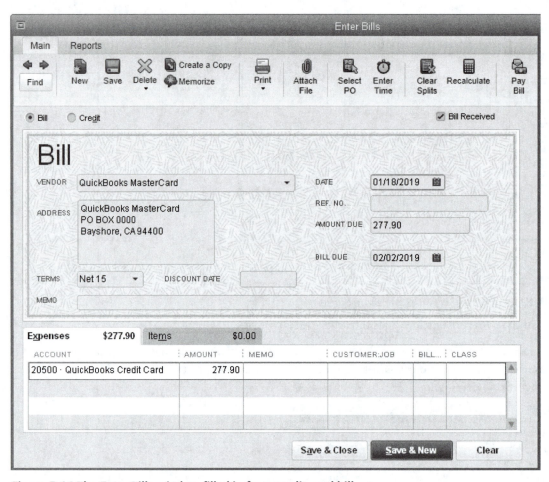

Figure 5-14 The Enter Bills window filled in for a credit card bill

> Tip: If you don't want to pay the entire amount due on your credit card, change the bill's *Amount Due* field to the amount that you want to pay. By doing that, you decrease the balance in the credit card liability account only by the amount you pay. That way, the amount that you *don't* pay remains in the credit card liability account and will match the account balance on your next credit card statement.

Resolving Bank Reconciliation Errors

If you mark all the transactions from your bank statement in the *Reconcile* window and the *Difference* field does not equal zero, there is a discrepancy between your records and those of your bank. Although QuickBooks has an adjustment feature that forces your QuickBooks ending balance to match your statement's ending balance, it's best to find the discrepancies and fix them. This section describes several techniques for doing just that.

Correcting the Beginning Balance Field

If you begin a reconciliation and the amount in QuickBooks' *Beginning Balance* field doesn't match the beginning balance on your bank statement, you need to correct that before you reconcile. Here are the most common reasons the beginning balances don't match:

- Voiding or deleting reconciled transactions.

- Editing a reconciled transaction's amount.

- Changing the cleared status of a reconciled transaction.

There are two techniques you can use to correct a beginning balance:

- Use the *Reconciliation Discrepancy Report* to find the changed transactions and then correct them.

- Undo the previous bank reconciliation.

Troubleshooting the beginning balance with the Reconciliation Discrepancy report

The *Reconciliation Discrepancy* report includes any changes or deletions to reconciled transactions. As shown in Figure 5-15, the *Type of Change* column identifies the type of change made to the transaction. In this example, someone deleted a bill payment.

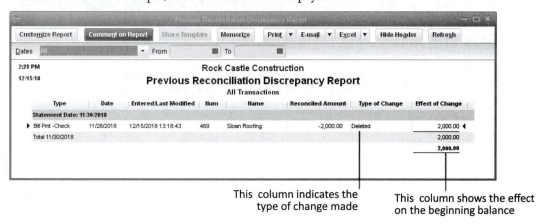

This column indicates the type of change made

This column shows the effect on the beginning balance

Figure 5-15 The Reconciliation Discrepancy report

Here is how you correct the discrepancies you find:

- For voided or deleted transactions, you have to recreate them. To see the details for a deleted transaction, on the *Reports* menu, choose *Accountant & Taxes*, and then choose *Voided/Deleted Transactions Detail*. This report includes all the transaction details you need to recreate the transaction. After you've restored the deleted transaction, re-reconcile the transaction (described next).

- For amount changes, double-click the transaction in the *Reconciliation Discrepancy* report to open it. Then, edit the transaction's amount back to the reconciled amount.

When you correct changes that were made to reconciled transactions, you have to re-reconcile those transactions. You don't have to redo the entire reconciliation. This section describes how to reconcile modified transactions:

1. On the *Banking* menu, choose *Reconcile*, and then, in the *Begin Reconciliation* window's *Account* drop-down list, choose the bank account you want to re-reconcile.

2. In the *Statement Date* field, change the date to the ending date on the bank statement that contains the corrected transaction. For example, if the corrected transaction is dated December 20, fill in the statement date for your December bank statement.

3. In the *Ending Balance* field, fill in the ending balance from the bank statement, and then click *Continue*.

4. In the *Reconcile* window, mark the corrected transactions. When you do that, the *Difference* value changes to 0.00.

5. Click *Reconcile Now* to complete this reconciliation. The next time you reconcile the account, the beginning balance will match your bank statement's beginning balance.

Undo the bank reconciliation

The *Previous Reconciliation Discrepancy* report shows changes to reconciled transactions from your most recent bank reconciliation. If the error occurred in an earlier reconciliation, the *Previous Reconciliation Discrepancy* report won't help. In that case, the other solution is to undo previous reconciliations until your QuickBooks records match those on the corresponding bank statement. To undo a reconciliation, in the *Begin Reconciliation* window, click the *Undo Last Reconciliation* button at the bottom of the window (Figure 5-16).

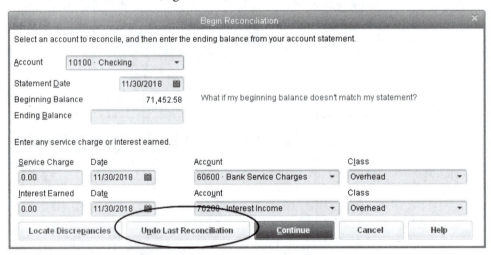

Figure 5-16 The Undo Last Reconciliation button

Note: When you undo a reconciliation, QuickBooks changes the beginning balance to the one from the previous reconciliation. However, it doesn't delete the bank service charges and interest income from the previous reconciliation (if any). When you redo the previous reconciliations, don't enter the bank service charges and interest income in the *Begin Reconciliation* window. You can mark those existing transactions as you re-reconcile the account.

Correcting Incorrectly Recorded Transactions

For discrepancies between your QuickBooks transactions and the ones on your bank statement, the method you choose to correct them depends on the discrepancy and the transaction date. In this section, you'll learn how to correct several types of discrepancies.

Correcting transactions in the current accounting period

Here's what you do when a discrepancy arises from a transaction dated within the current accounting period (that is, the period for which you have not yet filed tax returns or produced financial statements):

- If the error is in your QuickBooks transaction, you simply edit the transaction so it agrees with the bank statement transaction. For example, if you recorded a check for $50.25 in QuickBooks, but hand-wrote a check for $50.27, you change the check amount in Quick-Books to $50.27. To edit the check from within the *Reconcile* window, select the transaction and then click *Go To*. In the *Write Checks* window, edit the check, and then click *Save & Close*, which puts you back in the *Reconcile* window where you'll see the updated amount. (You can edit other types of transactions, such as deposits, using this same technique.)

- If the bank made the error, record a transaction in your QuickBooks bank account register (assign it to the *Reconciliation Discrepancies* account) to adjust your QuickBooks reconciliation ending balance so it matches the bank statement ending balance. Reconcile that transaction along with the others on your bank statement. Then, contact your bank and ask them to post an adjustment to your account to correct the error. The next bank statement you receive will contain the adjustment. Record that adjustment in your bank account register (also posted to the *Reconciliation Discrepancies* account). When you reconcile this bank statement, you mark the adjustment along with the other transactions on the statement. The two transactions offset each other, as shown in Figure 5-17.

  In Figure 5-17, the $10 adjustment on 12/31/2018 represents a shortage recorded so your QuickBooks account reconciles with the bank statement. The adjustment on 1/8/2019 is a deposit to correct the shortage from the previous month.

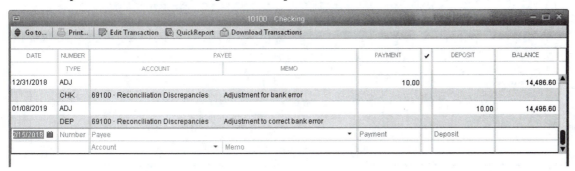

Figure 5-17 Adjustments to correct a bank error

Correcting transactions in a closed accounting period

If you find unreconciled transactions from closed accounting periods (that is, years for which you've already filed tax returns), you need to correct and/or reconcile them. One problem with these transactions is that they are part of the accounting records you used to prepare your tax returns, so you can't void them. However, you can't reconcile them as they are, because doing so would make your next bank reconciliation out of balance. To reconcile these transactions, you need an offsetting transaction dated within the current time period.

For example, suppose you find an unreconciled check dated December 15, 2017 and you've already

---

filed your company's 2017 tax return. To reconcile that check, record a deposit in the current period, for example, December 20, 2018, posted to the same account as the unreconciled check and for the same amount. Then, to reconcile these two offsetting transactions, in the *Begin Reconciliation* window, choose the date from your previous reconciliation so you don't throw QuickBooks statement dates off. In the *Ending Balance* field, type the *Beginning Balance* value. (The beginning and ending balances are equal because these two transactions offset one another). Click *Continue*. Mark the two transactions, and then click *Reconcile Now*.

Transferring Money between Accounts

You can easily transfer money between bank accounts using the *Transfer Funds Between Accounts* window.

Here are the steps to transferring money between bank accounts:

1. From the *Banking* menu, choose *Transfer Funds*.

    The *Transfer Funds Between Accounts* window opens.

2. In the *Transfer Funds From* field, choose the account that you are transferring money out of, in this example, *Checking*. In the *Date* field, enter the transfer date.

3. In the *Transfer Funds To* field, choose the account you are transferring money to, *Savings,* in this example.

4. In the *Transfer Amount* field, type the amount, in this example, *5000*.

    The window should look like the one in Figure 5-18.

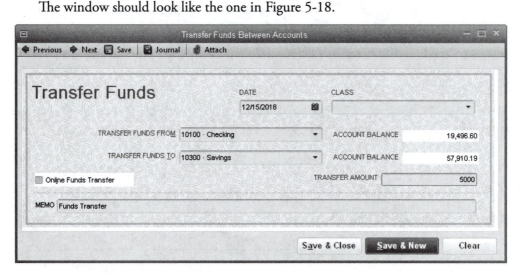

Figure 5-18 The Transfer Funds Between Accounts window

5. Click *Save & Close*.

    A message box opens warning you that the *Online Funds Transfer* check box is not selected so the transfer is recorded only in your QuickBooks company file. If you made the transfer in person or on your bank's website, click *OK*.

Handling Bounced Checks

You might hear bounced checks referred to as NSF checks (NSF stands for non-sufficient funds). Whether a customer pays you with a check that bounces or one of your checks overdraws your account, you have to do a few things to keep your records accurate. This section describes how to handle both situations.

Handling a Customer's Bounced Check

When a customer's check bounces, you have to perform several steps to straighten out your records. This section explains how to use QuickBooks' *Record Bounced Check* feature to do that.

Computer Practice

Here are the steps to recording a bounced check using the *Record Bounced Check* feature:

1. Open the *Receive Payments* window to the payment that bounced. In this example, open the *Customer Center* and select *Abercrombie, Kristy* on the *Customers & Jobs* tab. On the *Transactions* tab on the right side of the window, double click the payment dated 1*2/15/2018* for *$7,633.28*.

2. In the *Receive Payments* window, click *Record Bounced Check* (Figure 5-19) at the top of the window.

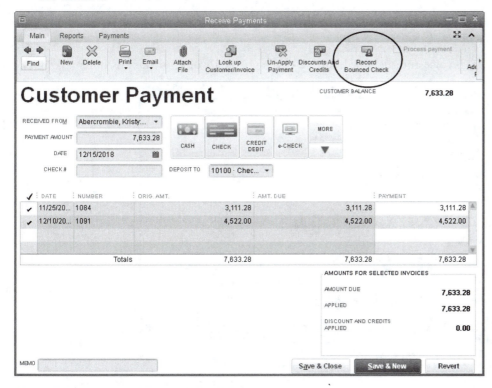

Figure 5-19 The Record Bounced Check icon

3. In the *Manage Bounced Check* window, enter the information in Figure 5-20.

    In the *Bank Fee* field, type the amount that your bank charged *you* because the customer's check bounced. In the *Expense Account* field, choose the account you use for bank service charges.

    In the *Customer Fee* field, type the additional amount you want to charge your customer for the bounced check.

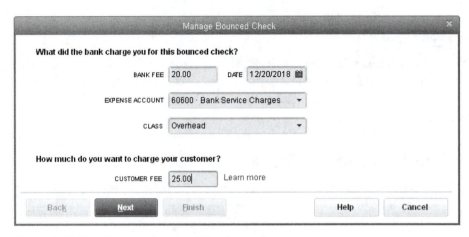

Figure 5-20 The Manage Bounced Check window

4. After you fill in the bounced check information, click *Next*. Review the *Bounced Check Summary* dialog box (see Figure 5-21), and then click *Finish*.

   The *Bounced Check Summary* dialog box identifies the steps that QuickBooks performs when you click *Finish*. First, it marks the invoices paid by this check as Unpaid. Second, it deducts the check amount and the bank fee from your QuickBooks bank account. Third, it creates an invoice for the fee you charge your customer.

5. Back in the *Customer Payment* window, you'll see a *Bounced Check* alert (as shown in Figure 5-22) on the payment. Click *Save & Close*.

6. Send the original invoice and the new bounced check charge invoice to your customer.

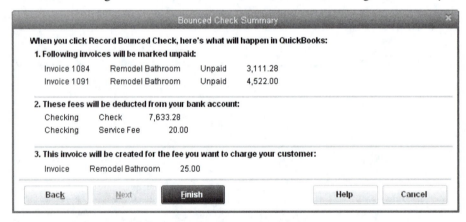

Figure 5-21 The Bounced Check Summary dialog box

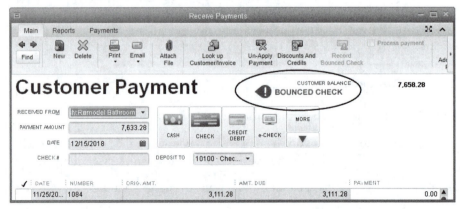

Figure 5-22 Bounced Check alert

Receiving and Depositing the Replacement Check

When you receive a replacement check from the customer for the original invoice *and* the new invoice, you record that payment as you would any other payment. This section shows you how.

Computer Practice

To record the replacement check payment, follow these steps:

1. On the *Customers* menu, choose *Receive Payments*.

2. In the *Receive Payments* window, in the *Received From* field, choose the customer or job that sent the replacement check.

3. Fill in the payment information as shown in Figure 5-23.

4. Be sure to apply the payment against the original invoice(s) and the service charge invoice that QuickBooks created.

5. Click *Save & Close*.

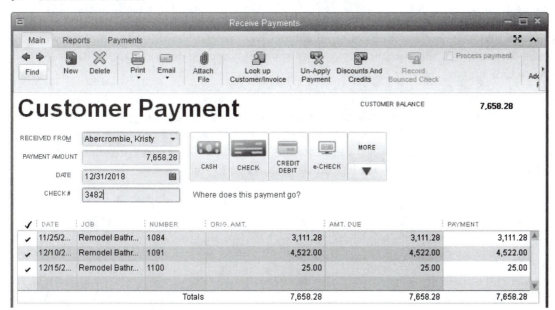

Figure 5-23 Recording the replacement check

Managing Bounced Checks You Write

If you write a check that overdraws your account, your bank returns the check to the person or company you paid. This section describes how to recover from this situation.

1. Talk to your vendor and decide whether the vendor will redeposit the check, you will send a new check, or you will pay by credit card.

2. Record a transaction for the bank's bounced check charge in your bank account register. Assign the transaction to your bank service charge account and fill in the date that the bank charged your account.

3. If you have enough money in the bank to cover the check, tell the vendor to redeposit it. If your balance is insufficient, pay by credit card or negotiate delayed payment terms with your vendor.

4. If your vendor charges a fee for bounced checks, enter a bill or write a check for the fee and assign it to the bank service charge account you use.

> Note: If you bounce a payroll check, you can use this same process. In this situation, reimburse your employee for any bank fees they incur due to your mistake.

Bank Feeds

With QuickBooks' *Bank Feeds* feature, you can set up online transactions, such as payments and transfers, to send to your bank and also download bank transactions from your bank into your QuickBooks company file. QuickBooks uses a secure Internet connection and high level of encryption to transfer information between your financial institution and your company file. By downloading transactions from your bank, you can spend less time entering data and also increase the accuracy of your records. However, you do need to review the transactions you download to make sure they are correct before you save them in your company file.

> Note: Some financial institutions charge fees for online banking services, such as online bill payments.

To use *Bank Feeds*, you need to set up your QuickBooks bank accounts so they communicate with your financial institutions. Because the steps you must perform depend on the financial institution you use, refer to QuickBooks Help for the details.

Once you have *Bank Feeds* set up for an account, you may be able to record online transactions, such as online bill payments, online customer payments, or transfers—depending on the services your financial institution offers. For example, Figure 5-24 shows how you set up a check in the *Write Checks* window to be paid online. When you turn on the *Pay Online* checkbox, QuickBooks changes the *No.* field to Send to indicate that it will send the transaction to your bank.

Turn on this checkbox to set up a
check for online payment

QuickBooks changes the
No. field to Send

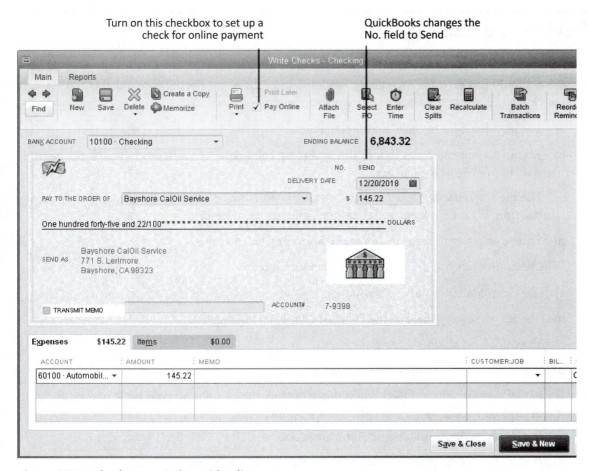

Figure 5-24 A check set up to be paid online

When you save an online payment, QuickBooks adds it to the queue of transactions to send in the *Bank Feeds Center*. To send online payments and other online transactions to your bank and download transactions from your bank, you click the *Bank Feeds Center*'s *Send Items* button, shown in Figure 5-25. Do not click the *Send Items* button now. (Your *Bank Feeds* window may vary from the one shown in Figure 5-25.)

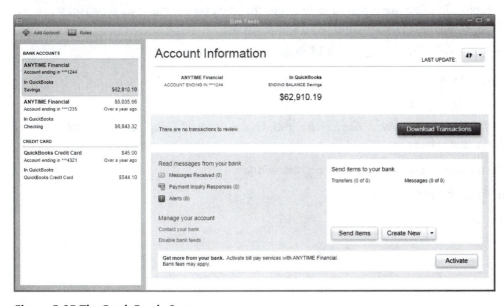

Figure 5-25 The Bank Feeds Center

Review Questions

Select the best answer(s) for each of the following:

1. What should you do if the *Beginning Balance* field in the *Begin Reconciliation* dialog box doesn't match the beginning balance on your bank statement?

    a) Record a bank fee to make up the difference.

    b) Record an adjustment to change the beginning balance in QuickBooks to match the bank statement's beginning balance.

    c) Use the *Discrepancy Report* and/or *Previous Reports* to see what changed since the last reconciliation. Fix the problem and then restart the reconciliation.

    d) Enter a statement charge to adjust the beginning balance.

2. Which features can you use to add bank service charges?

    a) The *Enter Statement Charges* window.

    b) The *Service Charge* field in the *Begin Reconciliation* dialog box.

    c) Download the charges using *Bank Feeds*.

    d) The *Write Checks* window before you reconcile.

3. If a transaction amount in QuickBooks doesn't match the amount on your bank statement, which method should you use to correct the amount?

    a) On the *Banking* menu, choose *Edit Transaction*.

    b) In the account's register window, edit the transaction's amount.

    c) In the *Reconcile* window, click *Go To*, and then edit the transaction's amount.

    d) Ask the bank to change the amount in their records.

4. To record a voided check from a closed accounting period:

    a) Void the check in the register.

    b) Make a deposit in the current period assigned to the same account as the check you want to void. Then reconcile the deposit and the original check.

    c) In the register, right-click the check, and then select *Void Check*.

    d) Change the check amount to zero.

5. To transfer money between accounts, you can:

    a) In the *Write Checks* window, write a check and, in the *Account* field, choose the account you want to transfer money to.

    b) Record a transfer in the first account's register window.

    c) Use the *Transfer Funds* feature.

    d) All of the above.

Bank Reconciliation Exercise 1

Applying Your Knowledge

> Note: For this exercise, restore Ch05_reconcile_forexercises 2015 (Portable).QBM if you are using QuickBooks 2015. If you run QuickBooks 2014, restore Ch05_reconcile_forexercises_2014 (Portable).QBM.

1. Using the bank statement shown in Figure 5-26, reconcile the credit card account for 12/31/2018.

		Statement Date	12/31/2018	
Credit Card Statement		Previous Balance as of	11/30/2018	$25.00
		New charges/fees	+	$3,653.31
		Payments/refunds	−	$3,552.10
		Ending Balance as of	12/31/2018	**$126.21**

Transactions

Ref. No.	Date	Description	Debits	Credits & Payments
109213	12/3/2018	Office supplies	$201.34	
301625	12/10/2018	Delivery	$69.20	
122481	12/10/2018	Equipment Rental	$3,290.42	
432077	12/17/2018	Tools	$92.35	
702362	12/18/2018	Office supplies		$52.10
123920	12/29/2018	Payment - thank you!		$3,500.00
			$3,653.31	$3,552.10

Figure 5-26 Bank statement to reconcile

2. Print a *Reconciliation Detail* report dated 12/31/2018.

Bank Reconciliation Exercise 2 (Advanced)

Applying Your Knowledge

> Note: For this exercise, restore Ch05_reconcile_forexercises 2015 (Portable).QBM if you are using QuickBooks 2015. If you run QuickBooks 2014, restore Ch05_reconcile_forexercises_2014 (Portable).QBM.

1. The check you received from *Anton Teschner* for his *Sun Room* job on *12/12/2018* bounced: check *#306* in the amount of *$3,500* as payment for Invoice *1085* (assigned to class *New Construction*).

    Record a bounced check transaction for this check. The bank charged a *$25* NSF fee to your checking account. Your company charges customers *$20.00* for bounced checks.

2. Record the transactions needed to record the receipt and deposit of Mr. Teschner's replacement check: check *#315* for *$3,500*. He didn't include the NSF charges in the replacement check.

    Record the payment and apply it to the correct invoice on *12/17/2018*. Record the deposit on *12/17/2018*.

3. Using the sample bank statement shown in Figure 5-27, reconcile the checking account through *12/31/2018*.

4. Print a *Reconciliation Detail* report dated *12/31/2018*.

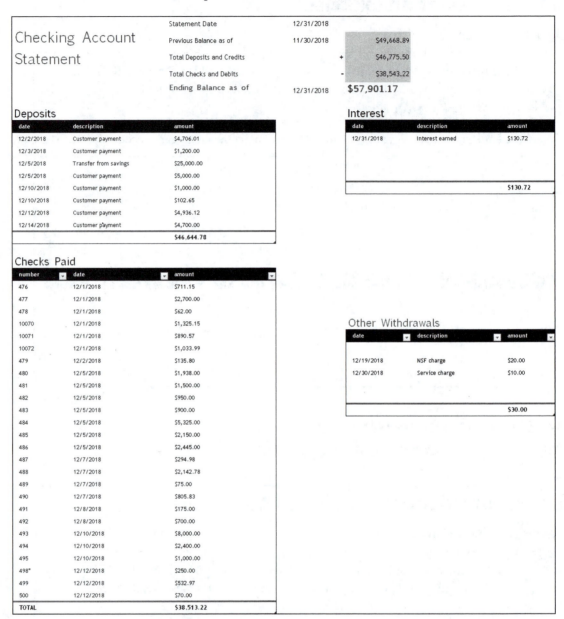

Checking Account Statement

Statement Date	12/31/2018	
Previous Balance as of	11/30/2018	$49,668.89
Total Deposits and Credits	+	$46,775.50
Total Checks and Debits	-	$38,543.22
Ending Balance as of	12/31/2018	**$57,901.17**

Deposits

date	description	amount
12/2/2018	Customer payment	$4,706.01
12/3/2018	Customer payment	$1,200.00
12/5/2018	Transfer from savings	$25,000.00
12/5/2018	Customer payment	$5,000.00
12/10/2018	Customer payment	$1,000.00
12/10/2018	Customer payment	$102.65
12/12/2018	Customer payment	$4,936.12
12/14/2018	Customer payment	$4,700.00
		$46,644.78

Interest

date	description	amount
12/31/2018	Interest earned	$130.72
		$130.72

Checks Paid

number	date	amount
476	12/1/2018	$711.15
477	12/1/2018	$2,700.00
478	12/1/2018	$62.00
10070	12/1/2018	$1,325.15
10071	12/1/2018	$890.57
10072	12/1/2018	$1,033.99
479	12/2/2018	$135.80
480	12/5/2018	$1,938.00
481	12/5/2018	$1,500.00
482	12/5/2018	$950.00
483	12/5/2018	$900.00
484	12/5/2018	$5,325.00
485	12/5/2018	$2,150.00
486	12/5/2018	$2,445.00
487	12/7/2018	$294.98
488	12/7/2018	$2,142.78
489	12/7/2018	$75.00
490	12/7/2018	$805.83
491	12/8/2018	$175.00
492	12/8/2018	$700.00
493	12/10/2018	$8,000.00
494	12/10/2018	$2,400.00
495	12/10/2018	$1,000.00
498*	12/12/2018	$250.00
499	12/12/2018	$532.97
500	12/12/2018	$70.00
TOTAL		**$38,513.22**

Other Withdrawals

date	description	amount
12/19/2018	NSF charge	$20.00
12/30/2018	Service charge	$10.00
		$30.00

Figure 5-27 Bank statement to reconcile

5. Print a statement for *Anton Teschner's Sun Room* job for the period *11/1/2018* through *12/31/2018*.

Chapter 6

Reports

Topics

This chapter covers the following topics:

- An Introduction to QuickBooks Reports
- Cash Versus Accrual Reports
- Accounting Reports
- Business Management Reports
- QuickBooks Graphs
- Processing Multiple Reports
- Printing Reports
- Exporting Reports to Spreadsheets
- Customizing Reports
- Memorizing Reports
- Adding Comments to Reports
- Finding Transactions

QuickBooks provides dozens of built-in reports that show what's going on with your company's finances. You can use these reports to manage your business, make crucial business decisions, and provide information to your accountant, the IRS, shareholders, and so on. In this chapter, you'll learn about many of the reports that QuickBooks offers, how to find the reports you need, and how to run them. If you need to produce several reports, you'll learn how to process multiple reports all at the same time. Then, you'll learn how to print reports or export them to a spreadsheet program for further analysis.

Despite the number of built-in reports you can choose from, they might not be exactly what you want. In this chapter, you'll learn how to customize reports to include the information you want to see, formatted in the way you want to see it. If you customize reports, you'll probably want to use those customized reports more than once. This chapter explains how to memorize reports so you can rerun them whenever you want.

Finally, this chapter explains how to find transactions in your company file.

> Note: For the computer practice in this chapter, restore the sample file, sample_product-based business 2015 (Portable).QBM. Or, if you are using QuickBooks 2014, restore sample_product-based business 2014 (Portable).QBM.

An Introduction to QuickBooks Reports

If you know which report you want to run, the *Reports* menu is the easiest way to get there. On the *Reports* menu, choose the report category, and then, on the category's submenu, choose the name of the report you want (Figure 6-1). On the other hand, the *Report Center* has several helpful features for finding and running reports, as this section explains.

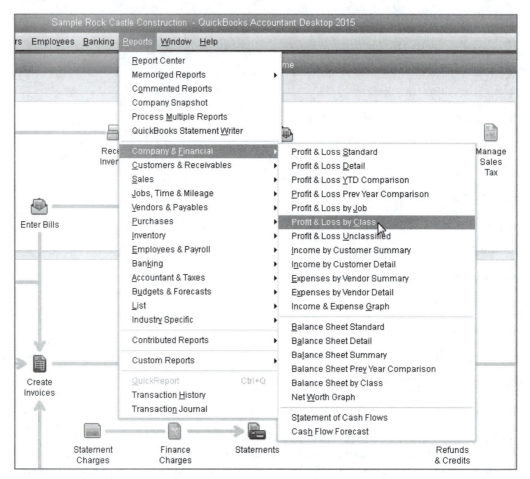

Figure 6-1 The Reports menu

Computer Practice

To work with reports in the *Report Center*, follow these steps:

1. To open the *Report Center*, on the *Reports* menu, choose *Report Center*.

   The *Report Center* window contains the same categories and reports as the *Reports* menu. The left side of the *Report Center* lists built-in report categories, which change depending on whether you select the *Standard*, *Memorized*, *Favorites*, *Recent*, or *Contributed* tab at the top of the window.

> Tip: The *Report Center* initially displays the *Standard* tab, which lists built-in categories and reports. To access memorized reports (see page 191), click the *Memorized* tab. The *Favorites* tab lists reports that you flag as your favorites (by clicking the *Heart* icon below a report). If you want to rerun a report you used recently, click the *Recent* tab to see a list of recently-run reports. Alternatively, you can type keywords in the *Search* box at the window's top right.

2. To see the reports in a category, click the category's name, in this example, *Company & Financials*.

    You can view reports in different ways by choosing a view icon at the window's top right (Figure 6-2): Carousel view, Grid view, and List view. Grid view, shown in Figure 6-2, displays thumbnails of reports, so you can see what they look like before you run them. You can change a report's date range before you run it. And you can click the icons below a report to run it, get more information about it, and so on. List view offers the same tools as Grid view without the report thumbnails. Carousel view provides much larger thumbnails, which makes it easy to tell whether the report is what you want. However, it takes longer to scroll through all the reports.

Click a report category to see the reports in the category

Click a tab to view the reports in that tab's category

Click these icons to switch between Carousel, List, and Grid View

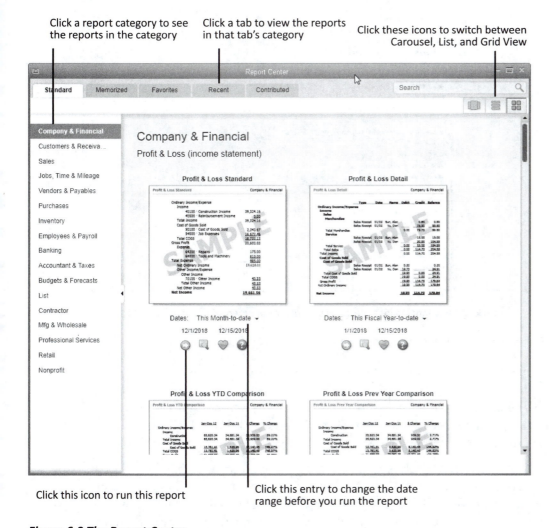

Click this icon to run this report

Click this entry to change the date range before you run the report

Figure 6-2 The Report Center

3. In this chapter, click the List view icon, which looks like three horizontal bars.

4. To change the date range before you run the report, click the *Dates* down arrow, and then choose the date range you want, in this example, *This Fiscal Year*.

5. Point your cursor at the *Profit & Loss Standard* report, and then click the *Run* icon.

   QuickBooks opens the report in its own window, as shown in Figure 6-3. The shading you see in this figure is new in QuickBooks 2015. In QuickBooks 2014, there is no shading in reports.

In QuickBook 2015, you can add comments to reports

Click this button to hide subaccounts in report

Click this button to refresh the report

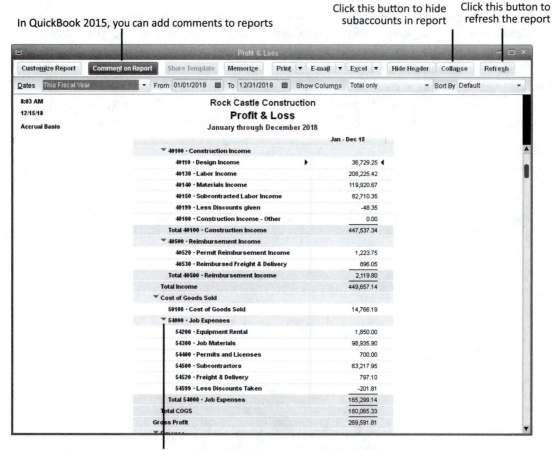

Clicking this triangle hides the subaccounts for the parent account

Figure 6-3 The Profit & Loss Standard report opened in a report window

Tip: You can run reports from many places within QuickBooks, as you'll learn throughout this book. For example, in a list window, such as the *Chart of Accounts* window, click the *Reports* button at the bottom of the window, and then choose the report you want to run on the drop-down list.

The *Customer, Vendor, Employee*, and *Inventory Centers* also include links to reports. For example, in the *Customer Center*, select a customer to display its information on the center's right. Then click one of the report links, like *QuickReport* or *Open Balance*. In a center's toolbar, you can choose *Print* or *Excel* to print a report or export it to Excel, respectively.

Cash Versus Accrual Accounting

Cash basis and accrual basis are the two different approaches companies use to track income and expenses. You can choose which basis QuickBooks uses for your reports by setting the program's *Summary Reports Basis* preference.

- **Cash accounting** shows income only when you've received a payment (regardless of when that happens), and shows expenses when you pay your bills.

- The **accrual method** matches income with its corresponding expenses. That way, income and expenses are linked to the same period, which provides a better picture of profitability. With accrual accounting, you recognize income when you record an invoice. For example, if you create an invoice in December 2018, the accrual method recognizes the income in 2018, even if you receive payment in January 2019. Similarly, you recognize expenses when you record bills, not when you pay them.

> Note: Although you can change QuickBooks' reporting basis easily, that doesn't mean you *should*. The basis you choose can have a significant effect on your financial reports. Once you select cash basis or accrual basis for your company, you should keep that setting in place. (In fact, if you decide to change your reporting basis, you must first get approval from the IRS. If, at some point, the numbers in your reports aren't what you expect, check the QuickBooks' Summary Reports Basis preference to make sure it wasn't changed inadvertently.

Computer Practice

To choose cash or accrual basis for your reports, follow these steps:

1. If your company file is in multi-user mode, you must switch to single-user mode to change company-wide preferences. Ask anyone who is working on the company file to log off. Then, on the *File* menu, choose *Switch to Single-user Mode*.

2. On the *Edit* menu, choose *Preferences*.

3. Click the *Reports and Graphs* category, and then click the *Company Preferences* tab.

4. In the *Summary Reports Basis* section (Figure 6-4), choose the *Cash* option or *Accrual* option. In this example, keep the basis set to *Accrual*.

5. To save changes (if any were made), click *OK*. Close the *Preferences* window.

> Tip: The *Reports & Graphs Company Preferences* tab has other settings that you might want to change. For example, you can choose how QuickBooks calculates invoice aging for reports, and whether you see names or descriptions for items and accounts. You can also change the formatting for reports by clicking the *Format* button.

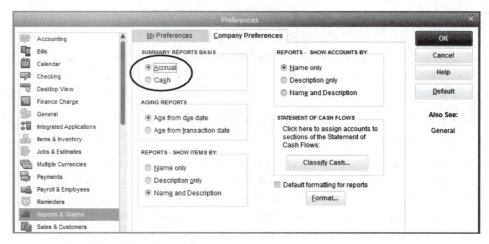

Figure 6-4 Reports & Graphs Preferences

Accounting Reports

Accounting reports contain important information about your company finances that your accountant, investors, and tax agencies want to see. The Financial Accounting Standards Board (FASB) has developed an accounting standard known as *GAAP* (generally accepted accounting principles), which includes three financial statements that convey company performance: the income statement (in QuickBooks, it's called the *Profit & Loss* report), the balance sheet, and the statement of cash flows. For example, the *Profit & Loss* report shows your company's income, expenses, and the resulting profit or loss.

Profit & Loss

The *Profit & Loss* report (the income statement) presents your income, expenses, and the resulting profit or loss over a period of time (such as a month, a quarter, or a full year). This report provides information that you need when preparing your tax return. In addition, it is a standard report that investors and financial analysts use to evaluate a business's performance. You can also use it to see whether your company is making or losing money—and how much. To learn more about how to analyze the *Profit & Loss* report, read the section, Interpreting the Profit & Loss report, on page 166.

To generate a *Profit & Loss* report, follow these steps:

1. On the icon bar, choose the *Reports* icon.

2. Click the Grid View icon, which is the third icon at the *Report Center* window's top right.

3. Select the *Company & Financial* category on the left, and then double-click the *Profit & Loss Standard* thumbnail (see Figure 6-2) to open it.

4. At the *Profit & Loss* window's top left, click the *Customize Report* button to open the *Modify Report* window (Figure 6-5).

5. In the *Dates* field, choose *This Fiscal Quarter*.

   You can also type dates in the *From* and *To* fields.

6. To switch your reporting basis, select the *Cash* option.

   Remember, once you choose a reporting basis, you need to keep that setting in place—unless you officially change your reporting basis with tax agencies.

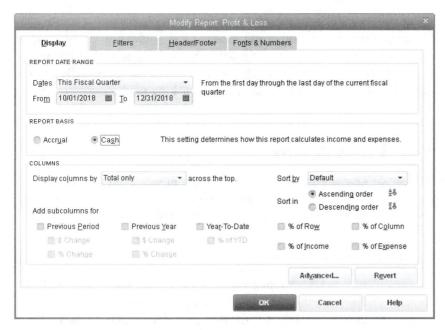

Figure 6-5 The Modify Report window

7. Click *OK* to display the cash basis *Profit & Loss* report for the fourth quarter of 2018 (shown in Figure 6-6).

8. Close the *Profit & Loss* report to return to the *Report Center.*

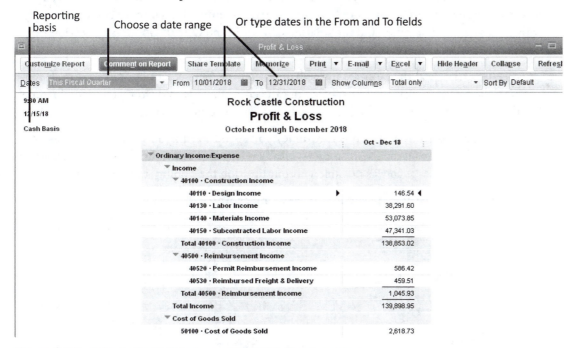

Figure 6-6 Cash basis Profit & Loss report for this fiscal quarter

Tip: Accounts appear in the *Profit & Loss* report in the order they appear in your company file's chart of accounts. You can rearrange the accounts in the *Chart of Accounts* window by pointing your cursor at the diamond to the left of an account's name and then dragging the account to where you want it. See page 400 to learn more about rearranging accounts in the *Chart of Accounts* window.

In addition, you can show or hide subaccounts in summary reports, which are reports that summarize your company's finances by account, customer, vendor, or other category. To hide subaccounts, click the downward-pointing triangle to the left of a parent account name, such as Construction Income in Figure 6-6. To expand that parent, click the triangle, which now points to the right to indicate that subaccounts are hidden. You can also show or hide all subaccounts by clicking the *Collapse* button in the report window's toolbar (see Figure 6-2).

Interpreting the Profit & Loss Report

The *Profit & Loss* report begins with the money your company makes: the money in all the income accounts in your chart of accounts. Beneath the income section, you see your company's costsincluding cost of goods sold and expenses. The last section shows your profit or loss, which is calculated by subtracting cost from your income.

Here is a description of each section in a *Profit & Loss* report:

- *Income* is the first section, which shows the revenue your company generates selling products and services. For example, in Figure 6-6, the *Income* section is broken down into Construction Income and Reimbursement Income. In addition, Construction Income has several subaccounts to show revenue from design, labor, materials, and subcontractors.

- *Cost of Goods Sold* represents the costs of the products and services that you sell. For example, if you use *Inventory Part* items to track inventory, the programs calculates cost of goods sold when you sell those items. To learn more about inventory, see Chapter 8, Inventory. If you don't sell inventory items, you might not have a *Cost of Goods Sold* section in your report. However, you can create *Cost of Goods Sold* accounts to track other costs associated with your sales, such as labor and materials, as shown in the *Cost of Goods Sold* section in Figure 6-6.

- *Gross Profit* is the total that appears immediately after the *Cost of Goods Sold* section. It represents your company's profit after subtracting the cost of goods sold from your total income. In other words, it's your profit before you subtract your overhead costs.

- *Expense* is the next section, which is the money you spend to run your business, such as office rent, bank fees, insurance, and so on (typically referred to as overhead). Companies strive to keep these expenses as low as possible without limiting their ability to make money.

- *Net Ordinary Income* is your profit after subtracting expenses.

64210 · Building Repairs	45.00
64220 · Computer Repairs	0.00
Total 64200 · Repairs	45.00
64800 · Tools and Machinery	350.00
65100 · Utilities	
65110 · Gas and Electric	154.40
65120 · Telephone	210.72
65130 · Water	48.00
Total 65100 · Utilities	413.12
Total Expense	41,017.37
Net Ordinary Income	8,214.22
Other Income/Expense	
Other Income	
70100 · Other Income	140.85
Total Other Income	140.85
Net Other Income	140.85
Net Income	8,355.07

Figure 6-7 Net income in a Profit & Loss report

- *Other Income/Expense* is the final section of the report. It represents income and expenses that don't relate to your primary business, such as interest income or interest you pay on loans.

- *Net Income* is the last entry in the report (see Figure 6-7). *Net income* is your income after subtracting all the costs and expenses you incur. If this number is positive, your company made money. If the number is negative, your expenses were greater than your income, and you lost money for the report period.

If your company lost money or didn't make as much as you had hoped, you can look at your expenses as a percentage of your total income to find areas where you might be able to cut costs.

Computer Practice

Here are the steps for modifying a *Profit & Loss* report to show expenses as a percentage of income:

1. In the *Profit & Loss* report window, click *Customize Report*.

2. On the *Display* tab (Figure 6-8), turn on the *% of Income* checkbox, and then click *OK*.

   The report now includes a *% of Income* column (Figure 6-9), which helps you identify expenses that represent a higher percentage of your total income.

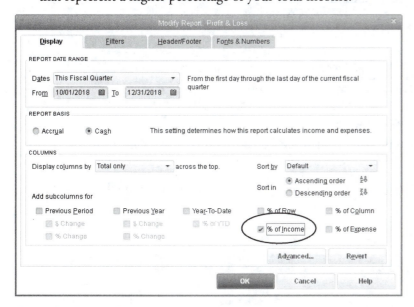

Figure 6-8 The % of Income setting

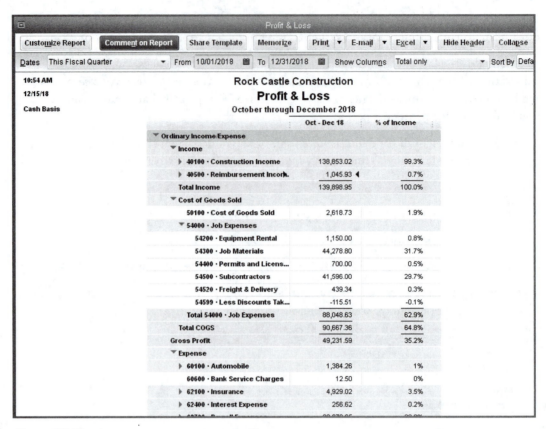

Figure 6-9 Viewing expenses as a percent of income

3.   If you want to examine the details behind a particular type of expense, such as the Subcontractors Cost of Goods Sold account, double-click the amount in that line to run a *QuickReport*.

QuickBooks runs a *Transaction Detail by Account* report for the account you double-clicked, as shown in Figure 6-10.

4.   Close both of the reports that are open.

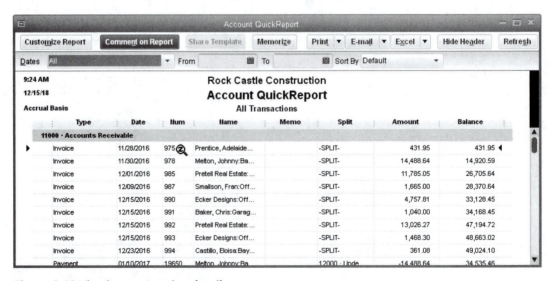

Figure 6-10 Viewing transaction detail

Profit & Loss by Class Report

If you use classes to classify your business, run the *Profit & Loss by Class* report to see how each class has performed.

Computer Practice

To create a *Profit & Loss by Class* report, follow these steps:

1. In the *Report Center*, click the List View icon at the window's top right (Figure 6-11).

2. In the *Company & Financial* category, double click the *Profit & Loss by Class* report to run it.

Double-click the report name to run it   Click this icon to display the List View

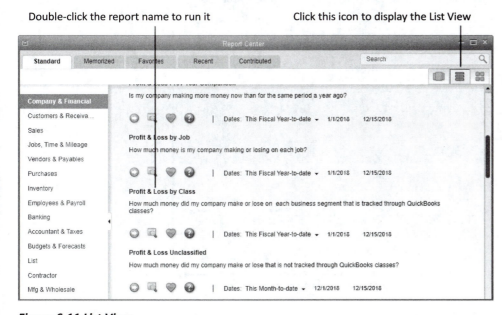

Figure 6-11 List View

3. In the report window's toolbar, enter *01/01/2018* in the *From* field and *1/31/2018* in the *To* field.

   QuickBooks displays the report, which should look like the one in Figure 6-12. Each class, in this sample file, New Construction, Remodel, and Overhead, appears in a separate column.

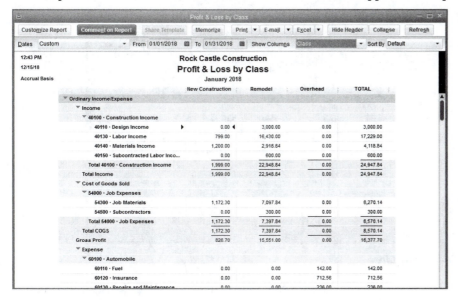

Figure 6-12 Profit & Loss Report by Class

If any transactions haven't been assigned to a class, this report will include an *Unclassified* column.

To see what unclassified results looks like, follow these steps:

1. Double-click the amount in the overhead column for *Automobile: Fuel.*

2. In the *Transaction Detail By Account* report that appears, double-click the *Debit* amount for the transaction.

3. In the *Write Checks* table, click the *Class* cell that contains *Overhead* (Figure 6-13), and then press the *Backspace* key to delete that value.

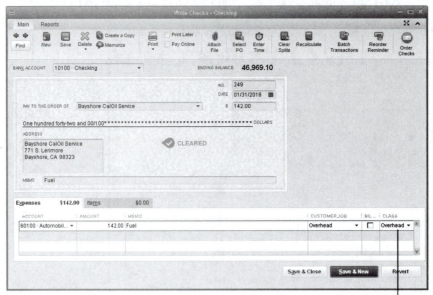

Click this cell and press Backspace to remove this value

Figure 6-13 Profit & Loss Report by Class

4. Click *Save & Close.*

5. Close the Transaction Detail By Account report.

6. To refresh the Profit & Loss by Class report, click the *Refresh* button at the window's top right.

   The *Profit & Loss by Class* report now includes an *Unclassified* column (see Figure 6-14).

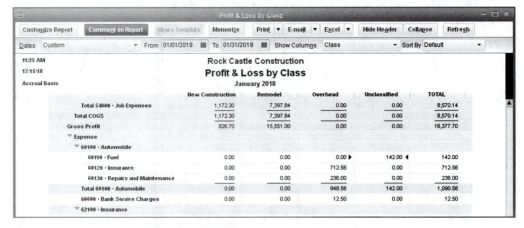

Figure 6-14 Profit & Loss Report by Class

7. To reassign the Overhead class to the Fuel transaction, repeat steps 1 through 6, except that in step 3, choose *Overhead* in the *Class* cell.

8. Close the *Profit & Loss by Class* report.

> Note: To ensure that you don't have any unclassified transactions, set up a class, such as the Overhead class in this sample file. That way, if a transaction doesn't apply to any other class, you can assign it to Overhead. In addition, you can modify a setting in QuickBooks preferences to tell the program to remind you if you try to save a transaction without assigning a class, as described on page 40.

Profit & Loss by Job Report

The *Profit & Loss by Job* report shows results categorized by customers and jobs. This report shows how much money you make or lose on each job so you can evaluate your profitability by job. It's also helpful for finding problems with pricing, excessive costs, or jobs where you forgot to bill for time and expenses. For example, if the cost for one job is much higher or lower than similar jobs, you might want to examine that job's transactions in more detail.

Computer Practice

Here are the steps to creating a *Profit & Loss by Job* report:

1. On the *Report* menu, choose the *Company & Financial* category, and then choose the *Profit & Loss By Job* report.

2. In the report window, set the report dates to *01/01/2018* and *01/31/2018*, then press Tab to update the report.

3. After you view the report (Figure 6-15), close it.

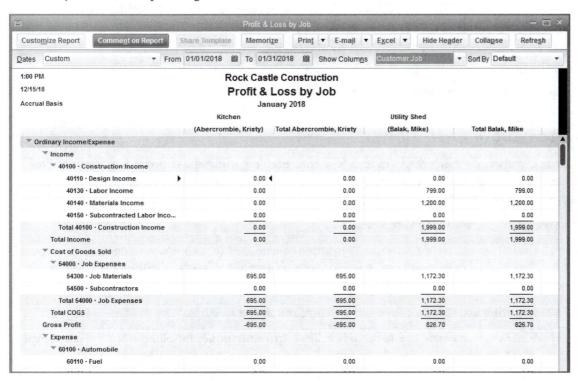

Figure 6-15 Profit & Loss by Job report

Balance Sheet Report

The *Balance Sheet* report shows your company's assets, liabilities, and equity on a specific date that you select, such as the end of the company fiscal year. While a Profit & Loss report shows whether your company is making money, the balance sheet helps you evaluate your company's financial strength.

Computer Practice

To create a *Balance Sheet* report, follow these steps:

1. On the *Report* menu, choose *Company & Financial*, and then choose *Balance Sheet Standard*.

2. In the *As of* field in the top left corner of the report, type *12/31/2018*, then press Tab to update the report (shown in Figure 6-16).

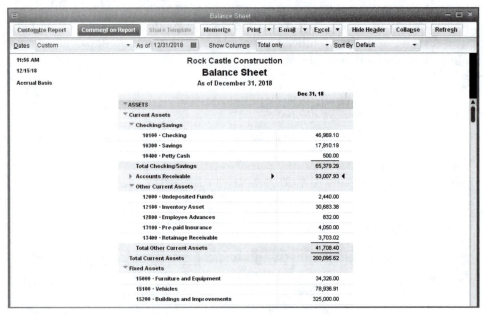

Figure 6-16 Balance Sheet Standard report

Statement of Cash Flows

Because of some accounting practices such as accrual basis reporting and depreciation, Profit & Loss reports don't actually identify how much cash comes in or goes out of your company. The *Statement of Cash Flows* report eliminates non-cash transactions so you can see your true cash flow.

Cash flow is divided into three categories:

*   Cash from **operating activities** is the money generated by a company's ongoing operations. This kind of cash means that the business can sustain itself without raising cash from other sources.

*   **Investing activities** are things like buying and selling buildings.

*   **Financing activities** include activities like borrowing money or selling stock in your company. (New companies often have to use financing activities until they begin to produce cash through operations.)

Computer Practice

To create a *Statement of Cash Flows* report, follow these steps:

1. On the *Report* menu, choose *Company & Financial*, and then choose *Statement of Cash Flows*.

2. In the *Dates* field, choose *This Fiscal Quarter-to-date*, then press Tab to update the report.

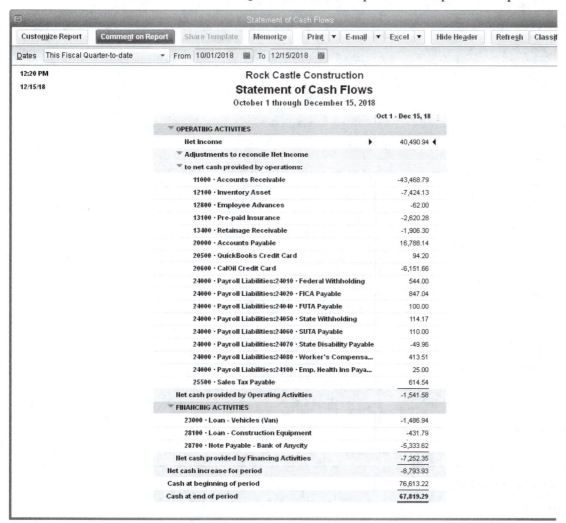

Figure 6-17 Statement of Cash Flows report

3. After you view the report, close it.

General Ledger

The *General Ledger* report shows all activity in every account in your chart of accounts for a specific time period.

Computer Practice

To create a *General Ledger* report, follow these steps:

1. In the *Report Center*, select the *Accountant & Taxes* category. In the *Account Activity* section, click the *General Ledger* report's *Run* icon to run it.

2. In the *Dates* field, choose *Today*, and then press Tab to update the report (Figure 6-18).

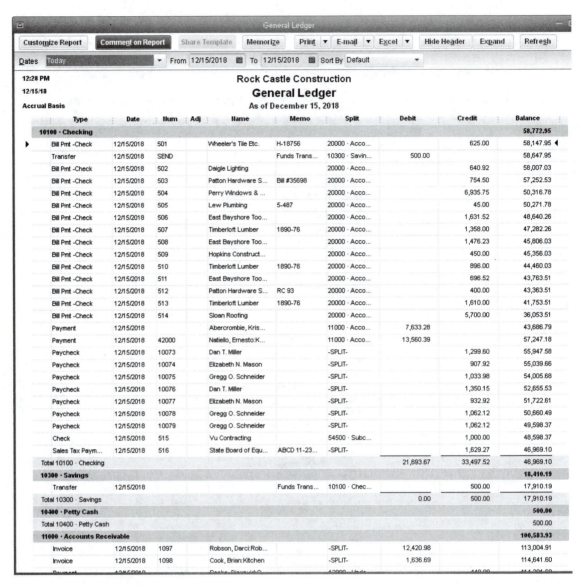

Figure 6-18 General Ledger report

3. After reviewing the report, close it.

> Note: Because this report shows every account (including those with a zero balance), the *General Ledger* report is very long. To make it more manageable, you can choose the accounts that you want to include. For example, you can choose only accounts with a balance. To do that, click the *Customize Report* button, then, in the *Modify Report* dialog box, click the *Advanced* button at the bottom right. In the *Include* section, select the *In Use* option to display only active accounts.

Trial Balance

The *Trial Balance* report shows the balances of all the accounts in your chart of accounts as of a specific date that you choose. Account balances appear in *Debit* and *Credit* columns. Typically, your accountant prepares this report at the end of each fiscal year to look for issues that might require attention.

Computer Practice

To run a *Trial Balance* report, follow these steps:

1. In the *Report Center*, choose the *Accountant & Taxes* category. In the *Account Activity* section, double-click the *Trial Balance* report.

2. In the *Dates* field, choose *This Fiscal Year*, then press Tab to update the report (Figure 6-19).

3. Close all report windows.

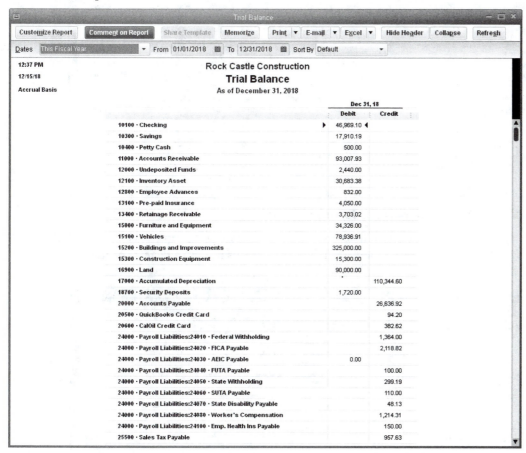

Figure 6-19 Trial Balance report

Voided/Deleted Transactions Summary Report

This report shows (Figure 6-20) all transactions in your company file that have been voided or deleted during a time period. This report can help you find errors or detect fraud. For example, if you have new users working on your company file, you can run this report to make sure they aren't voiding or deleting transactions by mistake. As you learned in Chapter 5, if your beginning reconciliation balance doesn't match the beginning balance on your bank statement, you can use this report to find transactions that contribute to that problem. On the *Reports* menu, choose *Accountant & Taxes*, and then choose *Voided/Deleted Transactions Summary* on the submenu.

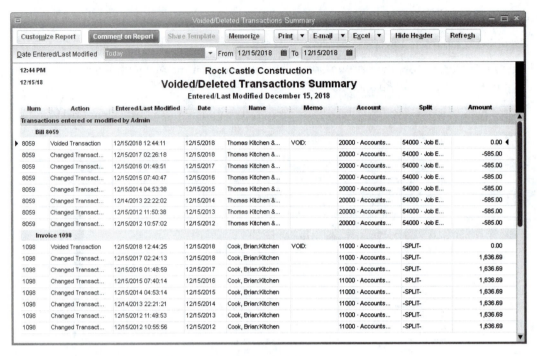

Figure 6-20 Voided/Deleted Transactions Summary report

To display all the line items for each transaction in the summary report, run the *Voided/Deleted Transactions Detail* report (Figure 6-21) instead. You can use this report to recreate or restore the original transactions.

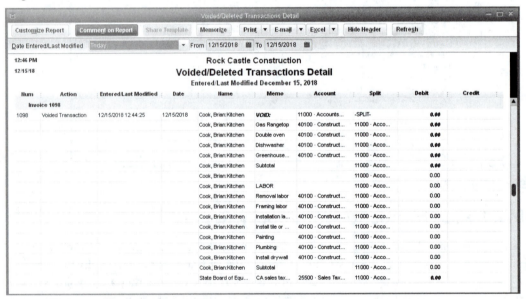

Figure 21 Voided/Deleted Transactions Detail report

Business Management Reports

QuickBooks provides many other reports that you can use to manage your business. You can review past performance and use that information to plan for the future. Some reports provide information you need to run your business, such as price lists for the things you sell and customer contact information. This section introduces you to several of these reports.

Customer Contact List

The *Customer Contact List*, shown in Figure 6-22, lists your customers and their contact information, such as address, primary contact, and phone number. To run this report, on the *Reports* menu, choose *Customers & Receivables*, and then choose *Customer Contact List* on the submenu.

Figure 6-22 Customer Contact List

Item Price List

The *Item Price List* lists the items you've created in your company file and includes the description, the preferred vendor, U/M (which stands for unit of measure and appears if you use QuickBooks Premier or Enterprise), and the sales price. To run this report, on the *Reports* menu, choose *Lists*, and then choose *Item Price List* on the submenu.

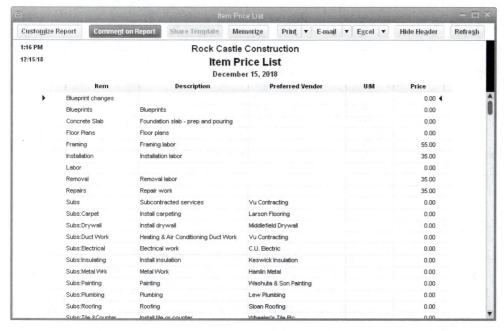

Figure 6-23 Item Price List

Check Detail Report

If you use accounts payable or payroll, the *Check Detail* report is helpful, because it shows the expense accounts associated with bill payments (see Figure 6-24) and payroll checks. For example, in the figure, Bill Pmt-number 480 shows the items and accounts associated with the bill. In contrast, if you look at a bill payment in the checking account register, the account assigned to the transaction is Accounts Payable.

To run this report, on the *Reports* menu, choose *Banking*, and then choose *Check Detail* on the submenu.

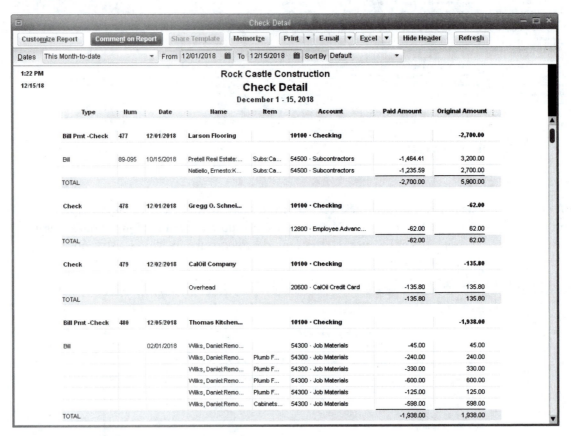

Figure 6-24 Check Detail report

A/R Aging Summary

The *A/R Aging Summary* report, shown in Figure 6-25, helps you find customers whose payments are late. As invoices grow older, it often becomes more difficult to collect the money you're owed. By checking the older columns in this report, you can see which customer you should follow up with. To run this report, on the *Reports* menu, choose *Customers & Receivables*, and then choose *A/R Aging Summary* on the submenu.

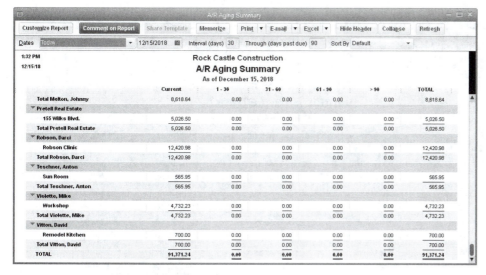

Figure 6-25 A/R Aging Summary report

Customer Balance Summary

The *Customer Balance Summary* report, shown in Figure 6-26, shows how much your customers owe you. To run this report, on the *Reports* menu, choose *Customers & Receivables*, and then choose *Customer Balance Summary* on the submenu.

If you want to examine the transactions that make up a customer's balance, double-click the customer's balance to run the *Customer Balance Detail* report, which shows every transaction that contributes to the balance. The *Customer Balance Detail* report is similar to the *Vendor Balance Detail* report shown in Figure 6-27.

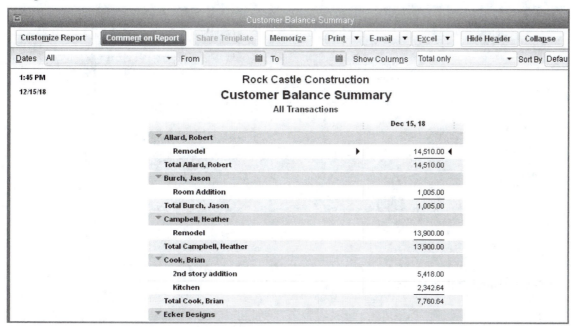

Figure 6-26 Customer Balance Summary report

Vendor Balance Detail

To see the transactions that contribute to your balances with vendors, run the *Vendor Balance Detail* report (Figure 6-27). To run this report, on the *Reports* menu, choose *Vendors & Payables*, and then choose *Vendor Balance Detail* on the submenu.

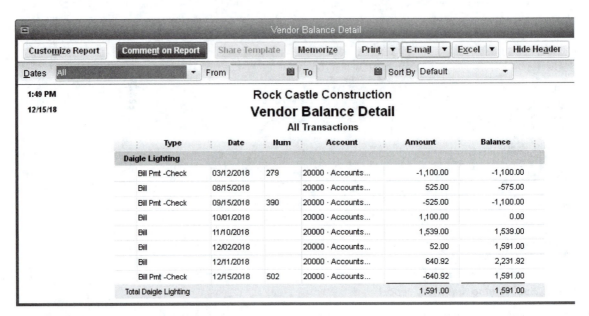

Figure 6-27 Vendor Balance Detail report

Unbilled Costs by Job

If you charge customers and jobs for billable time and expenses, it's important to get all those billable items onto the invoices you create. One way to view unbilled costs is by running the *Unbilled Costs by Job* report (Figure 6-28), which shows all transactions with unbilled time and expenses. To run this report, on the *Reports* menu, choose *Jobs, Time & Mileage*, and then choose *Unbilled Costs by Job* on the submenu.

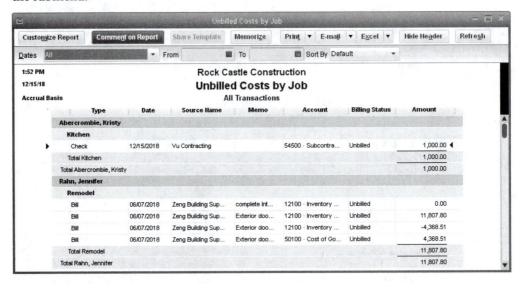

Figure 6-28 Unbilled Cost by Job report

QuickBooks Graphs

Graphs are invaluable tools for conveying information quickly. QuickBooks provides several graphs that help you evaluate your company's performance. This section shows you how to access these graphs and modify them.

Computer Practice

The *Income and Expense Graph* helps you keep track of your income, expenses, and, most importantly, how much you spend relative to what you earn. To earn a profit, your income must be higher than your expenses.

To create an *Income and Expense Graph*, follow these steps:

1. On the *Reports* menu, choose *Company & Financial*, and then choose *Income & Expense Graph*.

2. Click the *Dates* button at the top left, choose *This Quarter* in the drop-down list, and then click *OK*.

   A *QuickInsight* graph appears, showing income and expenses in the bar graph at the top. For example, in Figure 6-29, the green income bars (the left bar in each pair) are taller than the red expense bars (the right bar in each pair), so the company has made money each month this quarter. The pie chart at the bottom shows your company's expenses by account. The pie chart legend identifies the expense accounts in the pie chart and the percentage each represents of your total expenses.

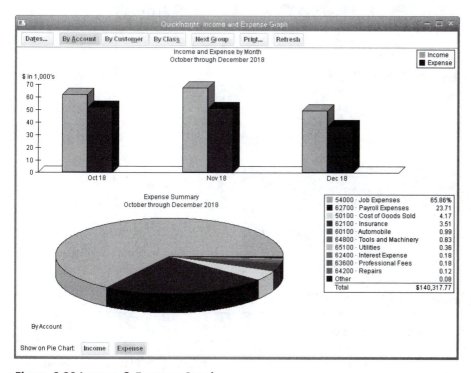

Figure 6-29 Income & Expense Graph

3. If you want to view your income and expenses by customer instead, click *By Customer* in the button bar.

> Tip: If you want to see the details behind a graph, put your cursor over a bar in the bar chart or a slice in the pie chart. When the cursor changes to a magnifying glass with a Z in the middle, double-click that element to generate a *QuickZoom Graph* for just that element. For example, double-click the November expense bar in the *Income and Expense Graph* to display a pie chart of November's expenses.

Processing Multiple Reports

You may run several reports at the same time, for example, your *Profit & Loss*, *Balance Sheet*, and *Statement of Cash Flows* reports at the end of each month. You can save time by processing several reports as a batch.

> Note: *Process Multiple Reports* works with regular reports, as well as memorized reports (see page 191) and commented reports (page 193).

Computer Practice

To process a batch of reports, follow these steps:

1. On the *Reports* menu, choose *Process Multiple Reports*.

2. In the *Select Memorized Reports From* drop-down list, choose *Customers* (shown in Figure 6-30).

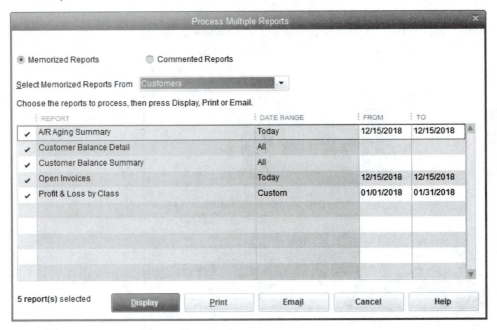

Figure 6-30 Process Multiple Reports dialog box

3. If you don't want to include a report in the batch, turn off its checkmark cell (to the left of its name). For example, turn off the *Customer Balance Detail* checkmark cell.

   The *From* and *To* cells show the date range covered by the reports. To change the range, type dates in these cells. In this example, keep the dates as they are.

4. To run the selected reports, click *Display*. (You can click *Print* or *Email* to print or email all the reports, respectively. Do not do this for this example.)

Each report opens in its own report window, as shown in Figure 6-31.

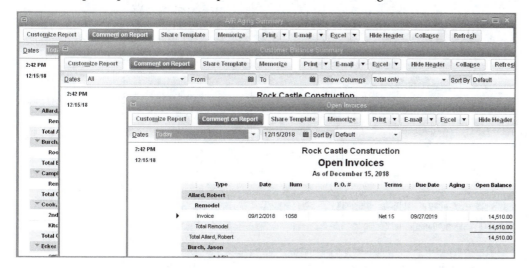

Figure 6-31 The batch of reports opened in separate report windows

Printing Reports

You can print any report you run in QuickBooks. Similar to other programs you use, you can specify print settings, such as the printer, page orientation, and so on.

Computer Practice

Do the following to specify print settings for a report and then print it:

1. Run a *Profit & Loss by Class* report for the current fiscal quarter.

2. To print the report, in the report window's button bar, click the *Print* button and then choose *Report*. (Alternatively, simply press Ctrl+P).

   The *Print Reports* dialog box (Figure 6-32) opens. Some of the settings you see in this window will differ from the ones shown here.

3. If necessary, in the *Printer* drop-down list, choose the printer you want to use.

   QuickBooks usually selects your default printer, but you can choose whichever printer you want.

4. In the *Orientation* section, choose *Landscape*.

5. In the *Page Breaks* section, make sure that the *Smart page breaks* checkbox is turned on.

   Smart page breaks help keep related data on the same page. When you turn on this checkbox, QuickBooks won't print a single line of a section on one page with the remaining lines of the section on the next page (a widow); it also won't print all but one line of a section on one page with the remaining line on the next page (an orphan). To insert page breaks only after major sections of a report, turn on the *Page break after each major grouping* check box. For example, if you turn on this checkbox for a *Profit & Loss* report, the income and cost of goods sold account might be on the first page, while the expense accounts (the next major grouping) appears on the next page.

Figure 6-32 Print Reports dialog box

6. To fit a report on a specific number of pages, turn on both *Fit report to* checkboxes and fill in the boxes with the number of pages you want (for width and height). In this example, keep the number 1 in each box, so the report prints on a single page.

7. To see what the report looks like before you print it, click the *Preview* button on the dialog box's right.

8. If the report looks the way you want, click *Print*.

9. Close all report windows.

Exporting Reports to Excel

If you need to modify reports in ways that QuickBooks can't, for example, to change column names or to perform calculations on the report contents, you can export them to Microsoft Excel. Because the changes you make to a report in Excel don't affect your QuickBooks data, you can customize exported reports in any way you want—even modifying their data.

> Note: QuickBooks Premier Accountant and QuickBooks Enterprise include a report application called QuickBooks Statement Writer, which creates reports in Excel using data from your company file.

Computer Practice

To export a report to Excel using the *Profit & Loss Standard* report as an example, follow these steps:

1. From the *Reports* menu, choose *Company & Financial*, and then choose *Profit & Loss Standard*.

2. In the *Dates* drop-down list, choose *This Fiscal Quarter*.

3. In the *Show Columns* drop-down list, choose *Month*.

   Your report should look like the one in Figure 6-33.

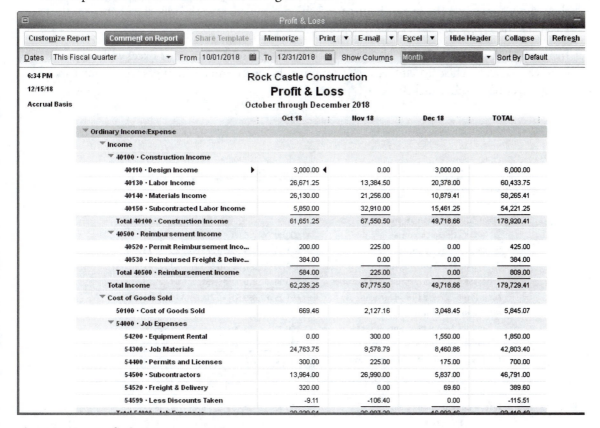

Figure 6-33 A Profit & Loss report to export

4. To export the report, click the *Excel* button, and then choose *Create New Worksheet* from the drop-down list.

   The *Send Report to Excel* window, shown in Figure 6-34, opens.

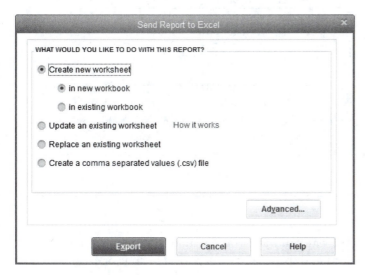

Figure 6-34 Send Report to Excel window

5. Click *Export*.

QuickBooks launches Excel (if it's not running already) and opens the report. Your Excel spreadsheet should resemble the one in Figure 6-35. If you want to save the report in Excel, on the Excel *File* menu, choose *Save* or simply press Ctrl+S.

In Excel, click the *QuickBooks* tab in the ribbon. To update the report in Excel with your current QuickBooks data, click *Update Report*. (You can't, however, import changes from your Excel spreadsheet back into QuickBooks.)

R24				f_x						
A B C D E				F	G	H	I	J	K	
1					Oct 18	Nov 18	Dec 18	TOTAL		
2		Ordinary Income/Expense								
3			Income							
4				40100 · Construction Income						
5				40110 · Design Income	3,000.00	0.00	3,000.00	6,000.00		
6				40130 · Labor Income	26,671.25	13,384.50	20,378.00	60,433.75		
7				40140 · Materials Income	26,130.00	21,256.00	10,879.41	58,265.41		
8				40150 · Subcontracted Labor Income	5,850.00	32,910.00	15,461.25	54,221.25		
9				Total 40100 · Construction Income	61,651.25	67,550.50	49,718.66	178,920.41		
10				40500 · Reimbursement Income						
11				40520 · Permit Reimbursement Income	200.00	225.00	0.00	425.00		
12				40530 · Reimbursed Freight & Delivery	384.00	0.00	0.00	384.00		
13				Total 40500 · Reimbursement Income	584.00	225.00	0.00	809.00		
14			Total Income		62,235.25	67,775.50	49,718.66	179,729.41		
15		Cost of Goods Sold								
16				50100 · Cost of Goods Sold	669.46	2,127.16	3,048.45	5,845.07		
17				54000 · Job Expenses						
18				54200 · Equipment Rental	0.00	300.00	1,550.00	1,850.00		
19				54300 · Job Materials	24,763.75	9,578.79	8,460.86	42,803.40		
20				54400 · Permits and Licenses	300.00	225.00	175.00	700.00		
21				54500 · Subcontractors	13,964.00	26,990.00	5,837.00	46,791.00		
22				54520 · Freight & Delivery	320.00	0.00	69.60	389.60		
23				54599 · Less Discounts Taken	-9.11	-106.40	0.00	-115.51		
24				Total 54000 · Job Expenses	39,338.64	36,987.39	16,092.46	92,418.49		
25			Total COGS		40,008.10	39,114.55	19,140.91	98,263.56		

Figure 6-35 Exported report opened in Excel

Note: When you export a report to Excel, QuickBooks doesn't export only numbers. It inserts formulas, such as the *Sum* function so the totals in your report actually add up the values in the appropriate cells.

Customizing Reports

If QuickBooks built-in reports aren't set up the way you want, you can modify them in several ways. For example, you can choose the columns to display, filter the report to include or exclude information, modify the header and footer, and choose the font and other formatting settings for the report's elements.

Report Settings

To modify a report, in the report window's button bar, click the *Customize Report* button to open the *Modify Report* window. This window has four tabs. Here's what you can do on each one:

- On the *Display* tab, you can change the date range, reporting basis, and columns that appear in the reports. You can also include subcolumns, such as a previous period or percentages of rows or columns. You can also specify how the report is sorted. The settings on this tab depend on the report you're working on. For example, in the *Modify Report* window for a summary report, such as a *Profit and Loss* report (see Figure 6-36), you can choose the category to use in the report columns by choosing an entry in the *Display columns by* drop-down list, such as Months. On the other hand, for a detail report or list report, such as the *Item Price List*, you can choose field columns, as shown in Figure 6-37.

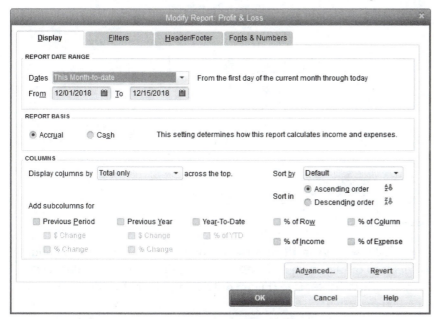

Figure 6-36 Modify Report window: Profit & Loss Standard Display tab

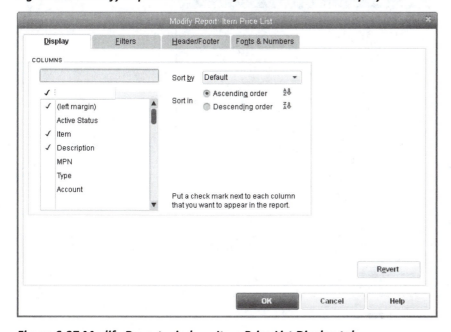

Figure 6-37 Modify Report window: Item Price List Display tab

- With the *Filters* tab, you can specify which information to include or exclude from a report, so you can focus on specific parts of your business. You can filter by many QuickBooks fields, although the most common include accounts, names, items, transaction types, and amounts. To apply a filter, first choose the field you want to filter by, such as Customer Type, as shown in Figure 6-38. Then, in the fields that appear to the field list's right (Customer Type, here), choose the value to filter for, in this example, Commercial. Click OK to apply the filter.

Figure 6-38 Modify Report window: Filters tab

- The *Header/Footer* tab includes settings that control what you see in the report header and footer. You can choose fields to display, such as *Company Name, Report Title, Subtitle, Date Prepared, Page Number,* and *Extra Footer Line* (Figure 6-39). The tab's right side has a drop-down list for the page orientation.

Figure 6-39 Modify Report: Header/Footer tab

- With the *Fonts & Numbers* tab, you can change fonts and the way numbers appear. The *Fonts & Numbers* tab also includes options for reducing numbers by multiples of 1000, hiding zero amounts, and showing dollar amounts without cents (Figure 6-40).

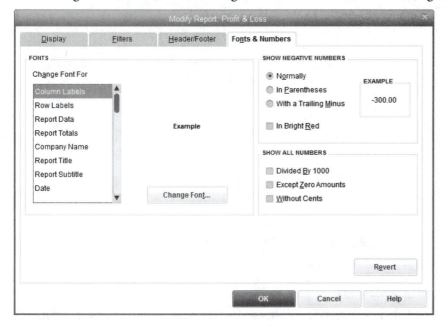

Figure 6-40 Modify Report window: Fonts/Numbers tab

Modifying a Report

To see how customizing a report works, suppose you want to create a report that shows your product sales to residential customers from July 1, 2018, through September 30. You want the report to be sorted and subtotaled by customer. In addition, you want to include the following columns: transaction type, date, transaction number, customer name, item, account, debit, and credit. The title "Q3 Residential Product Sales by Customer" should appear at the top of the report.

Computer Practice

To create a customer report like this, follow these steps:

1. On the *Reports* menu, choose *Custom Reports*, then choose *Transaction Detail* on the submenu.

   Because the *Transaction Detail* report is a custom report, the *Modify Report* window opens automatically.

2. In the *Dates* drop-down list, choose *Last Fiscal Quarter*.

   The *From* and *To* fields change to July 1, 2018 and September 30, 2018 (because the fiscal year in the sample file is 2018).

3. In the *Total by* drop-down list, choose *Customer*. Keep the *Sort by* field set to *Default* (which sorts in alphabetical order (A to Z).

4. To select the columns for the report, in the *Columns* section, click the checkmark cells to turn columns on or off (see Figure 6-41).

   In this example, the Type, Num, Name, Account, Debit, and Credit columns are already selected. However, you need to turn on the Item column and you need to turn off the checkmarks for Memo, Class, Clr, Split, and Balance.

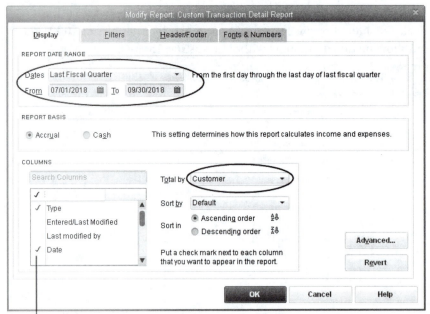

Click cell in this column to toggle columns on and off

Figure 6-41 An example of Display tab settings

6. To filter the report to show only residential customer, on the *Filters* tab, in the *Choose Filter* list, select *Customer Type*.

7. In the *Customer Type* drop-down list, choose *Residential,* as shown in Figure 6-42.

Figure 6-42 An example of Filter tab settings

8. On the *Header/Footer* tab in the *Report Title* field, change the name to *Q3 Residential Product Sales by Customer.* Remove the text from the *Subtitle* field.

9. Click *OK* to update your customized report.

    Your report should look like the one in Figure 6-43.

Note: Do not close this report. You use it in the next section.

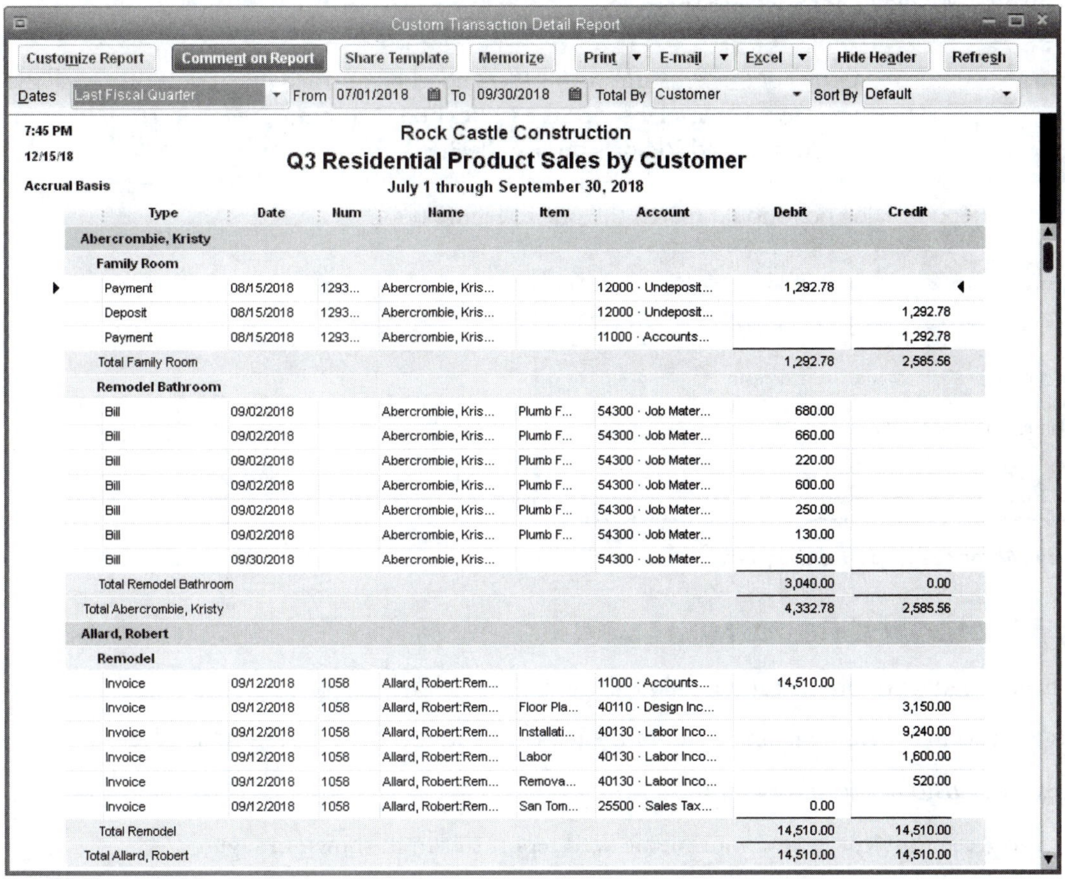

Type	Date	Num	Name	Item	Account	Debit	Credit
Abercrombie, Kristy							
Family Room							
Payment	08/15/2018	1293...	Abercrombie, Kris...		12000 · Undeposit...	1,292.78	
Deposit	08/15/2018	1293...	Abercrombie, Kris...		12000 · Undeposit...		1,292.78
Payment	08/15/2018	1293...	Abercrombie, Kris...		11000 · Accounts...		1,292.78
Total Family Room						1,292.78	2,585.56
Remodel Bathroom							
Bill	09/02/2018		Abercrombie, Kris...	Plumb F...	54300 · Job Mater...	680.00	
Bill	09/02/2018		Abercrombie, Kris...	Plumb F...	54300 · Job Mater...	660.00	
Bill	09/02/2018		Abercrombie, Kris...	Plumb F...	54300 · Job Mater...	220.00	
Bill	09/02/2018		Abercrombie, Kris...	Plumb F...	54300 · Job Mater...	600.00	
Bill	09/02/2018		Abercrombie, Kris...	Plumb F...	54300 · Job Mater...	250.00	
Bill	09/02/2018		Abercrombie, Kris...	Plumb F...	54300 · Job Mater...	130.00	
Bill	09/30/2018		Abercrombie, Kris...		54300 · Job Mater...	500.00	
Total Remodel Bathroom						3,040.00	0.00
Total Abercrombie, Kristy						4,332.78	2,585.56
Allard, Robert							
Remodel							
Invoice	09/12/2018	1058	Allard, Robert:Rem...		11000 · Accounts...	14,510.00	
Invoice	09/12/2018	1058	Allard, Robert:Rem...	Floor Pla...	40110 · Design Inc...		3,150.00
Invoice	09/12/2018	1058	Allard, Robert:Rem...	Installati...	40130 · Labor Inco...		9,240.00
Invoice	09/12/2018	1058	Allard, Robert:Rem...	Labor	40130 · Labor Inco...		1,600.00
Invoice	09/12/2018	1058	Allard, Robert:Rem...	Remova...	40130 · Labor Inco...		520.00
Invoice	09/12/2018	1058	Allard, Robert:Rem...	San Tom...	25500 · Sales Tax...	0.00	
Total Remodel						14,510.00	14,510.00
Total Allard, Robert						14,510.00	14,510.00

Figure 6-43 Customized Report

Memorizing Reports

If you've made a lot of changes to a report, you don't want to repeat all those steps the next time you run the report. To save a report with all your modifications, you can memorize it. (QuickBooks memorizes the report's settings, not its data.)

If you memorize a report with specific dates, such as 9/1/2018 and 12/31/2018, the report uses those exact dates the next time you run it. To make memorized reports more flexible, use date ranges, such as Last Fiscal Year or This Month-to-date, in the *Dates* field instead. That way, QuickBooks uses relative dates when you run the report. For example, if it's 1/3/2019, Last Fiscal Year represents the year 2018. If it's 4/12/2018, Last Fiscal Year is 2017.

Computer Practice

To memorize the customized report you created in the previous section, follow these steps:

1. In the *Custom Transaction Detail Report* window's button bar, click the *Memorize* button.

   The *Memorize Report* dialog box opens with your report title in the *Name* field (Figure 6-44). You can edit the title if you want to.

2. To save the memorized report in a group, turn on the *Save in Memorized Report Group* check-

box. In the drop-down list to the right of that label, choose *Customers*.

If you add a memorized report to a group, you can easily run all the reports in that group with the *Process Multiple Reports* feature (page 182).

> Note: Keep the *Share this report template with others* checkbox turned off. If you turn it on, you can share your report template with the QuickBooks community. To learn more, read the section Contributed Reports on page 193.

The *Memorize Report* dialog box should match the one in Figure 6-44.

Figure 6-44 Memorize Report dialog box

Using Memorized Reports

To use a memorized report in the future, follow these steps:

1. Click *Reports* in the icon bar, and then, in the *Report Center*, choose the *Memorized* tab.

2. Choose the *Customers* category on the left.

3. Click the green *Run* icon below your memorized report to run it, shown in Figure 6-45.

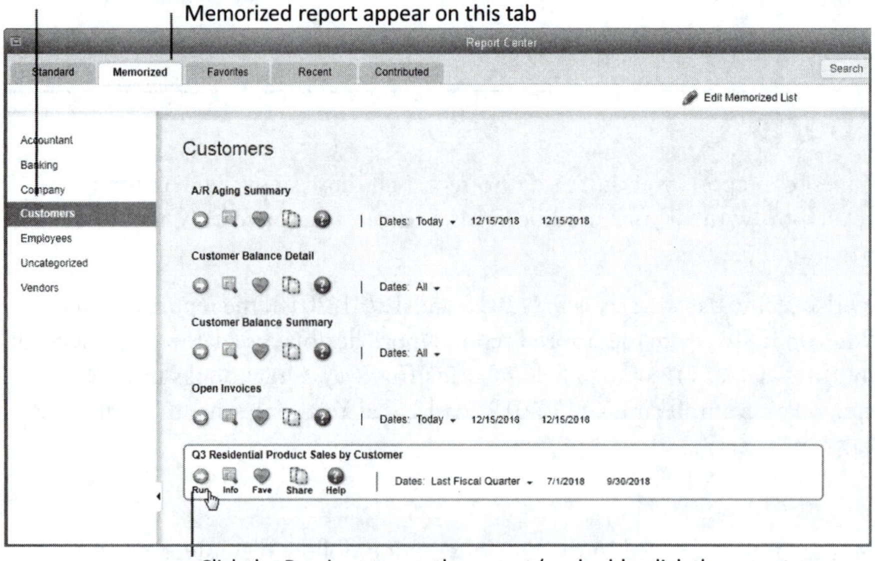

Memorized report groups

Memorized report appear on this tab

Click the Run icon to run the report (or double-click the report name

Figure 6-45 Memorized report in the Report Center

Note: If you use QuickBooks Premier, you can export memorized reports as report templates. A report template contains report settings you specify—for example, report date, format, and filters. Then, you can import report templates into another company and choose the reports from the *Memorized Report* list.

Contributed Reports

When you memorize a report, the *Memorize Report* dialog box that opens contains the *Share this report template* with others checkbox. If you want to share the report you've created with other QuickBooks users, turn this checkbox on. The *Share Template* window opens. The *Report Title* field is filled in automatically with your memorized report's title. You can fill in a description. After you click *Share*, the report becomes one of the QuickBooks community's contributed reports.

You can access contributed reports by clicking the *Report Center's Contributed* tab, shown in Figure 6-46. If contributed reports use features that you don't use, such as *Multiple Currencies*, you won't be able to run contributed reports that include those features.

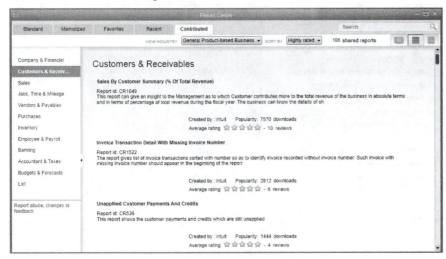

Figure 6-46 The Report Center's Contributed tab

Adding Comments to Reports

In QuickBooks 2015, you can now add comments to reports from within the program. Instead of printing a report and writing your comments on the hard copy, you can add a comment to any line in a report. For example, you might run a *Profit & Loss* report at the end of the year and you want to let your accountant know that you haven't recorded pension contributions yet. Or you run a *Budget vs. Actual* report and have questions for your accounting department.

If you are using QuickBooks 2015, here's how you add comments to a report:

1. Run the report you want, such as *Profit & Loss Standard*. (On the *Reports* menu, choose *Company & Financial*, and then choose *Profit & Loss Standard* on the submenu.)

2. In the report window's button bar, click the *Comment on Report* button.

   The *Comment on Report: [report name]* window opens. Small comment boxes appear to the right of the values in the rightmost column, as shown in Figure 6-47.

3. To add a comment to a line of the report, click that line's comment box.

   QuickBooks adds a number to the comment box and opens the *Comments* pane.

4. In the *Comment* pane's text box, type your comment, and then click *Save*.

   The comment you just added appears in the *Comments* pane, and the total number of comments in the report appears on the *Comments* tab. QuickBooks numbers comments as you add them, so they may not appear in sequence from top to bottom.

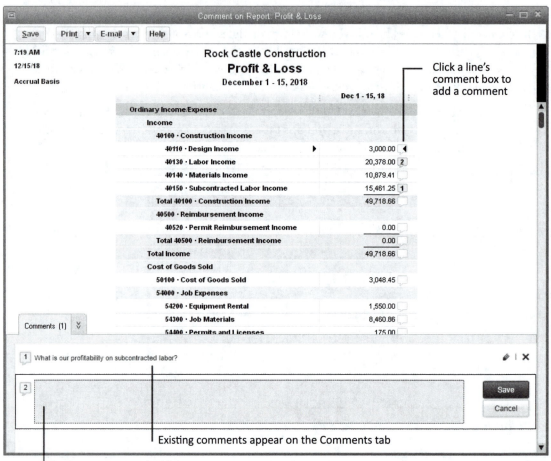

Figure 6-47 Commenting on reports

5. After you add all your comments, click the *Save* button at the *Comment on Report* window's top left.

6. In the *Save Your Commented Report* dialog box's *Name* box, type the name of your commented report, such as *P&L 2018 Questions about Labor Costs*, and then click *OK*. Click *OK* in the *Saved Successfully* message box.

7. Close the *Comment on Report* window.

8. To view commented reports, on the *Reports* menu, choose *Commented Reports*. In the *Commented Reports* window, double-click the report you want to open.

> Note: You can't customize commented reports. If you want to change something, like the date range, you have to run the report again and add new comments.

Finding Transactions

QuickBooks offers several ways to search for transactions. The best method to use depends on what you're trying to find. The *Find* feature is the best approach when you have specific values you're looking for, such as an invoice number, a specific item, customer, or amount. You can also search for transactions with the *Search* feature, in QuickBooks Centers, in account register windows, or with *QuickReports* and *QuickZoom*. This section explains how to use all these features.

Using the Find Feature

With QuickBooks' *Find* feature, you can search for transactions that match one or more criteria. For example, you can search for a specific invoice number, all bills within a specific date range, or all invoices from last year that include a specific product. If you have a transaction window open, such as the *Create Invoices* window shown in Figure 6-48, you can click the *Find* button to open the *Find [transaction type]* dialog box or simply press Ctrl+F. If you do that, the dialog box includes fields for finding that transaction type.

If you don't have a transaction window open and you choose *Find* on the *Edit* menu (or press Ctrl+F), a generic *Find* window opens.

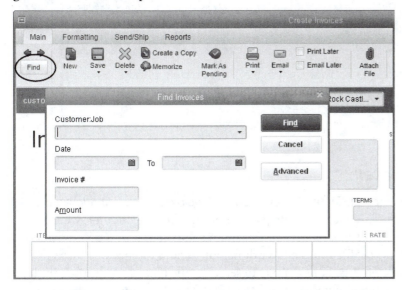

Figure 6-48 Opening the Find [transaction type] using the Find button

Using the Search Feature

The Search feature is helpful when you're looking for more than a single transaction or you're not sure where to look in your company file. For example, suppose you want to find all transactions for your customer Robert Allard. To do that, in the *Search* box at the top of the icon bar, type *Allard*, and choose *Search company file* from the drop-down menu. Then, click the *Search* icon.

In the *Search* window that opens (Figure 6-49), review the search results. (If necessary, in that window, type additional search terms in the *Search* field, and then click the *Search* icon. To view a transaction in the results, click its blue link text.

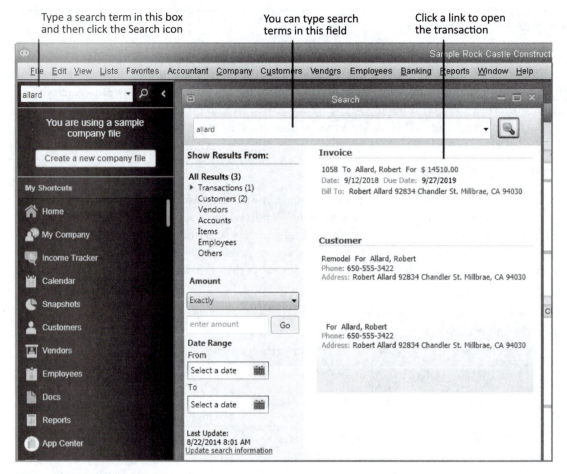

Type a search term in this box and then click the Search icon

You can type search terms in this field

Click a link to open the transaction

Figure 6-49 Search Results

Using a QuickBooks Center

QuickBooks Centers, such as the *Customer Center*, *Vendor Center*, *Employee Center*, and *Inventory Center*, have features that help you find transactions. For example, in the *Customer Center*, when you select a customer on the *Customers & Jobs* tab, that customer's transactions appear in the *Transactions* tab at the window's lower right (Figure 6-50). You can filter those transactions by choosing filters in the *Show*, *Filter By*, and *Date* drop-down lists. For example, to see a specific type of transaction, in the *Show* drop-down list, choose the transaction type like *Invoices* or *Received Payments*.

This tab lists customers and jobs

Click this tab to display a list of transaction types to search

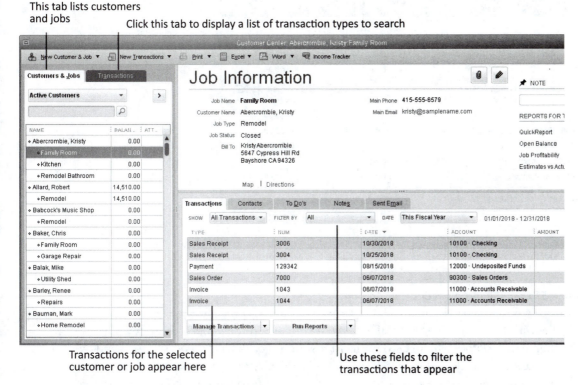

Transactions for the selected customer or job appear here

Use these fields to filter the transactions that appear

Figure 6-50 Finding Transactions in a Center

If you click the *Transactions* tab on the left side of the center, you can then click the type of transaction you want to look for. When you do, all the transactions of that type appear on the right side of the window. You can use the *Filter By* and *Dates* drop-down lists above the table to filter the transactions.

QuickReports

QuickReports are built-in reports that contain transactions for things like accounts, customers, vendors, and items. You can run *QuickReports* from the *Chart of Accounts* window, QuickBooks Centers, *List* windows, account register windows, and transaction forms. For example, if the *Chart of Accounts* window is open, you can create a *QuickReport* that shows all transactions for a specific account. If an account register window is open, the *QuickReport* shows transactions in the register with the same name as the selected transaction.

Computer Practice

Follow these steps to run a *QuickReport*:

1. On the *Home Page*, click the *Chart of Accounts* icon (or press Ctrl+A).

2. In the *Chart of Accounts* window, select the *Accounts Receivable* account.

3. In the *Reports* drop-down list (Figure 6-51), choose *QuickReport* (or press Ctrl+Q).

    The *QuickReport* contains all transactions posted to the Accounts Receivable account, as shown in Figure 6-52.

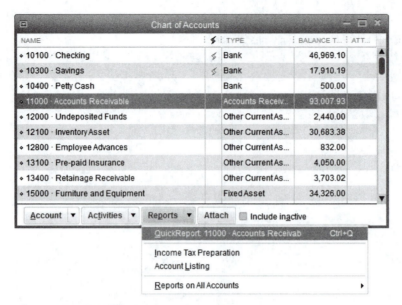

Figure 6-51 QuickReport from Chart of Accounts

Note: To run a *QuickReport* in the *Item List* window, in the *Reports* drop-down list, choose *QuickReport*. In an account register window, click *QuickReport* in the window's toolbar. In a QuickBooks Center, for example, the *Customer Center*, select the customer name on the *Customers & Jobs* tab. Then, in the *Customer Information* pane at the window's top right, click the *QuickReport* link.

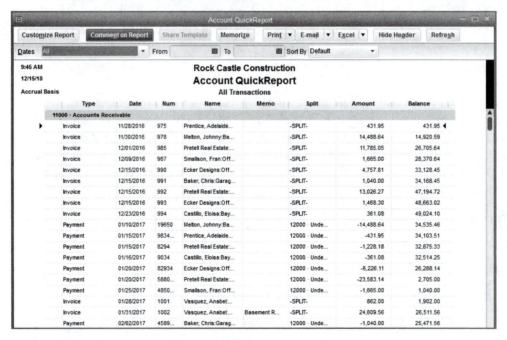

Figure 6-52 Accounts Receivable QuickReport

Note: Do not close this report. You use it in the next section.

Using QuickZoom

In any report, you can use *QuickZoom* to see more detail.

To *QuickZoom* within a report, follow these steps:

1. Place the cursor over *Invoice #975*. The arrow pointer turns into a magnifying glass with a Z in it, as shown in Figure 6-53.

2. Double click the invoice to open the original transaction.

Figure 6-53 Using QuickZoom

Review Questions

Choose the best answer(s) for each of the following:

1. If you run a summary report, you can modify it in the following ways:

    a) Choose the transaction fields that appear in report columns.

    b) Change the date range.

    c) Specify the categories for report columns.

    d) Apply a filter to include or exclude data.

2. You can make the following changes to reports in a *Modify Report* dialog box:

    a) Change the width of report columns.

    b) Choose the columns that appear.

    c) Specify the sort order.

    d) Memorize the report.

3. To examine your company's profitability, you should:

    a) Run a *Profit & Loss Standard* report.

    b) Run a *Statement of Cash Flows* report

    c) Include a *% of Income* column in a *Profit & Loss* report.

    d) Run a *Balance Sheet Standard* report.

4. You can create QuickReports for:

   a) Customers

   b) Items

   c) Invoices

   d) Accounts

5. After you customize a report, how can you reuse it in the future?

   a) Save the report as a template.

   b) Share the report with the QuickBooks community.

   c) Memorize the report.

   d) Reapply the customized settings each time in the *Modify Report* window.

Reports Exercise 1

Applying Your Knowledge

Restore the sample file, sample_product-based business 2015 (Portable).QBM. (Or, if you are using QuickBooks 2014, restore sample_product-based business 2014 (Portable).QBM.)

1. Print the *Profit & Loss Standard* report for *December 2018*.

2. Print the *Balance Sheet Standard* report as of *December 31, 2018*.

3. Print the *Statement of Cash Flows* report for *December 2018*.

4. Print the *Customer QuickReport* for *Brian Cook* for *December 2018*.

5. Print the *Customer Contact List* report.

6. Run an *Open Invoices Report* as of *December 31, 2018*. Filter the report to display only transactions under the *Remodel* class. Print the customized *Open Invoices* report.

Reports Exercise 2 (Advanced)

Applying Your Knowledge

Restore the sample file, sample_product-based business 2015 (Portable).QBM. (Or, if you are using QuickBooks 2014, restore sample_product-based business 2014 (Portable).QBM.)

1. Print the *Vendor Contact List.*

2. Print the *Profit & Loss Standard* report for the fourth quarter of 2018.

3. Print the *Profit & Loss by Class* report for the last month.

4. Print the *Trial Balance* report for *December 2018*.

5. Print the *Balance Sheet Standard* report as of *December 31, 2018*.

6. Create a customized report for customers who paid more than $3,000 in *December 2018*. Subtotal the report by customer. Change the title to *December Top Payments*. The report should look like the one in the figure.

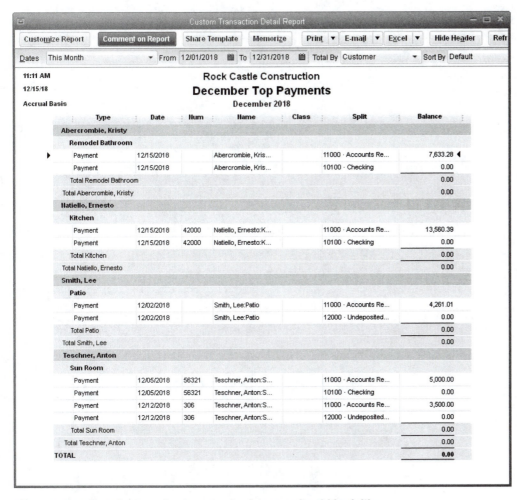

Figure 6-54 What the Exercise 2 customized report should look like

7. Memorize the report you created in step 6 in the *Customers* report group.

8. Run the *Profit & Loss by Class* report. Make sure there are no unclassified values. Modify the report to show only the *Remodel* and *New Construction* classes.

9. Run the *Profit & Loss by Job* report. Modify it to show *% of Income*. What is the gross profit for all of Kristy Abercrombie's jobs? Which job has the highest gross profit?

10. Create an *Income and Expense* graph for *This Year*.

Chapter 7

Customizing QuickBooks

Topics

This chapter covers the following topics:

- An Introduction to QuickBooks Preferences
- Customizing QuickBooks Menus
- QuickBooks Items
- Other QuickBooks Lists
- Custom Fields
- Customizing Form Templates

QuickBooks has hundreds of *preferences*, which are settings you can choose to tell the program how you want it to behave. When you install QuickBooks, it chooses settings that work for most companies. But you can change those settings if your company does things differently. This chapter introduces QuickBooks preferences and describes a few settings you might decide to change.

You can also customize QuickBooks' *Home Page*, menus, and icon bar so you can access the features you use most often. In this chapter, you'll learn how to customize all these elements.

You learned about several QuickBooks lists (the Customer:Job List, Vendor List, Item List, and so on) in earlier chapters. This chapter provides more information about QuickBooks items and introduces a few other QuickBooks lists you can use to streamline your bookkeeping.

QuickBooks comes with dozens of built-in business form templates. But you can customize those forms to modify their appearance and include the information you want. This chapter describes a few methods you can use to customize the business forms you produce.

> Note: For the computer practice in this chapter, restore the sample file, sample_product-based business 2015 (Portable).QBM. (Or, if you are using QuickBooks 2014, restore sample_product-based business 2014 (Portable).QBM.)

An Introduction to QuickBooks Preferences

QuickBooks has two types of preferences, which is why each category in the *Preferences* dialog box has the following two tabs (Figure 7-1):

- **My Preferences**: Think of the settings on this tab as user preferences. Each person who logs into a company file can choose settings that apply only to their QuickBooks sessions, such as the color scheme and whether you see multiple windows or one at a time.

- **Company Preferences**: Some preferences apply to the entire company, such as whether you use cash basis or accrual basis accounting. You find these global settings on *Company Preferences* tabs. To ensure that company preferences are set properly, only QuickBooks administrators can change the settings on these tabs.

> Note: This chapter provides a high-level look at how preferences work. Many QuickBooks preferences are described in detail in other chapters, such as settings for received payments in Chapter 3, Sales and Income. For more information about preferences, refer to *QuickBooks Help* (press F1).

Working with Preferences

Computer Practice

Here are the steps to viewing and setting QuickBooks preferences:

1. To open the *Preferences* dialog box, on the *Edit* menu, choose *Preferences*.

   The pane on the left side of the *Preferences* dialog box lists each preference category (Figure 7-1), such as *Accounting*, *Bills*, *Desktop*, and *Sales & Customers*.

2. Click the category you want to access.

   QuickBooks shades the category selected with a green background.

3. On the *My Preferences* tab, change any settings you want in the selected category. If you have administrator privileges, you can click the *Company Preferences* tab to change global preferences.

4. When you're done changing settings, click OK to save your changes and close the *Preferences* dialog box.

   If you change preferences in one category and then click another category, QuickBooks asks if you want to save the changes in the category you were working in. To save the changes before switching categories, click *Yes*.

Setting User Preferences

Computer Practice

To modify user preferences, follow these steps:

1. On the *Edit* menu, choose *Preferences*.

2. In the category list, select *Desktop View* (Figure 7-1).

   With the settings in this category, you can customize windows, the desktop, and color scheme for your sessions.

   The settings on the *Desktop View* category's *My Preferences* tab let you customize the windows you see when you log into QuickBooks. For example, the *Multiple Windows* option is selected initially, which is usually what you want. With this option selected, you can see more than one window at the same time, move them around, and resize them. The *Show Home page when opening a company file* checkbox is turned on initially, which means that the *Home Page* displays automatically when you open this company file.

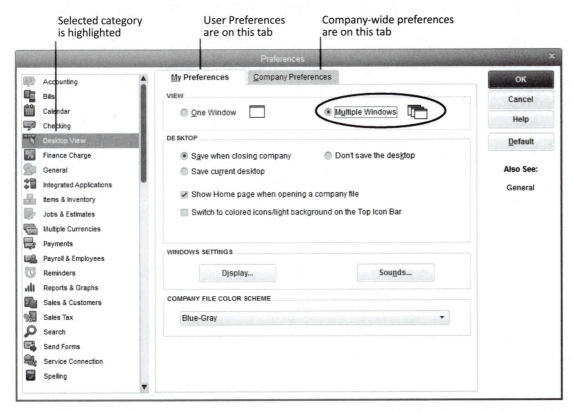

Figure 7-1 Desktop View Preferences window

3. To change the color scheme you see, in the *Company File Color Scheme* section, choose a color from the drop-down menu.

    When you choose a different color scheme, QuickBooks applies that color to the main Quick-Books window's title bar and to the title bars of other windows open in QuickBooks.

> Tip: If multiple users regularly use your company file, consider selecting the *Don't save the desktop* option to prevent a decrease in performance. If you choose *Save current desktop* instead, when you log in, QuickBooks reopens the windows that were open when you last exited the program, which could slow performance for other users.

Setting Company Preferences

Only administrators can change the settings on *Company Preferences* tabs. For example, on the *Desktop View* category's *Company Preferences* tab, you can choose settings to control which icons appear on the *Home Page*.

Computer Practice

To change company-wide preferences, follow these steps.

1. If you closed the *Preferences* dialog box, on the *Edit* menu, choose *Preferences*, and then select the *Desktop View* category.

2. Click the *Company Preferences* tab to display the *Desktop View* company-wide settings, shown in Figure 7-2.

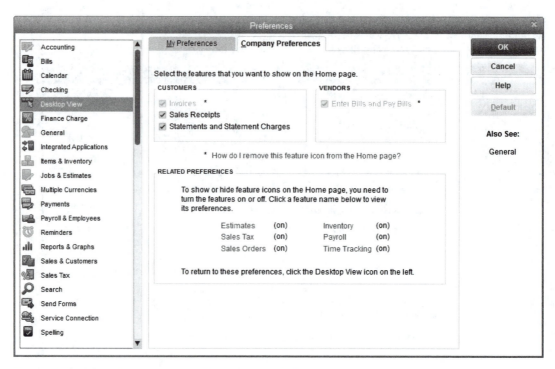

Figure 7-2 Desktop View Company Preferences window

3. To hide a *Home Page* icon, turn off its corresponding checkbox, in this example, the *Statements and Statement Charges* checkbox.

   When you turn off that checkbox, the *Statements* icon disappears from the *Home Page*, but the feature is still available from the *Customers* menu.

   The features in the *Related Preferences* section work differently. To remove them from the *Home Page*, you must disable them. To do that, click the link for that feature to jump to the corresponding category in the *Preferences* dialog box. There, you turn off the feature and its icon disappears from the *Home Page*.

Note: In Figure 7-2, the *Invoices* and *Enter Bills and Pay Bills* checkboxes are grayed out, which means you can't turn off those icons on the *Home Page*. They're grayed out because QuickBooks has automatically turned them on because of *other* selections you've made. For example, if you turn on estimates or sales orders, which require invoices, you can't turn off the *Invoices* icon.

---

4. To close the *Preferences* window, click *OK*. When the warning dialog box tells you it must close all windows, click *OK* again.

5. To reopen the *Home Page*, on the icon bar, click *Home*.

   The *Statements* icon no longer appears in the *Customers* section, as shown in Figure 7-3.

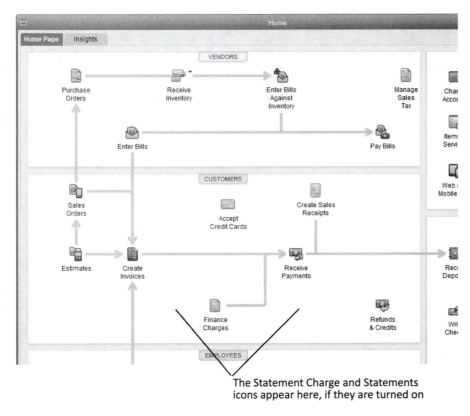

The Statement Charge and Statements
icons appear here, if they are turned on

Figure 7-3 The Home Page without Statement icons

Customizing QuickBooks Menus and Windows

You can customize QuickBooks' icon bar to include features you use frequently. You can also add features and windows you use often to the Favorites menu.

Customizing the QuickBooks Icon Bar

The QuickBooks icon bar initially includes shortcuts to popular features, like the *Home Page*, *Customer Center*, *Report Center*, and so on. The icon bar (Figure 7-4) has a dark blue background and appears on the left side of the QuickBooks main window by default. You can customize the icon bar to include features and windows you open frequently, or to remove entries for features you don't use. You can also change its appearance in several ways.

> Tip: If you want to hide the icon bar, for example, to make a transaction window larger, on the *View* menu, choose *Hide Icon Bar*. To restore the icon bar, on the *View* menu, click *Left Icon Bar*. To minimize the icon bar, click the left-pointing arrow to the right of the search box. You can also display the icon bar across the top of the QuickBooks window by choosing *Top Icon Bar* on the *View* menu. However, the icon bar doesn't have as many capabilities when it's displayed at the top, so you'll likely keep the icon bar on the left.

Figure 7-4 The QuickBooks Icon Bar

Computer Practice

To customize the icon bar, do the following:

1. On the *View* menu, choose *Customize Icon Bar*.

   QuickBooks opens the *Customize Icon* Bar window (Figure 7-5).

Figure 7-5 Customize Icon Bar window

2. To add an icon to the icon bar, first click the entry in the *Icon Bar Content* list where you want to insert the new icon, and then click *Add*.

    QuickBooks inserts the new icon below the entry you select.

3. In the *Add Icon Bar Item* dialog box, choose the entry you want to add, in this example, *Calculator* (Figure 7-6).

    QuickBooks automatically selects an icon and fills in the label and description. You can choose a different icon or type in a different label and description if you want.

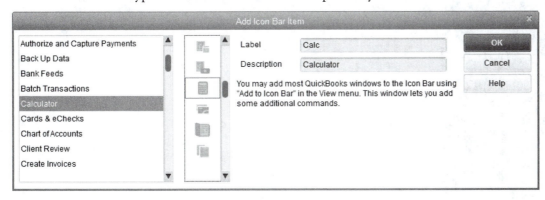

Figure 7-6 Choosing an entry in the Add Icon Bar Item window

4. Click *OK*.

5. To rearrange the order in which the icons appear, click the diamond next to an entry's name, and then drag it to where you want. In this example, drag the *Calc* icon so it appears below the *Feedback* icon, as shown in Figure 7-7.

Figure 7-7 Reordering icons

---

6. To save the customized icon bar, click *OK*.

The *Calc* icon now appears below the *Feedback* icon (see Figure 7-8).

Figure 7-8 Icon Bar with Calc icon

> Tip: You can easily add open windows to the icon bar, which is helpful if you want to add shortcuts to specific reports to the icon bar. To add a window shortcut to the icon bar, first open the window you want (for example, open a report window, such as *Balance Sheet*). With the window open and active, on the *View* menu, choose *Add "window name" to Icon Bar* (in this example, the menu entry is *Add "Balance Sheet" to Icon Bar*). In the *Add Window to Icon Bar* dialog box that opens, click *OK*. The new entry appears at the bottom of the *My Shortcuts* list.

Favorites Menu

The *Favorites* menu is another option for accessing your frequently-used QuickBooks features. If you use QuickBooks Accountant, the *Favorites* menu entry appears between the *Lists* and *Accountant* entries. If you use a different QuickBooks edition, *Favorites* appears between *Lists* and *Company*.

> Note: If you don't see the *Favorites* entry in the menu bar, on the *View* menu, click *Favorites Menu* to turn on its checkmark.

Computer Practice

Here are the steps to adding features to the *Favorites* menu:

1. In the menu bar, choose *Favorites*, and then choose *Customize Favorites*, as shown in Figure 7-9.

    In the *Customize Your Menu* dialog box, the *Available Menu Items* list contains *every* Quick-Books feature—all the entries that appear on the menu bar, and its menus and submenus. The *Reports* section includes built-in, custom, and memorized reports in your company file. The submenu entries are indented from the main menu entries.

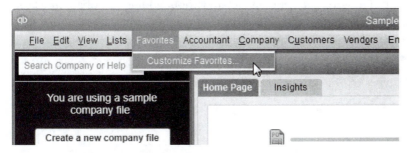

Figure 7-9 Choosing Customize Favorites

2. To add a menu item to the *Favorites* menu, select the item in the list (in this example, *Chart of Accounts*, as shown in figure 7-10), click *Add*, and then click *OK*.

    Chart of Accounts now appears on the *Favorites* menu, as shown in Figure 7-11.

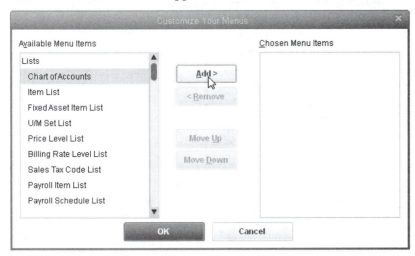

Figure 7-10 Adding an entry to the Favorites menu

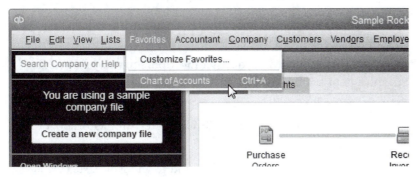

Figure 7-11 The Favorites menu with an entry added

QuickBooks Items

As you learned in Chapter 3, *items* represent not only the products and services you sell, but also things like subtotals, discounts, other charges, and sales taxes. When you create an item, you describe it and specify things like how much you pay for it and sell it for. But you also link items to accounts in your chart of accounts, so they tell QuickBooks how to move money between accounts behind the scenes.

> Note: Creating sales tax items is covered in Chapter 4 (page 125).

Items also help you track your financial performance in more detail without adding lots of accounts to your chart of accounts. For example, you might use two income accounts: one for services and one for products you sell. Then, you can create items for *each* type of service and product you sell so you can track sales and income in more detail.

This section describes the different types of QuickBooks items and what they do. It also explains how to create the most frequently-used item types.

Item Types

When you create an item, you must first select its type, as shown in Figure 7-12. When you do, the *New Item* window displays the fields associated with that type, as you'll see in the following sections.

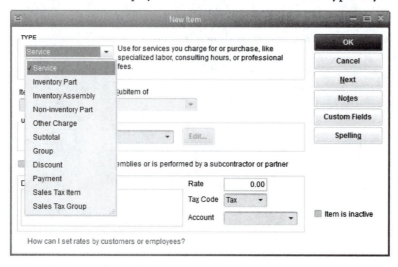

Figure 7-12 Item Types drop-down list

Here is a list of the item types in QuickBooks:

- **Service** items represent services you buy or sell, such as developing construction floor plans or performing repair work.

- **Inventory Part** items are products that you purchase and keep in stock to sell to customers.

- **Inventory Assembly** items represent products that you assemble from *Inventory Part* items, such as a door with hinges and a door knob. *Inventory Assembly* items are not available in QuickBooks Pro.

- **Non-inventory Part** items are products you purchase specifically for a customer or job, or for your company's use.

- **Other Charge** items cover various types of charges you might add to an invoice, such as shipping, bounced check fees, and finance charges.

- **Subtotal** items do one thing: calculate a subtotal for several lines in a sales form and display the subtotal on a separate line.

- **Group** items allow you to work with several separate items that typically go together, such as several services that you offer as a special package. *Group* items are similar to *Inventory Assembly* items, but they don't track quantity on hand for the group.

- **Discount** items calculate discounts and display them in a sales form.

- **Payment** items can be used to add received payments to invoices or to record refunds given on credit memos.

- **Sales Tax** items represent sales taxes you must collect for each sales tax location where you sell taxable goods and services.

- **Sales Tax Group** items can be used to collect taxes for locations that levy sales taxes from more than one tax agency.

Service Items

Services are skills, expertise, and other intangible things that you sell, like consulting time, hours of labor, or telephone support. In construction, services could represent phases of construction, such as demolition, foundation work, framing, electrical work, and so on. If the people who perform services are salaried, Service items are simple. However, if you sell services that you purchase from others, such as an electrician who subcontracts to you, your QuickBooks Service items require a few more fields of information. This section describes how to create both Service item variations.

Creating a Basic Service Item

If your employees perform services you sell, their salaries are part of you company's overhead. Your costs aren't directly connected to the income you earn from selling services. In that case, you only have to tell QuickBooks about the income side of the services you sell.

Computer Practice

To create a basic service item, follow these steps:

1. On the *Lists* menu, choose *Item List*.

   The *Item List* window opens (shown in Figure 7-13).

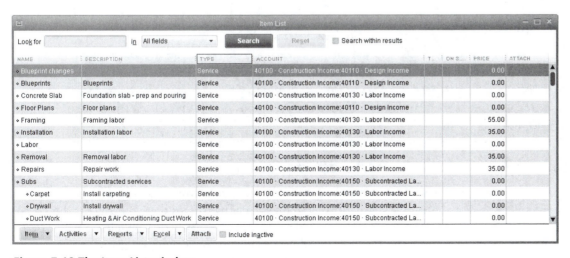

Figure 7-13 The Item List window

2. At the bottom of the window, click the *Item* button, and then choose *New* from the drop-down list. (Or simply press Ctrl+N.)

   The *New Item* window opens.

3. In the *Type* field, choose *Service* from the drop-down list, if it isn't already selected.

   > Note: The entries you see in the *Type* list depend on the QuickBooks edition you're using. If you have QuickBooks Premier or Enterprise, the list includes *Inventory Assembly*. If you use QuickBooks Pro, *Inventory Assembly* items aren't available.

4. In the *Item Name/Number* field, type the name for the service, in this example, *Demolition*.

5. To make the item a subitem to another item in the list, turn on the *Subitem of* checkbox. In the drop-down list below the *Subitem of* field, select *Labor*.

6. Fill in the remaining item details as shown in Figure 7-14.

Figure 7-14 New Item window filled in for a Service item

7. Click *OK* to save the item and close the *New Item* window.

   > Note: When you add the Demolition item to a sales form, QuickBooks fills in the *Rate* or *Price* field with the value from the *New Item* window's *Rate* field. If the item price varies, you can override the rate by typing the price you want in the sales form's *Rate* or *Price* field.

Creating an Item for Subcontracted Services

Subcontracted service items have a purchase and sales side. You charge your customer for the service and you also pay the subcontractor who performed the service. That means that your *cost* for the service is linked to the income you earn. (In some companies, such as law firms, people are paid based on the hours they bill. Their compensation is directly connected to the income earned.) For these situations, you create a *Service* item with information for both the purchase and sales side.

Tip: When you create *Service* items for subcontracted work, you can use them to track profitability by subcontractor (or partner). To simplify tracking profitability, set up a separate item for each contractor or partner.

Computer Practice

To create a subcontracted *Service* item, follow these steps:

1. Open the *Item List*, and choose *New* on the *Item* drop-down list (or press Ctrl+N).

2. On the *Type* drop-down list, choose *Service* and press the Tab key.

3. In the *Item Name/Number* field, type *Electrical Work*.

4. Turn on the *Subitem of* checkbox and select *Labor* on the *Subitem of* drop-down list.

5. Turn on the *This service is used in assemblies or is performed by a subcontractor or partner* checkbox.

   When you turn on this checkbox, QuickBooks includes fields for both purchase and sales transactions, as shown in Figure 7-15. When you purchase the service from a contractor, the money posts to an expense account. When you sell the service to a customer, the money posts to an income account.

6. Fill in item details as shown in Figure 7-15. (For the *Income Account*, choose *40150 Subcontracted Labor Income*.)

7. To save the item and create a new one, click *Next*.

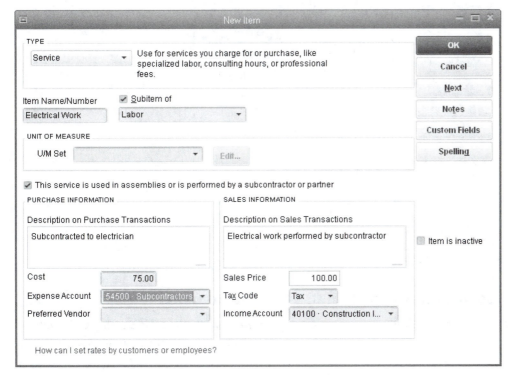

Figure 7-15 A subcontracted Service item

Non-inventory Part Items

Non-Inventory Part items are products you purchase but don't maintain as inventory. Similar to *Service* items, you can create basic *Non-inventory Part* items that include only one set of transaction information or you can create them with both purchase and sales information. For example, if you want to track office supplies you purchase for your business, create *Non-inventory Part* items for those supplies and add them to vendor bills. On the other hand, if you purchase materials specifically for customers or jobs, you would create *Non-inventory Part* items with how much you pay for the materials and how much you sell them for.

This section describes how to create both versions of *Non-inventory Part* items.

Creating a Basic Non-inventory Part Item

Computer Practice

To create a *Non-inventory Part* item, for example, for office supplies (Figure 7-16), follow these steps:

1. On the *Type* drop-down list, choose *Non-inventory Part*.

2. In the *Item Name/Number* field, type *Toner Cartridge*.

3. In the *Description* field, type *Color cartridges*.

4. In this example, choose the *Office Supplies* expense account, because you're purchasing supplies for your business.

5. To save the item and create a new one, click *Next*.

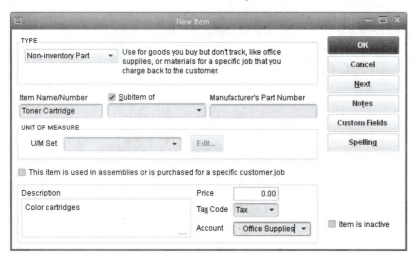

Figure 7-16 A basic Non-Inventory Part item

Creating a Non-inventory Part Item to Sell to Customers

When you order materials specifically for a customer, create *Non-Inventory Part* items that track both your expense and income. That way, you can track your profitability for customer- or job-specific goods.

Computer Practice

To create a *Non-inventory Part* item for products you purchase for a specific customer or job, follow these steps:

1. In the *Type* drop-down list, choose *Non-inventory Part*.

---

2. Fill in the fields, as shown in Figure 7-17.

The *This item is used in assemblies or is a reimbursable charge* checkbox is the key to tracking both expense and income for an item you sell. By turning that checkbox on, you see fields for both purchases and sales, as shown here. In this example, the assigned *Expense* account is the Cost of Goods Sold account, *Job Materials*. The income is assigned to the *Materials Income* account.

3. To save the item and create a new one, click *Next*.

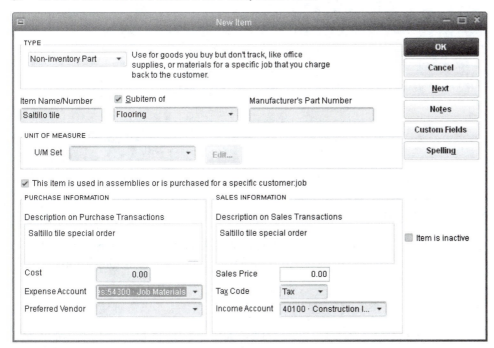

Figure 7-17 A Non-inventory Part item for products sold to customers

Other Charge Items

Use the *Other Charge* item type for any charges that don't fall into the service or product category, like shipping charges, bounced-check charges, or other fees. *Other Charge* items can be percentages or fixed amounts. For example, you could set up shipping charges to be the actual shipping cost, or you could calculate shipping as a percentage of the product cost.

> Note: You can use *Other Charge* items for reimbursable expenses. To set up an *Other Charge* item with both purchase and sales fields, turn on the *This item is used in assemblies or is a reimbursable charge* checkbox.

Computer Practice

To create an *Other Charge* item, follow these steps:

1. In the *Type* drop-down list, click *Other Charge*.

2. Fill in the fields, as shown in Figure 7-18.

3. Click *OK* to save the item.

Figure 7-18 A percentage-based Other Charge item

Other QuickBooks Lists

In Chapters 2 and 3, you used other lists like the Terms List when you created customers and vendors. In this section, you'll learn more about creating list entries and how to manage your QuickBooks lists.

The Terms List

This list (Figure 7-19) holds the payment terms you use for invoices and bills. The terms you apply to your customers' invoices and the terms vendors assign to you come from the same list in QuickBooks. When you assign terms to a transaction, QuickBooks uses the terms to calculate the due date. If terms include a discount for early payment, the program calculates the discount and the date when that early payment discount expires.

You can set up terms in two ways:

- **Standard Terms** specify the due date as a number of days from an invoice's or bill's transaction date. Terms such as these can also include an early payment discount.

- **Date-Driven Terms** define the due date as a specific date within a month, regardless of the date of the invoice or bill. This type of term is helpful if you send invoices on a schedule, such as the last day of the month. That way, you can set the due date, for example, as the 20th of every month.

If you assign terms in the customer and vendor records you create, QuickBooks uses those terms to fill in the *Terms* field on invoices and bills. However, you can choose different terms to override the value QuickBooks entered. QuickBooks takes the terms on invoices and bills into account when you run Accounts Receivable and Accounts Payable reports.

Computer Practice

Here are the steps to setting up new terms:

1. On the *Lists* menu, choose *Customers & Vendor Profile Lists*, and then choose *Terms List*.

   In the sample file, the *Terms List* (Figure 7-19) contains several built-in terms entries.

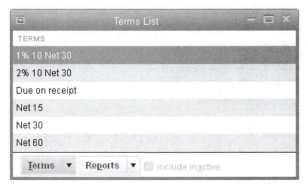

Figure 7-19 The Terms List window

2. Choose *New* on the *Terms* drop-down list, or press Ctrl+N.

3. To set up a *Standard* terms entry, fill in the *New Terms* window, as shown in Figure 7-20.

   In the *Net due in* field, type the maximum number of days after the bill or invoice transaction date that a customer (or you) can pay. In this example, the due date is 30 days after the transaction date.

   If the terms include a discount for early payments, type the discount percentage in the *Discount percentage is* field. In the *Discount if paid within* field, type the number of days after the bill or invoice date that a payment can arrive and still qualify for the early payment discount. In this example, you or the customer receive a 3 percent discount if the payment arrives within 5 days of the bill or invoice date.

4. To save this terms entry and create a new one, click *Next*.

Figure 7-20 Standard terms

5. In the *New Terms* window, select the *Date Driven* option.

6. Complete the *New Terms* window, as shown in Figure 7-21.

    In the *Net due before the __ th day of the month* field, type the day that the payment is due. In this example, the payment is due before the 14th of the month. To automatically push the due date to the following month when you issue invoices too close to the due date, type a number in the *Due the next month if issued within __ days of due date* field. In this example, if you created an invoice on the 10th of the month, QuickBooks would automatically change the due date to the 14th of the following month.

Figure 7-21 Date-driven terms

7. Click *OK* to save the new terms entries and close the *Terms List* window.

The Price Levels List

With QuickBooks price levels, you can set up custom pricing for different customers or apply discounts and markups when you create invoices. You can use price levels in two ways:

- **Assign a price level to a customer:** When you assign a price level to a customer's record (see Figure 7-22) and then choose that customer's name in a sales form (such as an invoice or sales receipt), QuickBooks automatically applies that price level to every sales item you add to that form. For example, you might set up a price level for customers who pay cash to give them a 10 percent discount on their purchases. Or you might define a price level that offers a 15 percent discount to contractors who hire your company.

- **Assign a price level to specific lines in an invoice:** You can also apply a price level to a line in an invoice to discount or mark up its price, as shown in Figure 7-23. To apply a price level to a line item, click the down arrow in the line's Rate cell, and then choose the price level you want.

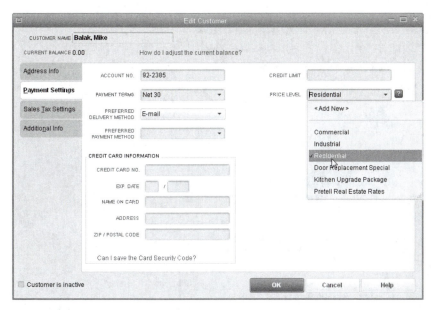

Figure 7-22 Assigning a price level to a customer

Price level assigned to the customer

Click the Rate down arrow to display
the Price Level drop-down list

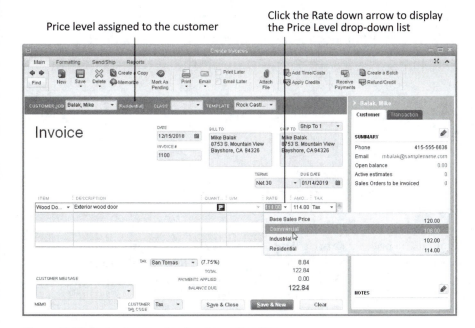

Figure 7-23 Assigning a price level to a line item

QuickBooks offers one or two types of price levels depending on which edition of the program you use:

- **Fixed %:** The *Fixed %* price level type (Figure 7-24) increases or decreases prices by a fixed percentage. If you have customers who always receive a discount, such as contractors, you should assign a *Fixed %* price level to their records. That way, as soon as you choose the customer in a sales form, QuickBooks automatically applies the appropriate discount to the items you add to the form. This price level type is your only option if you use QuickBooks Pro.

- **Per Item:** If you use QuickBooks Premier or Enterprise, you can create *Fixed %* or *Per Item* price levels. *Per Item* price levels allow you to apply different pricing levels to individual items in your item list, as shown in Figure 7-25.

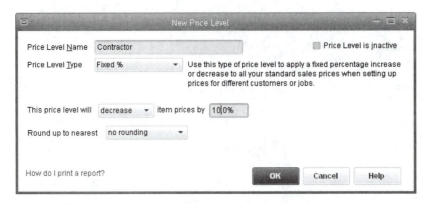

Figure 7-24 A Fixed % price level

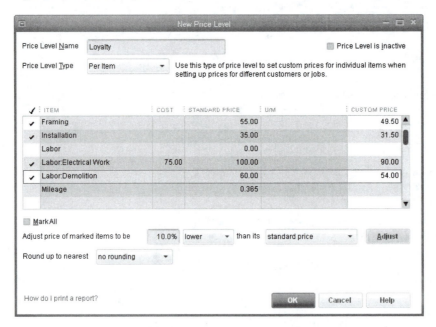

Figure 7-25 A Per Item price level

> Tip: If you want to round the prices that price levels calculate, choose an entry in the *Round up to nearest* drop-down list. For example, if you select *1.00 minus .01*, the programs rounds prices to the nearest dollar amount minus one cent ($10.00 rounds down to $9.99).

Printing Lists

You can print a QuickBooks list in a couple of ways:

Computer Practice

Follow these steps to explore both methods of printing lists:

1. Open the window for the list you want to print, in this example, the *Item List* window.

2. At the bottom of the window, click the button labeled with the list's name (in this example, *Item*), and then choose *Print List* (or press Ctrl+P).

    A message box suggests that you try list reports instead. Click *OK* to dismiss the message. (You'll create a list report shortly.)

3. In the *Print Lists* dialog box, change print settings, if necessary.

   QuickBooks selects the *Printer* option, fills in your default printer, and selects *Portrait* orientation.

4. Click *Print*.

   QuickBooks prints the list in a predefined layout.

5. To print a list report instead, on the *Reports* menu, choose *List*, and then choose the report you want, in this example, *Item Listing*.

   The *Item Listing* report opens in a report window, as shown in Figure 7-26. The advantage to running a list report is that you can click the *Customize Report* button in the report window to modify the report. (Refer to Chapter 6 to learn about report customization techniques.)

Item	Description	Type	Cost	Price	Sales Tax Code	Quantity On Hand	Quantity O...	Reorder Pt (Min)	Quantit
Labor:Electrical Work	Electrical work performed by subcontra...	Service	75.00	100.00	Tax				
Labor:Demolition	Hourly rate for interior demolition	Service	0.00	60.00	Tax				
Removal	Removal labor	Service	0.00	35.00	Non				
Repairs	Repair work	Service	0.00	35.00	Non				
Subs	Subcontracted services	Service	0.00	0.00	Non				
Subs:Carpet	Install carpeting	Service	25.00	0.00	Non				
Subs:Drywall	Install drywall	Service	25.00	0.00	Non				
Subs:Duct Work	Heating & Air Conditioning Duct Work	Service	25.00	0.00	Non				
Subs:Electrical	Electrical work	Service	25.00	0.00	Non				
Subs:Insulating	Install insulation	Service	25.00	0.00	Non				
Subs:Metal Wrk	Metal Work	Service	25.00	0.00	Non				
Subs:Painting	Painting	Service	25.00	0.00	Non				
Subs:Plumbing	Plumbing	Service	25.00	0.00	Non				
Subs:Roofing	Roofing	Service	25.00	0.00	Non				
Subs:Tile &Counter	Install tile or counter	Service	25.00	0.00	Non				
Cabinets	Cabinets	Inventory Part	0.00	0.00	Tax	0	0	15	
Cabinets:Cabinet P...	Cabinet Pulls	Inventory Part	3.00	0.00	Tax	423	0	15	
Cabinets:Light Pine	Light pine kitchen cabinet wall unit	Inventory Part	1,500.00	1,799.00	Tax	6	2	0	
Door Frame	standard interior door frame	Inventory Part	12.00	0.00	Tax	21	0		
Hardware		Inventory Part	0.00	0.00	Tax	0	0		
Hardware:Brass h...	standard interior brass hinge	Inventory Part	3.00	0.00	Tax	246	0		
Hardware:Doorkno...	Standard Doorknobs	Inventory Part	15.00	30.00	Tax	124	0	50	
Hardware:Lk Doork...	Locking interior doorknobs	Inventory Part	34.95	38.00	Tax	122	0	50	
Wood Door	Doors	Inventory Part	0.00	0.00	Tax	1	0		
Wood Door:Exterior	Exterior wood door	Inventory Part	590.39	120.00	Tax	16	0	5	
Wood Door:Interior	Interior wood door	Inventory Part	35.00	72.00	Tax	47	0	5	
Interior Door kit	complete Interior door	Inventory A...	0	0.00	Tax	20	0	5	

Figure 7-26 A list report for the Item List

Making List Items Inactive

You can delete list entries only if you haven't used them in any transactions. However, if you no longer sell an item, you can make it inactive. That way, the item still remains in your company file, but is hidden in the *Item List* and in item drop-down lists. (You can make any QuickBooks lists' entries inactive.)

To make a list entry inactive, in the list window, right-click the entry you want to make inactive. On the shortcut menu, choose *Make [listname] Inactive*. (In the *Item List* window, this menu entry is *Make Item Inactive*.) When you do that, the inactive entry disappears from the list.

To see inactive entries, turn on the *Include inactive* checkbox at the bottom of the list window. As shown in Figure 7-27, QuickBooks places an X to the left of the inactive entry names. To reactivate an entry, click the X to the left of its name.

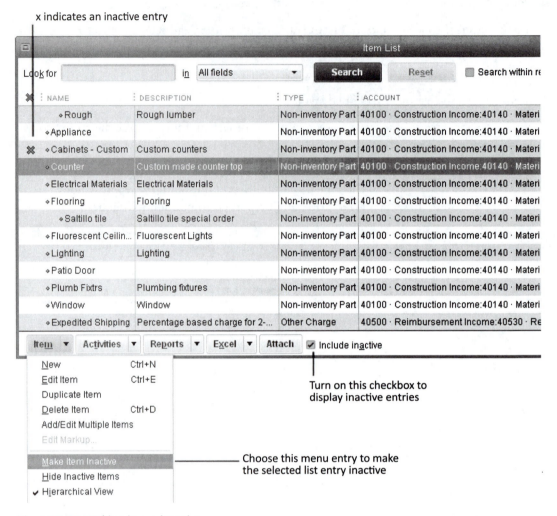

Figure 7-27 Making items inactive

Custom Fields

You can define custom fields to track information that QuickBooks doesn't record with its built-in fields. Then you can associate those custom fields with customers, vendors, employees, or items. For example, you might define a custom field to track the county in which your customers are located, so you know which building codes to use for jobs.

To define a custom field and choose the records to apply it to, follow these steps:

1. On the *Additional Info* tab of a Customer, Vendor, or Employee dialog box (such as *New Customer* or *Edit Vendor*), click the *Define Fields* button at the bottom right (Figure 7-28).

   The *Set up Custom Fields for Names* dialog box opens.

2. Type a name for your custom field.

3. To apply it to a customer, vendor, or employee, click the cell in the corresponding column.

4. To save it, click *OK*.

   The custom field appears in the *Additional Info* tab.

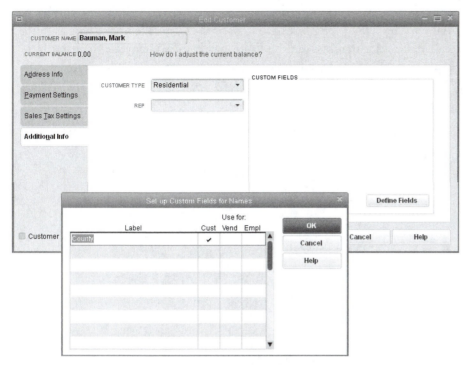

Figure 7-28 Define Field button

Note: You can also add custom fields to items. To do that, open the *New Item* or *Edit Item* window, and then click *Custom Fields* to open the *Custom Fields for [item name]* dialog box. In that dialog box, click *Define Fields*.

Modifying Form Templates

QuickBooks comes with templates that control the appearance of your sales forms. If the program's built-in templates aren't exactly what you want, you can create customized templates to specify the fields that appear on the screen and printed form, how fields are formatted, and so on. This section describes how to create a customized template.

Computer Practice

To customize a template, follow these steps:

1. On the *Lists* menu, choose *Templates*.

2. In the *Templates* window that appears, select the template you want to use as a basis for your customized template, in this example, *Custom Progress Invoice*.

3. Click the *Templates* button, and then choose *Duplicate* on the drop-down list.

4. In the *Select Template Type* dialog box (Figure 7-29), choose the template type you want to create, in this example, *Invoice*, and then click *OK*.

   Back in the *Templates* window, you'll see the new template in the list. (In this example, the new template's name is *Copy of: Custom Progress Invoice*.)

> Tip: When you duplicate a template, you don't have to choose the same template type as the original template. That means that you can duplicate a customized template to create templates with the same modifications for all the sales forms you use.

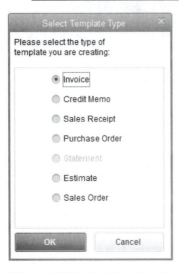

Figure 7-29 Select Template Type window with Invoice selected

5. If necessary, select the template you just created (*Copy of: Custom Progress Invoice*), and then, click the *Templates* button and choose *Edit Template* from the drop-down menu.

6. In the *Basic Customization* window that appears (Figure 7-30), click the *Manage Templates* button.

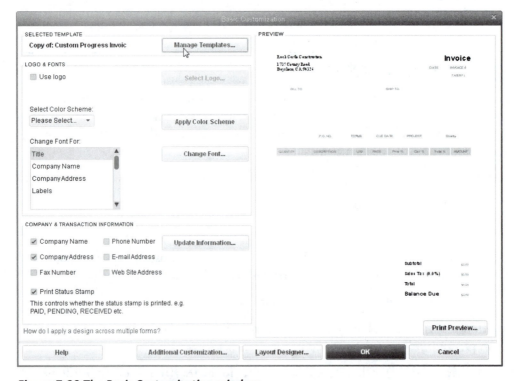

Figure 7-30 The Basic Customization window

7. In the *Manage Templates* window's *Template Name* field (Figure 7-31), type the new name for the template, in this example, *Rock Castle Product Invoice*, and then click *OK*.

Note: The Intuit website has more templates that you can download. To access them, click the *Download Templates* button at the bottom of the *Manage Templates* window.

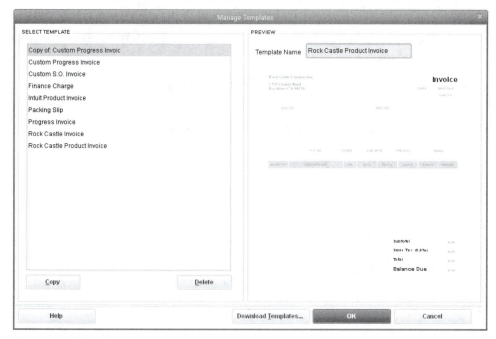

Figure 7-31 The Manage Templates window

8. To save the renamed template and close the *Manage Templates* window, click *OK*.

9. Back in the *Basic Customization* window, click the *Additional Customization* button at the bottom of the window.

    The *Additional Customization* window opens, as shown in Figure 7-32.

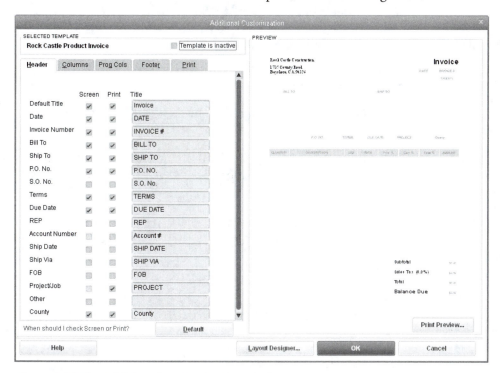

Figure 7-32 The Additional Customization window

10. To specify which fields appear in the form header, turn *Screen* and *Print* checkboxes on or off. In this example, to include the account number in the header, turn on the *Account Number* check box in the *Print* column.

    You can change the title that appears on your sales form by filling in the *Title* field.

11. To modify the columns in the form's table, click the *Columns* tab (Figure 7-33). For this example, don't change the settings on this tab.

    You can change the order of the columns in the form table by changing the numbers in the *Order* fields.

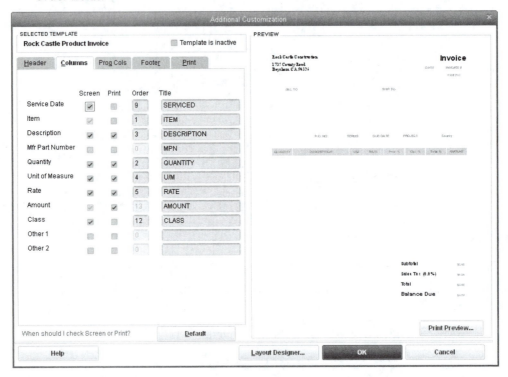

Figure 7-33 Additional Customization window with Columns tab

12. To return to the *Basic Customization* window, click *OK*.

13. To add a logo to your form, in the *Basic Customization* window, turn on the *Use logo* checkbox (see Figure 7-34).

14. In the *Select Image* window that appears, navigate to the folder that contains your student exercise files and find the *rockcastle_logo.gif* file. Select it, and then click *Open*.

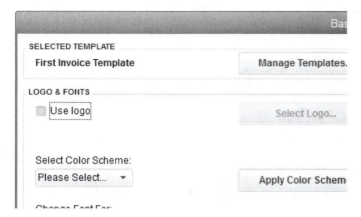

Figure 7-34 Add a logo to a template

15. In the warning dialog box that opens, click *OK*.

    In the form preview on the right side of the *Basic Customization* window, the logo appears at the upper left.

16. To add colors to your template, in the *Select Color Scheme* drop-down list, choose a color, and then click the *Apply Color Scheme* button.

17. To change the font and color of the title, in the *Change Font For* list, select *Title*, then click the *Change Font* button. In the *Example* window that opens, choose the font and color you want, as shown in Figure 7-35. Click *OK*.

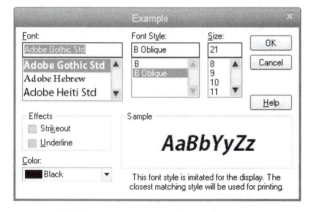

Figure 7-35 The Example window for changing font and font color

18. To close the *Basic Customization* window, click *OK*.

19. Close the *Templates* window.

20. To create an invoice with the new template, click the *Create Invoices* icon on the *Home Page*.

21. In the *Template* drop-down menu, choose *Rock Castle Product Invoice*.

22. To view the form, click the *Print* down arrow and choose *Preview* on the drop-down list.

23. Close the *Print Preview* window and the *Create Invoices* window.

> Note: With QuickBooks' *Layout Designer*, you can position the components in your customized templates. To access this feature, click the *Layout Designer* button at the bottom of the *Basic Customization* window.

Review Questions

Select the best answer(s) for each of the following:

1. The settings on the *Preferences* dialog box's *Company Preferences* tab:

    a) Apply to users with administrator privileges.

    b) Apply to every user who logs into the company file.

    c) Can only be changed by the Administrator user.

    d) Can be changed by anyone, but the Administrator user must approve the change.

2. Which features can you customize in QuickBooks?

    a) The *Home Page*

    b) The icon bar

    c) Entries on the menu bar's drop-down menus

    d) The *Favorites* menu

3. If you purchase products specifically for a customer or job, which type of item should you create for those products?

    a) Service item

    b) Non-inventory Part item

    c) Inventory item

    d) Group item

4. With price levels, you can:

    a) Adjust all prices for a customer by a percentage.

    b) Ensure that item prices remain consistent on every sales form you create.

    c) View the profitability of the items you sell.

    d) Adjust the price of an item on an invoice.

5. You can't set up custom templates for the following forms:

    a) Sales receipt

    b) Bill

    c) Statement

    d) Invoice

Customizing QuickBooks Exercise 1

Applying Your Knowledge

Restore the sample file, sample_product-based business 2015 (Portable).QBM. (Or, if you are using QuickBooks 2014, restore sample_product-based business 2014 (Portable).QBM.)

1. Create a new item using the information in the following table:

Table 7-1 New Item data

Field Name	Data
Item Type	Service
Item Name/Number	Excavating
Description	Excavating per hour
Price	$95.00
Tax Code	Non
Account	Labor Income

2. Create a *Terms* entry called *2% 8 Net 30*. Set up this entry so payment is due within 30 days and the payment qualifies for a 2 percent discount if it is received within 8 days of the transaction date.

3. Create an invoice using the information in the following table:

Table 7-2 Invoice data

Field Name	Data
Customer	Bauman, Mark
Class	New Construction
Date	04/10/2019
Invoice #	2019-100
Terms	2% 8 Net 30
Tax	San Tomas
Quantity	16
Item	Excavation
Item Description	Excavate foundation for new garage

4. Print the invoice.

5. Print the *Item List*.

Customizing QuickBooks Exercise 2 (Advanced)

Applying Your Knowledge

Restore the sample file, sample_product-based business 2015 (Portable).QBM. (Or, if you are using QuickBooks 2014, restore sample_product-based business 2014 (Portable).QBM.)

1. Set up each of the following *Terms* entries:

    a) 2% 5 Net 45

    b) 2% 10th Net 25th (Due on the 25th of the month with a 2 percent discount for paying by the 10th)

    c) Net 20

2. Create a report to view the terms you just created. Add the *Discount on day of Month* field to the report. Adjust the column widths so the column headings are entirely visible. Print the report.

3. Create a custom field called *Walkthrough Date* and apply it to customers. Add the following walkthrough dates to these customers and jobs:

Table 7-3 Walkthrough dates for jobs

Customer: Job Name	Walkthrough Date
Abercrombie, Kristy: Remodel Bathroom	02/20/2019
Allard, Robert: Remodel	03/01/2019
Baker, Chris: Family Room	03/02/2019

4. Create a *Customer Contact List* report. Modify it to show only the *Customer Name* and *Walkthrough Date* fields. Print the report.

5. Create a *Price Level* called *Long Distance*. Add the description, *Jobs more than 60 miles from office*. Set up the price level so it increases all prices by 5 percent.

6. Create an *Other Charge Item* using the information in the following table:

Table 7-4 Other Charge item data

Field Name	Data
Item Name/Number	Travel Reimbursement
Description	Lodging and ground transportation costs to be reimbursed
This item is used in assemblies or is a reimbursable charge	Turned on
Description fields	Lodging and ground transportation costs to be reimbursed
Cost	0
Expense Account	Reimbursable Expenses
Sales Price	0
Tax Code	Tax
Account	Reimbursement Income

7. Create a *Non-inventory Part* item using the information in the following table:

Table 7-5 Non-inventory Part item data

Field Name	Data
Item Name/Number	Kitchen remodel deluxe package
Description	Meals delivered while kitchen is unusable
Price	600
Tax Code	Tax
Account	Construction Income

8. Duplicate the *Intuit Product Invoice Template* and make the following customizations:

   a) Change the color scheme to *Maroon*.

   b) Change the template name to *Rock Castle Construction Invoice*.

   c) Add the *Walkthrough Date* custom field to the screen and printed invoice using the *Additional Customization* tab.

9. Create an invoice using the information in the following table:

Table 7-6 Invoice data

Field Name	Data
Customer	Cook, Brian: Kitchen
Class	Remodel
Date	04/12/2019
Invoice #	2019-101
Terms	2% 5 Net 45
Tax	San Tomas
Template	Rock Castle Construction Invoice
Quantity	1
Item	Kitchen Deluxe Package
Amount	$600
Price Level for item	Residential
Item	Travel Reimbursement
Item description	Mileage for delivery
Amount	$52.40
Walkthrough date	4/5/2019

10. Save and print the invoice.

Chapter 8

Tracking Inventory

Topics

This chapter covers the following topics:

- Should You Track Inventory?

- Tracking Inventory with QuickBooks

- Activating QuickBooks Inventory

- Setting up Inventory Part Items

- Purchasing Inventory

- Invoicing for Inventory

- Adjusting Inventory

- Using Group Items

- Inventory Assemblies

- Inventory Reports

Inventory is the name for products you keep in stock to sell to customers. When you stock inventory, you need to track it from your initial order until your customers pay for the products you sold them. QuickBooks tracks your inventory quantities and values each step of the way, as you record inventory-related transactions. This chapter begins with an overview of the inventory process in QuickBooks. Then, it describes how you turn on QuickBooks' inventory features and set up *Inventory Part* items.

After that, you'll learn how to record purchase orders so you can make sure that you receive what you ordered. This chapter then describes how to receive items into inventory and record bills for the inventory you receive. Recording inventory sales is similar to recording other sales. You'll learn what the program does behind the scenes as you record all these inventory transactions.

But the inventory process doesn't end with sales. This chapter explains how to adjust your inventory records to match what's actually in your warehouse, for example, to account for damage, theft, or other losses. You'll also learn how to track products that you assemble out of other inventory items.

Managing inventory involves knowing how many items you've sold, how many you have on hand, and how many are on order. In this chapter, you'll learn how to use QuickBooks' inventory reports to evaluate your inventory.

> Note: For the computer practice in this chapter, restore the sample file, sample_product-based business 2015 (Portable).QBM. Or, if you are using QuickBooks 2014, restore sample_product-based business 2014 (Portable).QBM.

Should You Track Inventory?

Because inventory requires more effort to track than business expenses or products you don't keep in stock, it's a good idea to determine whether your company *should* track inventory. Here are some guidelines to help you decide:

- **Track inventory if you stock products in a warehouse or store to sell to customers**. By tracking inventory, you'll know how many items you have on hand, when you need to order more, how much your inventory is worth, and the profit you make on sales.

- **Track inventory if you want to know when to reorder products**. QuickBooks keeps track of how many inventory items you have on hand and on order, so it can remind you to reorder when you run low.

- **Don't track inventory for products you purchase specifically for customers or jobs**. You don't need to track inventory for the products you custom-order for customers or jobs. When you receive these special orders, you deliver them to your customer or job. You don't have to track how many you have.

- **Don't track inventory for your business supplies**. It's much simpler to purchase supplies and record them as expenses, even if you store those products in a supply closet.

- **Don't track inventory if you sell unique products.** In QuickBooks, you can create no more than 14,500 items if you use QuickBooks Pro or Premier and the program's performance may decrease as you approach this limit. For that reason, QuickBooks inventory is intended to track commodity products, such as doors, cabinets, and hardware; not unique products.

Tracking Inventory with QuickBooks

QuickBooks automatically tracks how much inventory you have and moves inventory-related funds between accounts as you record transactions. You first need to set up your *Inventory Part* items properly, which you'll learn how to do in this chapter. After that, you must use those *Inventory Part* items in every inventory-related transaction, so the program can add and subtract the inventory quantities and values.

The Inventory Tracking Process

Whenever you record an inventory transaction in QuickBooks, it immediately updates the appropriate account balances and reports. This behavior is called *perpetual inventory*. The following list and Table 8-1 describe the QuickBooks inventory process.

1. If you want to make sure that you receive the inventory you order, you can record purchase orders in QuickBooks. If you do, the program tracks what you order and then compares your orders to what you receive. Purchase orders are non-posting transactions, so they don't affect your account balances.

2. When you purchase and pay for inventory, your checking or credit card account balance changes to show the money you spent on inventory.

3. The inventory you purchase has value, so QuickBooks debits (increases) your inventory asset account by the purchase amount.

4. When you sell inventory, the money from the sale goes to an income account (such as Materials Income) and the money your customer owes you appears in your *Accounts Receivable* account.

5. The products you sell leave inventory, so QuickBooks deducts their value from your inventory asset account and posts the value of the sold inventory to a cost of goods sold account.

Table 8-1 Inventory transactions and accounts

Transaction	Account	Debit	Credit
Order inventory (purchase order)	Non-posting		
Buy inventory	Checking Account		$800
Buy inventory	Inventory Asset	$800	
Sell inventory	Product Income		$1,400
Sell inventory	Accounts Receivable	$1,400	
Sell inventory	Inventory Asset		$800
Sell inventory	Cost of Goods Sold	$800	

In financial reports, gross profit represents your income minus the cost of goods sold. (Based on the transactions in Table 8-1, $1,400 income minus $800 cost of goods sold results in $600 gross profit.) When you turn on QuickBooks' inventory preference (page 238), the program automatically adds cost of goods sold and inventory asset accounts to your chart of accounts.

Calculating Inventory Cost

QuickBooks Pro, Premier, and Accountant calculate the cost of inventory using the average cost method, which divides the total cost of your available inventory by the number of units in stock. This method is most appropriate for inventory items whose prices don't change significantly or those with a high turnover rate.

> Note: QuickBooks Enterprise Solutions and QuickBooks Enterprise Accountant support the first-in first-out (FIFO) cost method and also offers other advanced inventory features, such as lot tracking and enhanced receiving if you use Advanced Inventory. This chapter, however, covers the inventory features available in QuickBooks Pro, Premier and Accountant, so it doesn't cover the FIFO inventory cost method.

Here is how QuickBooks uses the average cost method to calculate inventory cost as you record transactions:

- When you add an inventory item to a purchase order or bill, QuickBooks debits (increases) your inventory asset account with the *actual* inventory cost on the purchase order or bill. The program then calculates that inventory item's average cost by adding up what you paid for all the available units of that item, and then dividing that total by the number of units in stock.

- When you add an inventory item to a sales form, QuickBooks debits (increases) your cost of goods sold account and credits (decreases) your inventory asset account using the average cost for that item.

Activating QuickBooks Inventory

Before you can do anything with inventory in QuickBooks, you have to turn on the program's inventory features. This section describes how to turn on QuickBooks inventory and what the program does after that.

Computer Practice

To activate QuickBooks' inventory, do the following:

1. On the *Edit* menu, choose *Preferences*.

2. Click the *Items & Inventory* category, and then click the *Company Preferences* tab.

3. Turn on the *Inventory and purchase orders are active* checkbox (Figure 8-1).

4. Click *OK* to close the *Preferences* dialog box.

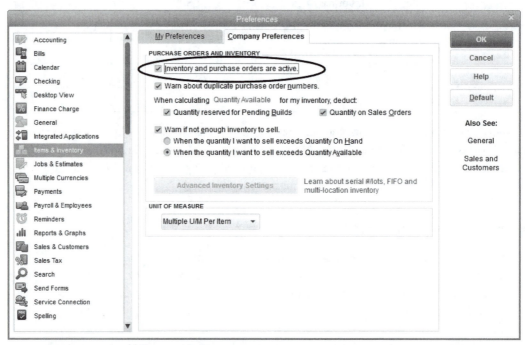

Figure 8-1 QuickBooks inventory preferences

When you turn on QuickBooks inventory, the program does the following:

- **Adds icons and menu entries for purchase orders**: Although purchase orders are optional, QuickBooks adds the *Purchase Orders* icon to the *Home Page* (and adds *Create Purchase Orders* to the *Vendors* menu).

- **Adds icons and menu entries for receiving inventory items**: The program adds the *Receive Inventory* icon to the *Home Page* and several menu entries, such as *Receive Items and Enter Bill*, to the *Vendors* menu.

- **Adds Inventory Part to the list of item types you see in the program:** In the *New Item* and *Edit Item* windows, you can choose *Inventory Part* from the *Type* drop-down list (Figure 8-2).

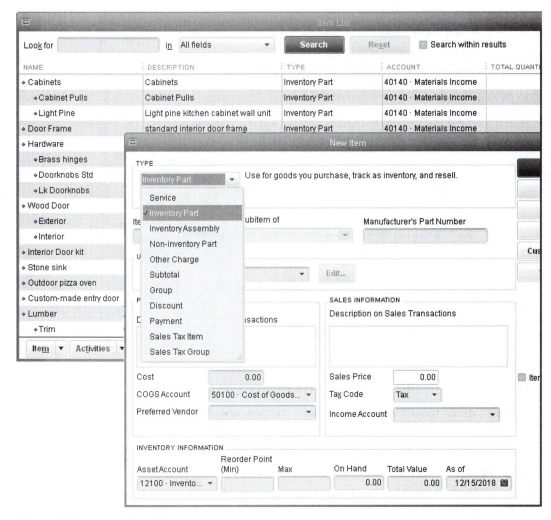

Figure 8-2 Inventory Part item type

- **Adds an entry to open the Inventory Center to the Vendors menu and Home Page (if you use QuickBooks Premier or Enterprise):** The *Inventory Center* (Figure 8-3) works in a similar fashion to, the *Customer Center*, *Vendor Center*, and *Employee Center*. It displays only inventory items. You can select an inventory item to see the transactions that include it. The Center has features for creating new inventory items and inventory-related transactions.

Note: To open the *Inventory Center*, on the *Home Page*, click the *Inventory Activities* icon in the *Company* section, and then choose *Inventory Center* from the drop-down menu. Or, on the *Vendors* menu, choose *Inventory Activities*, and then choose *Inventory Center* on the submenu

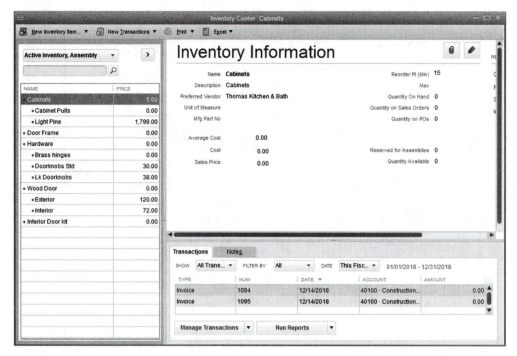

Figure 8-3 Inventory Center

When you create your first *Inventory Part* item, the program creates the following accounts:

- **An Other Current Asset account named Inventory Asset:** This account tracks the cost of the inventory you purchase. It increases by the actual purchase cost when you buy inventory, and then decreases by the average cost when you sell inventory.

- **A Cost of Goods Sold account:** This account increases by an inventory item's average cost when you sell one. QuickBooks calculates your gross profit by subtracting cost of goods sold from income.

Setting Up Inventory Part Items

To track inventory using QuickBooks inventory features, you must first create *Inventory Part* items for each product you keep in stock.

Computer Practice

To create an *Inventory Part* item, do the following:

1. In the *Inventory Center*'s toolbar, choose *New Inventory Item*, and then choose *New Inventory Item* from the drop-down list. Or simply press *Ctrl+N*.

2. In the *New Item* window, the *Inventory Part* type is already selected. Press *Tab* to move to the next field.

3. In the *Item Name/Number* field, type the name or part number, in this example, *Wood Trim*.

    If you assign part numbers to inventory items, you can enter the part number in the *Item Name/Number* field or in the *Manufacturer's Part Number* field.

4. In this example, skip the *Subitem of* field.

    If you want to make an item a subitem of another item, turn on the *Subitem of* checkbox, and then choose the parent item in the drop-down list.

5. In this example, skip the *Manufacturer's Part Number* field.

   You can fill in the manufacturer's part number or the part number that a vendor uses. This field can help you identify the items you add to purchase orders or bills.

6. In this example, skip the *Unit of Measure* section.

   This field comes in handy if you purchase items in one unit of measure and sell them in a different unit. For example, you might purchase products by the case, but sell them individually.

7. In the *Description on Purchase Transactions* field, type the default description you want to use on transactions like purchase orders and bills, in this example, *Standard wood trim for interior design*.

   In purchase transactions, you can edit the default description that QuickBooks fills in.

8. In the *Cost* field, type the typical price you pay a vendor for the item, in this example, *6.00*.

   When you add this item to a purchase order or bill, QuickBooks fills in the price or rate field with this value. If you pay a different amount on a purchase transaction, you can override the value that QuickBooks fills in.

9. In the *COGS Account* field (Figure 8-4), QuickBooks automatically selects the *Cost of Goods Sold* account. If you use other *Cost of Goods Sold* accounts, choose the one you want to use, in this example, *Job Materials*.

   This account represents the cost of the inventory items you sell. As described on page 237, QuickBooks calculates this cost using the average cost method.

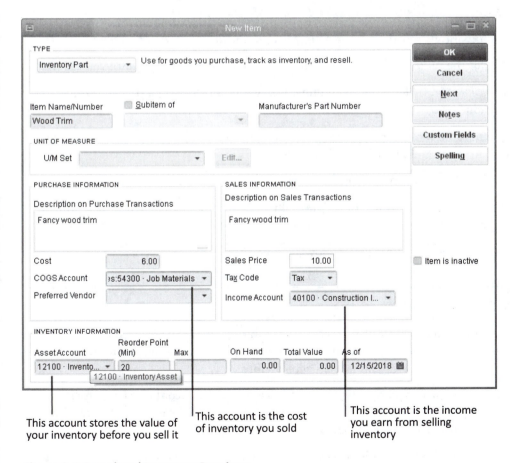

Figure 8-4 Completed Inventory Part item

10. In this example, skip the *Preferred Vendor* field.

   If you choose a vendor in this field, QuickBooks automatically fills in the vendor when you add this item to a purchase order or bill. In addition, you can sort or subtotal inventory reports using this field.

11. QuickBooks copies what you type in the *Description on Purchase Transactions* field to the *Description on Sales Transactions* field, but you can edit the *Description on Sales Transactions* field to be the default description you see on invoices and other sales forms. In this example, keep this field as it is.

12. In the *Sales Price* field, type the typical price you charge customers, in this example, *10.00*. (You can edit this value on individual sales forms.)

   Note: QuickBooks can calculate the *Sales Price* field based on the value you type in the *Cost* field. To do this, in the *Preferences* dialog box (on the *Edit* menu, choose *Preferences* to open it), click the *Time & Expenses* category, click the *Company Preferences* tab, and then fill in the markup percentage you want to use by default in the *Default Markup Percentage* field.

13. Skip the *Tax Code* field, since it is set to *Tax* by default.

   When the *Tax Code* field is set to *Tax*, QuickBooks calculates sales tax for this item when you add it to a sales form. See page 124 for more about *Sales Tax Codes*.

14. In the *Income Account* field, choose the income account you use to track income from selling inventory items, in this example, *Construction Income: Materials Income*.

15. QuickBooks automatically sets the *Asset Account* field to the *Inventory Asset* account.

   This account holds the value of your inventory from the time you purchase it until you sell it.

16. In the *Reorder Point (Min)* field, fill in the number that you want to use as a trigger to order more, in this example, *20*.

   When you set a minimum reorder point number and your inventory on hand drops below that minimum, QuickBooks reminds you to reorder this item.

17. Leave the *Max*, *On Hand*, and *Total Value* fields blank.

   The best way to set the *On Hand* and *Total Value* fields is by recording an inventory adjustment to specify your inventory on hand quantity and value (see page 412).

18. Click *OK* to save the item and close the window.

Purchasing Inventory

You can record inventory purchases in different ways depending on when you receive the inventory, when you receive the bill, and how you pay for it. This section explains how to record inventory purchases. Figure 8-5 and the following list explain your options:

- **Record a purchase order:** If you want to track what you order, record purchase orders for the orders you place with vendors. Then, when you receive orders, you can compare them to your purchase order. This step is optional.

- **Pay and receive at time of purchase:** If you purchase inventory at a store or vendor's location, and pay by check or credit card, you can record the inventory purchase in the *Write*

Checks window or *Enter Credit Card Charges* window.

- **Receive inventory first and record the bill later:** If you receive inventory without a bill, you can record the receipt of inventory in QuickBooks. Then, when you receive the bill, you can convert the item receipt into a bill.

- **Receive inventory and bill at the same time:** If the bill for inventory arrives with the products you purchased, you can record the item receipt and bill at the same time in QuickBooks.

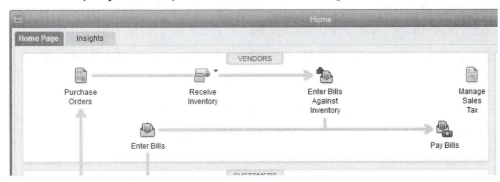

Figure 8-5 Workflow for ordering and receiving inventory

Purchasing Inventory by Check or Credit Card

If you pay for inventory at the time of sale, such as at a retail store, you can use the *Write Checks* window or *Enter Credit Card Charges* window to record your purchase. Because you must use *Inventory Part* items to track inventory, you add the inventory items you purchase on the *Items* tab, as shown in Figure 8-6.

> Note: Do not record the check in the figure; it is for reference only.

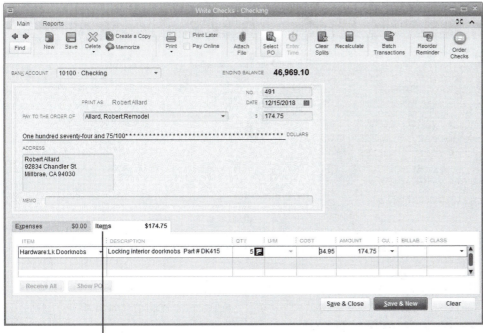

Add inventory items on the items tab

Figure 8-6 Add inventory items to the Items tab

Tracking What You Order with Purchase Orders

By creating purchase orders, you can keep track of what you have on order with vendors and when it's due to arrive. You can compare the items you receive to your purchase orders to make sure the quantities and prices match. This section describes how to create purchase orders.

Computer Practice

To create a purchase order, follow these steps:

1. On the *Vendors* menu, choose *Create Purchase Orders*.

2. In the *Vendor* field, choose the vendor you're ordering from, in this example, *Timberloft Lumber*.

3. In the *Class* drop-down list, choose the class for the order, in this example, *Remodel*.

4. In the *Date* field, choose the order date, in this example, *3/4/2019*.

5. If necessary, type the P.O. number you want to use in the *P.O. No.* field, in this example, *2019-100*.

   QuickBooks increments the number in the *P.O. No.* field for each purchase order you create, so you can usually skip this field.

6. If you want the order shipped directly to a customer or job, choose the shipping address in the *Drop Ship To* drop-down list. Leave this field blank in this example.

   QuickBooks initially fills in your shipping address in the *Ship To* box.

7. Add the inventory items you want to order in the purchase order table, as shown in Figure 8-7.

8. When your purchase order matches the one in Figure 8-7, click *Save & Close* to record it.

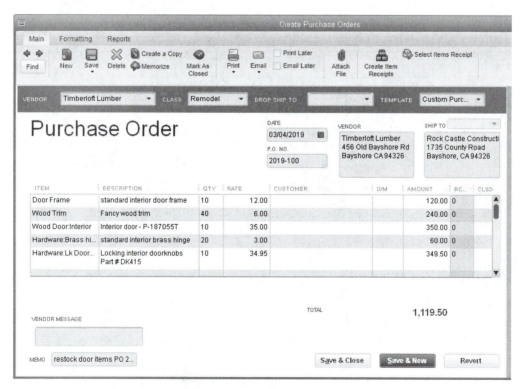

Figure 8-7 Create Purchase Order with inventory items

Receiving Inventory Before the Bill

If you receive inventory items before the bill arrives, you can record the receipt of inventory without the bill. See page 250 for the steps to receiving inventory and entering the corresponding bill at the same time.

Computer Practice

To receive inventory without the corresponding bill, follow these steps:

1. On the *Vendors* menu, choose *Receive Items*. Or, on the *Home Page*, click *Receive Inventory*, and then choose *Receive Inventory without Bill* from the drop-down menu.

2. In the *Create Item Receipt* window's *Vendor* field, choose the vendor you're ordering from, in this example, *Timberloft Lumber*.

3. If the *Open POs Exist* message box (Figure 8-8) appears, click *Yes* to record the receipt of inventory against one or more of the open purchase orders.

Figure 8-8 Open POs exist message

4. In the *Open Purchase Orders* dialog box that appears, turn on the checkmark cells for the purchase orders you want to receive, in this example, P.O. number *2019-100*, as shown in Figure 8-9.

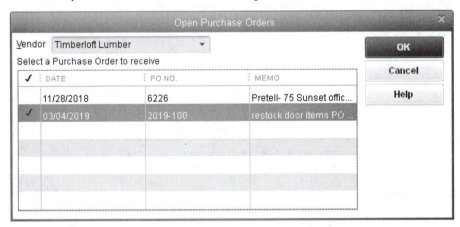

Figure 8-9 Open Purchase Orders dialog box

5. Click *OK* to apply the purchase order to the item receipt.

   The *Create Item Receipts* window opens with the information from the purchase order(s) you selected.

6. Fill in the *Date* and *Ref. No.* fields as shown in Figure 8-10.

   Fill in the *Ref. No.* field with the shipper's number on the packing slip that came with the shipment.

7. In the *Qty* field, fill in the quantities you received if they differ from what you ordered. In this example, in the *Hardware: Brass hinges* row, fill in *10* in the *Qty* cell.

    If the vendor doesn't send the quantity that you ordered, simply record the quantity you received. QuickBooks keeps the purchase order open so you can record the receipt of the backordered items when they arrive (page 248).

8. Click *Save & Close* to record the item receipt.

    When you record an item receipt, QuickBooks credits (increases) accounts payable and debits (increases) your inventory asset account. Although accounts payable increases, you haven't recorded a bill yet, so you won't see one for the item receipt in the *Pay Bills* window. However, the item receipt does appear in the *Unpaid Bills Detail* report and *A/P Aging* report, so you can see that you owe a vendor money even though you haven't received a bill yet.

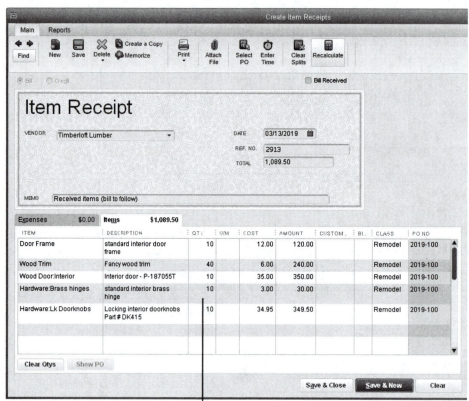

If the quantity you receive doesn't match the quantity on your purchase order, edit the value here.

Figure 8-10 Item Receipt for shipment received

Checking Purchase Order Status

To make sure you receive the products you order, you can run a report that shows your open purchase orders. You can also see a purchase order's status when you open it in the *Create Purchase Orders* window. This section describes both methods for checking order status.

Computer Practice

1. On the *Reports* menu, choose *Purchases*, then choose *Open Purchase Orders*.

    This report (see Figure 8-11) lists all open purchase orders and the value of the items you haven't yet received from that order.

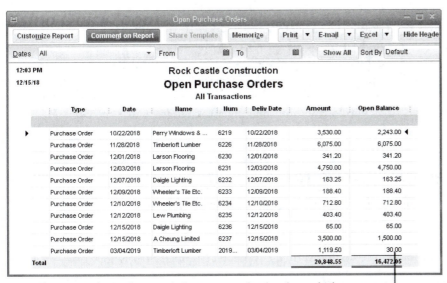

This report shows the open balance on purchase orders, which represents value of the items you haven't yet received.

Figure 8-11 Open Purchase Orders report

By editing a purchase order directly, you can see the status of the purchase order, and you can also make changes or even cancel it.

2. To view a specific purchase order, double-click it (in this example, the *Timberloft Lumber* purchase order dated *3/4/2019*).

The *Create Purchase Orders* window includes *Backordered* and *Rcv'd* columns. The *Rcv'd* column shows the quantity you've already received. The *Backordered* column shows the number you haven't received. In Figure 8-12, you can see the 10 hinges that weren't recorded in the item receipt in the previous section.

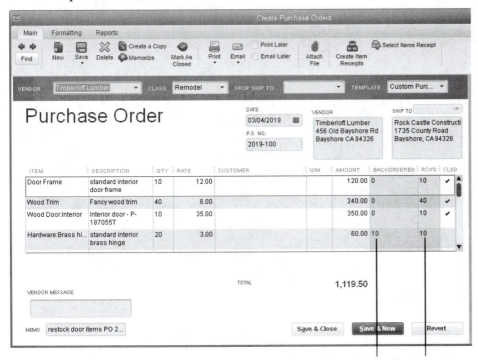

Quantity not yet received   Quantity received

Figure 8-12 Check status in the Create Purchase Orders window

> Note: If you know you aren't going to get the backordered items, you can close the purchase order. To do that, simply turn on the *Clsd* cell for the item you want to close. If several items are on backorder, you can cancel the rest of the order by clicking *Mark as Closed* at the top of the window.

3. Close the *Create Purchase Orders* window without making any changes. Close the *Open Purchase Orders* report.

Recording the Receipt of Backordered Items

When your backordered items arrive, you record a separate item receipt for them.

Computer Practice

1. On the *Vendors* menu, choose *Receive Items*, then choose *Receive Inventory without Bill*.

2. In the *Create Item Receipt* window's *Vendor* field, choose the vendor, in this example, *Timberloft Lumber*.

3. In the *Open POs Exist* message box, click *Yes*.

4. In the *Open Purchase Orders* dialog box, choose the purchase order for the backordered items, in this example, *2019-100*, and then click *OK*.

   QuickBooks automatically fills in the fields with the information from the purchase order.

5. Fill in the *Date* and *Ref.* No. fields, as shown in Figure 8-13.

6. If the items and quantities are correct, click *Save & Close* to record the item receipt.

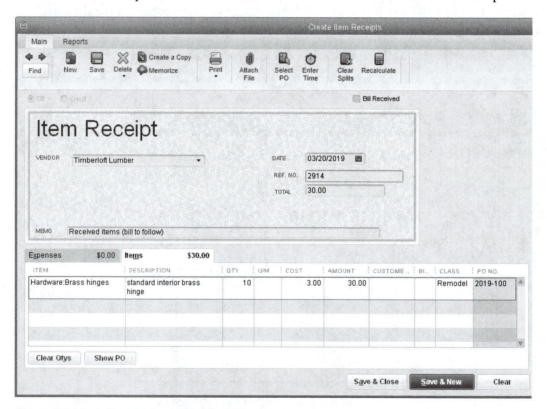

Figure 8-13 Item Receipt for backordered items

Entering Bills for Received Inventory

You can record bills when you receive them, whether they arrive with an inventory shipment or later. This section describes how to record them in both situations.

Converting an Item Receipt into a Bill

If you recorded an item receipt for inventory, you can convert it into a bill in QuickBooks when the bill from the vendor arrives. With this approach, the program converts the item receipt transaction in your *Accounts Payable* account into a bill transaction, so your *Accounts Payable* balance doesn't change. However, the bill will appear in the *Pay Bills* window and the *Unpaid Bills* report.

Computer Practice

To convert an item receipt into a bill, follow these steps:

1. On the *Vendors* menu, choose *Enter Bill for Received Items*. Or, on the *Home Page*, click *Enter Bills Against Inventory*.

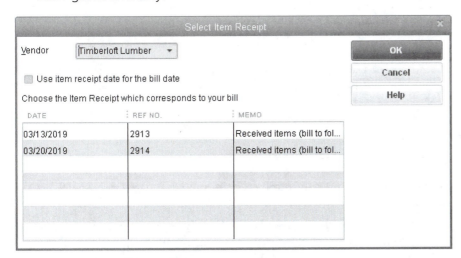

Figure 8-14 Select Item Receipt dialog box

2. In the *Select Item Receipt* window's *Vendor* field, choose *Timberloft Lumber*.

    QuickBooks fills in the *Date*, *Ref No.*, and *Memo* fields with your item receipts' information, as shown in Figure 8-14.

3. To select an item receipt, click its line in the table, in this example, click the row with Ref. No. *2913*. Click *OK*.

    In the *Enter Bills* window, QuickBooks automatically fills out the bill with the item receipt's information. In fact, QuickBooks doesn't create a new transaction. It converts the item receipt into a bill, as shown in Figure 8-15, by turning on the *Bill Received* checkbox.

4. Change the date to the bill's date, in this example, *3/20/2019*.

5. Click *Save & Close* to record the bill.

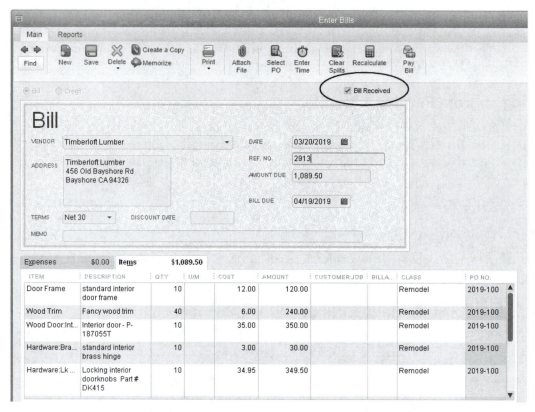

Figure 8-15 Convert item receipt to bill

6. If the *Recording Transaction* message appears, click *Yes*.

7. Repeat steps 1 through 6 to convert item receipt number *2914* into a bill dated *3/25/2019*.

> Note: You can't apply more than one item receipt to a bill. If the vendor sends one bill that covers multiple item receipts, create a bill for each item receipt. In the *Ref. No.* field, fill in the bill reference number from the vendor's bill. That way, in the *Pay Bills* window, you can identify all the bills that relate to the single vendor bill you received.

Receiving Inventory and the Bill at the Same Time

If you receive a bill with a shipment, you can record the item receipt and bill simultaneously.

Computer Practice

To record receipt of inventory and the corresponding bill at the same time, follow these steps:

1. On the *Vendors* menu, choose *Receive Items and Enter Bill*. Or, on the *Home Page*, click *Receive Inventory*, and then choose *Receive Inventory with Bill*.

2. In the *Enter Bills* window, in the *Vendor* drop-down list, choose the vendor who sent the shipment, in this example, *A Cheung Limited*.

3. In the *Open POs Exist* message box, click *Yes*.

4. In the *Open Purchase Orders* dialog box, turn on the checkmark cell for the purchase order whose items you received, in this example, P.O. number *6237*. Click *OK*.

    QuickBooks fills in the bill with the purchase order information, as shown in Figure 8-16. The *P.O. No.* column in the table displays the purchase order number for the received items.

5. Fill in the *Date* and *Ref*. No. fields as shown in Figure 8-16.

6. To save the bill and record the item receipt, click *Save & Close*.

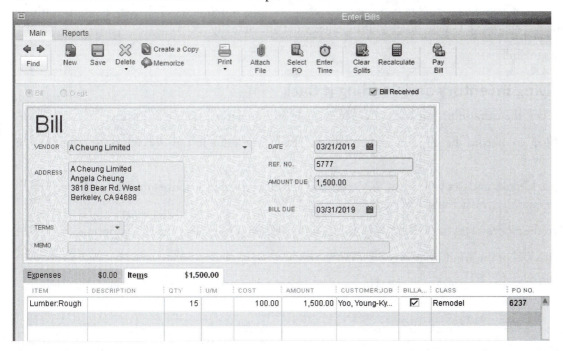

Figure 8-16 Record item receipt and bill simultaneously

Handling Overshipments

If a vendor ships more inventory than you ordered on a purchase order, you have three options. You can:

- **Refuse the extra shipment.** In this case, you send the extra shipment back to the vendor, and you don't record anything in QuickBooks.

- **Keep the extra shipment and pay for the extra items.** If you want to keep the extra items, you can record the receipt of the extra shipment and the corresponding bill. You pay for the extra inventory, in this situation.

- **Receive the items into inventory and then record a bill credit when you send the items back.** In this approach, you receive the extra shipment into inventory. However, you then record a bill credit for the items you return to the vendor.

This section describes the options that involve recording transactions in QuickBooks.

Keeping an Overshipment and Paying for it

This section describes the steps for recording and paying for an extra shipment.

> Note: Do not perform the following steps. They are for reference only.

1. When you record the shipment's item receipt, change the value in the *Qty* cell to the quantity you received.

   QuickBooks updates your inventory asset and accounts payable accounts to reflect the value of the quantity you actually received.

2. When you receive the vendor's bill, compare it to the item receipt you recorded and make sure the amount due is correct for the quantity you received.

Your purchase order won't match the item receipt or bill. When you decide to keep an overshipment, edit your purchase order so it matches what you actually received.

3. Pay the bill.

Receiving Inventory and Sending it Back

If you send the extra shipment back after receiving it into inventory, do the following:

1. When you record the shipment's item receipt, change the value in the *Qty* cell to the quantity you received.

QuickBooks updates your inventory asset and accounts payable accounts to reflect the value of the quantity you actually received.

2. On the *Home Page*, click *Enter Bills*. In the *Enter Bills* window, select the *Credit* option.

The label in the window changes to *Credit*.

3. Fill in the header portion of the window with the vendor, date, reference number, credit amount, and memo.

4. On the *Items* tab, choose the item you're returning and fill in the quantity you're sending back. Click *Save & Close* to save the credit.

If you receive a credit from the vendor, you don't have to record anything else in QuickBooks, because you've already recorded the bill credit. When you receive your next bill from the vendor, you can apply your credit to that bill.

5. If you receive a refund, record it in your next deposit transaction. You manually add a line for your refund in the deposit. In the *Received from* column, fill in the vendor's name. In the *From Account* column, choose *Accounts Payable*.

6. After you record the refund in a deposit, you can use the *Pay Bills* window to apply the deposit to the bill credit.

Handling Vendor Overcharges

If your purchase order and the vendor's bill don't match, you can handle the discrepancy in two ways. If the vendor overcharged you, ask them to send you a new bill. If they agree, wait until you receive the revised bill, and then record it in QuickBooks. The other approach is to pay the incorrect bill as it is, and then record a bill credit that you can apply to your next bill from the vendor. This section describes the steps you perform to pay the bill and record a bill credit.

Computer Practice

To correct a vendor's overcharge, follow these steps:

1. On the *Vendors* menu, choose *Enter Bills*.

2. In this example, click the *Previous* arrow at the window's top left to display the last bill you entered for *Timberloft Lumber*.

3. Click the *Expenses* tab.

4. In the first blank row, choose the account you want to assign the overcharge to, in this example, *Job Expenses*. In the *Amount* cell, type the overcharge, in this case, *20*. Choose *Overhead* in the *Class* cell.

5. Click *Recalculate* at the top of the window to adjust the value in the *Amount Due* field (Figure 8-17).

6. Click *Save & Close* to record your changes. When the *Recording Transaction* message appears, click *Yes*.

   Contact the vendor to discuss the overcharge. The vendor can issue a refund check if you've already paid the bill or issue a credit that you can apply to a future bill.

Figure 8-17 Edit bill to add overcharge

> Note: When you record the credit or refund, be sure to use the same account you used for the overcharge, such as *Job Expenses*.

Invoicing for Inventory Items

When you sell inventory, you record the sale with an invoice or sales receipt. That way, QuickBooks updates your inventory accounts and quantities.

Computer Practice

To record a sale of inventory, follow these steps:

1. On the *Customers* menu, choose *Create Invoices*.

2. In the *Customer:Job* field, choose the customer you need to invoice, in this example, *Teichman, Tim: Kitchen*.

3. Fill out the remaining fields of the invoice as shown in Figure 8-18.

4. Click *Save & Close* to record the invoice.

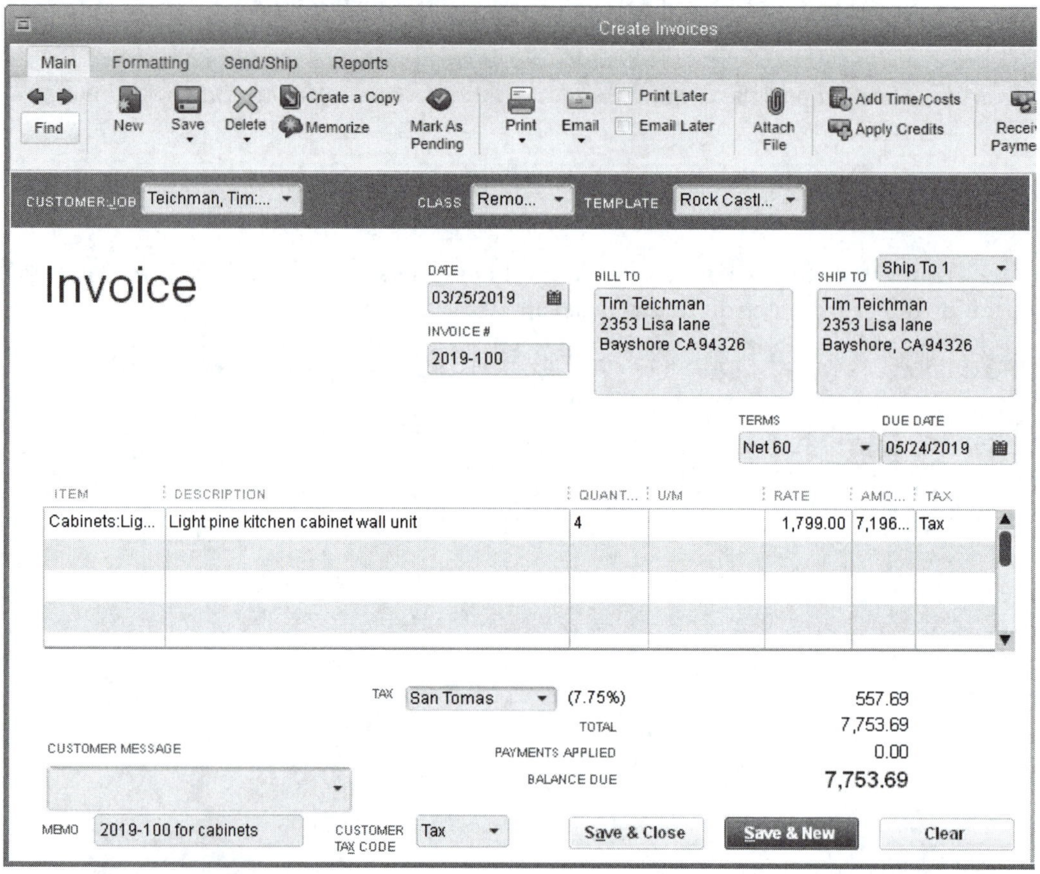

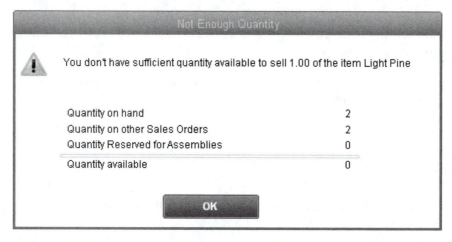

Figure 8-18 Invoice for inventory

Inventory Reminders

If you add inventory items to sales transactions and the quantity on hand falls below your reorder point, QuickBooks notifies you that you don't have enough quantity on hand to fulfill the customer's order (Figure 8-19). In addition, it adds a reminder to the QuickBooks *Reminders* list, as shown in Figure 8-20. (To open the *Reminders* window, click the *Reminders* icon at the QuickBooks window's top right, shown in Figure 8-20.)

Not Enough Quantity	
You don't have sufficient quantity available to sell 1.00 of the item Light Pine	
Quantity on hand	2
Quantity on other Sales Orders	2
Quantity Reserved for Assemblies	0
Quantity available	0
OK	

Figure 8-19 Message that you don't have enough inventory to fulfill an order

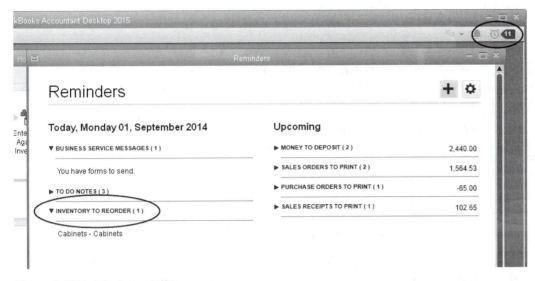

Figure 8-20 Reminders window

Note: The *Reminders* window has a new look in QuickBooks 2015. It shows reminders that are due as of today's date on the left and upcoming reminders on the right. You can click the triangles next to categories to hide or show individual reminders. If you want to modify your *Reminder* preferences, click the *Open Preferences* icon, which looks like a gear, at the window's top right.

In QuickBooks 2014, the *Reminders* window has three columns: *Due Date*, *Description*, and *Amount*. Reminders are grouped into categories. You can expand or collapse the categories by clicking *Collapse All* or *Expand All*.

Adjusting Inventory

As you've seen in previous sections, QuickBooks updates your inventory value and quantity as you buy and sell inventory items. However, sometimes, you need to manually adjust inventory, for example, to account for damage to the products in your warehouse. This section explains how to manually adjust inventory quantity and value.

Adjusting Inventory Quantity on Hand

If the quantity in QuickBooks doesn't agree with the quantity in your warehouse for whatever reason, you can adjust your QuickBooks inventory quantities. Adjusting inventory quantity is helpful when you perform a physical count of your inventory and need to update your QuickBooks records to match the number of units in your warehouse or store.

Computer Practice

To adjust the inventory quantity on hand, follow these steps:

1. On the *Home Page*, click the *Inventory Activities* icon in the *Company* section, and then choose *Adjust Quantity/Value on Hand*. (Or, on the *Vendors* menu, choose *Inventory Activities*, and then choose *Adjust Quantity/Value on Hand*.)

2. In the *Adjust Quantity/Value on Hand* window's *Adjustment Type* field, make sure *Quantity* is selected.

3. In the *Adjustment Date* field, choose the date for the adjustment, in this example, *03/31/2019*.

4. In the *Adjustment Account* field, choose the account you want to use for inventory adjustments.

   In this example, type *Inventory Adjustment*, and then press Tab. When the *Account Not Found* message box appears, click *Set Up*. In the *Add New Account* window, type 54900 in the Number box, and then click *Save & Close*.

5. In the *Ref. No.* field, fill in a reference number, in this example, *2019-1*.

6. Skip the *Customer:Job* field.

7. In the *Class* field, choose *Overhead*.

8. In the first *Item* line, choose the inventory item you want to adjust, in this example, *Doorknobs Std*.

9. In the *New Quantity* field, type the quantity you have on hand, in this example, *100*.

   When you click away from the *New Quantity* cell, QuickBooks automatically adds the difference in the *Qty Difference* field and adjusts the *Total Value of Adjustments* value at the window's bottom right. If you know the number of units you want to subtract, for example, to account for a box of 25 damaged doorknobs, you can type the value in the *Qty Difference* cell instead. Then, QuickBooks fills in the *New Quantity* cell for you.

10. In the *Memo* field, type a note about the adjustment, in this example, *Adjust inventory for physical count*.

11. When your screen matches the one in Figure 8-21, click *Save & Close*.

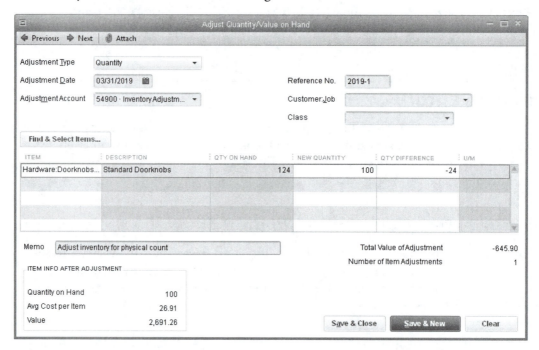

Figure 8-21 Adjust quantity on hand

Adjusting the Value of Inventory on Hand

In some instances, you need to adjust inventory because your inventory value has changed. This situation arises frequently with technology-related products that quickly lose value as newer, more capable products are introduced.

Computer Practice

To adjust inventory value, follow these steps:

1. On the *Home Page*, click the *Inventory Activities* icon in the *Company* section, and then choose *Adjust Quantity/Value on Hand*. In the *Adjust Quantity/Value on Hand* window, choose *Total Value* from the *Adjustment Type* drop-down list.

> Note: You can adjust both the quantity *and* value on hand at the same time by selecting *Quantity and Total Value* from the *Adjustment Type* drop-down list.

2. In the *Adjustment Date* field, choose the adjustment date, in this example, *3/31/2019*.

3. In the *Adjustment Account* field, make sure your adjustment account is selected (*Inventory Adjustment*, here).

4. Skip the *Ref. No.* field, since QuickBooks increments the number from the previous adjustment.

5. In the *Class* field, choose *Overhead*.

6. In the *Item* column, choose the item you want to adjust, in this example, *Cabinets: Light Pine*.

7. In the *New Value* field, type the new total value for the units you have in stock, in this example, *7,200.00*.

   When you click away from the field, QuickBooks adjusts the *Total Value of Adjustment*.

8. In the *Memo* field, type a note about the adjustment, in this example, *Adjustment for older goods*.

9. When your screen matches the one in Figure 8-22, click *Save & Close*.

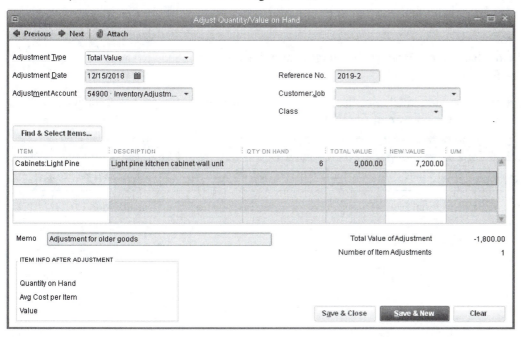

Figure 8-22 Adjust total value on hand

> Note: Whenever you adjust your inventory value, it affects your *Inventory Asset* account. If the *Total Value of Adjustment* is a positive number, then the *Inventory Asset* account increases by that amount, and the adjustment account you use decreases. If the *Total Value of Adjustment* is negative, the *Inventory Asset* account decreases and the adjustment account increases.

Using Group Items

A *Group* item represents several items that you often buy or sell together. For example, Rock Castle Construction stores individual door components in inventory. A *Group* item can include all the components needed to install a door (including services). In addition, you can also set up a *Group* item to show or hide the underlying items, which is useful when you create fixed-price invoices and don't want the customer to see the details. This section shows how to set up a *Group* item.

Computer Practice

To create a *Group* item, follow these steps:

1. On the *Home Page*, click *Items & Services*, or, on the *Lists* menu, choose *Item List*.

2. In the *Item List* window, click *Item*, and then choose *New*.

3. In the *Type* drop-down list, choose *Group*.

4. In the *Group Name/Number* field, type the name for the *Group* item, in this example, *Door Package*.

5. In the *Description* field, type the description, in this example, *Door components and installation labor*.

6. In the item table at the bottom of the window, add the individual items to the group, as shown in Figure 8-23.

   You can't see all the individual items in this table. The *Group* item in Figure 8-23 includes a quantity of *2* of the *Service* item, *Installation*.

   > Note: You don't enter sales prices when you create a *Group* item. QuickBooks uses the sales prices for the individual components when you add the *Group* item to a sales form.

7. If you want the individual items to appear on sales forms, turn on the *Print items in group* checkbox.

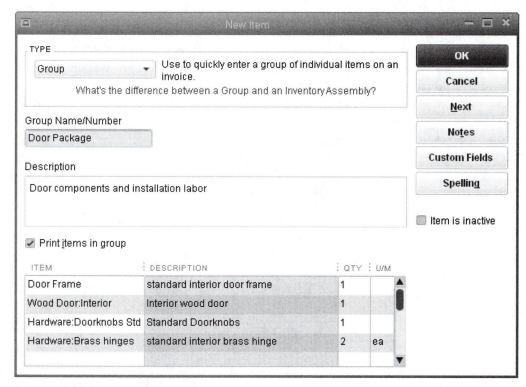

Figure 8-23 A Group item

8. When the window looks like the one in Figure 8-23, click *OK*.

Inventory Assemblies

QuickBooks Premier, Accountant, and Enterprise include an additional item type called *Inventory Assembly*, which you can use to track products you assemble from *Inventory Part* items or other *Inventory Assembly* items. When you build units of an *Inventory Assembly* item, QuickBooks automatically increases the number of assembled items you have on hand and decreases the quantity of the component parts you used up.

An *Inventory Assembly* item is similar to a *Group* item, but it has some added capabilities:

- You can combine several *Inventory Part* items and *Service* items into a single *Inventory Assembly* item.

- You can specify a price that's different than the sum of its component items.

- You can set a minimum build point so QuickBooks will automatically remind you to build more assembled items when stock is running low.

Inventory Reports

Managing inventory is a balance between keeping enough items in stock for sales, but not so many that your inventory grows stale. This section describes some of QuickBooks' built-in reports for tracking inventory.

Inventory Stock Status by Item Report

The *Inventory Stock Status by Item* report (Figure 8-24) provides an overview of each *Inventory Part* item, including the number of units on hand and how that number will change based on your outstanding sales orders and purchase orders. This report also has a column for sales per week, which helps you evaluate inventory turnover. To run this report, on the *Reports* menu, choose *Inventory*, and then choose *Inventory Stock Status by Item*.

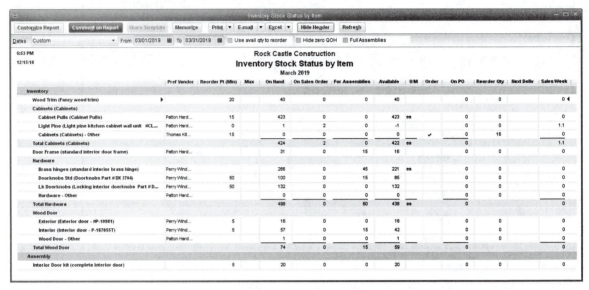

Figure 8-24 Inventory Stock Status by Item report

Inventory Stock Status by Vendor Report

The *Inventory Stock Status by Vendor* report (Figure 8-25) is similar to the *Inventory Stock Status by Item* report. This report groups the items by preferred vendors. To run this report, on the *Reports* menu, choose *Inventory*, and then choose *Inventory Stock Status by Vendor*.

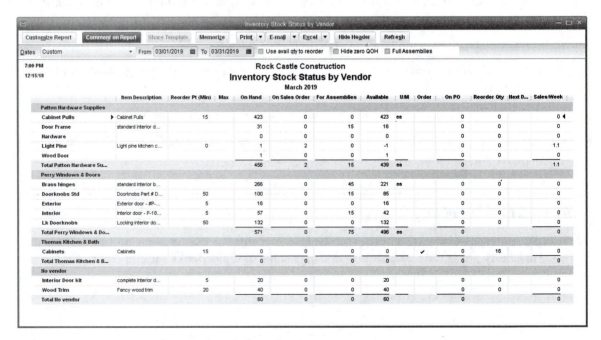

Figure 8-25 Inventory Stock Status by Vendor report

Inventory Valuation Summary

The *Inventory Valuation Summary* report, shown in Figure 8-26, tells you how much inventory you have on hand, what it's worth, and what it will be worth when you sell it.

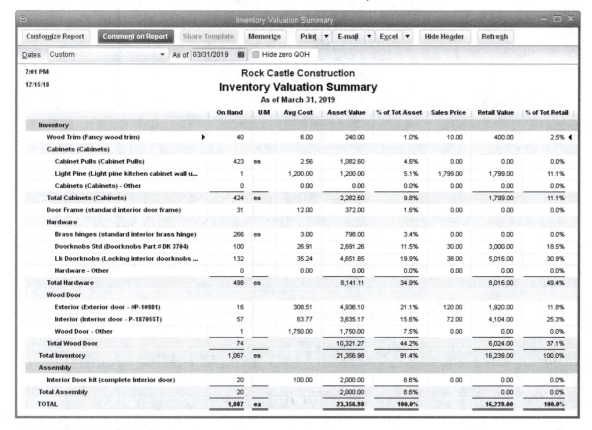

Figure 8-26 Inventory Valuation Summary report

Inventory Item QuickReport

To see all the transactions that include a specific inventory item, run the *Inventory Item QuickReport* (Figure 8-27).

Computer Practice

To create an *Inventory Item QuickReport*, follow these steps:

1. On the *Home Page*, choose *Inventory Activities* (in the *Company* section), and then choose *Inventory Center* from the drop-down list.

2. Select the item you want to run a report for, in this example, *Wood Door:Interior*.

3. On the right side of the *Inventory Information* section, click *QuickReport*.

4. In the *Dates* field, fill in the *From* and To fields (*3/1/2019* and *3/31/2019*, in this example).

5. When you are finished viewing the report, close it.

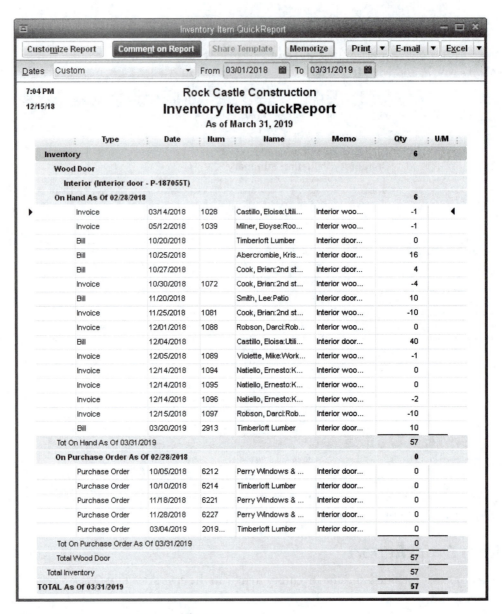

Figure 8-27 Inventory Item QuickReport

Review Questions

Select the best answer(s) for each of the following:

1. You record the sales price for a Group Item in:

   a) The Sales Price field

   b) The Rate field

   c) The Price Level field

   d) None of the above

2. When you sell an inventory item, which account(s) decrease in value?

   a) Inventory income account

   b) Inventory asset account

   c) Cost of goods sold account

   d) Expense account

3. If a vendor sends you more than the quantity on your purchase order, you can:

   a) Receive the extra shipment into inventory, and then send it back and record a bill credit.

   b) Refuse the extra shipment and send it back to the vendor without recording a transaction in QuickBooks.

   c) Receive the extra shipment and record an inventory adjustment.

   d) Receive the extra shipment and pay for it.

4. Which type of transaction applies only to inventory?

   a) Purchase order

   b) Item receipt

   c) Bill

   d) Invoice

5. QuickBooks Pro, Premier, and Accountant can't:

   a) Calculate gross profit on inventory sold.

   b) Report the status of inventory items including how many are on hand and how many are on order.

   c) Use the LIFO or FIFO method to calculate inventory cost.

   d) Track open purchase orders.

Tracking Inventory Exercise 1

Applying Your Knowledge

Restore the sample file, sample_product-based business 2015 (Portable).QBM. (Or, if you are using QuickBooks 2014, restore sample_product-based business 2014 (Portable).QBM.)

1. Create a new *Inventory Part* item in the *Item List* with the data in the following table.

Table 8-1 Data for new Inventory Part item

Item Type	Inventory Part
Item Name	Casement window
Purchase Description	Window for basement
Cost	$200.00
COGS Account	Cost of Goods Sold
Preferred Vendor	
Sales Description	Window for basement
Price	$400.00
Tax Code	Tax
Income Account	Materials Income
Asset Account	Inventory Asset
Reorder Point	20
Qty on Hand	0
Total Value	0
As of	Keep current date

2. Create purchase order *2019-1* dated *03/11/2019* to *Zeng Building Supplies* for *5 casement windows*. Use the *New Construction* class. Include a memo to identify the purchase order. Print the purchase order on blank paper.

3. Create an item receipt dated *03/28/2019* for *5 casement windows* from *Zeng Building Supplies* against PO 2019-1. The packing slip number is *180410*. The item receipt total is $1,000.

4. Create an invoice (#*2019-101*) for *Mark Bauman: Home Remodel* on *04/10/2019* for *2 casement windows*. Use the default sales price and assign the sale to the *Remodel* class. Add a memo to identify the invoice.

5. Run and print a *Casement Window item QuickReport* for *03/01/2019* to *04/30/2019*.

6. Run and print an *Inventory Stock Status by Item* report for *3/01/2019* to *4/30/2019*.

7. Run and print an *Inventory Valuation Summary* as of *04/30/2019*.

Tracking Inventory Exercise 2 (Advanced)

Applying Your Knowledge

Restore the sample file, sample_product-based business 2015 (Portable).QBM. (Or, if you are using QuickBooks 2014, restore sample_product-based business 2014 (Portable).QBM.)

1. Create new *Inventory Part* items with the data in the following tables.

Table 8-2 Data for New Inventory Part item

Item Type	Inventory Part
Item Name	Casement Wnd-White
Purchase Description	White casement window
Cost	$112.50
COGS Account	Cost of Goods Sold
Preferred Vendor	Leave blank
Sales Description	White casement window
Price	$225.00
Tax Code	Tax
Income Account	Materials Income
Asset Account	Inventory Asset
Reorder Point	20
Qty on Hand	0
Total Value	0
As of	Keep current date

Table 8-3 Data for New Inventory Part item

Item Type	Inventory Part
Item Name	Casement Wnd–Wood
Purchase Description	Casement window with unfinished wood
Cost	$179.50
COGS Account	Cost of Goods Sold
Preferred Vendor	Leave blank
Sales Description	Casement window with unfinished wood
Price	$351.50
Tax Code	Tax
Income Account	Materials Income
Asset Account	Inventory Asset
Reorder Point	20
Qty on Hand	0
Total Value	0
As of	Leave current date

2. Create purchase order *2019-1* dated *04/12/2019* to *Zeng Building Supplies*. Use the *New Construction* class. Include *5 white casement windows* and *2 casement windows with unfinished wood*. Add a memo to identify the purchase order. Print the purchase order on blank paper.

For the following transactions, unless specific values are provided, keep all defaults on transactions, such as dates, prices, and sales tax.

3. Create an item receipt dated *April 15, 2019* for *Zeng Building Supplies* against PO 2019-1 for *1 white casement window* and *1 casement window with unfinished wood*. The packing slip number is *5459*.

4. Create an item receipt dated *4/17/2019* for *Zeng Building Supplies* against PO 2019-1 for the remaining items on the purchase order. The packing slip number is *5472*.

5. Create an invoice *2019-102* dated *4/21/2019* to *Davies, Aaron: Remodel* for *2 white casement windows* and *2 casement windows with unfinished wood*. Use the *Remodel* class.

6. Record a bill for item receipt *5459* dated *4/22/2019* from *Zeng Building Supplies*. Delivery charges of *$32.50* were added to the bill. Use the *Expenses* tab to record delivery charges (using the *Postage and Delivery* expense account). Use the *Remodel* class. The total bill amount is $1419.00. (Hint: Use the *Recalculate* button to adjust the *Amount Due*.)

7. Record a bill for item receipt *5472* dated *4/22/2019* from *Zeng Building Supplies*. Use the *Remodel* class.

8. Record an inventory adjustment *(#2019-101)* dated 4/30/2019 for a white *Casement Window* item. Create the *Inventory Adjustment* account (*54530*). Use the *Remodel* class. Quantity on hand is *1*. Memo is *Damaged window*.

9. Run and print a *Casement Window – White item QuickReport* for all dates.

10. Run and print an *Inventory Stock Status by Item* report for *3/01/2019* to *4/30/2019*.

11. Run and print an *Inventory Valuation Summary* as of *04/30/2019*.

Chapter 9
Billable Time and Costs

Topics

This chapter covers the following topics:

- Reimbursable (Billable) Expenses

- Working with Billable Items

- Recording Time

- Billable Time and Costs Reports

When you incur costs that are billable to customers, it's important that you track all those costs—and charge your customers for them. If you don't, your company's profit won't be as much as it should be. QuickBooks can help you track all the billable costs you need to pass on to your customers: billable expenses, items you purchase specifically for customers or jobs, services you deliver that you purchase from others, and billable time.

This chapter begins with recording reimbursable expenses. You'll also learn how to set up items to track billable costs, such as products and services you purchase specifically for customers or jobs. Then you'll learn how to record purchases so they're billable to the correct customer or job. Finally, this chapter explains how to track time and invoice billable time to customers.

> Note: For the computer practice in this chapter, restore the sample file, sample_product-based business 2015 (Portable).QBM. Or, if you are using QuickBooks 2014, restore sample_product-based business 2014 (Portable).QBM.

Reimbursable (Billable) Expenses

You can make expenses billable when you record expense transactions, such as checks, credit card charges, or bills. All you have to do is choose the customer or job, and then turn on the *Billable?* cell (see Figure 9-1).

You can also assign expenses to customers or jobs without charging for them. That way, you can track your profit including those non-billable expenses. To do that, you choose the customer or job in the *Customer:Job* cell, but turn *off* the *Billable?* cell.

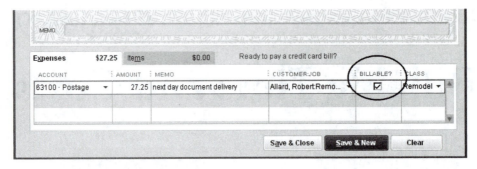

Figure 9-1 Billable Expense

> Note: The *Billable?* cell appears in a transaction table only if the account you choose is one of the following types of accounts: *Other Current Asset, Cost of Goods Sold, Expense,* and *Other Expense.* You won't see the *Billable?* cell for transactions posted to an income account.

If most or all of your expenses are non-billable, you can set a QuickBooks preference so that expenses are non-billable by default. To modify this preference, on the *Edit* menu, choose *Preferences*, click the *Time & Expenses* category, and then click the *Company Preferences* tab. In the *Invoicing Options* section, turn off the *Mark all expenses as billable* checkbox. Click *OK* to save your changes.

Setting Up Accounts to Track Reimbursable Expenses

Tracking reimbursable expenses as income makes it easy to compare income from reimbursable expenses with the reimbursable expenses to make sure you've invoiced for all those expenses. With this approach, QuickBooks posts reimbursable expenses from purchase transactions to an expense account as it does for any expense. However, when you invoice your customers, those reimbursements are recorded as income in an income account specifically for reimbursement income.

> Note: Ask your accountant whether you should track reimbursements as income before you apply the changes in this section to your company file.

To track reimbursable expenses as income, on the *Edit* menu, choose *Preferences*. In the *Time & Expenses* category, click the *Company Preferences* tab (Figure 9-2), and then turn on the *Track reimbursed expenses as income* checkbox. When you do that, QuickBooks adds a *Track reimbursed expenses in Income Acct.* checkbox to the *Add New Account* and *Edit Account* windows (Figure 9-4), so you can choose the income account for reimbursable expenses.

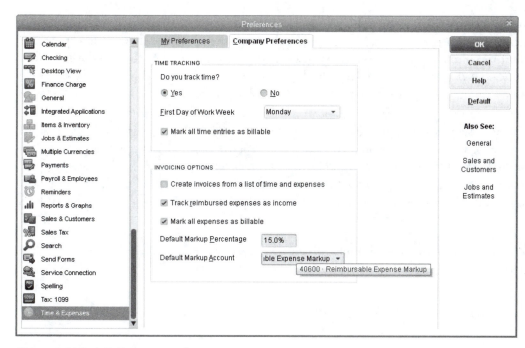

Figure 9-2 Time & Expense preferences

Computer Practice

Here are the accounts you need to track reimbursable expenses as income:

- **Income account for income from reimbursable expenses**: To track reimbursable expenses as income, you need an income account specifically for reimbursable expense income. The sample file already has an income account named *Reimbursement Income*.

- **Income account for markup**: If you mark up reimbursable expenses, create *another* income account to track your income from those markups. Create an income account, like the one shown in Figure 9-3.

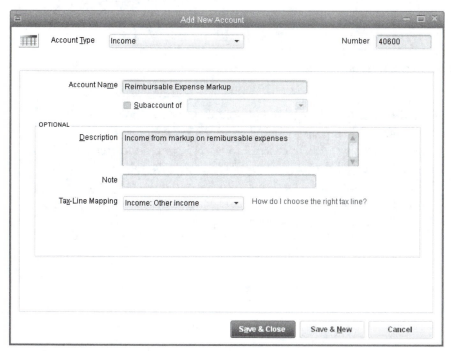

Figure 9-3 Income account for markup

- **Expense account for reimbursable expenses**: Although you can record reimbursable expenses to any expense account, it's easier to track them when you post them to an expense account specifically for reimbursable expenses, as shown in Figure 9-4. Turn on the *Track reimbursed expenses in Income Acct.* checkbox and then, in the drop-down list, choose the income account you use for income from reimbursable expenses.

> Note: If the expense account already exists and has been used in a closed accounting period (one for which you have filed tax returns or prepared financial statements), do not turn on its *Track Reimbursed Expenses in Income Acct.* checkbox. Doing so will create discrepancies between your QuickBooks reports and your tax returns and financial statements. Instead, create a *new* account for tracking reimbursable expenses.

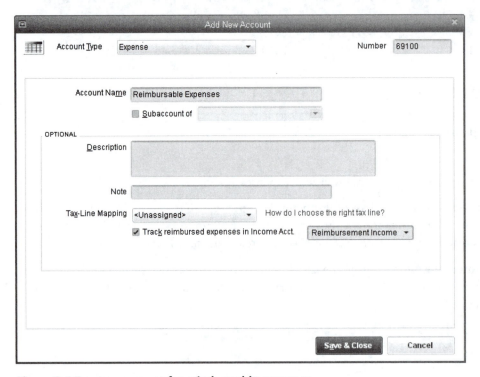

Figure 9-4 Expense account for reimbursable expenses

> Tip: If you want to track different types of reimbursable expenses, you can create *Other Charge* items for each type and set them up to include both purchase and sales information. (See the section, Working with Billable Items, to learn how to create items with both purchase and sales information.) You can assign those items to a single reimbursable income account, and you can run a *Sales By Item* report to track totals of each type of reimbursable expense. You can also set up a parent expense account for reimbursable expenses with subaccounts for each type of reimbursable expense.

Recording Reimbursable Expenses

Once you've created the accounts you need, recording billable expenses is easy.

Computer Practice

To record a reimbursable expense, follow these steps:

1. On the *Home Page*, click the *Write Checks* icon in the *Banking* section.

2. Fill in the *Write Checks* window with the information displayed in Figure 9-5.

   Choose an account in the row's *Account* cell, choose the customer or job to which the expense applies, and then turn on the row's *Billable?* cell. This approach also works with credit card charges and bills.

3. To save the transaction, click *Save & Close*.

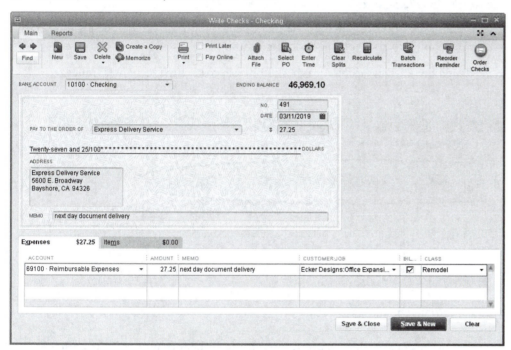

Figure 9-5 Recording a reimbursable expense in the Write Checks window

Invoicing Reimbursable Expenses

After you record reimbursable expenses, the next step is adding them to customer invoices. This section explains how to do that.

Computer Practice

To add reimbursable expenses to an invoice, follow these steps:

1. On the *Home Page*, click the *Create Invoices* icon. (Or choose *Invoice* in the icon bar, or simply press *Ctrl+I*.)

2. In the *Customer:Job* field, choose the customer or job, in this example, *Ecker Designs:Office Expansion*.

   If you choose a customer or job with billable time or costs, the *Billable Time/Costs* dialog box opens.

---

3. In the *Billable Time/Costs* dialog box (Figure 9-6), keep the *Select the outstanding billable time and costs to add to this invoice* option selected and click *OK*.

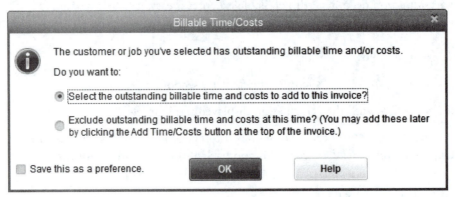

Figure 9-6 Billable Time/Costs dialog box

4. In the *Choose Billable Time and Costs* dialog box that opens (Figure 9-7), click the *Expenses* tab to display all reimbursable expenses for the customer or job.

    Each tab in the dialog box displays different types of billable costs: time, expenses, mileage, and items.

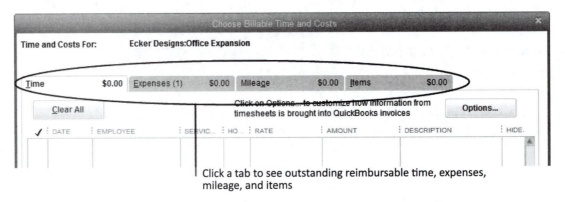

Figure 9-7 Choose Billable Time and Costs tabs

5. If you want to mark up expenses, in the *Markup Amount or %* field (Figure 9-8), type the markup amount or percentage, in this example, *15%*. In the *Markup Account* field, choose the account you use to track your income from the markup, in this example, *Reimbursable xpense Markup*.

    The markup you add increases the amount the customer owes. Typically, markup is added to cover the cost of processing reimbursable expenses. If you typically charge the same markup on all reimbursable expenses, you can set a default markup. To do that, in the *Edit* menu, choose *Preferences*, and then choose the *Time & Expenses* category. On the *Company Preferences* tab, in the *Default Markup* field, fill in your typical markup.

6. To select an expense to add to the invoice, turn on the checkmark cell in the first column of the expense's row (see Figure 9-8).

7. Turn on the *Print selected time and costs as one invoice item* checkbox.

    Turning on this setting tells QuickBooks to display a single line for all the reimbursable time and costs you select in the printed invoice. (Within QuickBooks, you'll still see the details of the reimbursable expenses and markup.)

In QuickBooks 2015 (not 2014), the number in parentheses shows the number of outstanding reimbursable expenses.

Turn on this cell to change the expense to non-billable and remove it from this screen.

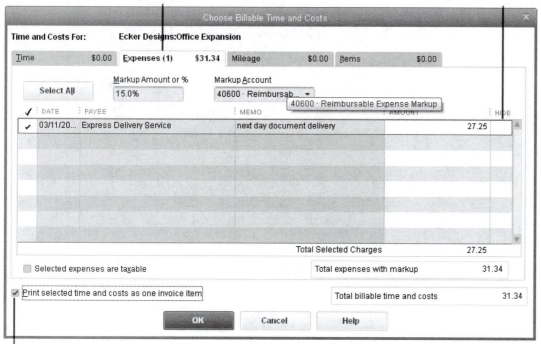

Turn on this checkbox to print a single invoice line for all reimbursable expenses.

Figure 9-8 Choose Billable Time and Costs dialog box filled out

8. Click *OK* to add the reimbursable costs to the invoice.

    As you can see in Figure 9-9, QuickBooks adds a group, *Reimb Group*, to contain all the reimbursable time and costs that you added. Within the group, you see the individual lines and markup.

9. In the *Create Invoices* window, fill in the remaining information (*Class, Date, Terms, Invoice #*) as shown in Figure 9-9.

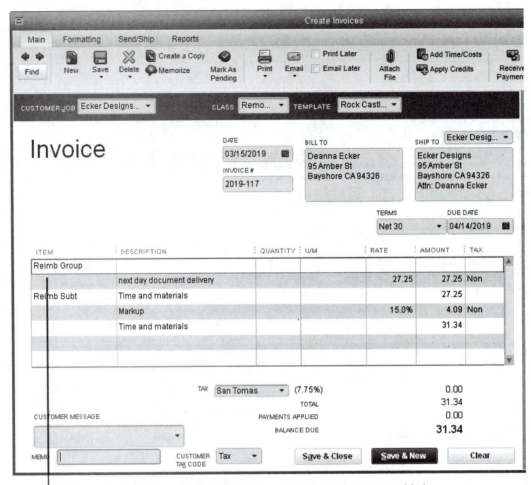

Reimbursement group contains all the reimbursable time and costs you added

Figure 9-9 Create Invoice window with billable expenses

10. To see what the printed invoice looks like, at the top of the *Create Invoices* window, click *Print*, and then choose *Preview* on the drop-down menu.

The printed invoice (Figure 9-10) includes only one line for reimbursable time and costs.

11. Click *Close* to close the preview window, and then click *Save & Close* to record the invoice and close the *Create Invoices* window.

Figure 9-10 Preview of printed invoice

The *Profit & Loss* report shown in Figure 9-11 is set to the date range that shows only the reimbursable expense and the corresponding income to demonstrate how reimbursable income and expense works.

- The Reimbursement Income account shows the amount you received from the customer for the reimbursable expenses.

- The Reimbursable Expense Markup account shows the income from marking up the reimbursable expenses.

- The Reimbursable Expenses account shows the original reimbursable expenses amount. In this example, this account's value equals the Reimbursable Income account's value, which means you invoiced and were reimbursed for all your reimbursable expenses. Another way to tell that you've been paid for your reimbursable costs is that the Net Income here equals the Reimbursable Expense Markup.

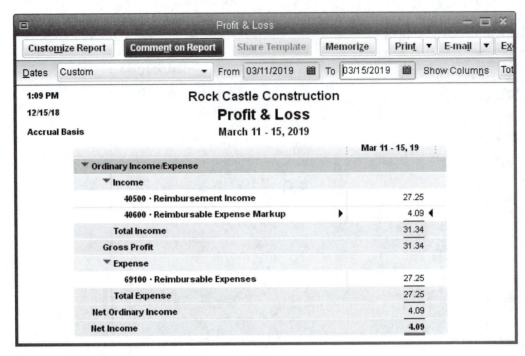

Figure 9-11 Profit and loss for invoiced reimbursable expense

Working with Billable Items

You can set up QuickBooks items to include both purchase and sales information to track billable costs and the corresponding income. By setting items up in this way, you can use them on purchase forms (checks, bills, credit card charges, and so on) and sales forms (invoices, sales receipts, and so on). Then, you can run reports to examine the profitability of those items.

Setting up items in this way helps you track the following types of billable costs:

- **Custom-ordered products**: If you purchase non-inventory products specifically for customers or jobs, you can create *Non-Inventory Part* items with purchase and sales information.

- **Subcontracted labor**: If you often hire subcontractors to perform work, you can create *Service* items with purchase and sales information.

- **Work performed by partners**: You can also track income and corresponding expense for the work partners perform, for example, as law firms frequently do.

This section explains how to create and work with items for all these situations.

Tracking Custom Orders

If you custom-order products specifically for customers or jobs (that is, products you don't stock as inventory), you create *Non-inventory Part* items that contain purchase and sales information. Then, when you add these items to purchase and sales transactions, QuickBooks automatically tracks the income and cost of these items. This section explains how to create items such as these and how to use them to track custom orders.

Creating an Item for Custom Orders

This section describes how you set up a *Non-inventory Part* item to track products you custom-order.

Computer Practice

To create an item for a product you order specifically for a customer or job, follow these steps:

1. On the *Lists* menu, choose *Item List* (or, on the *Home Page*, click *Items & Services*).

2. At the bottom of the *Item List* window, click *Item*, and then choose *New Item* on the drop-down menu. (Or press *Ctrl+N*.)

3. On the *Type* drop-down menu, choose *Non-inventory Part*.

4. In the *Item Name/Number* field, type the name of the product, in this example, *Stone sink*.

5. Turn on the *This item is used in assemblies or is purchased for a specific customer:job* checkbox.

   When you turn on this checkbox, the *New Item* window displays the *Purchase Information* section and *Sales Information* section.

6. Fill in the fields as shown in Figure 9-12.

   In Figure 9-12, the *Cost* and *Sales Price* fields are both equal to *0.00*, because custom-ordered product prices are likely to change each time you purchase or sell them. By setting these fields to zero in the item record, you can enter the price when you add the item to purchase or sales transactions.

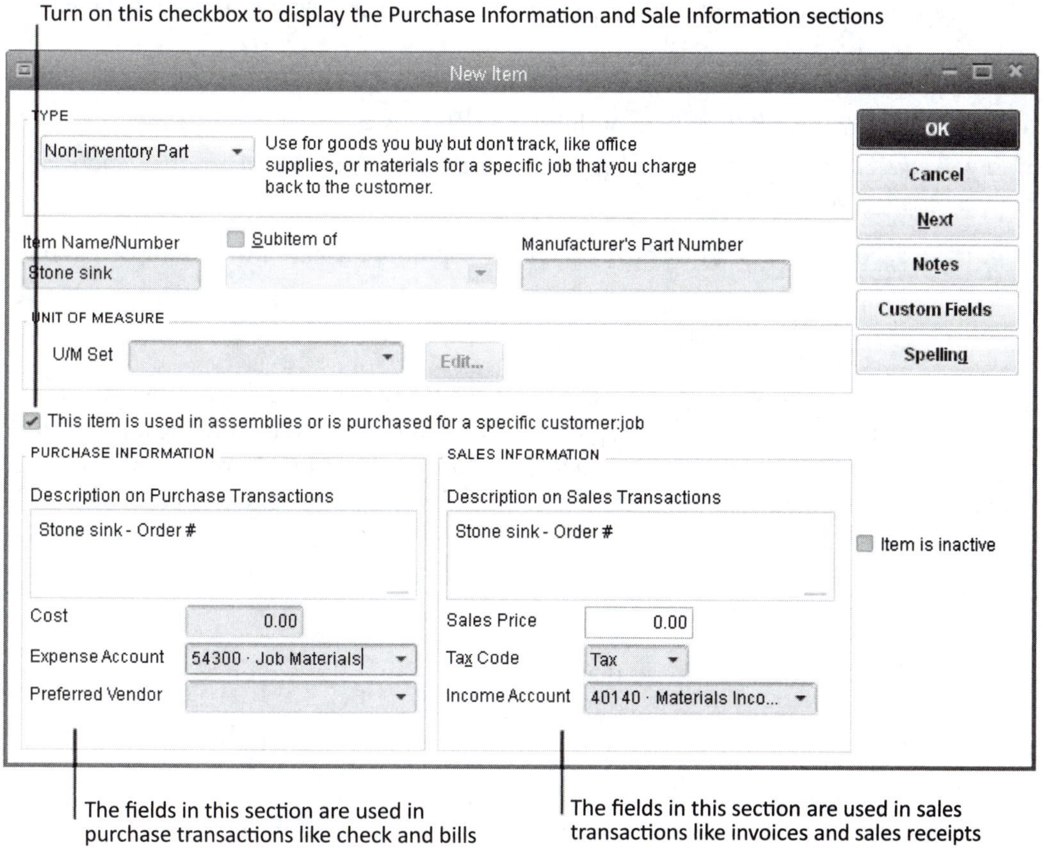

Turn on this checkbox to display the Purchase Information and Sale Information sections

The fields in this section are used in purchase transactions like check and bills

The fields in this section are used in sales transactions like invoices and sales receipts

Figure 9-12 Non-inventory part item with purchase and sales information

> Note: When you add a *Non-inventory Part* item like this to a check or bill, QuickBooks debits (increases) the expense account you chose in the *Expense Account* field. When you add the item to a sales transaction like an invoice, QuickBooks credits (increases) the income account you chose in the *Income Account* field.

7. When your *New Item* window matches the one in Figure 9-12, click *OK* to save the item and close the window.

    You can use this *Non-inventory Part* item for all custom orders for this type of product, regardless of the make or model you order. For example, when you record a bill for the purchase of a stone sink, you can change the description and price to match the specific sink you're buying. Similarly, you can change the description and price on the customer's invoice.

> Tip: To track details for several types of reimbursable expense, such as shipping, copying, and telephone calls, set up *Other Charge* items for each type of reimbursable expense you want to track. When you create an *Other Charge* item for reimbursable expenses, turn on the *This item is used in assemblies or is a reimbursable charge* checkbox to display the *Purchase Information* and *Sales Information* sections. Fill in these fields as described in this section. To purchase and invoice for these items, follow the instructions in the following sections.

Recording a Purchase for a Custom Order

This section describes how to record a purchase order for a custom-ordered *Non-Inventory Part* item.

Computer Practice

To create a purchase order for a custom order, follow these steps:

1. On the *Home Page*, click the *Purchase Orders* icon in the *Vendors* section, or, on the *Vendors* menu choose *Create Purchase Orders*.

2. In the *Vendor* field, choose the vendor you're ordering the product from, in this example, choose *Lew Plumbing*.

3. Fill in the *Purchase Order* fields, as shown in Figure 9-13.

    When you choose the item in the *Item* drop-down list, the *Description* cell displays the description from the item's record. Type the description for the specific item you're ordering and add the P.O. number to the end of the description. In addition, copy the description into the *Memo* field so you can identify this purchase order in the list of *Open Purchase Orders* that appears when you record the vendor's bill.

4. Click *Save & Close*.

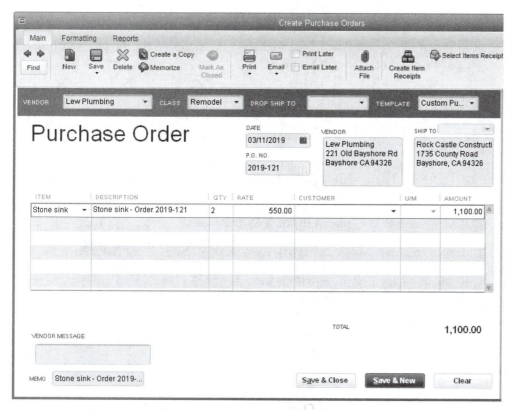

Figure 9-13 Create Purchase Orders window with custom-ordered Non-inventory Part item

To record the bill you receive from the vendor, follow these steps:

1. On the *Home Page*, click the *Enter Bills* icon in the *Vendor* section or choose *Enter Bills* on the *Vendor* menu.

2. In the *Vendor* field, choose the vendor who sent the bill, in this example, *Lew Plumbing*.

3. The *Open POs Exist* message box opens (Figure 9-14). Click *Yes* to associate the bill with one or more of the open purchase orders.

Figure 9-14 Open POs Exist window

4. In the *Open Purchase Orders* dialog box, turn on the checkmark cell for the purchase order you want to select, in this example, *PO No. 2019-121*, as shown in Figure 9-15.

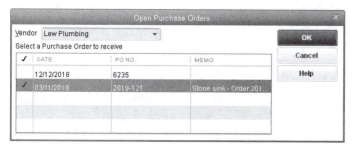

Figure 9-15 Select purchase orders in the Open Purchase Orders dialog box

---

5. Click *OK*.

QuickBooks fills in the *Enter Bills* window's fields with the information from the purchase order: the item you ordered, quantity, cost, and P.O. number.

6. On the *Items* tab, in the *Customer:Job* field, choose the customer or job that you ordered the product for, in this example, *Abercrombie, Kristy:Remodel Bathroom*.

When you choose the customer or job, QuickBooks turns on the *Billable?* checkbox. (If it doesn't, click the checkbox to turn it on.)

7. In the *Date* field, fill in the bill date, in this example, *3/15/2019*. Fill in the *Ref. No.* field, in this example, *2671*.

8. When your bill matches the one in Figure 9-16, click *Save & Close*.

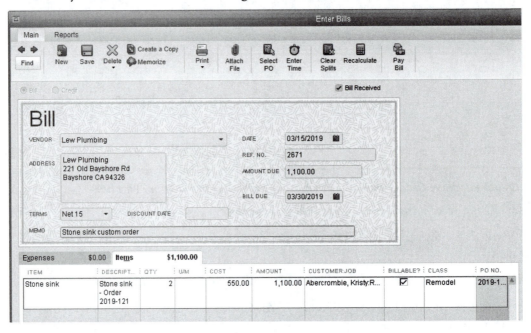

Figure 9-16 Enter Bills window for a custom order

> Note: When you record a bill such as this, QuickBooks automatically credits (increases) the *Accounts Payable* account and debits (increases) the *Cost of Goods Sold* account that you chose for the expense account when you created the *Non-inventory Part* item.

Recording the Sale for a Custom Order

When you create an invoice or sales receipt for this order, you can add the item to the sales form and add the markup.

Computer Practice

To create an invoice for a custom order, follow these steps:

1. On the *Home Page*, click the *Create Invoices* icon.

2. In the *Customer:Job* field, choose the customer or job that you want to invoice, in this example, *Abercrombie, Kristy:Remodel Bathroom*.

For this example, the *Available Estimates* dialog box appears. Click *Cancel* to dismiss it without selecting an estimate to invoice.

3. In the *Billable Time/Costs* window that opens, click *OK* to select the items you want to add to the invoice.

   QuickBooks automatically selects the *Select the outstanding billable time and costs to add to this invoice* option. If you don't want to add billable time and costs, select the other option, and then click OK.

4. In the *Choose Billable Time and Costs* dialog box, click the *Items* tab (Figure 9-17) to see the billable items for the selected customer or job.

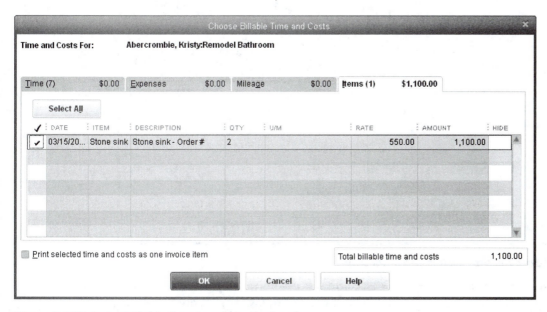

Figure 9-17 Select a billable item to add to the invoice

5. Turn on the checkmark cell(s) for the billable items that you want to add to the invoice. Then click *OK*.

   QuickBooks fills in the invoice table with the billable items you selected, as shown in Figure 9-18.

6. Fill in the remaining fields shown in Figure 9-18.

   QuickBooks fills in the *Rate* cell in the table with the amount recorded in the bill (Figure 9-16), in this example, *550.00*. To add your markup to the item, continue to the next step.

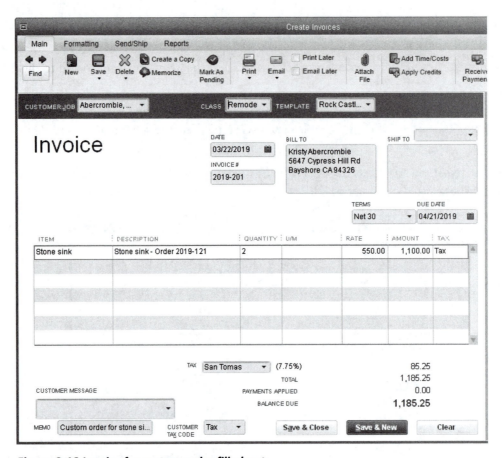

Figure 9-18 Invoice for custom order filled out

7. To mark up the item, click its *Rate* cell. In this example, you want to multiply the rate by 1 plus the markup percentage. To do that, press the asterisk key (*) on your numeric keypad for multiplication.

    The *QuickMath* popup appears. It looks like an adding machine tape, as shown in Figure 9-19.

8. To add the markup percentage to the existing rate, type 1 plus your markup percentage, in this example, *1.15* for a markup of 15%.

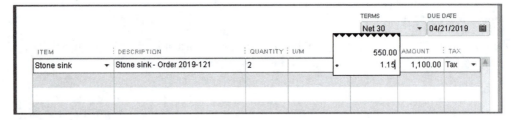

Figure 9-19 QuickMath popup

> Note: QuickBooks automatically opens the *QuickMath* feature when you press the asterisk (*), plus (+), minus (-), and back slash (/) keys, because it recognizes them as arithmetic functions.

11. Press *Tab* to update the invoice.

    QuickBooks recalculates the *Rate* and *Amount* fields, as shown in Figure 9-20.

12. Click *Save & Close*.

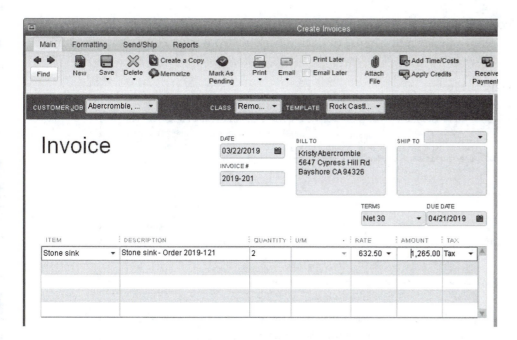

Figure 9-20 Custom order invoice with markup applied

Tracking Subcontracted or Partners' Work

If you hire subcontractors, you can track your income and cost for subcontracted work with *Service* items that contain both purchase and sales information. That way, you can track the profitability of subcontracted services. You can use the same approach to track income and cost for work performed by your company's partners.

Creating a Service Item for Subcontracted or Partners' Work

This section describes setting up a *Service* item for work performed by subcontractors or partners.

Computer Practice

To set up a *Service* item to track subcontracted work, follow these steps:

1. In the *Item List* window, double-click the *Concrete Slab* item to open the *Edit Item* window.

   You can create a new item for subcontracted work or edit an existing *Service* item.

2. Turn on the *This service is used in assemblies or is performed by a subcontractor or partner* checkbox.

   The *Edit Item* window displays the *Purchase Information* and *Sales Information* sections.

3. Fill in the fields as shown in Figure 9-21.

   Similar to setting up the *Non-inventory Part* item described on page 216, you fill in the descriptions you want to use on purchase and sales transactions. The *Cost* field represents what you pay subcontractors for the service on purchase transactions. In the *Expense Account* field, choose the *Cost of Goods Sold* account you use for subcontracted services, in this example, *Subcontractors*. (For work performed by partners, choose the *Cost of Goods Sold* account you use for work performed by partners.)

The *Sales Price* field is what you charge your customers for the service. In the *Income Account* field, choose the income account you use to track subcontracted work income, in this example, *Subcontracted Labor Income*.

4. Click *OK* to save the item.

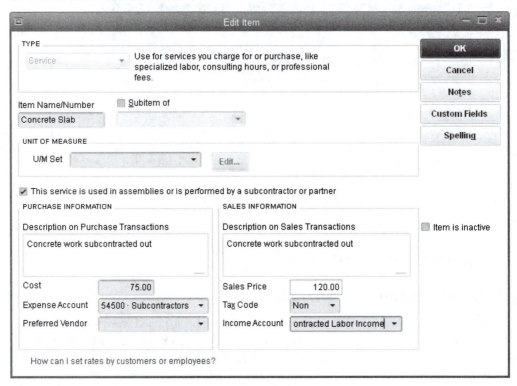

Figure 9-21 A Service item for subcontracted work

Recording a bill for subcontracted work

When you record a check, credit card charge, or bill for subcontractors' work, you use the *Service* item you set up for subcontracted services. (You can use this item when you write a check to pay partners based on the work they performed.)

Computer Practice

Here are the steps to recording a bill for subcontracted work:

1. On the *Home Page*, click the *Enter Bills* icon.

2. Fill out the fields as shown in Figure 9-22.

    By choosing the customer or job in the *Customer:Job* cell, you assign the cost to that customer or job. If you turn on the item's *Billable?* cell, QuickBooks flags this item as a billable cost to that customer or job.

3. Click *Save & Close* to record the bill.

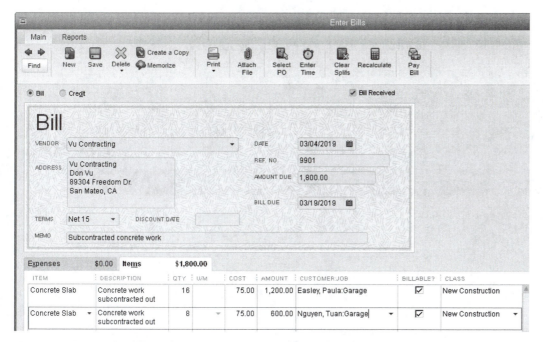

Figure 9-22 Enter Bills window with a bill for subcontracted work

Recording an invoice for subcontracted work

When you record an invoice for a customer or job with billable items, you'll see the *Choose Billable Time and Costs* dialog box.

Computer Practice

Here are the steps to recording an invoice for subcontracted work:

1. On the *Home Page*, choose the *Create Invoices* icon (or press Ctrl+I).

2. In the *Customer:Job* field, choose *Easley, Paula:Garage*.

3. In the *Billable Time/Costs* dialog box that opens, click *OK* to proceed to choosing billable time and costs.

4. In the *Choose Billable Time and Costs* dialog box (Figure 9-23), click the *Items* tab.

5. Turn on the checkmark cell to the left of the item you want to add to the invoice, in this example, *Concrete Slab*.

   The *Rate* field is set to *120.00*, which is the value you entered in the *Service* item's *Sales Price* field.

Figure 9-23 Choose Billable Time and Costs dialog box Items tab

6. Click *OK* to add the item to the invoice.

7. Fill out the *Class, Date* and *Invoice #* field, as shown in Figure 9-24.

8. Click *Save & Close* to save the invoice.

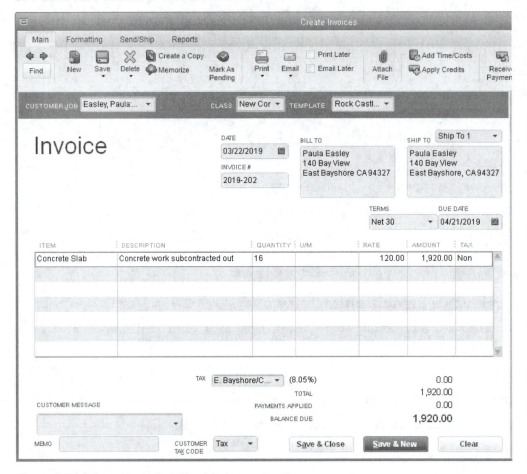

Figure 9-24 Subcontracted work added to an invoice

Recording Time

Time tracking in QuickBooks is easy to use and yet it can streamline bookkeeping for companies that provide time-based services to customers or pay employees hourly wages through QuickBooks Payroll. If you enter time in QuickBooks timesheets, you can flag that time as billable so you can easily add it to customer invoices just as you do other billable costs.

With QuickBooks time tracking, you can record time worked for each employee, subcontractor, partner, or owner and assign that time to customers, jobs, and classes. Once you do that, you can create invoices for billable time and calculate paychecks for hourly wages. This section explains how to set up time tracking, record time, and use it to create invoices. (Chapter 10, Setting Up Payroll, and Chapter 11, Processing Payroll, explain how to handle time worked in payroll.)

Activating Time Tracking in QuickBooks

The first thing you need to do is turn on the time tracking feature. Although it's already turned on in the sample file, this section shows you the steps:

1. On the *Edit* menu, choose *Preferences*.

2. Click the *Time & Expenses* category, and then click the *Company Preferences* tab (Figure 9-25).

3. If necessary, select the *Do You Track Time? Yes* option.

4. Click *OK* to save the setting.

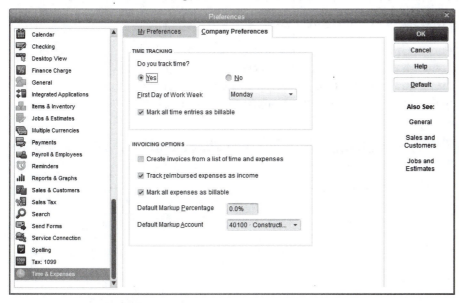

Figure 9-25 Time & Expenses Company Preferences tab

Filling In Timesheets

In QuickBooks, you can enter time using the *Weekly Timesheet* window or *Time/Enter Single Activity* window. If you're recording time for multiple days, customers, jobs, or tasks, the *Weekly Timesheet* is your best choice. Each line in the timesheet represents a unique activity: it uses the same customer or job, *Service* item, class, payroll item if it's for hourly wages, and even the same note. For example, you might record an activity for a subcontractor who is performing work that you'll bill to a customer.

> Note: If you're tracking your own time, the *Time/Enter Single Activity* window includes a stopwatch feature, so you can track how much time you spend on tasks.

Computer Practice

To record time in a weekly timesheet, follow these steps:

1. On the *Home Page*, click the *Enter Time* icon in the *Employees* section, and then choose *Use Weekly Timesheet*.

2. In the *Name* field, choose the name of the person whose time you want to record, in this example, *Gregg O. Schneider*.

   If you need to record the same activities and time for several people, at the top of the *Name* drop-down list, choose *Multiple Names (Payroll)* or *Multiple names (Non-payroll)*.

Note: You can use this same process to record billable time performed by partners or owners. Partners and owners typically take a draw from the company instead of being paid through payroll. If that's the case, you create an *Other Names* record for the partner or owner. Then you can record their time and add it to customer invoices. QuickBooks obtains the rate to charge from the *Service* item record.

3. Click the *Calendar* icon, and then click any day within the week that you want to record, in this example, *March 12, 2019.*

   QuickBooks sets the week to the one that contains the date you chose.

4. Fill in the timesheet rows, as shown in Figure 9-26.

   Similar to recording other types of billable costs, you can make time billable to a customer or job by choosing the customer or job in the *Customer:Job* cell and then turning on the activity's *Billable* checkmark in the rightmost column. If you aren't going to invoice the customer for the time, for example, for time that exceeds the hours the customer approved, keep the *Billable?* checkbox turned off.

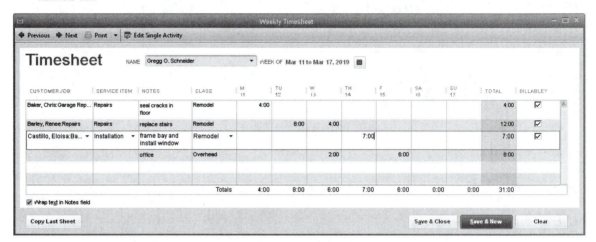

Figure 9-26 Weekly Timesheet

5. Click *Save & Close* to save the timesheet.

Note: If you use timesheets to generate paychecks, record all of the time worked for each employee, including non-billable time, such as administrative work, vacation, and sick time.

Printing Timesheets

If you need copies of timesheets, you can print them or save them to PDF format.

Computer Practice

To print timesheets, follow these steps:

1. On the *File* menu, choose *Print Forms,* and then choose *Timesheets.*

2. In the *Select Timesheets to Print* dialog box's *Dated* and *thru* fields, choose the date range for the timesheets you want to print (Figure 9-27).

3. Select the *Print full activity notes* option at the bottom of the dialog box.

4. Click *OK*.

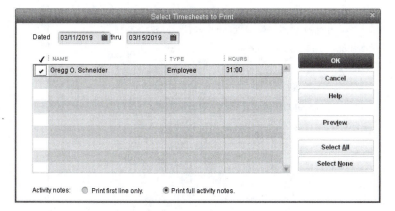

Figure 9-27 Select timesheets to print

Invoicing Billable Time

Invoicing customers for billable time works in the same way as invoicing for other billable costs. This section shows you how to add billable time to an invoice.

Computer Practice

To add billable time to an invoice, follow these steps:

1. On the *Home Page*, click the *Create Invoices* icon or press *Ctrl+I*.

2. In the *Create Invoices* window's *Customer:Job* field, choose the customer you want to invoice, in this example, *Barley, Renee:Repairs*.

3. In the *Billable Time/Costs* dialog box that appears, click *OK* to proceed to selecting outstanding billable time and costs.

4. Turn on the checkmark cells for the time you want to add to the invoice, as shown in Figure 9-28.

   To select all the time in the table, click the *Select All* button above the table.

   If you click the *Options* button, the *Options for Transferring Billable Time* dialog box opens. By default, QuickBooks chooses the option to combine activities that use the same service item and rate. However, you can tell the program to include each activity in the timesheet on a separate line on the invoice.

5. Click *OK* to add the selected time to the invoice, as shown in Figure 9-29.

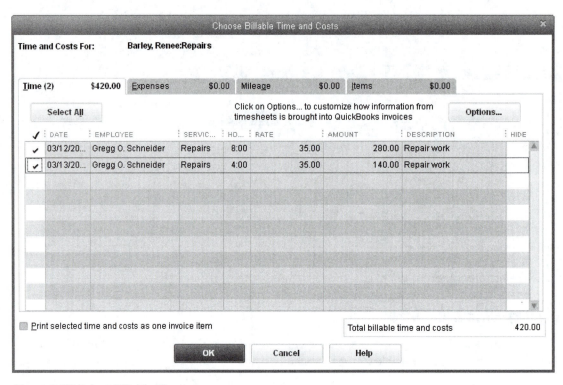

Figure 9-28 Select Billable Time

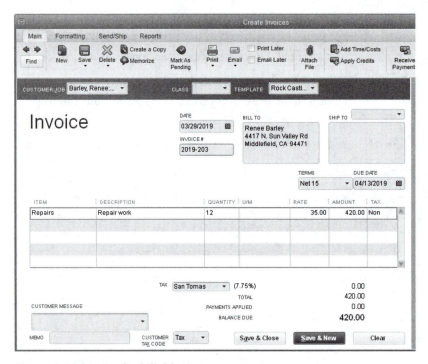

Figure 9-29 Invoice for billable time

Changing Activities Back to Billable

When you add time or other billable items to an invoice, QuickBooks changes the entries' status to *Billed*. (The icon in the *Billable?* cell changes from a checkmark to a small gray invoice icon, as shown in Figure 9-30.) If you void or delete an invoice that contains billable time or other costs, the program doesn't change those items' statuses back to *Unbilled*.

Here are the steps to change time activities back to *Unbilled*:

1. Open the timesheet with the activities you want to change.

2. Click an activity's *Billable?* cell.

   QuickBooks changes the icon in the *Billable?* cell back to a checkmark to indicate its status has been changed to *Unbilled*.

3. In the message box that tells you that the row has already been billed, click *Yes* to make the activity billable.

4. Click *Save & Close* to save your changes and close the *Weekly Timesheet* window.

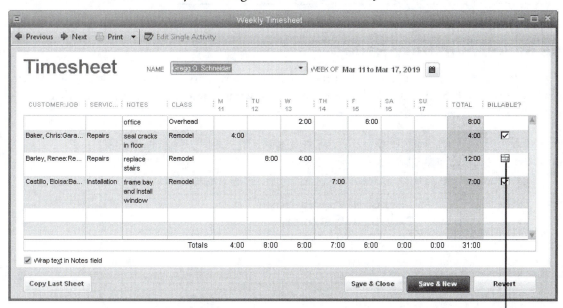

This icon represents billed status

Figure 9-30 The icon for Billed status

Billable Time and Costs Reports

To make the profit you deserve, it's important to invoice for all your billable time and costs. This section describes a few QuickBooks features to help you review billable time and costs—and identify the ones that are unbilled.

Finding Unbilled Costs by Job

The *Unbilled Costs by Job* report includes billable expenses and items that you haven't yet added to invoices. However, it doesn't include unbilled time.

Computer Practice

To run the *Unbilled Costs by Job* report, follow these steps:

1. On the *Reports* menu, choose *Jobs, Time & Mileage*, then choose *Unbilled Costs by Job*.

2. In the *From* and *To* fields for this example, fill in *3/1/2019* and *3/31/2109*, respectively.

   This report shows billable expenses and items that you haven't yet added to invoices (Figure 9-31).

3. When you are finished reviewing the report, close it.

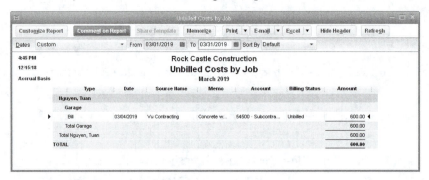

Figure 9-31 Unbilled Cost by Job report

Time by Job Summary Report

The *Time by Job Summary* report shows the time assigned to jobs for the date range you specify, which is helpful for reviewing the time worked on each job, as shown in Figure 9-32. You can modify the report to show both billed and unbilled time.

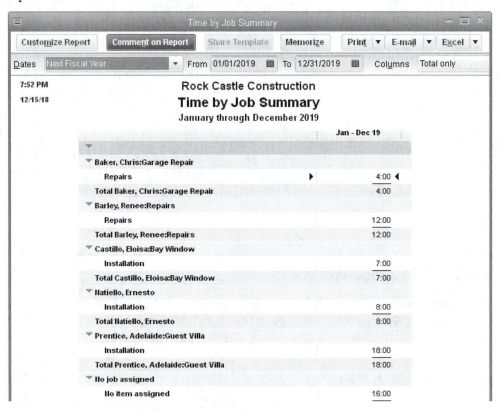

Figure 9-32 The Time by Job Summary report

Here are the steps to customizing this report to show billed and unbilled time:

1. On the *Reports* menu, choose *Jobs, Time & Mileage*, and then choose *Time by Job Summary*. In the report's window, click the *Customize Report* button to open the *Modify Report* dialog box.

2. In the *Add subcolumns for* section at the bottom of the dialog box, turn on the *Billed* and *Unbilled* checkboxes (Figure 9-33), and then click *OK*.

   When you do that, columns for *Billed* and *Unbilled* time appear, as shown in Figure 9-34.

3. When you are finished viewing the report, close it.

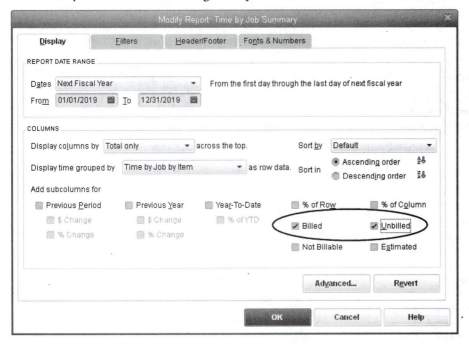

Figure 9-33 Modify Report window

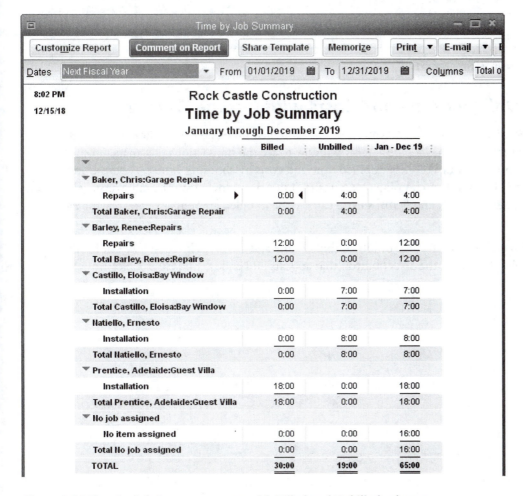

Figure 9-34 Time by Job Summary report with Billed and Unbilled columns

Time by Name Report

The *Time by Name* report summarizes the hours worked by each employee, owner, or partner, broken down by customer or job, as shown in Figure 9-35. On the *Reports* menu, choose *Jobs, Time & Mileage*, and then choose *Time by Name*.

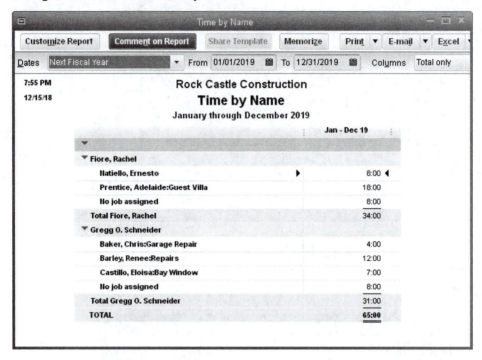

Figure 9-35 Time by Name report

Viewing Unbilled Time and Costs with Income Tracker

In QuickBooks 2015, *Income Tracker* can show your unbilled time and costs. Click the *Time & Expenses* bar at the top of the *Income Tracker* window to see the transactions that make up the bar's total (Figure 9-36). You can also view unbilled time and costs by choosing *Time & Expenses* in the *Type* drop-down list, and then choosing *Open* in the *Status* drop-down list. The table displays columns for *Time, Expenses, Mileage*, and *Items*, so you can see the unbilled amounts by category for each customer and job.

To create an invoice for a customer's or job's unbilled time and costs, click the *Action* cell for that customer or job. Then, click the *Select* button that appears and choose *Choose Billables* from the drop-down menu.

2. Or, choose Time & Expenses in this drop-down list

1. Click this bar to filter the table to show billable time and costs

Choose Open to filter for unbilled time and costs

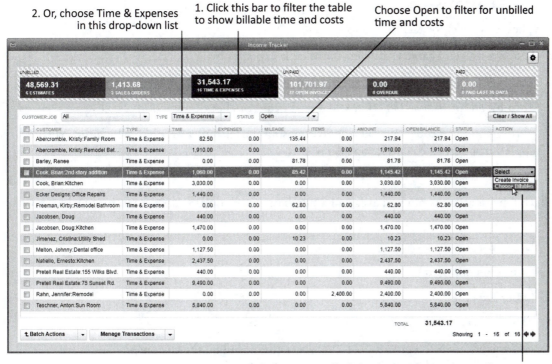

Click the Action cell, click Select, and then choose Choose Billables to create an invoice for unbilled time and costs.

Figure 9-36 Unbilled time and costs in Income Tracker

Review Questions

Select the best answer(s) for each of the following:

1. In QuickBooks, you charge customers for billable expenses by:

    a) Turning on the *Billable?* checkbox in a bill's line item row.

    b) Turning on the *Billable?* checkbox in a credit card or check transaction.

    c) Turning on the *Billable?* checkbox and choosing the customer or job to which the expense applies in a purchase transaction's expense row.

    d) None of the above.

2. Which type of account can you assign in a purchase transaction's *Expenses* tab for billable expenses?

    a) Expense

    b) Cost of Goods Sold

    c) Other Expense

    d) All the above

3. How do you assign expenses to a *Customer:Job* without billing the customer?

    a) In the expense row, choose the *Customer:Job* and turn off the *Billable?* checkmark.

    b) Assign the *Customer:Job* to the purchase transaction. Then, in the customer invoice, delete the expense.

    c) Enter the *Customer:Job* in the *Memo* field.

    d) a or b.

4. Which types of billable expenses can you add to invoices?

    a) Items

    b) Expenses

    c) Time

    d) Mileage

5. In an invoice, you can automatically mark up billable expenses using the *Markup Account* option on which tab of the *Choose Billable Time and Costs* window?

    a) *Items* tab

    b) *Expenses* tab

    c) *Time* tab

    d) All of the above

Billable Time and Costs Exercise 1

Applying Your Knowledge

Restore the sample file, sample_product-based business 2015 (Portable).QBM. (Or, if you are using QuickBooks 2014, restore sample_product-based business 2014 (Portable).QBM.)

1. Create a *Non-inventory Part* item that you can use for billable products, using the data in the following table:

Table 9-1 Non-inventory Part item for billable products

Field	Data
Item Type	Non-inventory Part
Item Name	Custom-made entry door
Description on Purchase Transactions	Custom-made oak entry door – order #
Description on Sales Transactions	Custom-made oak entry door – order #
Cost	$0
Sale Price	$0
Expense Account	Job Expenses: Job Materials
Tax Code	Tax
Income Account	Materials Income

2. Create a purchase order for custom-made entry doors using the data in the following table:

Table 9-2 Purchase order for billable entry doors

Field	Data
Vendor	Miller, Dan
Class	Remodel
Date	3/25/2019
P.O. No.	2019-101
Item	Custom-made entry door
Description	Custom-made oak entry door – order #2019-101
Qty	2
Rate	$750
Customer	Bauman, Mark: Home Remodel
Memo	Entry door PO #2019-101

3. Record bill # *12206* on *4/2/2019* from *Dan Miller* for the purchase order.

   Use *P.O. No. 2019-101*, Customer:Job: *Bauman, Mark: Home Remodel*, Class: *Remodel*, Memo: *Custom oak front entry doors Order #2019-101*. Make the item billable.

4. Create an invoice # *2019-106* dated *4/8/2019* for *Mark Bauman: Home Remodel* for the custom doors.

   Use *QuickMath* to mark up the doors by *20%*. Class is *Remodel*.

   Invoice total is *$1,939.50*.

Billable Time and Costs Exercise 2 (Advanced)

Applying Your Knowledge

Restore the sample file, sample_product-based business 2015 (Portable).QBM. (Or, if you are using QuickBooks 2014, restore sample_product-based business 2014 (Portable).QBM.)

1. Create an *Other Charge* item for billable expenses using the data in the following table:

Table 9-3 Other Charge item for billable expenses

Field	Data
Item Type	Other Charge
Item Name	Delivery and install
Description on Purchase Transactions	Delivery and installation charges
Description on Sales Transactions	Delivery and installation charges
Cost	$150
Sale Price	$200
Expense Account	Job Expenses: Subcontractors
Tax Code	Non
Income Account	Subcontracted Labor Income

2. Create a *Non-inventory Part* item for a billable product using the data in the following table:

Table 9-4 Non-inventory Part item for billable product

Field	Data
Item Type	Non-inventory Part
Item Name	Outdoor pizza oven
Description on Purchase Transactions	Propane outdoor pizza oven – order #
Description on Sales Transactions	Propane outdoor pizza oven – order #
Cost	$1,400
Sale Price	$2,000
Expense Account	Job Expenses: Job Materials
Tax Code	Tax
Income Account	Materials Income

3. Create a purchase order using the data in the following table:

Table 9-5 Purchase order for billable product

Field	Data
Vendor	McClain Appliances
Class	Remodel
Date	3/25/2019
P.O. No.	2019-101
Item	Outdoor pizza oven
Description	Propane outdoor pizza oven – order #2019-101
Qty	1
Customer	Prentice, Adelaide: Guest Villa
Memo	Outdoor pizza oven PO #2019-101

4. Record bill # *32196* on *3/28/2019* from *McClain Appliances* for the purchase order.

   Use P.O. No. *2019-101*, Customer:Job: *Prentice, Adelaide: Guest Villa*, Class: *Remodel*, Memo: *Outdoor pizza oven Order #2019-101*. Make the item billable.

   Add the *Delivery and install* charge to the bill and make it billable to the customer.

5. A new partner, *Rachel Fiore*, has joined Rock Castle Construction. Add her to the *Other Names* list.

6. Use the *Weekly Timesheet* to record Rachel's hours for the week of *April 15 – 19, 2019* using the hours in the following table:

Table 9-6 Hours for week of April 15-19, 2019

Day	Hours	Customer:Job	Item	Notes	Class	Billable
4/15/2019	6	Prentice, Adelaide: Guest Villa	Installation labor	Prep patio area	Remodel	Yes
4/16/2019	8	Prentice, Adelaide: Guest Villa	Installation labor	Stone work around oven	Remodel	Yes
4/17/2019	4	Prentice, Adelaide: Guest Villa	Installation labor	Stone work around oven	Remodel	Yes
4/18/2019	8	Natiello, Ernesto	Installation labor	Patio	Remodel	Yes
4/19/2019	8				Overhead	No

7. Print the *Unbilled Costs by Job* report for *3/1/2019* to *4/30/2019*.

8. Create invoice # *2019-116* dated *4/25/2019* for the *Prentice, Adelaide: Guest Villa* job.

   Use the *Rock Castle Invoice* template, Class: *Remodel*. Memo: *Outdoor pizza oven order #2019-101*. Select all open billable items for this job (including older entries).

9. Print the invoice.

10. Print the *Profit and Loss by Job* report for *March 1, 2019* to *April 30, 2019*.

x

Chapter 10
Payroll Setup

Topics

This chapter covers the following topics:

- QuickBooks Payroll Services

- The QuickBooks Payroll Setup Process

- Payroll Accounts

- Payroll Items

- Using the Payroll Setup Interview

- Setting up Employee Defaults

In this chapter, you'll learn how to set up payroll in QuickBooks. (You'll learn how to run payroll in Chapter 11.) To run payroll and track payroll amounts, you need to set up payroll accounts, payroll items, and employees. You'll learn how to set up all these elements in this chapter.

> Note: Intuit sometimes modifies its payroll service features between QuickBooks releases, so the material in this chapter may differ from what you see in your version of Quick-Books.

> Note: For the computer practice in this chapter, restore the sample file, sample_product-based business 2015 (Portable).QBM. Or, if you are using QuickBooks 2014, restore sample_product-based business 2014 (Portable).QBM. Because you will continue to use this file in Chapter 11, when you restore the file, be sure to name it payroll_chapterwork. qbw.

QuickBooks Payroll Services

Intuit offers several payroll services. Here's what each one does:

- With **Basic Payroll**, you set up everything at the beginning. When you run payroll, you enter hours or payroll amounts, and QuickBooks uses its tax tables to calculate payroll taxes and deductions. With this service, you can run reports to get the information you need to fill out the federal and state tax forms you have to file. After you run payroll, you print the paychecks QuickBooks creates (or use direct deposit), make tax deposits, and file your payroll tax forms.

> Tip: Intuit payroll services offer free phone, chat, and email support to help you set up your payroll.

- **Enhanced Payroll** includes up-to-date tax forms so it can prepare federal *and* state payroll forms with most of the tax-form information already filled in. With this service, you can make your tax deposits and file your tax forms electronically from within QuickBooks. It sends you email reminders when payroll, forms, and payroll taxes are due. It also notifies you via email when payroll is direct deposited, taxes have been paid, and tax authorities have accepted your tax forms. At the same, the *Payroll Center* in QuickBooks reminds you when payroll and payroll taxes are due, and shows the status of direct deposit payments, electronic tax payments, and tax forms you submit through QuickBooks. It also archives your tax forms as PDFs on your desktop.

- **Full Service Payroll** is a payroll service in which Intuit takes care of everything for you. It sets up payroll. (If you previously used another payroll service, Full Service Payroll transfers that data into your Intuit payroll records.) It handles federal and state payroll tax deposits, files required tax reports, and prepares W-2 and W-3 forms at the end of the year. In addition, Intuit guarantees that your payroll and payroll tax deposits and filings will be accurate and on time, as long as you send Intuit the correct data when you're supposed to.

> Note: Intuit Online Payroll offers many of the same features as Enhanced Payroll. Because you access it online, you don't need QuickBooks to use it. This chapter does not cover this service.

To learn more about Intuit's various payroll services, on the *Employees* menu, choose *Payroll*, and then choose *Learn About Payroll Options* on the submenu.

The QuickBooks Payroll Setup Process

To ensure that your payroll works the way you want, you need to set up QuickBooks payroll features properly. Here is an overview of payroll setup:

1. Gather your employee information, such as names, addresses, Social Security numbers, and W-4 information.

> Note: When you hire employees, they must fill out W-4 forms with their name, address, Social Security number, and withholding information. To learn about the forms required by the IRS and states, go to payroll.intuit.com/support/compliance.

2. Turn on QuickBooks payroll (in the *Preferences* dialog box).

3. Set up payroll accounts, such as Gross Wages, Payroll Tax Expense, and Payroll Tax Liabilities.

4. Enable your company file to process payroll by signing up for an Intuit payroll service or enabling it manually.

5. Use *QuickBooks Payroll Setup* to set up payroll items, vendors, employee records, and employee defaults. You can also record year-to-date payroll amounts if you are setting up payroll in Quick-Books in the middle of a year.

6. Create any additional payroll items in the *Payroll Item List*.

7. If necessary, edit payroll items to use the correct vendors and accounts.

8. If you're setting up payroll mid-year, enter year-to-date information for your additional payroll items and liability payments.

9. Review your payroll accounts, payroll items, payroll-related vendors, and employee setup.

10. Use the *Payroll Checkup* wizard (not covered in this chapter) to check for issues. Compare your QuickBooks payroll reports and setup with reports from your accountant or prior payroll service's reports.

Payroll Accounts

You need *some* accounts for payroll in your chart of accounts, but you don't need to add accounts or subaccounts for every aspect of payroll. Payroll items (described in the next section) help you track payroll details. Figure 10-1 and Figure 10-2 show the payroll accounts that are already set up in your practice file. You'll see how these accounts are used throughout this chapter.

Figure 10-1 Payroll liability accounts

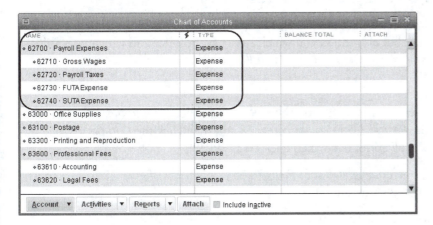

Figure 10-2 Payroll expense accounts

Payroll Items

Similar to the items you use to track income and business expenses, *Payroll Items* track things like employee compensation, deductions, additions, and employer-paid expenses. For example, you might have *Payroll Items* for salary, wages, commissions, benefits, taxes, retirement plans, and so on—basically, all the items you see on paychecks.

Payroll Items are associated with accounts in your chart of accounts. That means when you run payroll, QuickBooks posts your payroll expenses and liabilities to the correct accounts. You can see all your

Payroll Items by opening the *Payroll Item List*. To do that, on the *Lists* menu, choose *Payroll Item List*. Figure 10-3 shows examples of *Payroll Items*.

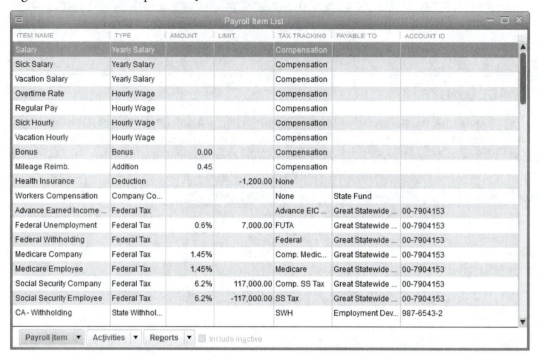

ITEM NAME	TYPE	AMOUNT	LIMIT	TAX TRACKING	PAYABLE TO	ACCOUNT ID
Salary	Yearly Salary			Compensation		
Sick Salary	Yearly Salary			Compensation		
Vacation Salary	Yearly Salary			Compensation		
Overtime Rate	Hourly Wage			Compensation		
Regular Pay	Hourly Wage			Compensation		
Sick Hourly	Hourly Wage			Compensation		
Vacation Hourly	Hourly Wage			Compensation		
Bonus	Bonus	0.00		Compensation		
Mileage Reimb.	Addition	0.45		Compensation		
Health Insurance	Deduction		-1,200.00	None		
Workers Compensation	Company Co...			None	State Fund	
Advance Earned Income ...	Federal Tax			Advance EIC ...	Great Statewide ...	00-7904153
Federal Unemployment	Federal Tax	0.6%	7,000.00	FUTA	Great Statewide ...	00-7904153
Federal Withholding	Federal Tax			Federal	Great Statewide ...	00-7904153
Medicare Company	Federal Tax	1.45%		Comp. Medic...	Great Statewide ...	00-7904153
Medicare Employee	Federal Tax	1.45%		Medicare	Great Statewide ...	00-7904153
Social Security Company	Federal Tax	6.2%	117,000.00	Comp. SS Tax	Great Statewide ...	00-7904153
Social Security Employee	Federal Tax	6.2%	-117,000.00	SS Tax	Great Statewide ...	00-7904153
CA - Withholding	State Withhol...			SWH	Employment Dev...	987-6543-2

Payroll Item ▼   Activities ▼   Reports ▼   ☐ Include inactive

Figure 10-3 Payroll Item List

The QuickBooks Payroll Setup Interview

QuickBooks Payroll Setup guides you through all the steps to setting up payroll. It not only helps you set up your *Payroll Items* correctly, but also shows you which steps are complete and which ones still remain. This section shows you how to use *QuickBooks Payroll Setup*.

Computer Practice

1. If payroll isn't activated in your company file, on the *Edit* menu, choose *Preferences*. In the *Preferences* dialog box, click the *Payroll & Employees* category, and then click the *Company Preferences* tab. Select the *Full payroll* option, and then click *OK*.

2. Once payroll is turned on, open the *QuickBooks Payroll Setup* interview (Figure 10-4) by choosing *Payroll Setup* on the *Employees* menu.

   The *Welcome to QuickBooks Payroll Setup* screen appears.

3. Click *Continue* to proceed to *Company Setup*, which is described in the following sections.

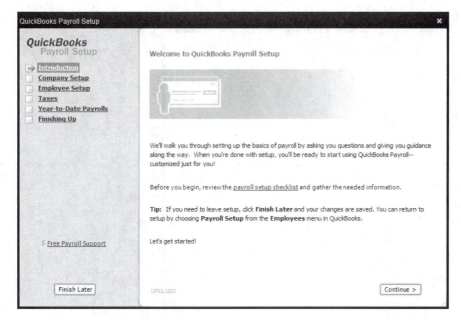

Figure 10-4 QuickBooks Payroll Setup wizard

Setting up Compensation Payroll Items

This section covers setting up compensation items, such as hourly wages, salary, bonuses, and commissions.

Computer Practice

To create a new compensation item, do the following:

1. On the *Set up your company compensation and benefits* page, click *Continue*.

   The *Review your Compensation list* screen displays compensation items that have already been added, such as *Overtime Rate*, *Regular Pay*, *Salary*, *Bonus*, and *Mileage reimb*.

2. To create an additional compensation item, for commission, in this example, click the *Add New* button below the list.

3. In the *Add New* dialog box's *Other compensation* section (Figure 10-5), turn on the *Commission* checkbox, and then click *Next*.

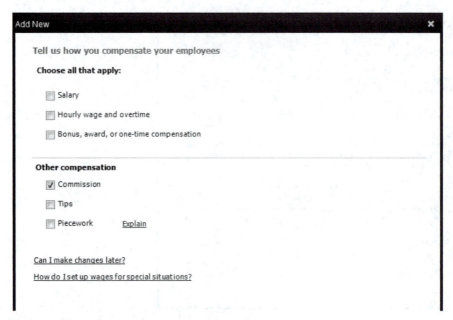

Figure 10-5 Add new compensation item

4. On the *Tell us about commissions* screen (Figure 10-6), select the *Percentage of sales (or other amount)* option, and then click *Finish*.

    Back in the *Review your Compensation list* screen, you can see the Commission item you just added, as shown in Figure 10-7.

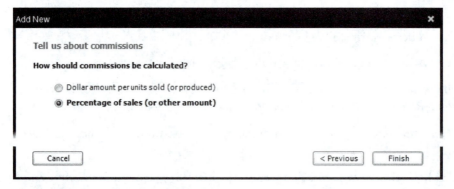

Figure 10-6 Commission calculation

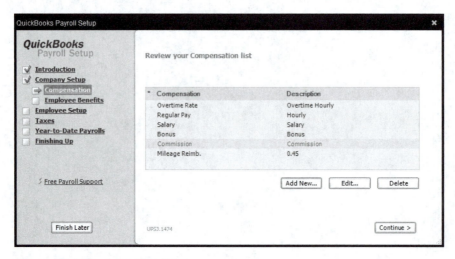

Figure 10-7 Compensation list

You can also edit existing compensation items. To practice doing this, follow these steps:

1. In the *Review your Compensation list* screen, select the *Regular Pay* item, and then click the *Edit* button below the table.

   The *Edit: Hourly* dialog box opens.

2. In the *Show on paychecks as* field, type the name you want to see on paychecks, in this example, *Hourly Wage* (see Figure 10-8).

3. In the *Account name* drop-down list, choose the account you want to use to track this compensation. In this example, keep *Payroll Expenses: Gross Wages*.

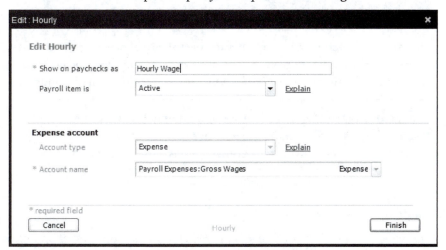

Figure 10-8

4. Click *Finish*.

5. Click *Continue* to proceed to the *Employee Benefits* section.

You'll learn how to set up and edits benefits in the next several sections.

Health Insurance Deduction

When you click *Continue* in the *Compensation* category, the interview switches to the *Employee Benefits* category. In this section, you set up the benefits you offer your employees, such as health insurance, retirement benefits, and so on, as shown in Figure 10-9. You can also set up additions and deductions that affect employees' gross income, such as expense reimbursements, dues, and wage garnishments.

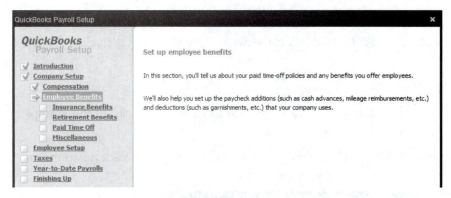

Figure 10-9 Set up employee benefits

There are three options for who pays for benefits: the company can cover the total expense; the company and employee share the expense; or the employee pays the entire expense. If you share the expense with employees or they pay the entire amount, you use a *Deduction* item to track the benefit funds.

> Note: If your company pays for a benefit, you need a payroll item only if you need to include benefits on employees' W-2s. If you aren't sure whether you need to set up a payroll item for a company-paid benefit, ask your accountant or tax professional.

Computer Practice

To set up an insurance benefit, follow these steps:

1. To display the *Review your Insurance Benefits list* screen, either click *Continue* on the *Set up employee benefits* screen or click the *Insurance Benefits* category on the left side of the dialog box.

2. Click the *Add New* button.

3. To set up a health insurance benefit, turn on the *Health Insurance* checkbox (see Figure 10-10), and then click *Next*.

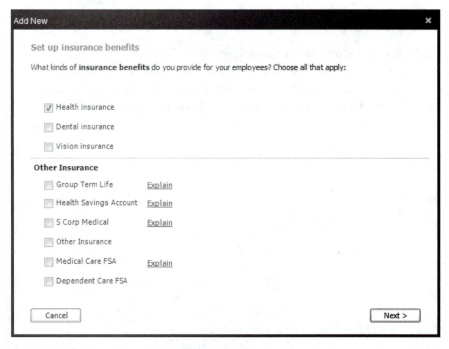

Figure 10-10 Set up insurance benefits window

4. On the *How is Health Insurance paid?* screen (Figure 10-11), select the *Both the employee and company pay portions* option. Click *Next*.

    In this example, keep the *Payment is deducted after taxes* option selected.

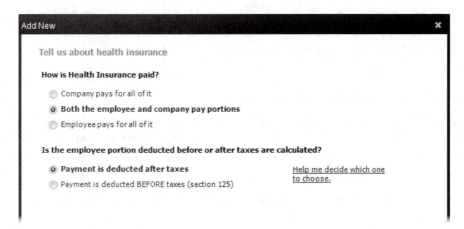

Figure 10-11 Setting up a health insurance deduction

5. On the *Set up the payment schedule for health insurance* screen (Figure 10-12), keep the fields as they are. Make sure the *I don't need a regular payment schedule* option is selected, and then click *Finish*.

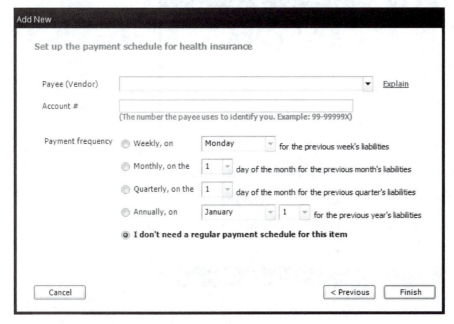

Figure 10-12 Health insurance payment schedule

The *Review your Insurance Benefits list* screen reappears. Two new Health Insurance items appear on the list (Figure 10-13): *Health Insurance (company paid)* represents the portion that the company pays and *Health Insurance (taxable)* is what the employee pays.

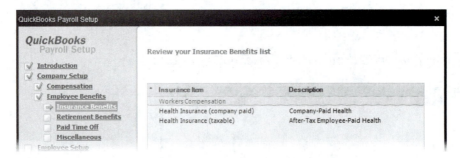

Figure 10-13 Insurance Benefits list with health insurance added

In this example, the employer pays the health insurance bill and assigns it to the *Health Insurance* expense account. Then, the employer deducts the employee's portion from the employee's paycheck. With this approach, you can delete the *Health Insurance (company paid)* item, because the employer's portion doesn't go through payroll.

6. To delete *Health Insurance (company paid)*, select it, and then click *Delete*. In the *Delete Payroll Item* message box, click *Yes*.

7. To edit the *Health Insurance (taxable)* item, select it, and then click the *Edit* button.

8. In the *Show on paychecks as* field (see Figure 10-14), type *Medical Insurance*, and then click *Next*.

Figure 10-14 After-Tax Employee-Paid Health benefit

9. In the *Edit the payment schedule for After-Tax Employee-Paid Health* screen, click *Next*.

10. In the *Account type* field, choose *Expense* from the drop-down list.

11. In the *Account name* field, choose *Insurance: Less Employee Portion – Health* (shown in Figure 10-15). Click *Next* to continue.

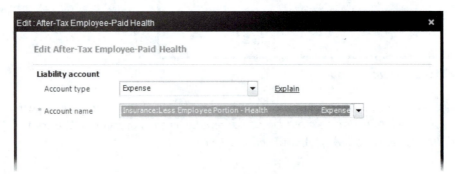

Figure 10-15 Change account type and name

12. Click *Next* to skip the *Tell us which taxes apply to this item* screen.

13. On the *Tell us how to calculate the amount* screen (Figure 10-16), in the *Default rate* field, type the amount the employee pays, in this example, *100.00*, and then click *Finish*.

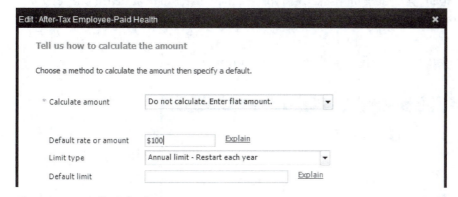

Figure 10-16 Edit default rate

14. Back in the *Review your Insurance Benefits list* screen, click *Continue* to proceed to the *Retirement Benefits* section.

401(k) Employee Deduction and Company Match Items

When you click *Continue* in the *Employee Benefits* category, the interview moves to the *Retirement Benefits* section, where you can set up benefits for the retirement plan that your company offers. This section describes how you set up payroll items for employer and employee contributions to a 401(k) plan.

Computer Practice

To set up 401(k) benefits, follow these steps:

1. If the *Review your Retirement Benefits list* screen isn't visible, click the *Retirement Benefits* category on the dialog box's left.

2. Click *Add New*.

3. On the *Tell us about your company retirement benefits* screen (Figure 10-17), turn on the *401(k) (most common)* checkbox, and then click *Next*.

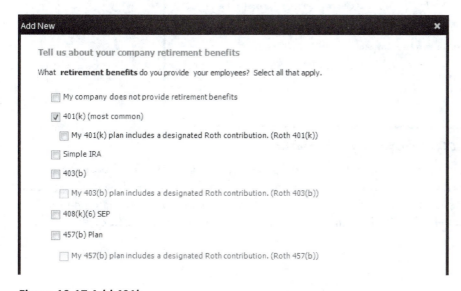

Figure 10-17 Add 401k

4. On the *Set up the payment schedule for 401(k)* screen, click *Finish* to skip the payment schedule.

Back in the *Review your Retirement Benefits list* screen, you see the two retirement items: one for company matching and one for employee's contributions (Figure 10-18). To edit these items, do the following:

1. Select the *401k Co. Match* item, and then click the *Edit* button.

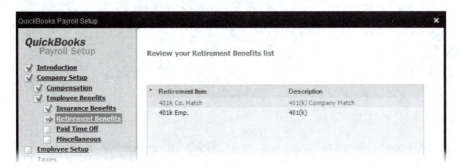

Figure 10-18 401k items

2. In the *Show on Paychecks as* field, type *401k Company Matching*, and then click *Next*.

3. In the *Payee (Vendor)* field, enter the name of the company that handles the 401(k) plan, in this example, type *Great Statewide Bank*, as shown in Figure 10-19. In the *Account #* field, type your account number (*99-12344*), and then click *Next*.

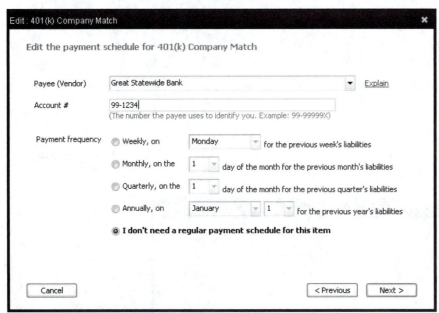

Figure 10-19 Modifying 401k Company Match information

4. In the *Expense account* section's *Account name* drop-down list (Figure 10-20), choose the account you use to track your company's expense for matching, in this example, *Payroll Expenses*. In the *Liability account* section, choose the account you use to hold your company matching funds until you deposit them in the 401(k) plan, in this example, *Payroll Liabilities*. Click *Next*.

Figure 10-20 Choose expense and liability account

5. In the *Tell us which taxes to apply to this item* screen, keep the *Use standard tax settings* option selected, and then click *Next*.

6. On the *Tell us how to calculate the amount* screen, fill in the fields as shown in Figure 10-21, and then click *Finish*.

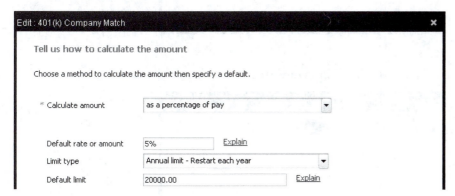

Figure 10-21 Calculating company matching

The *Review your Retirement Benefits list* screen reappears. Now, you can edit the item for employees' 401(k) contributions.

1. Select *401k Emp.*, and then click the *Edit* button.

2. In the *Show on paychecks as* field, type *401k Deduction* (shown in Figure 10-22), and then click *Next*.

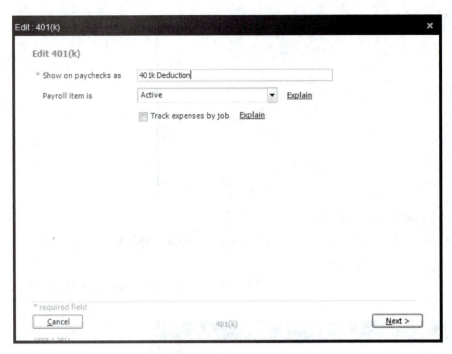

Figure 10-22 Edit 401k name

3. Enter the schedule information displayed in Figure 10-23, and then click *Next*.

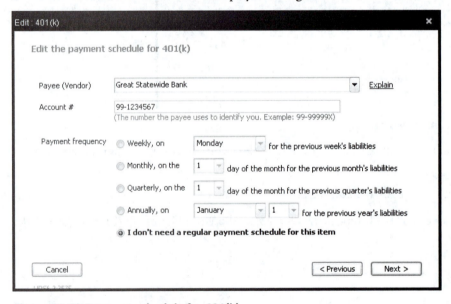

Figure 10-23 Payment schedule for 401(k)

4. In the *Liability account* section's *Account name* field (Figure 10-24), choose the account you use to hold employee 401(k) contributions until you deposit them in the 401(k) plan, in this example, *Payroll Liabilities*. Click *Next*.

Figure 10-24 Account type and name

5. In the *Tell us which taxes apply to this item* screen, keep the *Tax tracking type* and the *Use standard settings* option as they are, and then click *Next*.

6. On the *Tell us how to calculate the amount* screen, fill in the information shown in Figure 10-25. Click *Finish*.

   The wizard takes you back to the *Review your Retirement Benefits list* screen where the edited retirement items appear.

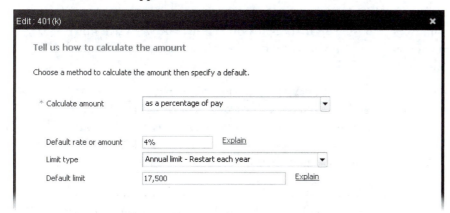

Figure 10-25 Settings for calculating 401k contribution

7. Click *Continue* to proceed to the *Paid Time Off* category.

> Note: You can set up separate *Deduction* items for each employee to track 401(k) deductions. To distinguish between them, enter the employee's account number in the *Enter the number that identifies you to agency* field. Another option is to use one Deduction item and send your *Payroll Summary* report and 401(k) payment to the 401(k) administrator. With this option, filter the *Payroll Summary* report to show only the 401(k) payroll items. You can add the employee's account number to the report by commenting on the report (see page 293 to learn about this 2015 feature) or simply by hand-writing the accounts on a hard copy.

Paid Time Off Payroll Items

When you click *Continue* in the *Retirement Benefits* category (or click the *Paid Time Off* category), the interview moves to the *Paid Time Off* section, where you can set up paid time off benefits. This section describes how you set up these payroll items.

Computer Practice

To set up payroll items for paid time off, follow these steps:

1. In the *Review your Paid Time Off list* screen, click the *Add New* button.

    The interview adds *Hourly Vacation* and *Salary Vacation*, as shown in Figure 10-26.

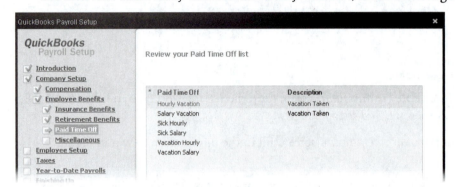

Figure 10-26 Paid time off payroll items

> Note: If you offer employees paid time off that doesn't differentiate between sick time and vacation, you can choose either *Paid sick time off* or *Paid vacation time off* to track this combined paid time off.
>
> To change what appears on paychecks and paystubs, on the *Edit* menu, choose *Preferences*, click the *Payroll* category, and then click the *Company Preferences* tab. Click the *Pay Stub & Voucher Printing* button. In the appropriate *Print as* field, type *Paid Time Off*. Turn off the checkbox for the paid time off category you aren't using. Click *OK* to close the *Payroll Printing Preferences* dialog box, and click *OK* again to close the *Preferences* dialog box.

2. Select *Salary Vacation*, and then click the *Edit* button. Fill in the fields as shown in Figure 10-27, and then click *Finish*.

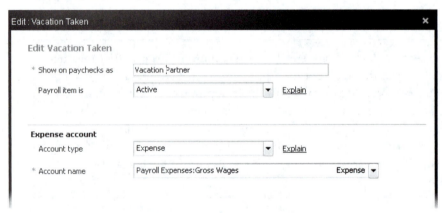

Figure 10-27 Paid time off settings

3. Select *Hourly Vacation*, and then click the *Delete* button.

4. Instead of clicking *Continue* to move to additions and deductions, click the *Employee Setup* category on the dialog box's left to set up your employees.

Setting Up Employees

You need to create an employee record for each person who will receive a W-2 from your company. This section shows how to do this. To set up employees, you can click *Continue* from the paid time off section or you can click the *Employee Setup* category on the dialog box's left.

Computer Practice

To create a new employee record, follow these steps:

1. On the *Set up your employees* screen, click *Continue*.

2. Click the *Add New* button and enter the information shown in Figure 10-28. Click *Next*.

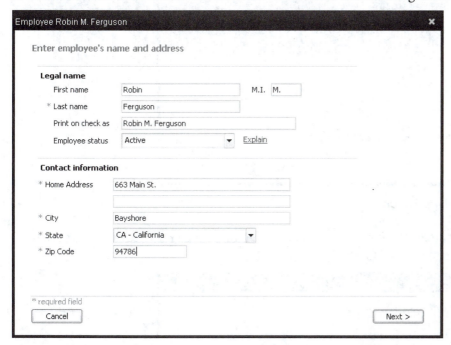

Figure 10-28 Enter employee information

3. On the hiring information screen, enter the information shown in Figure 10-29, and then click *Next*.

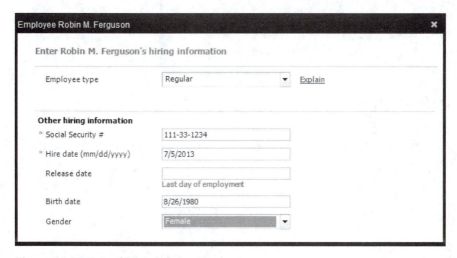

Figure 10-29 Enter hiring information

4. On the *Tell us how you plan to pay <name>* screen, enter the information shown in Figure 10-30. Click *Next*.

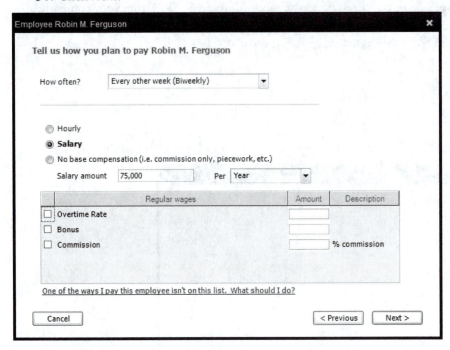

Figure 10-30 Enter salary information

5. On the *Tell us about additional items for <name>* screen, turn on all the checkboxes. Edit the values as shown in Figure 10-31. Click *Next*.

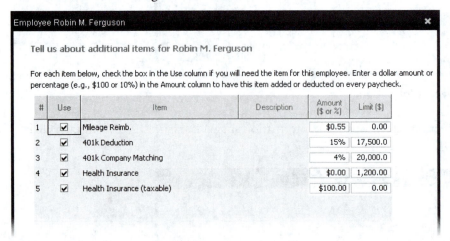

Figure 10-31 Choose benefits for employee

6. On the *How is sick time off calculated for <name>* screen, enter the values shown in Figure 10-32, and then click *Continue*.

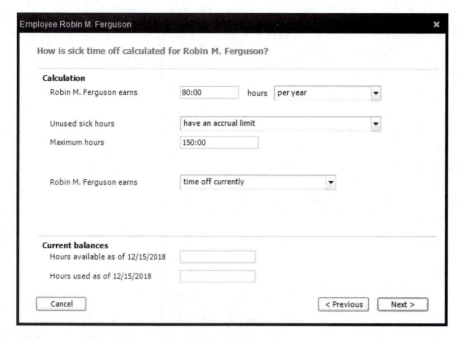

Figure 10-32 Specify how sick time is calculated

7. On the *How is vacation time off calculated for <name>* screen, enter the values shown in Figure 10-33, and then click *Continue*.

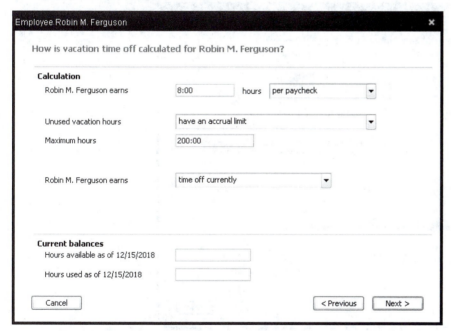

Figure 10-33 Specify how vacation time is calculated

8. Click *Next* to skip the direct deposit window.

9. On the *Tell us where <name> is subject to taxes* screen, keep the default settings, and then click *Next*.

10. On the federal tax information screen, change the *Filing Status* to *Married*, and in the *Allowances* field, type *2*. Click *Next*.

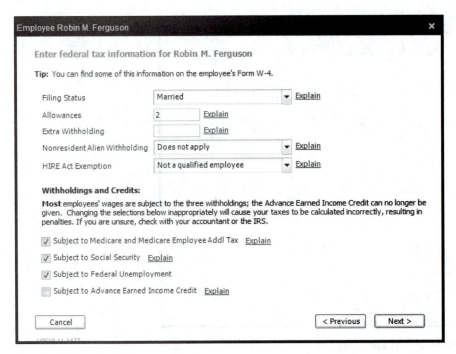

Figure 10-34 Edit federal tax information

11. Enter the state tax information shown in Figure 10-35, and then click *Next*.

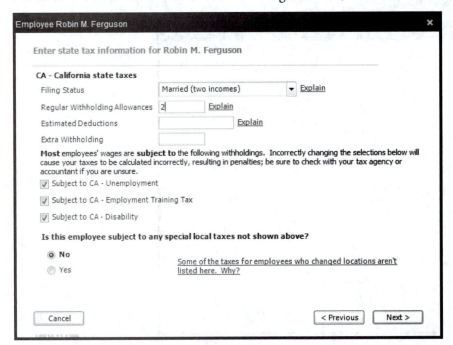

Figure 10-35 Edit state tax information

12. On the *Setup wage plan information for <name>* screen in the *Wage Plan Code* drop-down list, choose *S (State Plan For Both UI and DI)*, and then click *Finish*.

   Back in the *Review your Employee list* screen, the employee appears in the employee list, as show in Figure 10-36.

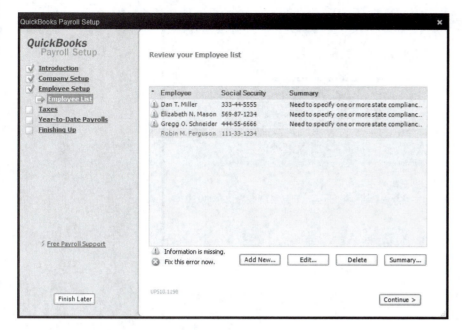

Figure 10-36 Employee list with new employee

13. Click *Continue* to set up payroll tax items.

Setting Up Payroll Tax Items

You need to set up payroll tax items for all the payroll taxes you and your employees must pay. To set up these items, you can click *Continue* from the *Employee Setup* section or you can click the *Taxes* category on the dialog box's left. This section shows you the payroll tax items already set up in the sample file.

Computer Practice

To set up payroll tax items, do the following:

1. On the *Set up your payroll taxes* screen, click *Continue*.

   The federal tax screen lists the federal tax items already added to your payroll setup, as shown in Figure 10-37).

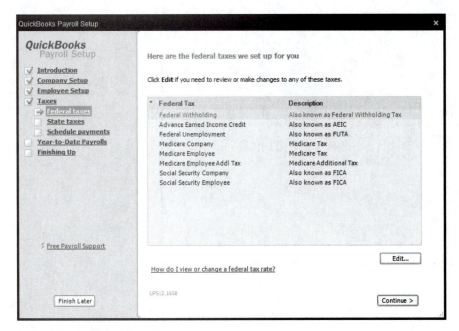

Figure 10-37 Federal tax list

2. Click *Continue*.

    The state tax screen lists the state tax items already added to your payroll setup, as shown in Figure 10-38).

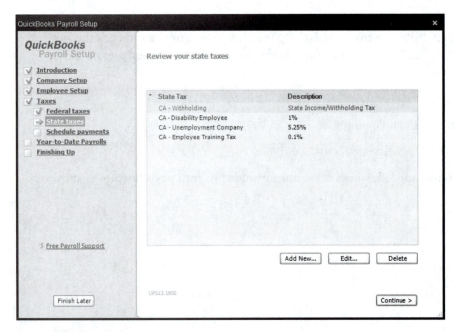

Figure 10-38 State tax list

3. Click *Continue*.

Scheduling Your Tax Payments

Another part of the payroll setup process is to specify who you send tax payments to and how often you must do so, such as paying California state withholding and disability insurance each month. This section shows you how to schedule your tax payments.

Computer Practice

To schedule tax payments, follow these steps:

1. To access the *Schedule payments* settings, click *Continue* from the *Payroll Tax Item* section or click the *Schedule payments* category on the dialog box's left.

    The *Review your Scheduled Tax Payments list* screen, shown in Figure 10-39, appears.

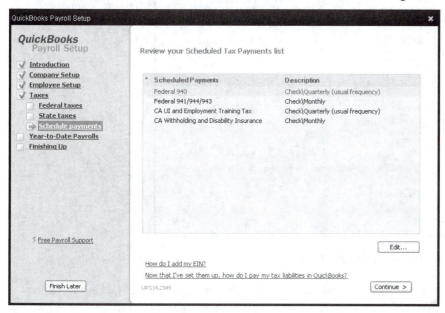

Figure 10-39 Scheduled Tax Payments list

2. To edit the *Federal 940* scheduled payment, select the entry, and then click *Edit*.

3. On the *Set up payment schedule for Federal 940* screen (Figure 10-40), in the *Payee* field, choose the vendor to whom you pay your federal tax liabilities. If you make payments using the Electronic Federal Tax Payment System (EFTPS), choose *EFTPS*.

4. In the *Payment (deposit) frequency* field, keep *Quarterly (usual Frequency)* selected. Click *Finish*.

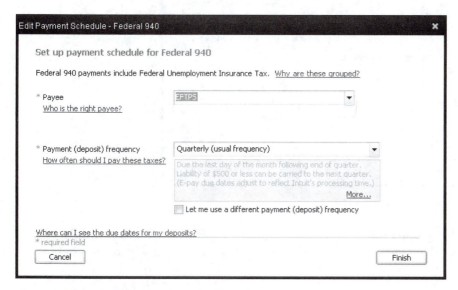

Figure 10-40 Scheduled payment for federal taxes

5. To set up payments for *Federal 941/944/943*, select that entry in the list, click *Edit*, and then enter the values shown in Figure 10-41. Then click *Next*.

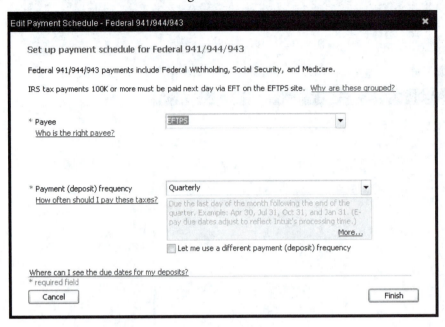

Figure 10-41 Scheduled payment for Federal 941/944/943 taxes

6. To set up payments for a state tax, select the entry in the list, in this example, *California UI and Employment Training Tax*, and then enter the data shown in Figure 10-42. Click *Finish*.

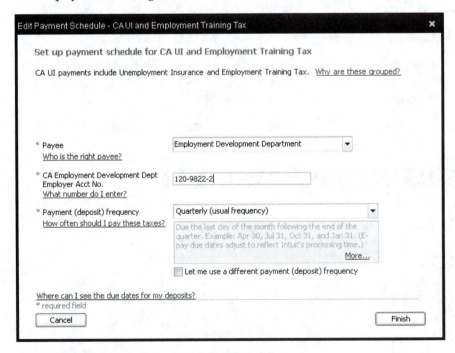

Figure 10-42 Scheduled payment for state taxes

7. To set up payments for another state tax, select the entry in the list (in this example, *California Withholding and Disability Insurance*), click *Edit*. Use the same values from Figure 10-42. Then click *Next*.

8. When you're done setting up tax payments, click *Continue* to enter year-to-date payroll totals, if you're starting payroll in the middle of the year.

Setting up Year-to-Date Payroll Amounts

If you start running payroll in QuickBooks mid-year, you need to tell the program your year-to-date payroll totals. That way, the program can produce the reports, W-2s, and other forms you need at the end of the year. This section shows you where to add this information if you need to.

Computer Practice

To view or record year-to-date payroll totals, do the following:

1. On the dialog box's left, click *Year-to-Date Payrolls*, and then click *Continue*.

2. If you're setting up payroll in the middle of the year, you would keep the *Yes* option selected. In this example, click *No* (see Figure 10-43), and then click *Continue*.

   If you select the *Yes* option, the wizard guides you through setting up each employee's payroll history for the current year.

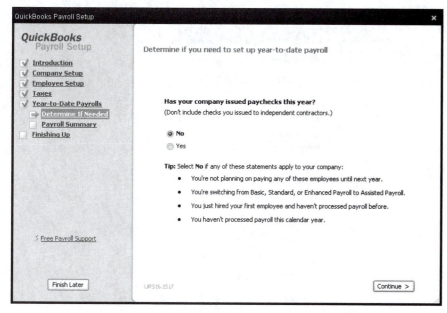

Figure 10-43 Entering year-to-date payroll

Finishing Up the QuickBooks Payroll Setup

The last category in the *QuickBooks Payroll Setup* interview is named *Finishing Up*. The good news is that you're already done. Whether you click *Continue* in the *Year-to-Date Payrolls* section or click the *Finishing Up* category, you'll see a screen that says payroll setup is finished. At the dialog box's bottom right, click *Go to Payroll Center*. There you can run payroll, pay liabilities, or file payroll forms, all of which are described in Chapter 11.

Setting Up Employee Defaults

If you have payroll policies in place so that the same payroll settings apply to most of your new employees, you can define them with the *Employee Defaults* feature. That way, QuickBooks fills in those default values automatically when you create new employee records. You only need to edit an employee record's fields if they differ from your defaults. For example, if you pay all your employees bi-weekly, you make that schedule the default, and then you won't have to enter the pay period each time you set up a new employee.

> Note: Employee default settings only apply to new employee records. Setting them won't change existing employee records in QuickBooks.

Computer Practice

To set up employee defaults, follow these steps:

1. On the *Employees* menu, choose *Employee Center*.

2. In the *Employee Center* (Figure 10-44), choose *Manage Employee Information*, and then choose *Change New Employee Default Settings*.

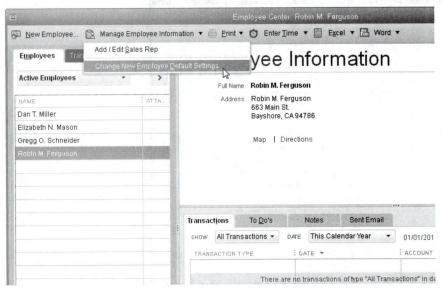

Figure 10-44 Employee Center

3. In the *Employee Defaults* dialog box, in the *Payroll Schedule* field, choose *<Add New>* from the drop-down list.

    Setting up a payroll schedule simplifies running payroll. With a payroll schedule, you can group employees who are paid on the same frequency (such as weekly, bi-weekly, and so on), and run payroll for all of them.

4. Enter the new payroll schedule information as shown in Figure 10-45, and then click *OK*.

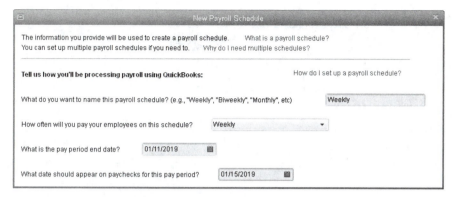

Figure 10-45 Add new payroll schedule

5. In the *Employee Defaults* dialog box, enter the defaults shown in Figure 10-46.

   When you select items in the *Additions, Deductions, and Company Contributions* table, Quick-Books fills in the amounts and limits you specified in the individual payroll items.

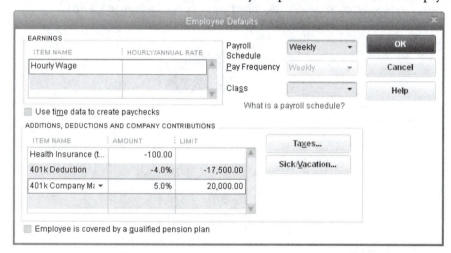

Figure 10-46 Employee defaults

6. Don't click *OK* yet. The following sections cover features in the *Employee Defaults* dialog box.

Default Settings for Taxes

If most of your employees pay the same taxes, you can set those as defaults in the *Employee Defaults* dialog box.

Computer Practice

To specify default taxes, follow these steps:

1. In the *Employee Defaults* dialog box, click the *Taxes* button.

2. In the *Taxes Defaults* dialog box that opens, keep the defaults selected on the *Federal* tab (see Figure 10-47).

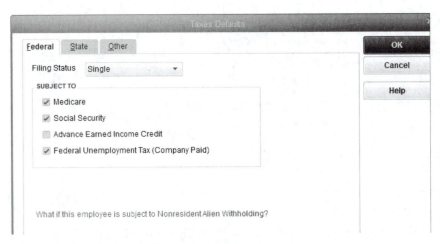

Figure 10-47 Default settings for Federal taxes

3. Click the *State* tab, and then choose the state you want to set defaults for, in this example, *CA* for both the *State worked* and *State subject to withholding* sections (shown in Figure 10-48).

    The settings you see depend on which state you choose.

Figure 10-48 Default settings for State taxes

4. On the *Other* tab, choose additional items to set as defaults. In this example, choose *CA – Employee Training Tax* (see Figure 10-49).

    If your state has local taxes, they will appear on the *Other* tab. You can add local taxes if QuickBooks supports them. If not, you can manually add a User Defined – Other Tax. For help with setting up an unsupported local tax, search for *Payroll Taxes (Other)* in QuickBooks Help.

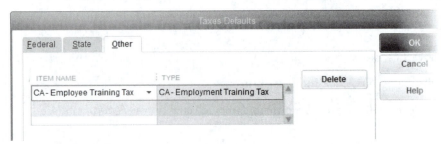

Figure 10-49 Default settings for other taxes

5. Click *OK*.

Default Settings for Sick/Vacation Time

If you give all your new employees the same starting paid time off and have that time accrue at the same rate, you can set those up as defaults in the *Employee Defaults* dialog box. For example, you can specify the number of hours of sick time and vacation time, how much they accrue and how often, and the maximum amount. This section describes how to set up these default settings.

Computer Practice

To specify default vacation and sick time, follow these steps:

1. In the *Employee Defaults* dialog box, click the *Sick/Vacation* button.

2. In the *Sick and Vacation Defaults* dialog box, fill in the fields, as shown in Figure 10-50.

3. When your screen matches Figure 10-50, click *OK*.

Figure 10-50 Default settings for paid time off

4. Click *OK* to close the *Employee Defaults* dialog box.

Changing Employee Payroll Information

After you create employee records, you can edit their payroll information, for example, to change their salaries or the percentage for their 401(k) contribution. In the *Employee Center's Employees* tab, double-click an employee's name to open the *Edit Employee* window. Click the *Payroll Info* tab (shown in Figure 10-51). When you change information here, it will apply to future paychecks.

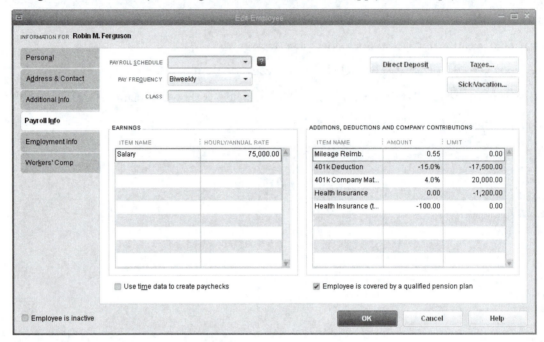

Figure 10-51 Edit Employee Payroll Info

The Employee Contact List Report

You can print a list of employees (Figure 10-52). On the *Reports* menu, choose *List*, and then choose *Employee Contact List*.

Figure 10-52 Employee Contact List

Review Questions

Select the best answer(s) for each of the following:

1. Which *Payroll Items* can you set up in *QuickBooks Payroll Setup*?

   a) Commission

   b) Bonus

   c) Medical Insurance Deduction

   d) All of the above

2. Which sick and vacation time accrual option is not available in QuickBooks?

   a) At beginning of year

   b) Every two weeks

   c) At end of month

   d) Per hour worked

3. If you pay employees on different payroll schedules, you can simplify running payroll by:

   a) Switching to a single payroll schedule.

   b) Using the *QuickBooks Payroll Schedule* feature.

   c) Defining the payroll schedule in each employee's record.

   d) Setting up reminders for each payroll schedule.

4. Which of the following payroll periods is not an option in QuickBooks?

   a) Quarterly

   b) Biweekly

   c) Daily

   d) Semiannually

5. In *QuickBooks Payroll Setup*, you can't:

   a) Edit *Payroll Item* names.

   b) Add two employees with the same name.

   c) Associate deduction and withholding items with vendors.

   d) Set the pay rate for an employee.

Payroll Setup Exercise 1

Applying Your Knowledge

> Note: For this exercise, restore the sample file, sample_product-based business 2015 (Portable).QBM. Or, if you are using QuickBooks 2014, restore sample_product-based business 2014 (Portable).QBM. Because you will continue to use this file in Chapter 11, when you restore the file, be sure to name it payroll_exercise1.qbw.

1. Using *QuickBooks Payroll Setup*, add the *Payroll Items* shown in the following table.

Table 10-1 Payroll Items

Item Name	Expense account
Hourly Wages	Payroll Expenses: Gross Wages
Flex Holiday (Paid Time Off)	Payroll Expenses: Gross Wages

2. Set up a new employee with the information in the following table:

Table 10-2 Employee data

Field	Data
First Name	Donna
M.I.	
Last Name	Baylor
Print on check as	Donna Baylor
Employee Status	Active
Address	9902 48th Ave., Bayshore, CA 94786
Employee Tax Type	Regular
SS No.	199-45-6789
Hire Date	6/16/2013
Release Date	Leave blank
Date of Birth	9/14/1981
Gender	Female
Pay Period	Biweekly
Earnings	Hourly Wages – Rate $25 per hour (Leave all other fields blank.)
Vacation settings	2 hours vacation time per paycheck, maximum 160 hours
Direct Deposit	No direct deposit
Employee works and lives	In California and did not live or work in another state.
Federal filing status	Single, 0 Allowances Nonresident Alien Withholding: Does not apply HIRE Act Exemption: Not a qualified employee Subject to Social Security, Federal Unemployment, Medicare
State filing status	CA – Filing Status Single 0 regular withholding allowances; Subject to Unemployment, Employment Training tax, and Disability Not subject to any special local taxes
Wage Plan Code	S (State Plan For Both UI and DI)

3. Fill in the additional payroll setup information shown in the following table.

    Table 10-3 Additional payroll setup information is below.

Field	Data
State Unemployment Rate	3.4%
Federal Tax Payee	EFTPS
Payment frequency (all payroll taxes)	Quarterly
State Tax Payee	Employment Development Department
CA EDD Employer Acct No.	100-2223-9
Year-To-Date-Payroll	None

4. Run a *Payroll Item Listing* report. (On the *Reports* menu, choose *List*, and then choose *Payroll Item Listing*. Print the report.)

5. Print an *Employee Contact List* report.

Payroll Setup Exercise 2 (Advanced)

Applying Your Knowledge

> Note: For this exercise, restore the sample file, sample_product-based business 2015 (Portable).QBM. Or, if you are using QuickBooks 2014, restore sample_product-based business 2014 (Portable).QBM. You will continue to use this file in Chapter 11. For that reason, when you restore the file, be sure to name the restored file payroll_exercise2.qbw.

1. Using *QuickBooks Payroll Setup*, add or edit the *Payroll Items* shown in the following table.

Table 10-4 Payroll setup information to add or apply to existing items

Item Name	Setup Notes
Salary Regular ✓	Payroll Expenses: Gross Wages
Hourly Wages ✓	Payroll Expenses: Gross Wages
Hourly Time-and-a-half	Payroll Expenses: Gross Wages
Commission ✓	4%; Calculated as percentage of sales. Payroll Expenses: Gross Wages.
Health Insurance (HSA)	Employee pays for all of it (deducted after taxes). Leave the payee and account number fields blank. Use HSA Emp. (Taxable) for tax tracking. Use Payroll Liabilities to track the withholding.
401(k) Employee	Traditional 401(k) not a Roth 401(k). Payee is Great Statewide Bank and account number is 10-9999999. Liability account: Payroll Liabilities Tax Tracking type: 401(k) and use the standard tax settings. Default rate is 4% as a percentage of pay and default limit is $16,000.00.
Match 401(k)	Track as expense. Payee is Great Statewide Bank and account number is 10-9999999. Liability account: Payroll Liabilities Expense is Payroll Expenses Tax Tracking type is 401(k) Co. Match Use standard tax settings. Default rate is 4% and the default limit is $6,000.00.
Vacation Salary	Payroll Expenses: Gross Wages
Vacation Hourly	Payroll Expenses: Gross Wages
Sick Time Salary	Payroll Expenses: Gross Wages
Sick Time Hourly	Payroll Expenses: Gross Wages

2. Set up a new employee with the information in the following table:

Table 10-5 Employee setup information

Field	Data
First Name	Duane
M.I.	
Last Name	Marshall
Print on check as	Duane Marshall
Employee Status	Active
Address	152 Partridge Lane, Bayshore, CA 94786
Employee Tax Type	Regular
SS No.	444-44-1234
Hire Date	2/4/2007
Release Date	
Date of Birth	05/01/1970
Gender	Male
Pay Period	Weekly
Earnings	Hourly Wages – Rate $30 per hour (leave all other fields blank)
Additions, Deductions, and Company Contributions	401(k) Employee (4%), limit $16,000.00 Match 401(k) (4%), limit $6,000.00 Health Insurance ($49.50)
Sick/Vacation Settings	3 hours sick time per paycheck, maximum 80 hours 3 hours vacation time per paycheck, maximum 160 hours
Direct Deposit	No Direct Deposit
Employee Works and lives	In California and did not live or work in another state.
Federal Filing Status	Single, 0 AllowancesNonresident Alien Withholding: Does not apply HIRE Act Exemption: Not a qualified employee Subject to Social Security, Federal Unemployment, Medicare
State Filing Status	CA – Filing Status Single, 0 regular withholding allowances Subject to Unemployment, Employment Training tax, and DisabilityNot subject to any special local taxes
Wage Plan Code	S (State Plan For Both UI and DI)

3. Select *EFTPS* as the *Payee (Vendor)* for *Federal Withholding* and *Federal Unemployment* and deposit your taxes quarterly to pay your Federal tax liabilities.

4. California state tax payee is *Employment Development Department* with account number *222-1234-5*. State taxes are paid *Quarterly* and the State Unemployment rate is *3.5%*.

5. Set employee defaults based on the values in the following table.

Table 10-6 Employee default values

Field	Data
Payroll Schedule	Monthly
Pay Period End Date	1/4/2019
Paycheck Date	1/9/2019
Earnings	Hourly Wage – Rate $25 per hour
Additions, Deductions, and Company Contributions	401(k) Employee (4%), limit $16,000.00 Match 401(k) (4%), limit $6,000.00 Health Insurance ($49.50)
Sick Time Accruals	Accrual period is beginning of year Hours accrued: 40 Maximum hours: 80. Do not reset each year.
Vacation Time Accruals	Accrual period is beginning of year Hours accrued: 80 Maximum hours: 160. Do not reset each year.
Employee Works and lives	In California and did not live or work in another state.
Federal Taxes	Single Subject to Social Security, Federal Unemployment, Medicare
State Taxes	Default state worked: CA Default state subject to withholding: CA
Other Taxes	CA – Employment Training Tax

6. Run a *Payroll Item Listing* report. (On the *Reports* menu, choose *List*, and then choose *Payroll Item Listing*. Print the report.)

7. Print an *Employee Contact List* report.

Chapter 11
Payroll Processing

Topics

This chapter covers the following topics:

- Payroll Processing Checklist
- Payroll Tax Tables
- Paying Employees
- Editing Paychecks
- Paying Payroll Liabilities
- Running Payroll Reports
- Preparing Payroll Tax Returns

After you set up your employees and other payroll information (covered in Chapter 10), you're ready to process payroll. In this chapter, you'll learn how to create and print paychecks for employees. You'll also learn how to edit paychecks, if their information is incorrect. This chapter also covers paying payroll liabilities such as employee withholdings and employer payroll taxes. Finally, you'll learn how to run payroll reports and use them to prepare payroll tax returns.

This chapter uses QuickBooks Basic Payroll, which automatically calculates the payroll taxes for the paychecks you create. (Although it doesn't perform as many payroll tasks as Intuit's other payroll services, you can experiment with Basic Payroll in a sample file without signing up for a payroll subscription.

> Note: For the computer practice in this chapter, back up the company file that you worked on in Chapter 10, and then restore it to work on in this chapter. Name the restored file *ch11_payroll_chapterwork.qbw*.

Payroll Processing Checklist

Payroll processing comprises several tasks that must be performed on specific schedules, depending on how often you process payroll. Follow the steps below to make sure that you complete all your payroll tasks on time and with a minimum of errors.

Each Time You Run Payroll

Regardless of the payroll frequency you use, perform these steps for each payroll you run:

1. Make sure your payroll tax tables are up to date.

2. Create, review, and (if necessary) edit paychecks.

3. If necessary, print paychecks and pay stubs.

> Note: The left side of the *Employee Center* (on the *Home Page*, click *Employees*, or click *Employees* in the icon bar) includes an *Employee* tab and a *Transactions* tab, which are similar to the tabs you learned about in the *Customer Center* and *Vendor Center*. The *Employees* tab lists your employees; and the *Transactions* tab displays transactions (such as paychecks, liability checks, payroll liability adjustments, and so on) associated with the selected employee. Before you process payroll, review the payroll activity for each employee for the last pay period. (On the *Employees* tab, select an employee, and then review the transactions listed on the *Transactions* tab at the center's lower right. If you notice any errors, you can fix them before you process the next payroll.

When Tax Liability Deposits are Due (Bi-weekly or Monthly)

The tax agencies to which you remit payroll tax liabilities specify the frequency of your payments. Perform these steps when tax liabilities are due:

1. Create, review, and (if necessary) edit payroll tax liability payments.

2. If you don't make payments electronically, print payroll tax liability payment checks.

For Each Calendar Quarter

Perform these steps after the end of every calendar quarter:

1. Check the previous quarter's payroll activity for accuracy.

2. If necessary, edit your payroll activities. Once the payroll is correct, run payroll reports for the previous quarter and the year-to-date.

3. Create payroll tax returns, such as Federal Form 941 and state quarterly returns.

Each January

Perform these steps after the end of every calendar year:

1. Review the previous year's payroll for accuracy.

2. If necessary, make changes to the payroll activity. Once the payroll is correct, run payroll reports for the previous quarter and the entire year.

3. Prepare payroll tax returns, such as Federal Form 941, Federal Form 940, and state yearly returns.

Payroll Tax Tables

Payroll tax tables specify payroll tax rates and the tax amounts the employer must withhold from employees' paychecks. When you use QuickBooks Payroll, the tax tables you download provide the information that QuickBooks needs to automatically update the payroll tax forms you print from within the program (Federal Form 940, Form 941, and W-2). Figure 11-1 shows an example of a tax table from IRS Publication 15, which illustrates the types of information that QuickBooks Payroll tax tables contain.

(For Wages Paid in 2014)

TABLE 1—WEEKLY Payroll Period

(a) SINGLE person (including head of household)—				(b) MARRIED person—			
If the amount of wages (after subtracting withholding allowances) is:		The amount of income tax to withhold is:		If the amount of wages (after subtracting withholding allowances) is:		The amount of income tax to withhold is:	
Not over $43		$0		Not over $163		$0	
Over—	But not over—	of excess over—		Over—	But not over—	of excess over—	
$43	—$218	$0.00 plus 10%	—$43	$163	—$512	$0.00 plus 10%	—$163
$218	—$753	$17.50 plus 15%	—$218	$512	—$1,582	$34.90 plus 15%	—$512
$753	—$1,762	$97.75 plus 25%	—$753	$1,582	—$3,025	$195.40 plus 25%	—$1,582
$1,762	—$3,627	$350.00 plus 28%	—$1,762	$3,025	—$4,525	$556.15 plus 28%	—$3,025
$3,627	—$7,834	$872.20 plus 33%	—$3,627	$4,525	—$7,953	$976.15 plus 33%	—$4,525
$7,834	—$7,865	$2,260.51 plus 35%	—$7,834	$7,953	—$8,963	$2,107.39 plus 35%	—$7,953
$7,865		$2,271.36 plus 39.6%	—$7,865	$8,963		$2,460.89 plus 39.6%	—$8,963

TABLE 2—BIWEEKLY Payroll Period

(a) SINGLE person (including head of household)—				(b) MARRIED person—			
If the amount of wages (after subtracting withholding allowances) is:		The amount of income tax to withhold is:		If the amount of wages (after subtracting withholding allowances) is:		The amount of income tax to withhold is:	
Not over $87		$0		Not over $325		$0	
Over—	But not over—	of excess over—		Over—	But not over—	of excess over—	
$87	—$436	$0.00 plus 10%	—$87	$325	—$1,023	$0.00 plus 10%	—$325
$436	—$1,506	$34.90 plus 15%	—$436	$1,023	—$3,163	$69.80 plus 15%	—$1,023
$1,506	—$3,523	$195.40 plus 25%	—$1,506	$3,163	—$6,050	$390.80 plus 25%	—$3,163
$3,523	—$7,254	$699.65 plus 28%	—$3,523	$6,050	—$9,050	$1,112.55 plus 28%	—$6,050
$7,254	—$15,667	$1,744.33 plus 33%	—$7,254	$9,050	—$15,906	$1,952.55 plus 33%	—$9,050
$15,667	—$15,731	$4,520.62 plus 35%	—$15,667	$15,906	—$17,925	$4,215.03 plus 35%	—$15,906
$15,731		$4,543.02 plus 39.6%	—$15,731	$17,925		$4,921.68 plus 39.6%	—$17,925

Figure 11-1 An IRS tax table

Tax tables change frequently, so it's important to keep them up to date. To ensure that you're using up-to-date tax tables, use a QuickBooks Payroll service subscription so you can download the current tax tables before you process payroll. That way, QuickBooks Payroll can correctly calculate paychecks and fill out your payroll forms.

Paying Employees

In this section, you'll learn how to assign employees to a payroll schedule, so it's easy to select the employees you want to pay and create their paychecks.

Assigning Employees to a Payroll Schedule

In this chapter's company file, the three original employees are assigned to the Biweekly payroll schedule, which hasn't been used for several years. In addition, the employee that you created in Chapter 10 is set up to be paid bi-weekly, but hasn't been assigned to a payroll schedule. Because QuickBooks payroll schedules make it easy to select and pay employees, this section explains how to assign employees to a payroll schedule (in this example, the Weekly payroll schedule that you created in Chapter 10).

Computer Practice

To assign an employee to a payroll schedule, do the following:

1. On the *Employees* menu, choose *Employee Center*.

2. On the *Employees* tab, double-click the person's name in the *Name* list, in this example, *Robin M. Ferguson*.

   The *Edit Employee* window opens.

3. Click the *Payroll Info* tab.

4. In the *Payroll Schedule* drop-down list (see Figure 11-2), choose the schedule you want for the employee, in this example, *Weekly*, and then click *OK*.

   Repeat steps 2 through 4 to assign other employees to the payroll schedule. In this example, reassign *Dan T. Miller*, *Elizabeth N. Mason*, and *Gregg O. Schneider* to the *Weekly* payroll schedule.

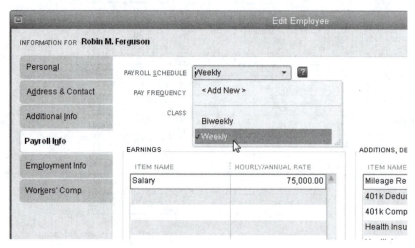

Figure 11-2 Choose Payroll Schedule

> Tip: An easy way to see the payroll schedule for your employees is by adding the *Pay Schedule* column to the *Employee Center*'s *Employees* tab. To do that, right-click any employee in the *Employees* tab, and then choose *Customize Columns*. Scroll in the *Available Columns* list until you see *Pay Schedule*, select that field, and then click *Add*. Click *OK* to close the *Customize Columns* dialog box.

Running a Scheduled Payroll

After you assign employees to payroll schedules, it's easy to create their paychecks.

Computer Practice

To run a *Scheduled Payroll* that you've defined, follow these steps:

1. In the *Employee Center*, click the *Payroll* tab on the window's left.

2. On the window's right (below the *Create Paychecks* heading), select the *Weekly* payroll schedule, as shown in Figure 11-3.

3. Click the *Start Scheduled Payroll* button.

Figure 11-3 Select a payroll schedule

4. In the *Enter Payroll Information* window that opens, keep the default dates that QuickBooks enters in the *Pay Period Ends* and *Check Date* fields, as shown in Figure 11-4. (If the dates that the program enters aren't correct, edit them.)

   The *Pay Period Ends* field specifies the end date for the pay period, that is, the date through which employees are paid. The *Check Date* field is the date that appears on the paychecks you create. When you run payroll, the program automatically calculates the dates for the next pay period based on the previous payroll dates.

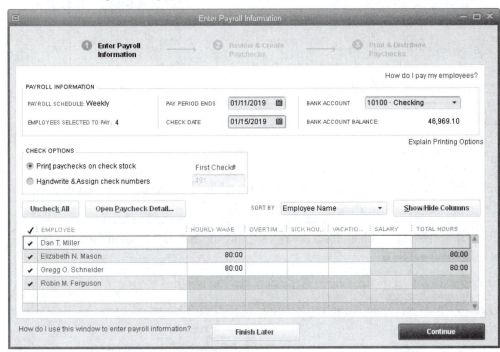

Figure 11-4 The Enter Payroll Information window

> Note: The *Check Date* field also determines when some payroll expenses appear on all reports. For example, if you pay your employees on the 18th for their wages for the first half of the month, reports you run show wage expenses for that payroll if the report's date range includes the 18th of the month.

5. To preview a paycheck, select the employee's name in the *Employee* column, in this example, *Robin M. Ferguson*.

   The *Preview Paycheck* dialog box that opens (Figure 11-5) shows the employee's earnings, payroll deductions, and company payroll liabilities based on the tax tables and settings you set in Chapter 10.

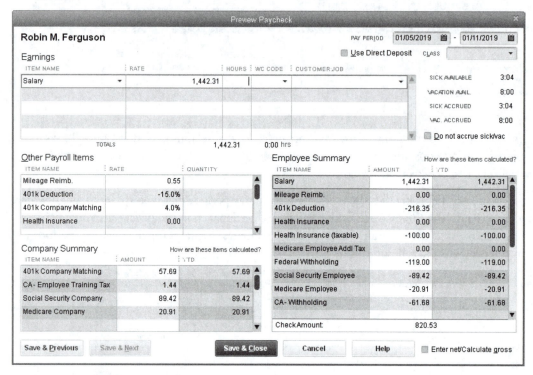

Figure 11-5 Preview a paycheck

> Note: The tax withholdings shown in Figure 11-5 may differ from the ones you see on your computer. If your computer contains different tax tables than the ones used in this chapter, your results will vary from the ones shown here.

6. In the *Earnings* table, in the first blank *Item Name* cell, add another payroll item, in this example, *Vacation Salary*.

   QuickBooks automatically splits the salary evenly between the two items.

7. In the *Salary* row's *Hours* cell, type *32*; in the *Vacation Salary* row's *Hours* cell, type *8* (as shown in Figure 11-6).

   For salaried employees, QuickBooks calculates gross pay for the pay period by dividing the annual rate by the number of pay periods. The program then allocates the gross pay equally to the *Earnings* items. To track sick and vacation hours used, type the hours used in each line, so that QuickBooks can prorate the salary to each *Earnings* line.

Figure 11-6 Edited earnings items in the Preview Paycheck dialog box

8. Review the *Other Payroll Items* section to confirm that the items and values are correct. In this example, the *401k Deduction* rate should be *-15%*; the *401k Company Matching* rate should be *4%*; and *Health Insurance* should be *-25.00* (you need to enter this value).

   Your *Preview Paycheck* dialog box should look like the one in Figure 11-7 (although the tax item values may vary).

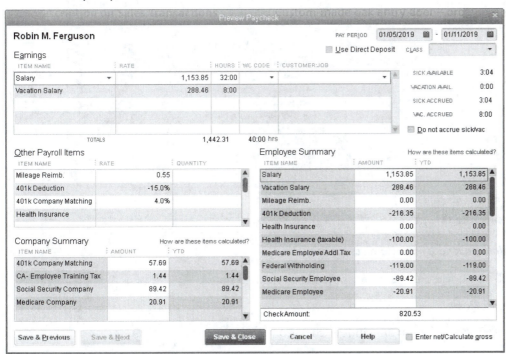

Figure 11-7 Edited paycheck (tax item values may vary)

9. In this example, click *Save & Previous* to view another paycheck (Figure 11-8). (To save the paycheck and close the *Preview Paycheck* dialog box, click *Save & Close*.)

   When you click *Save & Previous*, the previous paycheck in the list appears. In this paycheck, the earnings item name is *Hourly Wage*. QuickBooks automatically fills in the hours from the previous paycheck.

10. In this example, in the *Hourly Wage's Hours* cell, type *32*.

11. In this example, click *Save & Previous*.

> Note: If you turned on the *Use Time Data to Create Paychecks* checkbox in an employee's record, QuickBooks fills in the paycheck's Earnings section with data entered in the employee's Weekly Timesheet for the paycheck period. If you discover errors in the timesheet, it's best to click *Cancel* in the *Preview Paycheck* dialog box, correct the timesheet, and then recreate the paycheck. Although you can edit information copied from a timesheet, those changes don't affect the original timesheet.

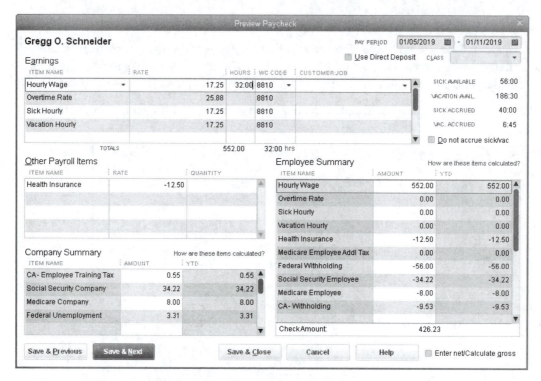

Figure 11-8 Edited paycheck – tax item values may vary

12. Edit Elizabeth N. Mason's record to show she worked 40 hours.

13. Click *Save & Close*.

14. In the *Enter Payroll Information* window, click *Continue*.

The *Review and Create Paychecks* window opens (Figure 11-9). In the *Check Options* section, the *Print paycheck on check stock* option is selected automatically. Keep that option selected.

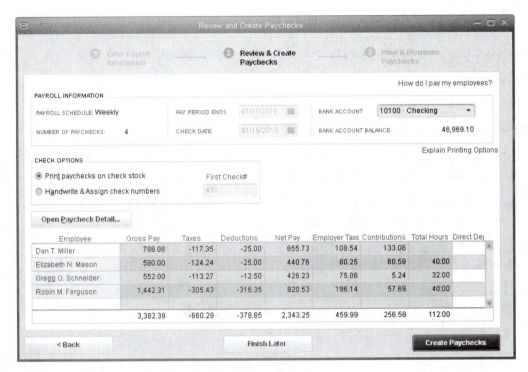

Figure 11-9 Review and Create Paychecks window

15. If the paychecks match the ones in Figure 11-9 (except for possible differences in taxes), click *Create Paychecks*.

The *Confirmation and Next Steps* dialog box opens (Figure 11-10). You'll use this dialog box in the next section, so keep it open.

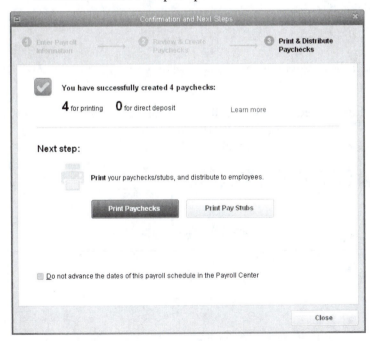

Figure 11-10 Confirmation and Next Steps dialog box

Printing Paychecks

Printing paychecks is similar to printing other types of checks in QuickBooks.

Computer Practice

To print paychecks, follow these steps:

1. In the *Confirmation and Next Steps* dialog box, click *Print Paychecks*.

    If you didn't keep the *Confirmation and Next Steps* dialog box open from the previous section, on the *File* menu, choose *Print Forms*, and then choose *Paychecks*.

2. In the *Select Paychecks to Print* dialog box, in the *First Check Number* field, fill in the number on the first paycheck in your printer, in this example, type *15001*, as shown in Figure 11-11.

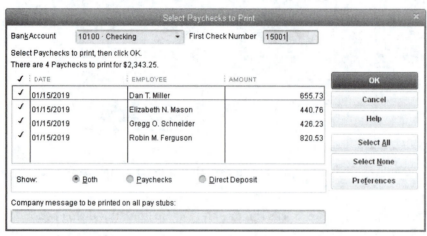

Figure 11-11 Select Paychecks to Print dialog box

3. Click *OK*.

    The *Print Checks* dialog box opens. It shows the number of checks waiting to print and the total amount of those checks, as shown in Figure 11-12.

    Voucher checks are the best choice for paychecks, because QuickBooks prints payroll item details in the voucher area. If you don't use voucher checks, you can print pay stubs for your employees (by clicking *Print Pay Stubs* in the *Confirmation and Next Steps* dialog box.)

Figure 11-12 Print Checks dialog box

---

348   Chapter 11: Payroll Processing

4. To print the paychecks, click *Print*. Figure 11-13 shows an example of a paycheck printed on blank paper. (You don't see the check number in this example, because it is pre-printed on your check stock.)

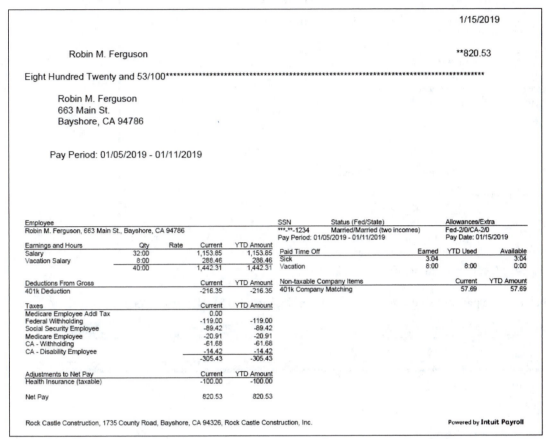

Figure 11-13 Printed paycheck

Printing Pay Stubs

If you don't print paychecks from within QuickBooks (for example, handwriting a few paychecks), you can print the pay stubs. And you can print them any time you want, whether or not you have printed paychecks.

Computer Practice

To print pay stubs, follow these steps:

1. On the *File* menu, choose *Print Forms*, and then choose *Pay Stubs*.

    The *Select Pay Stubs* dialog box opens (Figure 11-14).

2. Keep the values in the *Check Date* and *thru* fields as they are.

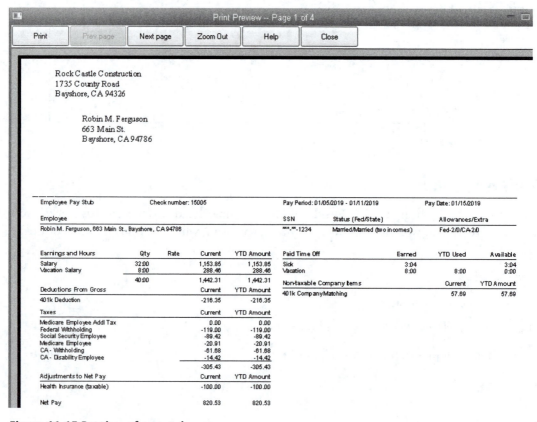

Figure 11-14 Select Pay Stubs window

3. To review the pay stubs before you print them (Figure 11-15), click the *Preview* button.

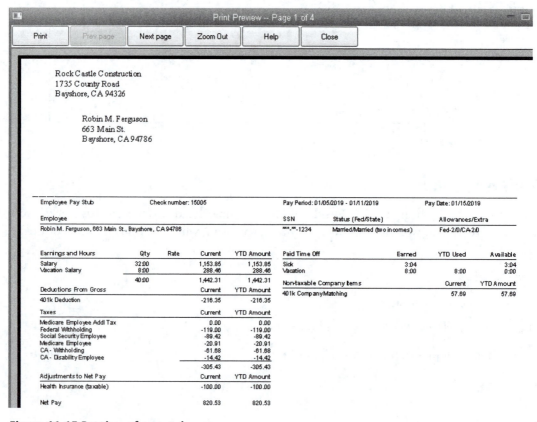

Figure 11-15 Preview of pay stub

4. To close the *Print Preview* window, click *Close*.

   To print the pay stubs, click *Print*. (Don't do that in this exercise.)

5. Click *Close* to close the *Select Pay Stubs* window.

Editing Paychecks

If you notice an error on a paycheck, you can edit or void it. (You can also delete a paycheck in QuickBooks, but it's better to void it instead.)

> Note: Editing or voiding paychecks affects your financial records. Consult your accountant to see whether editing or voiding a paycheck is the correct action to take. You shouldn't edit paychecks that have already been printed and sent to employees. In addition, don't edit an employee's paychecks if he or she has received paychecks dated after the one you want to edit, because the changes you make could invalidate the tax calculations on more recent paychecks.

Computer Practice

To edit a paycheck, do the following:

1. On the *Payroll Center's Pay Employees* tab, in the *Activities* section at the bottom of the window, click the *Edit/Void Paycheck* link (see Figure 11-16).

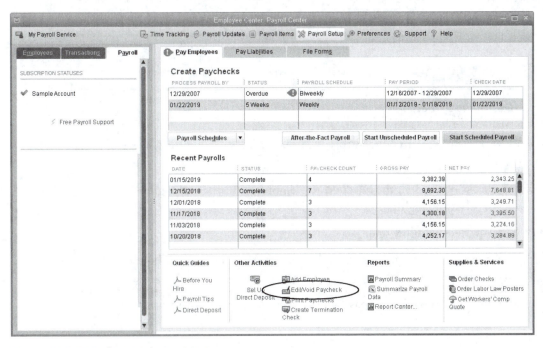

Figure 11-16 Edit/Void Paycheck link

> Note: Another method for editing a paycheck is to double-click it in the checking account register. The *Review Paycheck* window opens. Continue with step 4 in this numbered list.

2. In the *Edit/Void Paychecks* window, fill in the date range for the paychecks you want to edit or void, in this example, choose *1/1/2019* and *1/15/2019*.

Notice the message at the top of the window (Figure 11-17). If you aren't editing or voiding paychecks because you created them by mistake, click the *Tell me how to handle other situations* link to learn what to do.

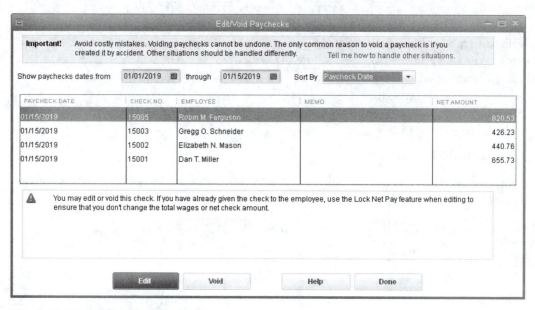

Figure 11-17 Edit/Void Paycheck link

3. Select the check you want to edit, in this example, number *15003* for *Gregg O. Schneider*, and then click *Edit*.

4. To edit paycheck items, click the *Paycheck Detail* button (circled in Figure 11-18) at the *Paycheck* window's bottom right.

The *Review Paycheck* window opens.

5. Make the changes you want, in this example, change the Hourly Wage hours to *28:00* and the Sick Hourly hours to *4:00*.

If you see a message about the net pay being locked, click *Yes* to dismiss it.

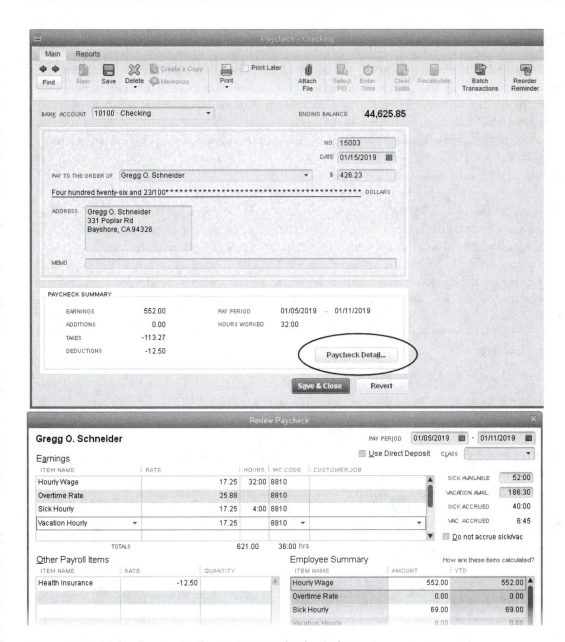

Figure 11-18 Make changes in the Review Paycheck window

> Note: You can't edit values in cells shaded in gray. To change year-to-date amounts, use the *Adjust Liabilities* feature or override the amounts on one of this employee's future paychecks.

6. In this example, click *Cancel*, so you don't save the changes. (If you want to save changes, in the *Review Paychecks* dialog box, click *OK* instead.)

7. In the *Paycheck* window, click *Save & Close*. Click *Done* to close the *Edit/Void Paychecks* window.

Paying Payroll Liabilities

After you run payroll, the next step is to pay the liabilities (employee withholdings and employer payroll taxes) associated with that payroll run. For accurate payroll records, you must pay these liabilities on the *Pay Liabilities* tab in the *Payroll Center*—not with the *Write Checks* window. When you use the *Pay Liabilities* feature, QuickBooks debits (decreases) the payroll liability accounts and the balances due for payroll items. Those payments also appear in payroll liability reports and on payroll tax forms, such as Forms 940 and 941. This section shows you how to use the *Pay Liabilities* tab of the *Payroll Center* to pay your payroll liabilities correctly.

> Note: IRS publication, Circular E, Employer's Tax Guide, contains the rules for when payroll taxes must be paid. Depending on the size of your payroll, you need to deposit taxes monthly or semi-weekly. Monthly depositors must pay payroll liabilities by the 15th of the month following the payroll date. Semi-weekly depositors must pay by the Wednesday after the payroll date, if that date falls on a Wednesday, Thursday, or Friday; or you must pay by the following Friday if your payroll date is Saturday, Sunday, Monday or Tuesday.

Computer Practice

To pay payroll liabilities, follow these steps:

1. On the *Home Page*, in the *Employees* section, choose *Pay Liabilities*.

   If the *Payroll Center* is already open, click the *Pay Liabilities* tab.

2. In the *Pay Taxes & Other Liabilities* table, turn on the checkmark cells for the payments you want to select, in this example, all three payments, as shown in Figure 11-19.

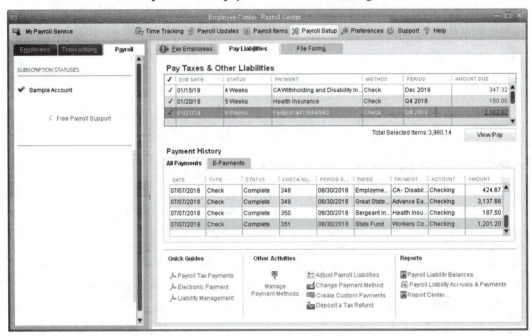

Figure 11-19 The Pay Liabilities tab

3. Click the *View/Pay* button.

   The first liability payment appears, as shown in Figure 11-20. In this example, it is a payment to the California Employment Development Department.

Figure 11-20 Payment 1 of 3

4. Change the *Date* field to *1/15/2019* in this example, and then click *Save & Next*.

    The second payment window appears.

5. For the second payment, change the date to *1/15/2019* and the *Payee* to *Sergeant Insurance* (Figure 11-21).

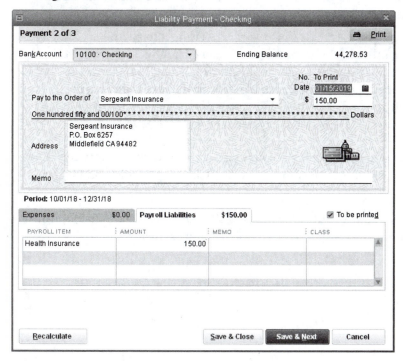

Figure 11-21 Payment 2 of 3

6. Click *Save & Next* to display the third payment. Change the date for the *EFTPS* payment to *1/31/2019*.

7. Click *Save & Close*.

The *Payment Summary* window (Figure 11-22) appears, displaying the liability payments you've recorded.

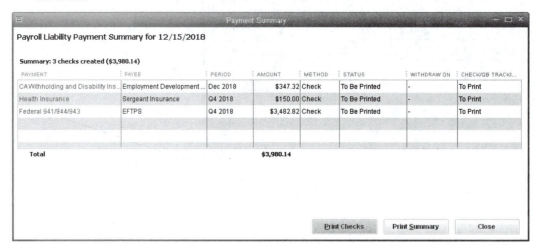

Figure 11-22 The Payment Summary window

8. Click *Print Checks*.

In the *Select Checks to Print* dialog box, complete the printing process. In this example, keep the *First Check Number* field set to *15006*.

9. Close the *Payment Summary* window.

On the *Pay Liabilities* tab, you can see the checks you printed in the *Payment History* table.

> Tip: The liabilities that QuickBooks payroll calculates may differ from what the tax agencies say you owe. Discrepancies such as these can arise due to changes to payroll tax rates (such as your state unemployment rate) that you haven't changed in QuickBooks. In that case, edit the payroll item to reflect the new rate, and then use a liability adjustment to correct the taxes for that payroll period. Discrepancies might be due to liability payments being made incorrectly, such as using the *Write Checks* window, or an incorrect payment date. For errors such as these, void the incorrect payment and record a new one.

10. To view the payments you made in the checking account register, on the *Home Page*, click *Check Register*, choose your checking account in the drop-down list (Checking in this example), and then click *OK*.

The liability checks you produced are identified by the type *LIAB CHK* (see Figure 11-23), which is the only type of transaction that properly records payroll liability payments.

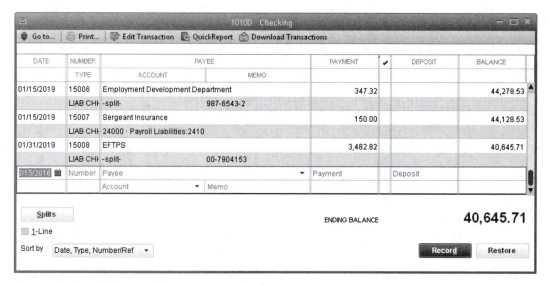

Figure 11-23 Liability check in checking account register

Running Payroll Reports

QuickBooks offers several reports you can use to view your payroll. This section describes the ones you might use most often.

Payroll Summary Report

The *Payroll Summary* report displays each employee's earnings, taxes, and net pay.

Computer Practice

To run the *Payroll Summary* report (Figure 11-24), follow these steps:

1. On the *Reports* menu, choose *Employees & Payroll*, and then choose *Payroll Summary*.

2. Change the *From* and *To* fields to *1/1/2019* and *1/31/2019*, respectively. Click *Refresh* in the window's tool bar.

   The *Payroll Summary* report includes *Hours*, *Rate*, and payroll subcolumns for each employee.

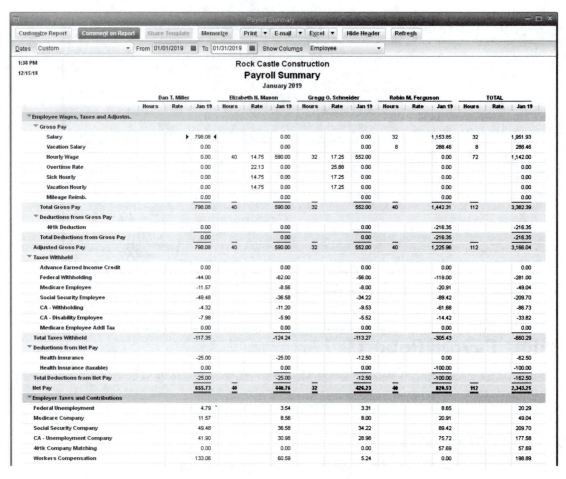

Figure 11-24 Payroll Summary report

3. To hide the hours and rate columns, click the *Customize Report* button, and then turn off the *Hours* and *Rate* checkboxes (see Figure 11-25). Click *OK* to update the report (Figure 11-26).

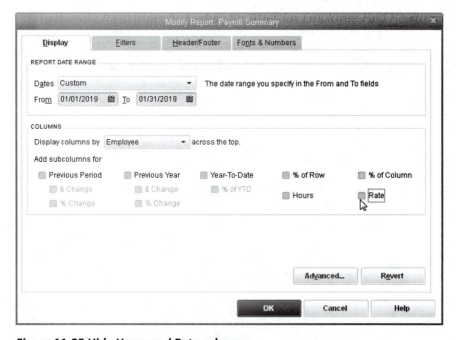

Figure 11-25 Hide Hours and Rate columns

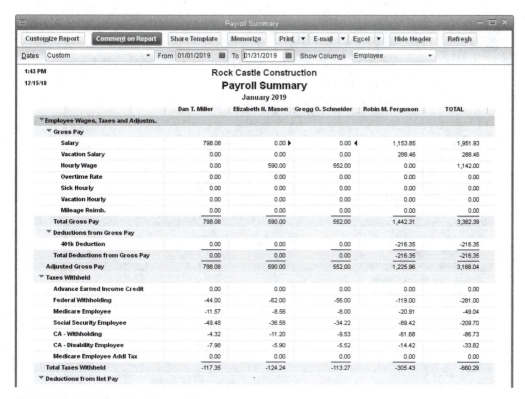

Figure 11-26 Customized Payroll Summary report

4. To print the report, click *Print* (or press Ctrl+P).

Payroll Liability Balances Report

The *Payroll Liability Balances* report shows payroll liability status for each *Payroll* item you use.

Computer Practice

To create a *Payroll Liability Balances* report, follow these steps:

1. On the *Reports* menu, choose *Employees & Payroll*, then choose *Payroll Liability Balances*.

2. In the *Dates* field, for this example, choose *Next Calendar Year*.

3. In the *Show Columns* field, choose *Year*.

    Figure 11-27 shows the payroll liability balances for 2019.

4. To print the report, choose *Print* (or press Ctrl+P).

5. Close all the reports that are open.

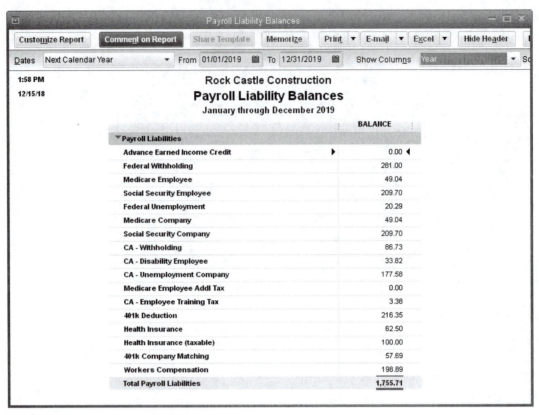

Figure 11-27 Payroll Liability Balances report

Sales Rep Commissions

The *Sales by Rep Summary* and *Sales by Rep* detail reports help you calculate the commissions you owe sales reps. If you want to see only sales that the company has received payment for, change the report basis from accrual to cash.

> Note: These steps are for reference only. Do not perform them. The sample file does not include sales reps.

To run the *Sales by Rep Summary* report, do the following:

1. On the *Reports* menu, choose *Sales*, then choose *Sales by Rep Summary*.

2. Click the *Customize Report* button.

3. In the *Report Basis* section, choose *Cash*, then click *OK* to update the report.

Preparing Payroll Tax Forms

You must pay payroll taxes and other liabilities, and submit payroll tax forms associated with those payments on time. If you signed up for an Enhanced Payroll subscription, you can process forms, such as Form 940, Form 941, and W-2s, from the *Payroll Center's File Forms* tab.

Before you process forms, perform the following steps:

1. Update your tax tables.

2. Pay tax liabilities using the *Pay Liabilities* tab before you prepare Quarterly and Annual Payroll Forms.

When QuickBooks prepares Form 941, it uses those payments to calculate the value for *Deposits made*. Form 940 uses those payments to calculate your Federal Unemployment tax based on 940 contributions, State Unemployment liabilities, and any payments you made during the year. If you use Enhanced Payroll, it automatically calculates the values on payroll tax forms using information from paychecks and payroll liability payments.

Review Questions

Select the best answer(s) for each of the following:

1. When you print voucher-style paychecks, you can include:

   a) Federal filing status

   b) Earnings and tax withholdings

   c) Adjustments to net pay

   d) All of the above

2. To run a payroll, you should:

   a) On the *Home Page*, click the *Write Checks* icon.

   b) On the *Home Page*, click the *Pay Employees* icon.

   c) On the *Employees* menu, choose *Pay Employees*, and then choose *Scheduled Payroll*.

   d) On the *Employees* menu, choose *Process Payroll*.

3. The *Payroll Liability Balances* report identifies:

   a) Liability payments during a date range

   b) Liability amounts you owe by *Payroll Item*

   c) Liability amounts for employee deductions

   d) Liabilities for employer taxes

4. Which *Home Page* icon should you click to pay payroll taxes?

   a) Write Checks

   b) Pay Bills

   c) Pay Employees

   d) Pay Liabilities

5. Which statement is true?

   a) You can't void a paycheck.

   b) You can print pay stubs at any time.

   c) If a paycheck that you sent to an employee contains an error, delete it and create a new one.

   d) You can only print voucher-style paychecks.

Payroll Processing Exercise 1

Applying Your Knowledge

> For this exercise, use the company file that you created in Chapter 10 for exercise 1, payroll_exercise1.qbw.

1. Run an unscheduled payroll to create printable paychecks for the payroll period ending on *1/11/2019*. The checks should be dated *01/15/2019* and drawn on the *Checking* bank account. Use the payroll information in the following table.

Table 11-1 Payroll information

Field	Data
Donna Baylor	
Earnings	Hourly Wages: 80 hours
Payroll Item Deductions	Health Insurance (taxable): -$100
Gregg O. Schneider	
Earnings	Hourly Wages: 80 hours Rate $30 per hour
Payroll Item Deductions	Health Insurance: -$100

2. Print voucher paychecks on blank paper.

3. Print a *Payroll Liability Balances* report for *01/01/2019* through *1/31/2019*.

Payroll Processing Exercise 2 (Advanced)

Applying Your Knowledge

> For this exercise, use the company file that you created in Chapter 10 for exercise 2, payroll_exercise2.qbw.

1. Assign all four employees to the *Monthly* pay schedule.

2. Run a *Monthly* payroll to create printable paychecks for the payroll period ending on *1/4/2019*. The checks should be dated *01/9/2019* and drawn on the *Checking* bank account. Use the payroll information in the following table.

Table 11-2 Payroll information

Field	Data
Dan T Miller	Use default values
Duane Marshall	Hourly Wages: 120 hours Vacation Hourly: 40 hours Bonus: $2,000 401k Deduction: -15% 401k Company Match: 4% Health Insurance:-$100
Elizabeth N. Mason	Hourly Wages: 120 hours Rate $35 per hour Sick Time Hourly: 40 hours Bonus: $2,500 401k Deduction: -15% 401k Company Match: 4% Health Insurance: -$100
Gregg O. Schneider	Hourly Wages: 120 hours Rate $35 per hour Hourly Time-and-a-half: 15 hours Vacation Hourly: 40 hours Bonus: $2,000 401k Employee: -10% 401k Company Match: 4% Health Insurance: -$100

3. Print voucher paychecks on blank paper.

4. On *1/21/2019*, pay the *Federal* and *California* liabilities due on *01/15/2019*. Print the payroll liability checks on blank paper.

5. Print a *Payroll Summary* report for *1/1/2019* through *1/15/2019*. Hide the *Hours* and *Rate* columns.

6. Print a *Payroll Liability Balances* report for 0*1/01/2019* through *1/31/2019*.

Chapter 12

Adjustments and Year-end Procedures

Topics

This chapter covers the following topics:

- Recording General Journal Entries

- Editing, Voiding, and Deleting Transactions

- Memorizing Transactions

- Closing Your Books

This chapter covers several methods for adjusting your financial records, which you do at the end of each year or other accounting period. In this chapter, you'll learn how to record journal entries for adjustments that aren't possible using other QuickBooks transactions. You'll also learn how to edit, void, and delete transactions. This chapter describes how you can memorize transactions so you can reuse them. Finally, you'll learn how to close your books in QuickBooks including setting the *Closing Date*.

> Note: For the computer practice in this chapter, restore the sample file, sample_product-based business 2015 (Portable).QBM. Or, if you are using QuickBooks 2014, restore sample_product-based business 2014 (Portable).QBM.

General Journal Entries

Most of the time, you can record your financial transactions using QuickBooks forms, such as the *Create Invoices* window, *Enter Bills* window, *Make Deposits* window, and so on. But those forms won't work for some types of adjustments. In those situations, you record journal entries. QuickBooks refers to these transactions as *General Journal Entries*. For simplicity, this chapter refers to them as journal entries.

It's good accounting practice to document the reason for the journal entries you create. In QuickBooks, you can fill in *Memo* fields with that information. These memos are helpful as reminders for the reasons for journal entries and especially for answering questions during audits.

> Note: In QuickBooks, it's best to use QuickBooks' forms whenever possible, only turning to journal entries for transactions you can't record in any other way, such as recording depreciation.

Here are some reasons you might record journal entries in QuickBooks:

- Record non-cash expenses, such as depreciation.

- Reclassify transactions from one account to another.

- Reclassify transactions from one *Class* to another.

- Close the *Owners Draw* account into the *Owners Equity* account.

- Allocate prepaid expenses to each month throughout the year.

Creating a Journal Entry

If you don't have permission to create journal entries in QuickBooks, ask the company file administrator to change your user access so you can create them.

Computer Practice

To create a journal entry, follow these steps;

1. On the *Company* menu, choose *Make General Journal Entries*.

   If you use QuickBooks Accountant, you can also choose *Make General Journal Entries* from the *Accountant* menu.

2. If the *Assigning Numbers to Journal Entries* dialog box opens, turn on the *Do not display this message in the future* box, and then click *OK*.

3. In the *Date* field, choose the date for the journal entry, in this example, 12/31/2018.

   > Note: If you use QuickBooks Pro or Premier, the *Make General Journal Entries* window may look different than the one in Figure 12-1.

4. In the *Entry No.* field, type a journal entry number, if QuickBooks hasn't automatically filled in the correct number. In this example, type 2018-1.

   When you type a number in the *Entry No.* field, QuickBooks automatically increments the entry number when you create the next journal entry. For example, in this example, when you create a second journal entry, the program automatically fills in the *Entry No.* field with 2018-2.

5. In this example, turn off the *Adjusting Entry* checkbox.

   An adjusting journal entry alters a company's records so they follow accrual basis accounting. In this example, the journal entry is reclassifying income to a new account, so it isn't an adjusting entry.

6. In the first line of the table, click the *Account* cell, type *Journal Entries*, and then press the *Tab* key. In the *Account Not Found* message box, click *Set Up*. Choose the *Bank* account type, and then save the account.

   > Note: Adding the *Journal Entries* account to the first line of each journal entry makes it easy to see all the journal entries you create. By setting this account up as a bank account, you can open the account in a register window. You can view all your journal entries by scrolling through the register. You don't debit or credit the account, so its balance is always zero.

7. In the first row's *Memo* cell, type the reason for the journal entry, in this example, *Reclassify income*.

8. Click the second row's account cell, and then enter the information shown in Figure 12-1.

    The totals at the bottom of the *Debit* and *Credit* columns must be equal to one another. If your journal entry includes only one debit and credit, QuickBooks helps you balance your debits and credits. If you fill in the second row's *Debit* cell with a value, QuickBooks automatically adds that number to the *Credit* cell in the next row.

9. Click *Save & Close*.

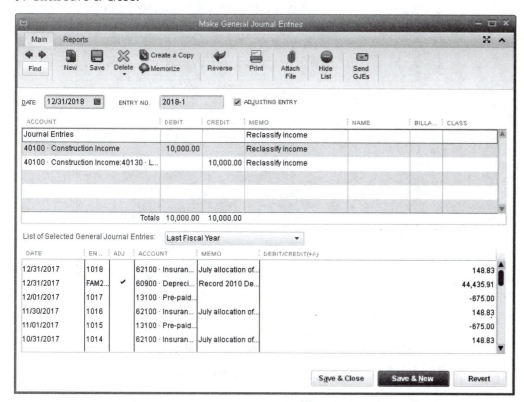

Figure 12-1 Make General Journal Entries window - your window may vary

Adjusting Expense Related to Items

If you use *Items* to track expense details, you may need to make adjustments for those items and the accounts to which they're assigned. The *Make General Journal Entries* window doesn't have fields for items, so you can't record item adjustments with a journal entry. However, you can make adjustments such as these by recording a transaction (such as a check). The check has an amount of zero, because the debits and credits offset each other. Use the *Journal Entries* bank account created in the previous section as the bank account. That way, your real checking account won't include these adjustment transactions.

> Do not perform the following steps. They are for reference only.

To create a check that acts as a journal entry, do the following:

1. Open the *Write Checks* window.

2. In the *Bank Account* field, choose the *Journal Entries* account. In the *No.* field, type *ZB* to identify the check as a zero-balance check.

3. For debits, enter positive *Items* amounts. For credits, enter negative *Items* amounts, as shown in Figure 12-2.

   Remember, the value in the *$* field at the top of the check must be zero.

4. Click *Save & New*.

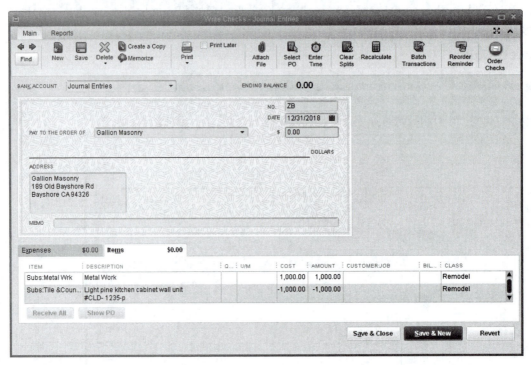

Figure 12-2 Check used as a journal entry

5. Click the *Previous* arrow at the *Write Checks* window's top left to display the check again.

6. To see the transaction results, on the *Reports* menu, choose *Transaction Journal*.

   QuickBooks displays the report shown in Figure 12-3.

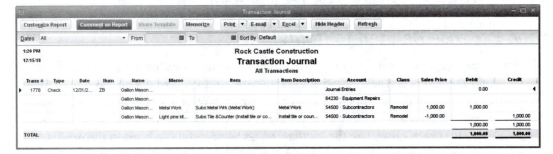

Figure 12-3 Transaction Journal report

This type of check transaction is also useful for making adjustments to a combination of *Items* and expenses. Similarly, you can record zero-dollar *Sales Receipts* to adjust items that affect income accounts.

Editing, Voiding, and Deleting Transactions

Unlike many other accounting programs, QuickBooks lets you change transactions at any time (as long as you have the QuickBooks privileges to do so). However, you shouldn't change transactions dated in closed accounting periods or that have been reconciled with a bank statement.

> Note: A closed accounting period is one for which you've issued financial statements and/or filed tax returns.

When you change or delete a transaction, QuickBooks updates the corresponding accounts as of the transaction's date. That means, if you modify or delete transactions in a closed accounting period, your QuickBooks financial statements will change for that period, which creates discrepancies between your QuickBooks reports and your tax return.

> Note: Before you change a transaction, be sure to check whether it's dated in a closed accounting period. If it is, see page 149 to learn how to record the change you want.

Editing Transactions

You may need to modify transactions to correct errors. You can do that in QuickBooks by editing the values for the transaction in its corresponding transaction window. For example, suppose you forgot to add a charge to an invoice that you haven't sent to the customer. You can make the change to the existing invoice. (If you've already sent the invoice to the customer, you must create a new invoice with the charge, instead.)

Computer Practice

To edit an existing transaction, in this example, an invoice, follow these steps:

1. On the *Customers* menu, choose *Create Invoices*.

2. Click *Previous* to display invoice 1098 dated 12/15/2018.

3. In the *Installation* row's *Amount* cell, type *250*. Press *Tab*. (See Figure 12-4.)

4. Enter *3* in the *Removal* row's *Quantity* column and then press *Tab*.

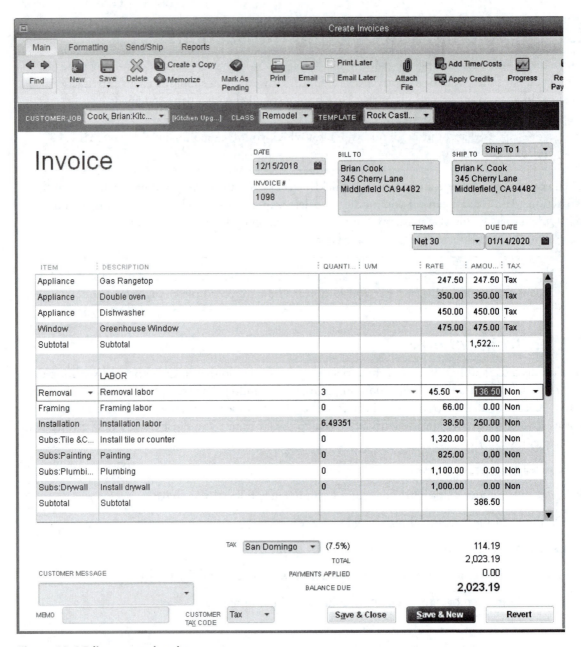

Figure 12-4 Edit an open invoice

5. Click *Save & Close* to save the invoice.

6. In the *Recording Transaction* message box (see Figure 12-5), click *Yes* to confirm that you really want to change the transaction.

   The message wording can vary. For example, if there are no linked transactions, the message is "You have changed the transaction. Do you want to record your changes?"

Figure 12-5 Recording Transaction message box

Voiding and Deleting Transactions

When you void or delete transactions, QuickBooks removes the debits and the credits associated with the transactions. However, you should almost always void transactions, rather than delete them. That's because deleting transactions removes all record of those transactions from your company file. If you void a transaction instead, QuickBooks changes the amounts to zero, but keeps a record of the date, number, and other details. In addition, you can fill in the voided transaction's *Memo* field with the reason you voided it.

In QuickBooks, the *Audit Trail* feature tracks transaction changes and deletions, which you can see by running the *Audit Trail* report. For more information about the *Audit Trail*, see QuickBooks *Help*. In addition, the *Voided/Deleted Transactions* report lists all voided and deleted transactions. This report is useful when you have several users working on a company file and you want to find out why transactions are disappearing when they shouldn't. The *Voided/Deleted Transactions* report includes the time, date, and user name for each void or deletion.

Computer Practice

To void a transaction, follow these steps:

1. In a transaction window or form, display the transaction you want to void. In this example, open the *Write Checks* window to check number 515 dated 12/15/2018.

2. On the *Edit* menu, choose *Void* (or right-click the transaction, and then choose *Void* from the shortcut menu).

3. In the *Memo* cell, type a note explaining why you're voiding the check, in this example, *Check never arrived, issuing new check.*

4. Click *Save & Close*.

5. In the *Recording Transaction* message box, click *Yes*.

    If you void a transaction that's been reconciled, QuickBooks displays the message shown in Figure 12-6. Click *No* and turn to page 146 to learn how to record a change to a reconciled transaction.

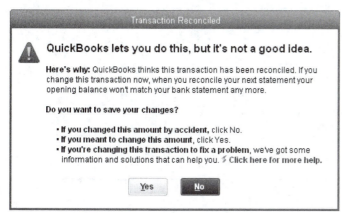

Figure 12-6 Recording Transaction message box

Note: Do not perform the following steps. They are for reference only.

To delete a transaction, do the following:

1. Open the transaction you want to delete in a transaction window (or select it in a register window).

2. On the *Edit* menu, choose *Delete* (or simply press *Ctrl+D*).

3. In the *Delete Transaction* message box, click *OK*.

> Note: For proper accounting, you shouldn't delete transactions. However, in some cases, you can delete transactions without causing problems in your financial records. For example, if you recorded a check by mistake and haven't printed it yet, you can delete it. However, if you already printed it, void the check so you have a record of the voided check and your check numbering sequence remains intact.

Deleting All Transactions

Suppose you want to create a new company file with all your existing lists (customers, vendors, employees, and so on) and preferences, but you don't want any of your existing transactions. QuickBooks' *Condense Data Utility* gives you the option to delete all transactions or transactions prior to a date you specify. To use the *Condense Data* feature, on the *File* menu, choose *Utilities*, and then choose *Condense Data* on the submenu. In Figure 12-7, the third option, *Transactions outside of a date range*, is available only in QuickBooks Accountant.

> Note: Do not use *Condense Data* with your exercise file.

Figure 12-7 Condense Data dialog box

Memorizing Transactions

If you record the same transactions again and again, you can save time by memorizing them in QuickBooks. For example, by memorizing your monthly rent check, the program can fill in the vendor, account, and amount, and remind you when it's time to pay the bill. Or you can memorize invoices if you perform similar services to multiple customers. Once you memorize transactions, you can choose the one you want to reuse, make sure the values in the new transaction are what you want, and then save it to create a new transaction. This section shows you how to memorize and then reuse a transaction.

Computer Practice

To memorize a transaction, in this example, a bill, follow these steps:

1. Open the bill you want to memorize in the *Enter Bills* window. In this example, click the *Previous* arrow at the window's top left until you see the bill to Cal Gas & Electric dated 12/15/2018 (see Figure 12-8).

2. At the top of the *Enter Bills* window, click *Memorize*.

   The *Memorize Transaction* window dialog box (Figure 12-9) opens.

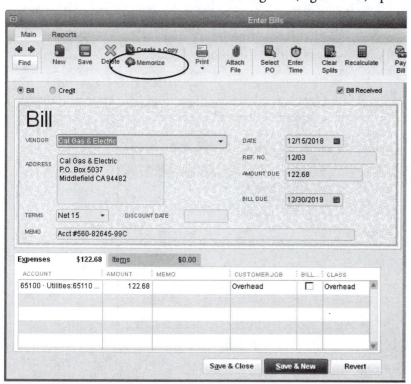

Figure 12-8 Opening a bill to memorize

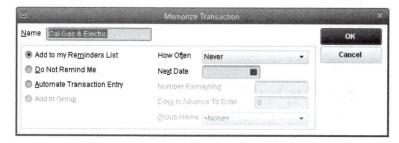

Figure 12-9 The Memorize Transaction dialog box

3. In the *Name* field, type a brief description so it's easy to identify the memorized transaction, in this example, *Gas & Electric Bill*.

4. Because the amount for this bill changes each month, keep the *Add to my Reminders List* option selected.

5. In the *How Often* drop-down list, choose *Monthly*.

6. In the *Next Date* field, choose the date you want to be reminded next, in this example, *1/15/2019*.

7. Click *OK*.

   QuickBooks adds the memorized transaction to the *Memorized Transaction* list.

8. Close the *Enter Bills* window.

To reuse a memorized transaction at any time, do the following:

1. On the *Lists* menu, choose *Memorized Transaction List*.

2. In the *Memorized Transaction List* window that opens, select the transaction you want (Gas & Electric Bill), and then click *Enter Transaction* at the bottom of the window.

   The corresponding transaction window opens with the memorized values filled in. Modify the data if necessary.

   If you reuse a memorized invoice, journal entry, or other transaction that QuickBooks numbers for you, the program fills in the next transaction number and the current date.

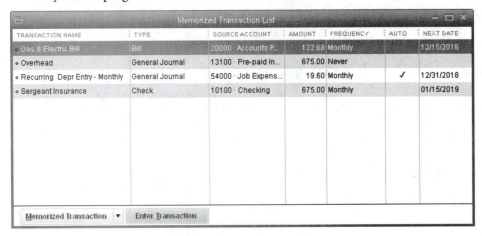

Figure 12-10 The Memorized Transaction List window

3. Edit the values if necessary. In this example, change the date to *1/15/2019* and the amount to *145.10*.

4. Click *Save & Close* to record the new transaction.

5. Close the *Memorized Transaction List* window.

Rescheduling or Renaming Memorized Transactions

You can rename a memorized transaction or change its schedule. This section describes the steps.

Computer Practice

To edit a memorized transaction's name or schedule, follow these steps:

1. On the *Lists* menu, choose *Memorized Transaction List*, or press *Ctrl+T*.

2. Select the transaction you want to edit (in this example, *Sergeant Insurance*), and then press *Ctrl+E* (or click *Memorized Transaction*, and then choose *Edit Memorized Transaction* from the drop-down list).

The *Schedule Memorized Transaction* window opens (see Figure 12-11). You can type a new name or choose different schedule options. You can't edit the actual transaction values. (The next section describes how to do that.)

3. In this example, change the name to *Annual Insurance Premium* and change the *How Often* field to *Quarterly*.

4. Click *OK*.

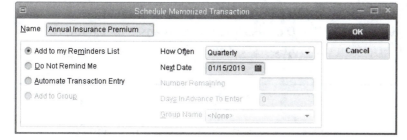

Figure 12-11 The Schedule Memorized Transaction window

Editing Memorized Transactions

Sometimes, you need to edit the contents of a memorized transaction, for example, to change prices, choose different items, or switch to a new vendor. To do that, you re-memorize the transaction. This section shows you how.

Computer Practice

To edit the contents of a memorized transaction, follow these steps:

1. On the *Lists* menu, choose *Memorized Transaction List*, or press *Ctrl+T*.

2. Double-click the transaction you want to edit, in this example, *Annual Insurance Premium*.

    The memorized transaction opens in its corresponding window with the memorized values filled in.

3. Change any fields you want. In this example, change the *Disability Insurance* value to *100*.

4. To re-memorize the transaction, click *Memorize* at the top of the window or press *Ctrl+M*.

    The *Replace Memorized Transaction* message box appears (Figure 12-12).

5. To re-memorize the edited transaction, click *Replace*.

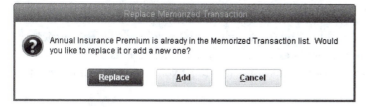

Figure 12-12 The Replace Memorized Transaction message box

6. If you don't want to save the actual transaction you created in order to memorize it, in the transaction window, click the *Clear* button at the bottom right, and then close the window.

Deleting Memorized Transactions

If you no longer need a memorized transaction, you can delete it by following these steps:

> Note: Don't perform these steps. They are for reference only.

1. On the *Lists* menu, choose *Memorized Transaction List*, or press *Ctrl+T*.

2. Select the transaction you want to delete.

3. To delete the memorized transaction, press *Ctrl+D* or click *Memorized Transaction*, and then choose *Delete Memorized Transaction* on the drop-down menu.

Closing Your Books

This section describes tasks you may perform to close your books for an accounting period. You'll also learn how to use QuickBooks' *Closing Date* field to lock transactions dated in closed accounting periods.

At the end of each year, QuickBooks automatically records an adjusting journal entry to transfer the year's net income or loss into the *Retained Earnings* (or *Owners Equity*) account. (This journal entry is known as the closing entry.) Table 12-1 demonstrates how the closing entry works. The *Net Income* on 12/31/2018 is $75,000 and *Retained Earnings* is $100,000. On January 1, 2019, the first day of the next fiscal year, QuickBooks transfers *Net Income* to *Retained Earnings*, so *Net Income* drops to zero, and *Retained Earnings* increases to $175,000. (In a QuickBooks *Balance Sheet* report, the program adds up net income for all prior years to calculate the *Retained Earnings* balance.)

Table 12-1 Anatomy of a QuickBooks closing entry

Equity on 12/31/2018		Equity on 1/1/2019	
Opening Balance Equity	0	Opening Balance Equity	0
Common Stock	50,000	Common Stock	50,000
Retained Earnings	100,000	Retained Earnings	175,000
Net Income	75,000	Net Income	0
Total Equity	225,000	Total Equity	225,000

Closing an Accounting Period

This section describes tasks you should perform at the end of each accounting period to close your company's books. Some companies close monthly or quarterly, while others close yearly. The entries that you record to close a period may include prepaid expense allocations, adjustments to equity, and non-cash entries, such as depreciation, so that your books correctly reflect your company's finances at the close of the period.

At the end of the accounting period, perform some or all of the following tasks:

1. Record depreciation of assets.

2. Reconcile bank, credit card, cash, and loan accounts with the statements through the end of the accounting period.

3. If you sell inventory, perform a physical inventory count on the last day of the period.

After the inventory count is complete, record an *Inventory Adjustment* transaction so that inventory quantities and values in QuickBooks match what's in your warehouse. Refer to Chapter 8 to learn how to adjust inventory.

4. If you use accrual basis accounting, create journal entries to accrue expenses and revenues. Ask your accountant for help with these entries.

5. For partnerships, record a journal entry to distribute net income for the period to each of the partner's capital accounts. For a sole proprietorship, record a journal entry to close the owner's draws into owner's equity. (The following section provides the details on recording these transactions.)

6. Run reports for the period and check them for accuracy. If necessary, record adjusting entries and rerun the reports.

7. Print or save PDF files for the following reports as of your closing date: *General Ledger*, *Balance Sheet Standard*, *Statement of Cash Flows*, *Trial Balance*, *Inventory Valuation Summary*, and *Profit & Loss Standard* for the accounting period.

8. Back up your data file (naming it something like Close2018.qbb) and store the backup in a safe place.

9. Set the closing date to the last day of the period. Set a closing date password to prevent users from changing transactions in the closed period. See page 376 to learn how to set the closing date.

Recording Investments and Closing Entries for Sole Proprietorships

In a sole proprietorship's chart of accounts, you use an *Owners Draw* account and *Owners Equity* account to keep track of owner investments, withdrawals, and equity in the company. In this section, you'll learn about how to record owner's transactions using these accounts.

> Note: Do not enter the transactions in this section. They are for reference only.

To record an owner's investment in a sole proprietorship, record a deposit in the company's checking account (or whichever account you deposit the money into). In the *From Account* field, choose

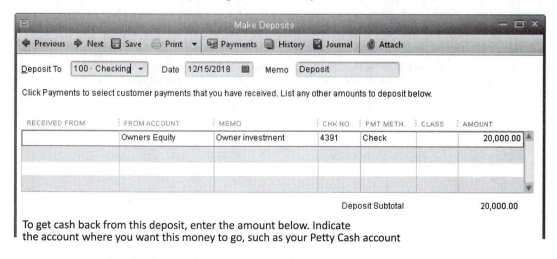

Figure 12-13 Depositing owner's investments in a sole proprietorship

Owners Equity (see Figure 12-13), which increases the owner's equity in the company.

To record an owner's withdrawal from the company, record a check written on the company checking

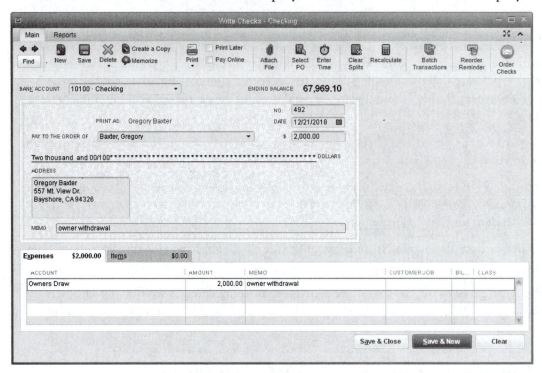

Figure 12-14 Taking an owner's draw from a sole proprietorship

account and made out to the owner. Choose *Owners Draw* in the *Account* field (see Figure 12-14), which decreases the owner's equity in the company.

At the end of each year, you record a journal entry to zero out the *Owners Draw* account and close it into the *Owners Equity* account, that is, you move the balance in the *Owners Draw* account to the *Owners Equity* account, as shown in Figure 12-15.

> Tip: To determine the value to use in the journal entry to close the *Owners Draw* account, run a *Trial Balance* report for the entire year. Then, use the balance in the *Owners Draw* account as the value for the journal entry. For example, if the *Owners Draw* account has a debit balance of $2,000.00 in your *Trial Balance* report, in the closing journal entry, enter $2,000.00 in the *Owners Draw* row's *Credit* cell to zero out the account. Then, enter a debit for the same amount in the *Owners Equity* account's row.

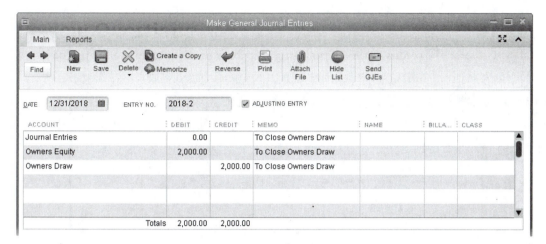

Figure 12-15 Closing out the Owners Draw account

Closing Entries and Distributing Net Income for Partnerships

A partnership's chart of accounts has a *Partners Draw* and *Partners Equity* account for each partner, such as Partner1 Draw, Partner1 Equity, Partner2 Draw, Partner2 Equity, and so on. Although a partnership has a *Retained Earnings* account, you zero it out at the end of each year. Similar to a sole proprietorship, you record transactions using the partners' draw and equity accounts to show additions to or withdrawals from the partners' equity. For example, you record deposits to partner equity accounts when partners make an investment in the partnership. Likewise, you write checks to partners if they withdraw money from the partnership.

> Note: Do not enter the transactions in this section. They are for reference only.

To close partner draw accounts into each partner's equity account, record a journal entry like the one shown in Figure 12-16. Run a year-end *Trial Balance* report to determine the value you need to use in the journal entry to zero out the partner draw accounts.

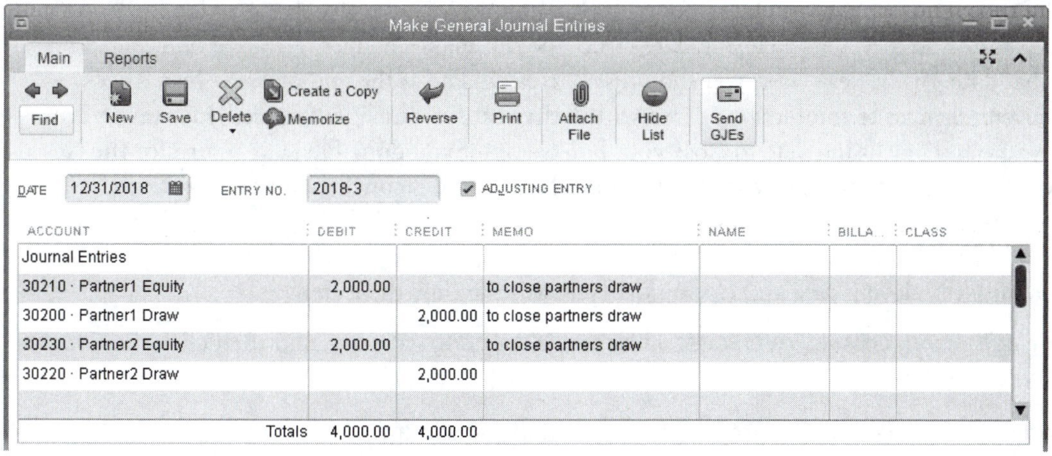

Figure 12-16 Closing out Partners' Draw accounts

To distribute the company profits into each partner's equity account, you need to record another journal entry. To determine the amount each partner receives, first make all your year-end adjustments, and then run a *Profit & Loss* report for the entire year. You then allocate the *Net Income* value at the bottom of the *Profit & Loss* report to the partners based on their ownership in the partnership, as shown in Figure 12-17. In this example, two equal partners share net income of $114,800.

In Figure 12-17, the journal entry debits *Retained Earnings*. Because QuickBooks automatically closes net income into the *Retained Earnings* account each year, you debit *Retained Earnings* in order to reduce its balance to zero. The credits in the journal entry distribute the net income to the partners.

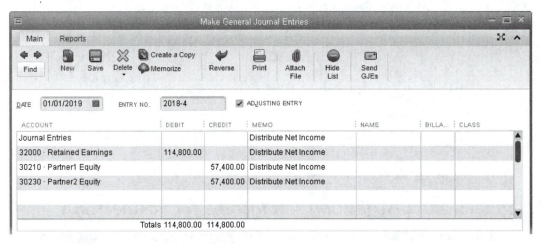

Figure 12-17 Distributing partners' profits

> Tip: The distribution journal entry date is January 1 because QuickBooks doesn't have a way to produce an after-closing *Balance Sheet* report. By recording this journal entry on January 1 of the next year, the December 31 *Balance Sheet* report represents before- closing and the January 1 *Balance Sheet* shows after-closing values. To reserve the January 1 *Balance Sheet* for the after-closing balance sheet, record all normal business transactions that occur on January 1 using January 2 as the transaction date.

Setting the QuickBooks Closing Date

Depending on your company, you may close your books monthly, quarterly, or yearly. In order to prevent changes to transactions in closed periods, QuickBooks includes a preference that lets someone with administrator privileges set a closing date so no one can make changes to transactions dated on or before that date. At the very least, you should set a closing date at the end of every year. That way, you can prevent changes to transactions dated within the year for which you've filed your tax returns. However, you can set a closing date to close your books even if you don't file a tax return for the closed period. For example, you can close your books monthly after you reconcile your bank account.

Computer Practice

To set or modify the closing date and closing date password, follow these steps:

1. On the *Edit* menu, choose *Preferences*, click the *Accounting* category, and then click the *Company Preferences* tab.

2. Click the *Set Date/Password* button at the bottom of the window.

    The *Set Closing Date and Password* window opens (see Figure 12-18).

3. In the *Closing Date* field, choose the closing date you want, in this example, *12/31/2018*.

    After you save the closing date, users without administrator privileges can't make changes to transactions dated on or before that date.

4. In the *Closing Date Password* and *Confirm Password* fields, type a password, in this example, *Student1234*. In a production environment, you should create a strong password.

    Setting a password protects transactions in closed periods from being edited or deleted. When you set a password, all users, including the administrator, must enter that password before they can add, change, or delete transactions dated on or before the closing date. If you don't set a closing date password, the company file administrator can bypass the closing date by ignoring the warning that appears.

    > Tip: When you set up new users, always choose the setting that prevents them from changing or deleting transactions recorded on or before the closing date.

5. In this example, click *Cancel*, so you don't save the closing changes. Click *OK* to save the dialog box, and then click *OK* to close the *Preferences* dialog box.

Figure 12-18 Setting a closing date and password

Review Questions

Select the best answer for each of the following questions:

1. Voiding transactions is preferable to deleting transactions because:

    a) Voiding transactions keeps a record of the date, number, and transaction detail.

    b) Deleting transactions completely removes all record of the transactions.

    c) You can add a memo to a voided transaction to explain the reason you voided it.

    d) All of the above.

2. QuickBooks automatically performs which tasks at year-end?

    a) Creates journal entries to zero out income and expense accounts.

    b) Creates a journal entry to zero out Retained Earnings.

    c) Adjusts the Retained Earnings account balance to reflect the net income or loss for the year.

    d) Automatically backs up the company file.

3. Which transactions can you use to make an adjustment to *Items* and their associated accounts?

    a) General Journal Entry

    b) Deposit

    c) Check for zero dollars

    d) Credit card charge for zero dollars

4. Choosing a date in the *Closing Date* field:

    a) Sets the date that QuickBooks automatically enters your closing journal entries.

    b) Locks transactions dated on or before the *Closing Date* so users can't add, change, or delete those transactions unless they have administrator privileges.

    c) Locks transactions dated on or before the *Closing Date* so users must enter a password in order to add, change, or delete those transactions.

    d) Defines your company's fiscal year.

5. At the end of the year, you should perform the following tasks:

    a) Enter depreciation entries.

    b) Perform a physical inventory.

    c) If your business is a partnership, record journal entries to distribute net income for the year to each of the partner's capital accounts.

    d) If your business is a sole proprietorship, record a journal entry to close owner's draw and owner's investments into the Owners Equity account.

Adjustments and Year-end Procedures Exercise 1

Applying Your Knowledge

Restore the sample file, sample_product-based business 2015 (Portable).QBM. (Or, if you are using QuickBooks 2014, restore sample_product-based business 2014 (Portable).QBM.)

1. Create journal entry *2018-1* on *12/31/2018* to recategorize *$10,000.00* in the Labor Income account from the *Remodel* class to *New Construction* class. Enter the *Journal Entries* account in the first row of the journal entry. (Hint: Debit the *Remodel* class and credit the *New Construction* class.) Enter a memo *Reclassify class* in each line of the journal entry.

2. Void check number *474* and create journal entries to balance the accounts affected by the check.

3. Run and print a *Journal* report. (On the *Reports* menu, choose *Accountant & Taxes*, and then choose *Journal*.) Set the *Date* field to *This Fiscal Quarter*. Filter the report to only show journal transactions.

Adjustments and Year-end Procedures Exercise 2 (Advanced)

Applying Your Knowledge

Restore the sample file, sample_product-based business 2015 (Portable).QBM. (Or, if you are using QuickBooks 2014, restore sample_product-based business 2014 (Portable).QBM.)

1. Create journal entry *2018-1* on *12/31/2018* to recategorize *$69.20* from Postage to Job Expenses: Freight & Delivery. Enter the *Journal Entries* account in the first row of the journal entry. Use class *Remodel*. Enter a memo *Reclassify account* in each line of the journal entry.

2. Create journal entry *2018-2* on *12/31/2018* to record *$43,321* in depreciation for the company's fixed assets. (Hint: Debit Depreciation Expense, credit Accumulated Depreciation.) Use the *Journal Entries* account in the first row of the journal entry. Enter a memo *Depreciation for fixed assets* in each row. Class: *Overhead*.

3. Memorize the depreciation journal entry from Step 2 using the *Memorize* feature and schedule it to be automatically entered every year on *December 31* (the next occurrence is *12/31/2019*) for *5* more years. Name the transaction *Annual Depreciation*.

4. Run and print a *Balance Sheet Standard* report as of *12/31/2018*. Collapse categories so you can see the accumulated depreciation.

5. Run and print a *Journal* report for *12/01/2018* through *12/31/2018* filtered to show only journal entries.

Chapter 13

Setting Up a Company File

Topics

This chapter covers the following topics:

- Choosing a Start Date
- Creating a Company File in QuickBooks
- Fine-tuning the Chart of Accounts
- Setting Up Other QuickBooks Lists
- Defining Account Opening Balances
- Entering Open Transactions
- Entering Year-to-Date Income and Expenses
- Adjusting the Opening Balance for Sales Tax Payable
- Adjusting Inventory
- Setting Up Fixed Assets
- Setting Up Payroll and Year-to-date Payroll Information
- Verifying Your Trial Balance
- Closing Opening Balance Equity
- Setting the Closing Date
- Creating Additional Users

When you create a new company file in QuickBooks, the program performs a lot of the setup for you. However, there's more to do before you can start keeping your books in earnest: fine-tuning your chart of accounts, defining account balances, and so on. You'll also learn how to set up additional users if other people work on your company file.

> Note: The steps in this chapter work whether you're just starting your company, you're switching from another accounting program to QuickBooks, or you're starting over because the previous company file has too many issues to fix.

Choosing a Start Date

Before you create a company file, you need to choose a start date for your records. The date that you choose should be the day *before* you start tracking your finances with QuickBooks:

- If you're just starting your business, the start date is the day you form your company.

- If the business is already established and you use the calendar year for tax reporting, December 31 of the previous year is the best start date.

- If you use a fiscal year other than the calendar year, choose the last day of your previous fiscal year.

- If you don't want to start at the end of the previous year, you can choose the last day of the previous quarter or month. However, if you choose this option, your company file won't contain all your financial details for the year.

You have to record all transactions between your start date and the date you set up your company file. For example, if you set up your company file on January 10 and use December 31 of the previous year as the start date, you must enter all your company's transactions between December 31 and January 10.

See page 391 to learn how to define the start date in QuickBooks.

Creating a Company File in QuickBooks

QuickBooks provides two main methods for creating a company file. *Express Start* requires only a few fields of information, which means you have to set more QuickBooks preferences and perform more cleanup once your company file exists. On the other hand, the *EasyStep Interview* helps you set preferences and fill in company details, so your company file setup is closer to being complete at the end of the interview. This section describes how to use the *EasyStep Interview*.

> Note: If you use *Express Start*, the only information you have to provide is a company name, industry, company type, and tax ID. Once the company file exists, you can enter customers, vendors, employees, items, and bank accounts. QuickBooks sets up the chart of accounts and selects preferences based on the industry you choose.

Setting Up a Company File Using the EasyStep Interview

The *EasyStep Interview* asks you a series of questions and uses your answers to set up the company file and several QuickBooks preferences.

Computer Practice

To create a new company file using the *EasyStep Interview*, follow these steps:

1. On the *File* menu, choose *New Company*. In the *QuickBooks Setup* dialog box, click *Detailed Start*. (If you use an edition other than QuickBooks Accountant, the button is labeled *Advanced Start*.

   The *EasyStep Interview* dialog box appears.

2. On the *Enter your company information* screen (Figure 13-1), fill in your company name, tax ID, and contact information. Then, click *Next*.

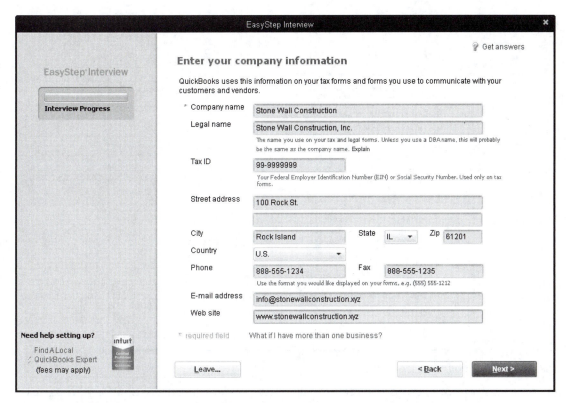

Figure 13-1 The Enter your company information screen

> Note: After you fill in the fields in one of the interview's screens, click *Next* to proceed to the next screen. If you want to go back to an earlier screen, click *Back* until you see the screen you want. If you want to exit the interview before you've completed all the steps, click *Leave*. (If you click *Leave* before QuickBooks creates the company file, you'll lose all the data you've entered so far.) If the company file has been created and you click *Leave*, QuickBooks saves your data. The next time you open the company file, the program re-opens the *EasyStep Interview*.

3. On the *Select your industry* screen (Figure 13-2), choose the industry that is the closest match to your company's industry, in this example, *Construction Trades*. Then, click *Next*.

    QuickBooks recommends features, such as sales tax, estimates, and inventory, based on the industry you choose. If none of the industries are what you want, scroll to the bottom of the list, and then choose either *General Product-based Business* or *General Service-based Business*.

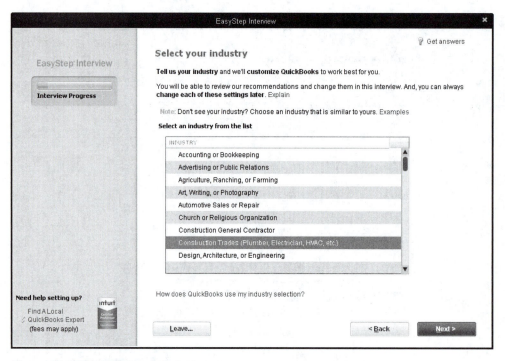

Figure 13-2 The Select your industry screen

4. On the *How is your company organized?* screen (Figure 13-3), select the option for your company's type of business entity, in this example, *S Corporation*. Then, click *Next*.

QuickBooks uses this selection to choose appropriate accounts for your chart of accounts, the tax form your business must file, and the tax lines to assign to your accounts.

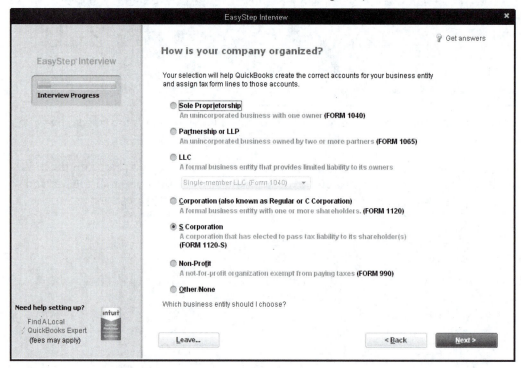

Figure 13-3 The How is your company organized? screen

5. On the *Select the first month of your fiscal year* screen (Figure 13-4), choose the first month of your fiscal year, in this example, *January*. Then, click *Next*.

    This field specifies the month that QuickBooks uses as the first month of the year in year-to-date reports.

Figure 13-4 The Select the first month of your fiscal year screen

6. On the *Set up your administrator password* screen (Figure 13-5), you would fill in the *Administrator password* and *Retype password* fields. In this example, leave these fields blank, because you are only creating a practice file. Then, click *Next*.

    The administrator password is optional. However, you should assign a password to the administrator user to protect your data. The administrator is the only user with access to all areas of the company file.

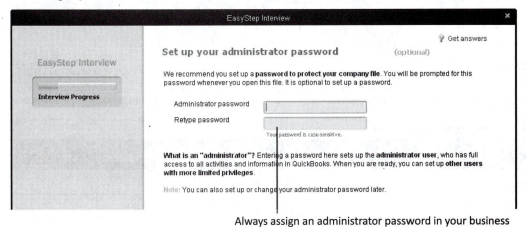

Always assign an administrator password in your business company files. In the practice file, leave these fields blank.

Figure 13-5 The Set up your administrator password screen

7. On the *Create your company file* screen, click *Next*.

8. In the *Filename for New Company* dialog box, navigate to the folder where you want to store your company file, as shown in Figure 13-6. In this example, choose your student data file folder.

    QuickBooks automatically fills in the *File name* field with your company's name followed by *.qbw* and sets the *Save as type* field to *QuickBooks Files (*.QBW, *.QBA)*. If you want to use a different file name, edit the *File name* field.

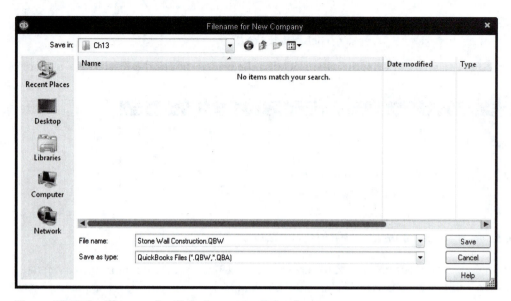

Figure 13-6 The Filename for New Company dialog box

9. Click *Save*.

   QuickBooks creates your company file. At this point, you can click *Leave* without losing any of the data you entered so far. When you open this company file the next time, QuickBooks opens the *EasyStep Interview* to the screen you were on when you clicked *Leave*.

10. When the *Customizing QuickBooks for your business* screen appears, click *Next*.

    The next several screens that appear guide you through setting preferences and customizing your company file. Use Table 13-1 to answer the *EasyStep Interview* questions. Click *Next* to proceed to each screen.

Table 13-1 EasyStep Interview questions

Questions	Answers
What do you sell?	Both services and products
Do you charge sales tax?	Yes
Do you want to create estimates in QuickBooks?	Yes
Do you want to track sales orders before you invoice your customers?	Yes (Note: this question doesn't appear if you use QuickBooks Pro, because it doesn't offer sales orders.)
Do you want to use billing statements in QuickBooks?	Yes
Do you want to use progress invoicing?	Yes
Do you want to keep track of bills you owe?	Yes
Do you want to track inventory in QuickBooks?	Yes
Do you want to track time in QuickBooks?	Yes
Do you have employees?	Yes (and turn on the *We have W-2 employees* checkbox and the *We have 1099 contractors* checkbox)

11. On the *Using accounts in QuickBooks* screen, click *Next*.

12. On the *Select a date to start tracking your finances* screen (Figure 13-7), select your QuickBooks company file start date. (See page 386 for more information on selecting a start date.) In this example, select the *Use today's date or the first day of the quarter or month* option, and then type *12/31/2018* in the box. Click *Next*.

Figure 13-7 The Select a date to start tracking your finances screen

The *Review income and expense accounts* screen (Figure 13-8) lists the accounts recommended for your industry.

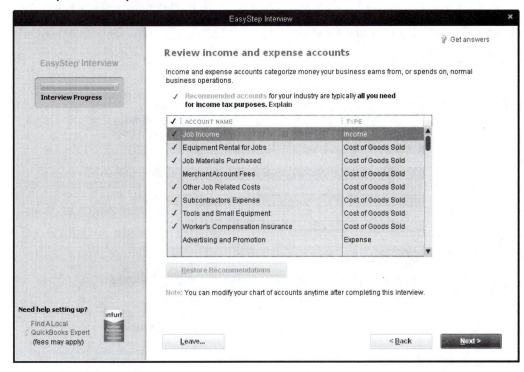

Figure 13-8 The Review income and expense accounts screen

13. On the *Congratulations!* Screen (Figure 13-9), click *Go to Setup*.

The *EasyStep Interview* is now complete. The *QuickBooks Setup* dialog box opens to the *You've got a company file! Now add your info* screen. This screen provides an easy way to add customers, vendors, employees, items, and bank accounts to your company file.

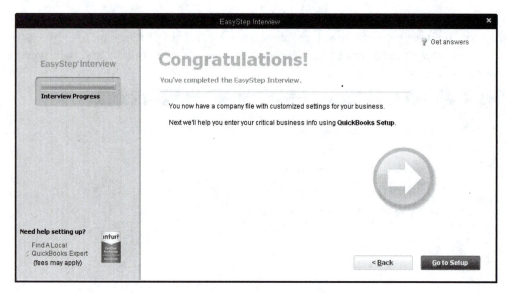

Figure 13-9 The Congratulations! Screen

The *Now add your info* screen (Figure 13-10) contains *Add* buttons you can click to add that type of information.

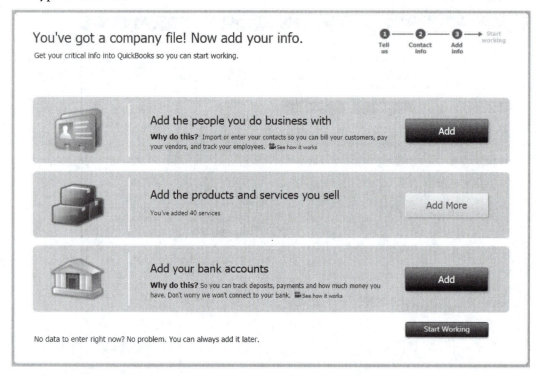

Figure 13-10 The You've got a company file! Now add your info screen

14. Click the *Add* button in the *Add the people you do business with* panel.

    The *Add the people you do business with* screen appears (Figure 13-11). You can import names from Outlook, Yahoo, or Gmail. Alternatively, you can paste data from an Excel spreadsheet. In this example, click *Cancel* to return to the previous screen without adding names.

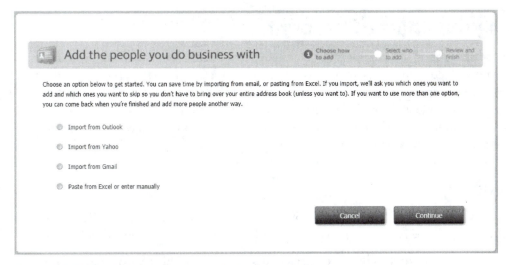

Figure 13-11 *The Add the people you do business with screen*

15. Click the *Add* button in the *Add your bank accounts* panel. In this example, fill in the values shown in Figure 13-12 to add a checking account to the company file.

    Fill in the *Account number* cell with the account number assigned to your bank account by your financial institution.

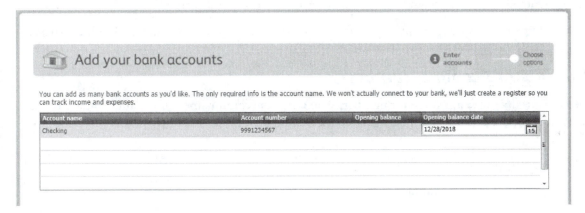

Figure 13-12 *Adding a bank account to your company file*

16. After you add your checking account, click *Continue*. Select the *No Thanks* option to decline ordering Intuit checks. If other offers appear, decline them, too.

17. Click *Continue*.

18. When the screen for adding info reappears, click the *Start Working* button at the screen's bottom right.

19. Close the *Quick Start Center* window that appears.

Your company file now has a default chart of accounts including a checking account. In addition, several QuickBooks preferences are set based on the answers you provided during the *EasyStep Interview*. You're ready to proceed to the next task in company file setup: fine-tuning the chart of accounts, which is described in the next section.

Fine-tuning the Chart of Accounts

In bookkeeping and accounting, an *account* is like a category that tracks money used for a specific purpose. Money you earn goes into an income account. When you buy materials, services, or supplies, that money ends up in an expense account. If you buy a car, its value is tracked in an asset account. And if you owe money to someone, your loan appears in a liability account. Your *chart of accounts* is a list of all the accounts you use to track your business finances. This section describes how to add, edit, and remove accounts in your chart of accounts.

Account Types

The chart of accounts is made up of five basic types of accounts (used in either *Profit and Loss* reports or *Balance Sheet* reports). These basic account types are broken down further in QuickBooks:

- **Assets**: Asset account types include Bank, Accounts Receivable, Other Current Asset, Fixed Asset, and Other Asset.

- **Liabilities**: Liability account types include Accounts Payable, Credit Card, Other Current Liability, and Long Term Liability.

- **Equity**: Equity doesn't have any subtypes.

- **Income**: Income account types include Income and Other Income.

- **Expenses**: Expense account types include Cost of Goods Sold, Expense, and Other Expense.

Turning on Account Numbers

QuickBooks doesn't require account numbers. You can use account names only to differentiate accounts. However, if you want to assign account numbers, you must first turn on that preference in QuickBooks.

Computer Practice

Here's how to turn account numbers on:

1. On the *Edit* menu, choose *Preferences*. Choose the *Accounting* category, and then click the *Company Preferences* tab.

   You have to be a QuickBooks administrator to turn on account numbers.

2. Turn on the *Use account numbers* checkbox, as shown in Figure 13-13.

3. Click *OK* to close the *Preferences* dialog box.

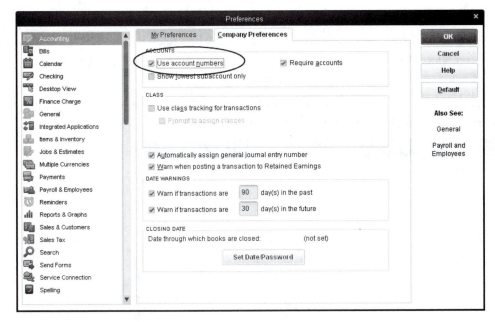

Figure 13-13 Turning on account numbers

Adding Accounts

If the chart of accounts that QuickBooks creates doesn't include accounts you want to use, you can create them. (Figure 13-14 shows some of the accounts QuickBooks creates for a company file when you choose the Construction Trades industry.) If you aren't sure which accounts you need, ask your accountant or QuickBooks Pro Advisor for help.

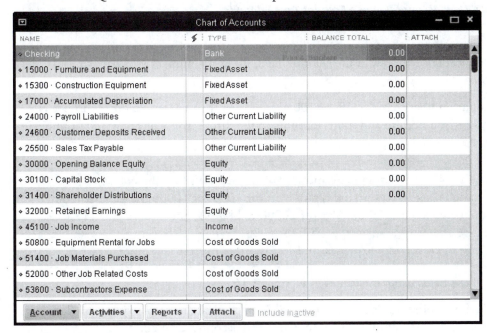

Figure 13-14 The Chart of Accounts window

Computer Practice

To add a new account to your company file's chart of accounts, follow these steps:

1. On the *Home Page*, click the *Chart of Accounts* icon (in the *Company* panel) or press *Ctrl+A*.

2. At the bottom of the window, click the *Account* button, and then choose *New*. (Alternatively, you can simply press *Ctrl+N*.)

3. In the *Add New Account: Choose Account Type* window (Figure 13-15), select the radio button for the type of account you want to add, in this example, *Expense*.

   If the account type you want doesn't have a corresponding radio button, select the *Other Account Types* radio button, and then choose the type from the drop-down list.

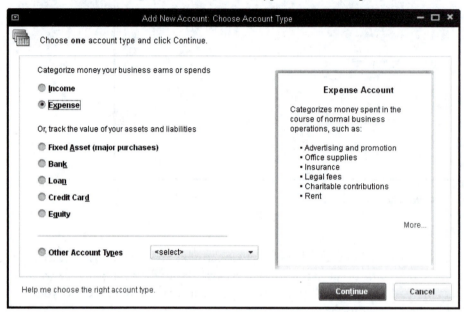

Figure 13-15 The Add New Account: Choose Account Type window

4. Click *Continue*.

5. In the *Add New Account* window, in the *Number* field, fill in the number you want, in this example, *64400*.

   Choose an account number that is 5, 10, or 100 greater than the previous account number in the list. That way, if you need to add more accounts in the future, you won't have to renumber existing accounts.

   > Tip: The accounting world has standard numbering conventions for different types of accounts. For example, asset accounts are typically in the 1000 (or 10000) range. Liabilities usually are numbered from 2000 to 2999 (or 20000 to 29999). Equity covers the 3000 (or 30000) range and income spans the 4000 (or 40000) range. After that, the remaining ranges cover cost of goods sold, expenses, and finally, other income and other expenses.

6. Fill in the rest of the fields using the values in Figure 13-16.

   If you use TurboTax or other QuickBooks-compatible tax software to prepare your company's tax return, select the tax line on your tax return to which this account corresponds.

7. Click *Save & Close*.

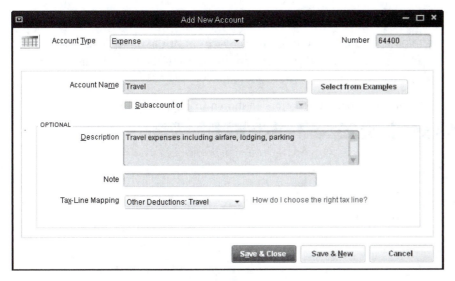

Figure 13-16 The Add New Account window

> Note: You can edit an account to change its values, for example, to add an account number or edit the description. To edit an account, in the *Chart of Accounts* window, right-click the account you want to edit, such as *Checking*, and then choose *Edit Account* on the shortcut menu. Or, click the *Account* button at the bottom of the window, and then choose *Edit Account* on the drop-down menu. For the *Checking* account, fill in the *Number* field with *10000*.

Adding Subaccounts

To track your finances in more detail, you can create subaccounts within your chart of accounts. Subaccounts also help when you need to assign similar expense types to different lines on tax forms. For example, meal and entertainment expenses are only partially deductible, whereas other travel expenses are fully deductible. You might create *Meals and Entertainment* as a separate subaccount within the *Travel* parent account.

Computer Practice

You can create up to five levels of subaccounts. (A subaccount must be the same account type as its parent account.) To create a subaccount, follow these steps:

1. On the *Home Page*, click the *Chart of Accounts* icon (in the *Company* panel) or press *Ctrl+A*. (You can also open this window by choosing *Chart of Accounts* from the *Lists* menu.)

2. At the bottom of the window, click the *Account* button, and then choose *New*.

3. In the *Add New Account: Choose Account Type* window, select the radio button for the type of account you want to add, in this example, *Expense*. Click *Continue*.

4. In the *Add New Account* window, in the *Number* field, fill in the number you want, in this example, *64410*.

5. In the *Account Name* field, type the account name, in this example, *Lodging*.

6. Turn on the *Subaccount of* checkbox, and then choose the parent account in the drop-down list, in this example, *Travel*.

7. Fill in the rest of the fields using the values in Figure 13-17.

8. Click *Save & Close*.

9. Edit the *Meals and Entertainment* account to make it a subaccount of the travel parent account. (Right-click the account and then choose *Edit Account* on the shortcut menu.) Change its account number to *64420*.

Subaccounts are indented from their parent accounts as shown in Figure 13-18.

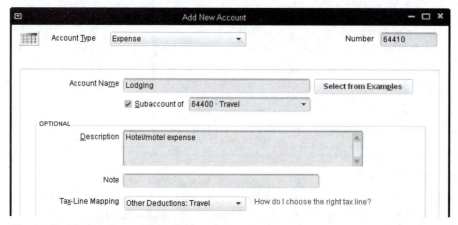

Figure 13-17 Creating a subaccount

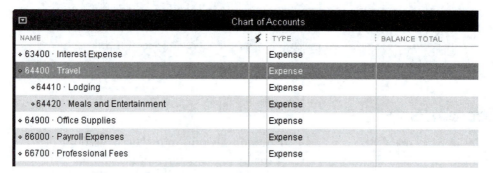

Figure 13-18 Subaccounts in the Chart of Accounts window

> Note: If you create subaccounts, you should use only those subaccounts in transactions, not the parent account. If you assign a transaction to a parent account, QuickBooks creates another account with "-Other" appended to the end of the parent account name.

If you use subaccounts, consider turning on the *Show lowest subaccount only* checkbox (below the circled checkbox in Figure 13-13). That way, QuickBooks displays only the lowest level accounts in account drop-down lists so you can't choose parent accounts by mistake.

Removing Accounts from the Chart of Accounts

If you no longer need an account, you can remove it from the Chart of Accounts window in a couple of ways. (This technique works with entries in most QuickBooks lists, including customers, vendors, and items.)

> Note: If an account hasn't been referenced in any way in your company file, you can delete it. To do so, select the account in the *Chart of Accounts* window and then press *Ctrl+D* (or click the *Account* button, and then choose *Delete Account*). If the account has been used in even one transaction or is referenced in an item record, you can't delete it.

Making Accounts Inactive

The best way to remove an account from the *Chart of Accounts* window is to make it inactive. With this method, your historical records are preserved and you can reactivate the account if you discover you need it in the future.

> Note: Do not perform the following steps. They are for reference only.

To make an account inactive, follow these steps:

1. In the *Chart of Accounts* window, select the account you want to make inactive.

2. Click the *Account* button, and then choose *Make Account Inactive*, as shown in Figure 13-19.

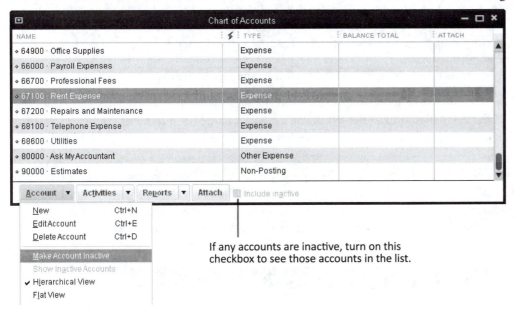

Figure 13-19 Making an account inactive

> Tip: To view both active and inactive accounts in the *Chart of Accounts* window, turn on the *Include inactive* check box below the table. When you do that, an *X* appears to the left of the name of each inactive account. You can reactivate the account by clicking its *X*.

Merging Accounts

If you no longer need an account because you already have another account you can use, you can merge one account into another. When you merge two accounts, QuickBooks reassigns all the transactions to the account that remains and removes the obsolete account from the list. (You can't undo account merging.)

> Note: Do not perform the following steps. They are for reference only.

To merge two accounts, follow these steps:

1. In the *Chart of Accounts* window, select the account you no longer need, for example, an account called *Entertainment*.

2. Click the *Account* button, and then choose *Edit Account*.

3. In the *Name* field, type the exact same name as the account you want to keep, such as *Meals & Entertainment*.

4. Click *Save & Close*.

5. When QuickBooks asks if you want to merge the two accounts, click *Yes*.

Reordering the Chart of Accounts

In the *Chart of Accounts* window, if you don't use account numbers, accounts are initially sorted by account type and then alphabetically by account name within each account type category. If you use account numbers, accounts are sorted by account number. You can sort accounts in the *Chart of Accounts* window by other fields. You can also drag accounts within the list.

> Note: Do not perform the following steps. They are for reference only.

- To sort accounts by a field, click the field name at the top of the list.

- To drag an account to another position within the same account type category, put your cursor over the small diamond to the left of the account's name (or number if you use account numbers). Then drag until the account is where you want it, as shown in Figure 13-20.

> Note: To keep accounts in your financial reports in the correct order, you can rearrange accounts only within the same account type category. In addition, QuickBooks treats a parent account and its subaccounts as a group. Because of that, you can't drag an account into the middle of a parent/subaccount group. You can drag it above or below the group.

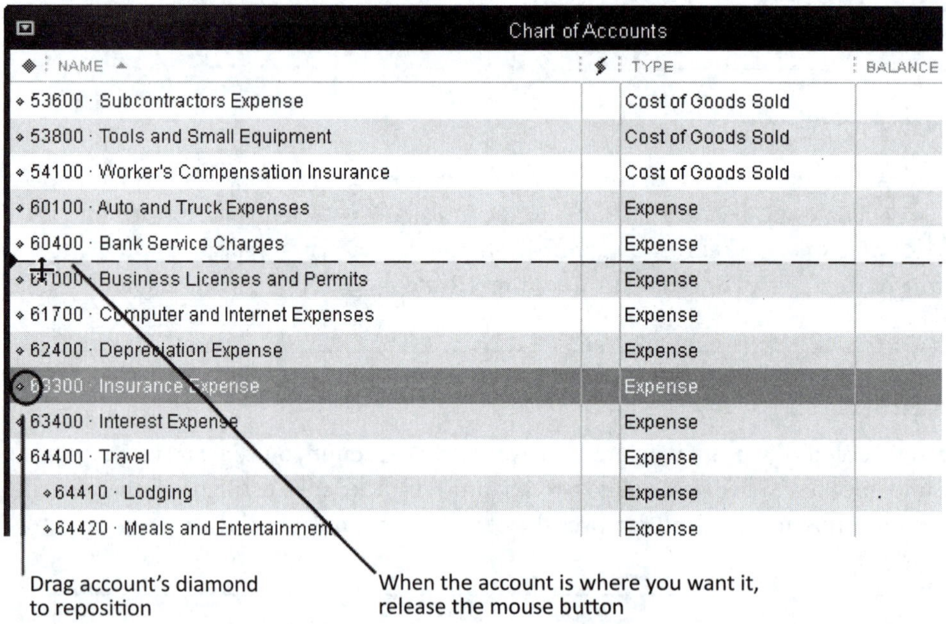

Figure 13-20 Repositioning an account in the Chart of Accounts window

Setting Up Other QuickBooks Lists

At this point in company file setup, you can add information to other QuickBooks lists, such as the *Customers and Jobs List*, *Vendors List*, *Class List*, *Terms List*, and so on. You can use the *QuickBooks Setup Add Info* screen (see page 392) to add information about customers, vendors, employees, and items. Refer to the other chapters in this book to learn about creating customers, jobs, vendors, employees, items, and other list entries.

Computer Practice

For this example, create the sales tax items shown in Table 13-2.

Table 13-2 Sales tax items

Item Type	Item Name	Description	Account	Amount
Sales Tax Item	Illinois State sales tax	Illinois State sales tax Sales tax is paid to the Illinois Department of Revenue. (Use QuickAdd to add as vendor.)	Sales Tax Payable	6.25%
Sales Tax Item	Rock Island City sales tax	Rock Island City sales tax Sales tax is paid to the Illinois Department of Revenue.	Sales Tax Payable	1.25%
Sales Tax Group	Rock Island City total tax	Rock Island City total tax Note: Add Illinois State sales tax and Rock Island City sales tax to group.	Sales Tax Payable	

Note: For the computer practice in the remainder of this chapter, use *QuickAdd* to add customers, jobs, vendors, and employees as needed.

Defining Account Opening Balances

After your chart of accounts is set up, it's time to enter opening balances for your accounts. Before you can do that in QuickBooks, you need to collect the paperwork and reports that document those opening balance values. Here are two methods for obtaining your account opening balances if your company has been operating for some time:

- Use the trial balance as of your company file start date that you get from your accountant or your previous accounting program.

  If you chose the end of your fiscal year as your start date, use the after-closing trial balance, which is the trial balance after income and expenses have been closed into *Retained Earnings*. Table 13-3 shows a sample after-closing trial balance for Stone Wall Construction as of the start date of 12/31/2018.

- Use an after-closing *Balance Sheet* report and a year-to-date *Profit & Loss* report as of your start date.

Note: If you're just launching your company, your account opening balances are zero.

Table 13-3 Trial Balance for Stone Wall Construction

Account	Debit	Credit
Checking	10,850.22	
Accounts Receivable	6,075.00	
Inventory	1,914.00	
Furniture and Equipment	10,000.00	
Accumulated Depreciation		1,000.00
Accounts Payable		1500.00
Payroll Liabilities		350.00
Sales Tax Payable		165.00
Capital Stock		10,000.00
Retained Earnings		15,839.22
Total	**28,839.22**	**28,839.22**

Gathering Opening Balance Values

This section identifies where you can obtain your opening balance values.

- **Bank statements**: Collect your most recent statements from each bank account (and credit card account) with ending dates prior to your company file start date. For example, if your start date is *12/31/2018*, use the bank statements with ending dates just before *12/31/2018*. Figure 13-21 shows the checking account bank statement that ends on *12/29/2018*.

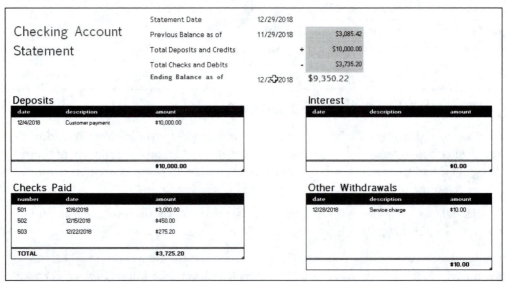

Figure 13-21 Checking account statement

- **Outstanding checks and deposits**: You also need a list of the checks and deposits that haven't cleared your bank between your bank statement ending date and your company file start date. In this example, suppose you have an outstanding customer deposit of *$2,000* dated *12/30/2018* and check number *504* for *$500* dated *12/30/2018*.

Tip: You can simplify your bookkeeping by asking your bank to change your statement dates to the end of the month. In addition, your bank's web site might offer a feature that lets you run a statement that ends on the date you choose.

- **Unpaid Bills**: List each vendor's bill with bill date, amount due, and the expenses or items you purchased, as shown in Table 13-4.

Table 13-4 Unpaid bills

Bill No.	Bill date	Vendor	Amount	Account or item	Customer: Job	Class	Terms
1201	12/22/2018	Rock It	1500.00	Job Materials Purchased	Customer – Ryan, Anna Job – Remodel	Retail	Net 30

- **Open Invoices**: List each open (unpaid) customer invoice including invoice date, amount due, and items sold (Table 13-5).

Note: For this example, assign the *Rock Island City total tax* item to the retail customer and make the *Site Work* performed taxable.

Table 13-5 Open invoices

Inv. No.	Invoice date	Customer: Job	Amount	Items	Qty	Class	Terms
412	12/18/2018	Customer – Ryan, Anna	1000.00	Site Work: Demo		Retail	Net 15
414	12/20/2018	Customer – Rock Castle Construction	5000.00	Masonry		Wholesale	Net 30

- **Employee list and W-4 information for each employee**: You need each employee's full name, address, social security number, and withholding information.

- **Payroll information**: If your start date is in the middle of a calendar year and you want to track payroll with QuickBooks (creating payroll reports, Form 940, Form 941, W-2s and so on), you need to collect the amount due as of your start date for each of your payroll liabilities (Federal withholding, employer Social Security, employee Social Security, and so on). You also need gross earnings, withholdings, employer taxes, and any other deductions for each employee year to date. Finally, you need to know any payroll tax deposits you've made during the year by payroll item.

Note: If your start date is 12/31, you can skip this payroll information and simply enter the payroll liabilities account opening balances, as shown later in this chapter.

- **Physical inventory**: List the quantity and cost for each product you keep in inventory as of your start date (see Table 13-6).

Table 13-6 Physical Inventory as of start date

Item	Quantity on hand	Value
Flagstone – gray	7,200	$864.00
Sandstone - flat	7,000	$1,050.00

Recording Account Opening Balances

A journal entry is the best way to record opening balances for most of your accounts. With a journal entry, you can record account opening balances for several accounts at the same time. In addition, you can specify the accounts to debit and credit.

The exceptions for your opening-balance journal entry are bank accounts, Accounts Payable (AP), Accounts Receivable (AR), Inventory, Sales Tax Payable, and Retained Earnings:

- **Bank accounts**: In an opening-balance journal entry, you can enter the ending balance from the bank statement dated just prior to your company file start date. However, after you record the journal entry, you need to record any transactions that occurred between that statement date and your company file start date.

- **Accounts Payable (AP)**: To define your AP balance, you record unpaid bills in QuickBooks (page 407). You can add your *Accounts Payable* account to a journal entry, but you need to fill in a vendor name to do that and you can add the *Accounts Payable* account to only one line in the journal entry.

- **Accounts Receivable (AR)**: To define your AR balance, you record open invoices in QuickBooks (page 408). Although you can add your *Accounts Receivable* account to a journal entry, you need to fill in a customer name to do that and you can add the *Accounts Receivable* account to only one line in the journal entry.

- **Inventory**: To record your inventory value, you record an inventory adjustment, as you'll learn on page 412.

- **Sales Tax Payable**: You need to adjust sales tax payable to reflect collected sales taxes, as described on page 411.

- **Retained Earnings**: After you record the opening balances for all your other accounts, you close any outstanding values in the *Opening Balance Equity* account to *Retained Earnings*. (See page 414.)

> Note: The *New Account* and *Edit Account* windows include an *Enter Opening Balance* button. Clicking that button lets you specify the opening balance for the account that you're creating or editing. If you do that, QuickBooks adds that balance to the *Opening Balance Equity* account.

Computer Practice

Use the information from the trial balance in Table 13-3 to create an opening-balance journal entry. Here are the steps to record this journal entry:

1. On the *Company* menu, choose *Make General Journal Entries*.

   If the *Assign Numbers to Journal Entries* dialog box appears, turn on the *Do not display this message in the future* checkbox, and then click *OK*.

2. In the *Make General Journal Entries* window (Figure 13-22), in the *Date* field, choose your com-

pany file start date, in this example, *12/31/2018*.

If you are using a QuickBooks edition other than QuickBooks Accountant, your *Make General Journal Entries* window may differ from the one in Figure 13-22.

3. Turn off the *Adjusting Entry* checkbox.

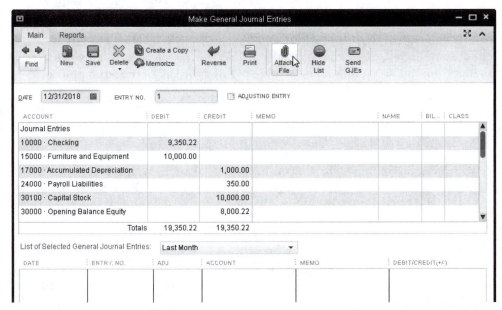

Figure 13-22 An opening-balance journal entry

4. In the first *Account* cell, type *Journal Entries* and press *Tab*. In the *Account Not Found* message box, click *Set Up*. Select the *Bank* option, click *Continue*, and then click *Save & Close*.

    Creating a bank account called *Journal Entries* and adding it to the first line of each journal entry you create enables you to look at all your journal entries in a QuickBooks register window. Because this account never has a balance, it won't appear on financial statements.

5. In the second *Account* cell, choose your first opening balance account, in this example, *Checking*. In the *Debit* cell, type the account's opening balance. In this example, it is the ending balance from the last statement before the start date, *$9,350.22*.

    When you enter opening balances for bank accounts and credit cards, be sure to use the ending balance from the bank statement dated on or just prior to your start date. Page 406 explains how to update your bank and credit card account balances to reflect transactions recorded after the last statement date.

6. Click the next *Account* cell.

    Because total debits always equal total credits, QuickBooks automatically calculates the amount required to make the total debits and credits match as you fill in each line in the journal entry. To change the amount in a debit or credit cell, simply fill in the correct value.

7. In the third *Account* cell, choose the next account in your trail balance, in this example, *Furniture and Equipment*. In the *Debit* cell, fill in the value, in this example, *$10,000*.

    Remember, you don't add *Accounts Receivable* or *Inventory* to your opening-balance journal entry. You'll learn how to record these opening balances later in this chapter.

8. Fill in the rest of the lines with opening balances, as shown in Figure 13-22.

   For liability accounts, type the opening balance in the *Credit* cell.

9. In the *Account* cell for the line where QuickBooks adds the amount to make debits and credits match, choose *Opening Balance Equity*.

   The amount in this line may be a debit or credit, depending on the other values in the journal entry. The trial balance doesn't show a balance for *Opening Balance Equity*. This account keeps everything in balance while you set up your company file. As you'll learn later in this chapter, you transfer the balance from this account into *Retained Earnings* at the end of the setup process.

10. Click *Save & Close*.

   In this example, you'll see a message box about transactions more than 30 days in the future. Click *Yes*.

   You'll also see a message about setting up fixed assets using *Fixed Asset* items from the *Fixed Asset Item List*. Click *OK*. If you see the *Items not assigned classes* dialog box, click the *Save Anyway* button.

   The *Payroll Liability Account Selected* message box warns you that journal entries don't affect payroll liabilities. In this example, the journal entry records the opening balance for the *Payroll Liabilities* account directly without first setting up the Payroll feature. By doing this, you can finalize your opening balances without going through the payroll setup steps (see Chapter 10). Because these initial payroll liabilities have been set up outside of payroll, you must record a check (you can use the *Write Checks* window) to record your first payroll liability payment (for last year's liability). (Alternatively, you could use the *Adjust Liabilities* window with the *Do not Affect Accounts* setting to define payroll liability balances, and then use the *Pay Liabilities* window to pay your opening *Payroll Liability* balances.)

Using Opening Balance Equity Properly

As you enter opening balances for asset and liability accounts, QuickBooks automatically updates the *Opening Balance Equity* account to keep things balanced. In addition, you can quickly view the details of your setup transactions by looking at this account's register window. However, it is important to use this account properly. After you record all account opening balances, you close the *Opening Balance Equity* balance into *Retained Earnings* (or *Owner's Equity*), as described on page 414. After you complete your company file, you must maintain a zero balance in the *Opening Balance Equity* account.

Recording Open Transactions

As you learned in the previous section, some account opening balances can't be recorded (or recorded completely) in a journal entry. This section describes how to update bank account opening balances to reflect transactions recorded after the last bank statement. It also describes how to record opening balances for Accounts Payable and Accounts Receivable.

Entering Outstanding Checks and Deposits

In your opening-balance journal entry, you use the ending balance from the bank statement dated on or just prior to your start date. (If your bank statement end date is the same as your start date, your QuickBooks bank account balances are already up to date and you can skip to the section on recording unpaid bills.) If your bank statement end date is earlier than your QuickBooks company file start date, you need to record outstanding checks, deposits, charges, and payments that occurred after the bank or credit card statement end date. That way, you'll be able to reconcile your account when you receive your *next* statement.

Computer Practice

To record outstanding transactions, follow these steps:

1. In the *Chart of Accounts* window, double-click the account you want to update, in this example, *Checking*.

    The account's register window opens.

2. Record the outstanding transactions directly in the register (Figure 13-23). In this example, use the outstanding checks and deposits described on page 402.

    The outstanding transactions appear before the opening balance transaction in the register when the register is sorted by date. The account balance including the outstanding transactions must match your bank account balance from your trial balance.

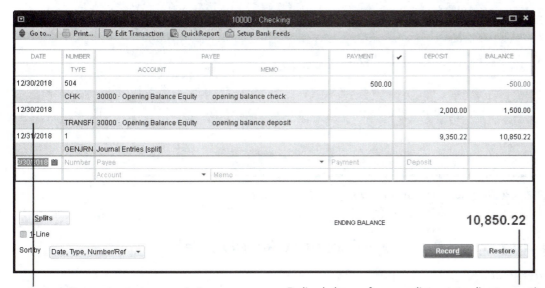

Outstanding transactions appear before the opening balance transaction

Ending balance after recording outstanding transactions matches the bank account balance on trial balance

Figure 13-23 Recording outstanding transactions in a register window

Recording Unpaid Bills (Accounts Payable)

Computer Practice

To create your *Accounts Payable* opening balance, record all the bills you've received but haven't paid:

1. On the *Home Page*, click *Enter Bills*.

2. Record the unpaid bill (Figure 13-24) described in Table 13-4. Use *QuickAdd* to create the vendor and the customer.

3. Click *Save & Close*.

   If you have more than one unpaid bill, click *Save & Next* to record the next bill.

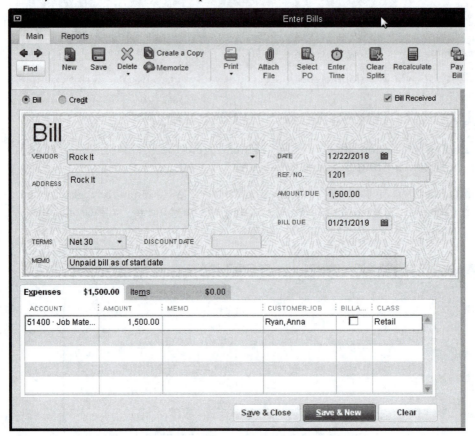

Figure 13-24 Creating your Accounts Payable opening balance

Recording Open Invoices (Accounts Receivable)

Computer Practice

To create your *Accounts Receivable* opening balance, record all open invoices as of your start date:

1. On the *Home Page*, click *Create Invoices*.

2. Record the open invoices described in Table 13-5. Use *QuickAdd* to create the customers. Figure 13-25 shows the two invoices.

   If you have more than one open invoice, click *Save & Next* to record the next invoice.

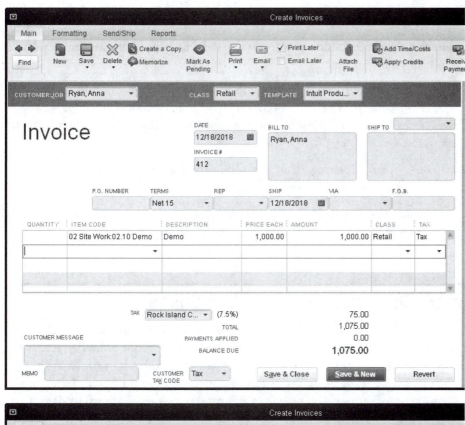

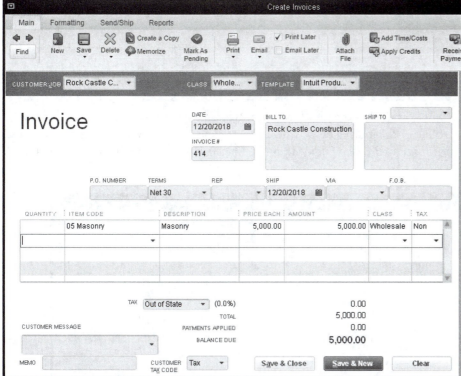

Figure 13-25 Creating your Accounts Receivable opening balance

Recording Open Non-posting Transactions

In addition to transactions that affect account balances, you also need to record non-posting transactions that are open as of your start date:

- **Purchase orders**: After you set up vendors and items in QuickBooks, record purchase orders (see page 244) for items you've ordered from vendors, but haven't received yet. That way, when you receive those items, you can use the purchase orders to record the vendors' bills and receive items into inventory.

- **Estimates**: Record any open estimates you created for customers. Then, if customers accept those estimates, you can use them to create invoices.

- **Sales orders**: If you use QuickBooks Premier or Enterprise, record any open sales orders for products. Then, when you have the products to ship, you can produce invoices from your sales orders.

Entering Year-to-Date Income and Expenses

At the end of a fiscal year, QuickBooks automatically totals the values from all your income and expense accounts to calculate your net profit (or loss) and then transfers that profit or loss value to *Retained Earnings*. In this chapter's example, the start date is the end of the calendar year. Later in this chapter, you'll see the income and expense accounts zeroed out and the net profit transferred to *Retained Earnings* on the first day of the year (1/1/2019, in this case). However, if your start date is not the end of the fiscal year, you need to create a journal entry to record your year-to-date income and expenses (see Figure 13-26).

> Note: Do not create this journal entry in your chapter file. It is for reference only to show how to set up a company file started mid-year.

Record amounts for income accounts in the *Credit* column. Record expense account amounts in the *Debit* column. In the last line of the journal entry where QuickBooks fills in a value to make debits and credits match, choose the *Opening Balance Equity* account. That records your net income or loss for the year to date.

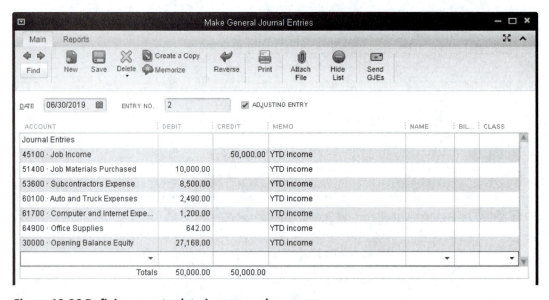

Figure 13-26 Defining year-to-date income and expenses

Adjusting the Opening Balance for Sales Tax Payable

If you record open invoices that include sales tax during your company file setup, the *Sales Tax Payable* account will include entries for the sales tax from those invoices. These entries represent uncollected sales tax. However, the total sales tax liability shown on your trial balance (Table 13-3) is the total of collected and uncollected sales tax. You need to adjust the balance in the *Sales Tax Payable* account to reflect the taxes you've already collected, but haven't yet paid to tax agencies.

To determine the unpaid collected tax that you owe, you subtract the uncollected tax (the amount in the Sales Tax Payable account) from the sales tax liability account on your trial balance. Here are the formulas to use:

Total sales tax liability = Collected sales tax + Uncollected sales tax

Uncollected sales tax = Sales tax on open invoices

Adjustment amount = Collected sales tax (in other words, Total sales tax liability – Uncollected sales tax

In this example, the uncollected sales tax is $75. The collected sales tax is $75, that is, the amount on the trial balance ($150) minus the uncollected sales tax ($75). In this example, you must record a *Sales Tax Adjustment* to increase the *Sales Tax Payable* balance to reflect the collected tax amount.

Computer Practice

To record a sales tax adjustment, follow these steps:

1. On the *Vendors* menu, choose *Sales Tax*, and then choose *Adjust Sales Tax Due*.

2. In the *Sales Tax Adjustment* window, fill in the fields, as shown in Figure 13-27.

3. Click *OK*.

   If you see the *Items not assigned classes* dialog box, click the *Save Anyway* button.

4. If you pay sales tax to more than one sales tax agency, repeat these steps to record a separate adjustment for each agency.

Figure 13-27 Adjusting sales tax due

> Note: When you record a *Sales Tax Adjustment*, QuickBooks creates a journal entry and fills in the *Entry No.* field with the next number in your journal entry sequence.

Adjusting Inventory

If you have inventory, you need to record an inventory adjustment to enter the inventory quantity and value on hand as of your start date. You record this adjustment after you record unpaid bills and open invoices. That way, your inventory quantities and values will be correct, even if those bills and invoices include inventory items. This section describes how you adjust inventory to match the inventory balance on your trial balance and the quantities from your physical count.

Computer Practice

To record an inventory adjustment, follow these steps:

1. In this chapter's example, no inventory items exist yet. Create the inventory items shown in Table 13-7.

Table 13-7 New inventory items

Item Name	Description	Tax Code	Income Account	Cost	Sales Price
Sandstone - flat	1" thick flat sandstone per pound	Tax	Job Income	$0.15	$0.24
Flagstone - gray	1" thick flagstone - gray	Tax	Job Income	$0.12	$0.22

2. On the *Home Page* in the *Company* panel, click the *Inventory Activities* down arrow, and then choose *Adjust Quantity on Hand*.

3. In the *Adjustment Type* drop-down list, choose *Quantity and Total Value*.

4. In the *Adjustment Date* field, type your start date, in this example, *12/31/2018*.

5. In the *Adjustment Account* drop-down list, choose *Opening Balance Equity*.

   When you click away from the *Adjustment Account* field, the *Income or Expense expected* message box appears. Click *OK* to close it.

6. In the first *Item* cell, choose the *Flagstone - gray* item. In the *New Quantity* cell, enter the quantity on hand, in this example, *7200*. In the *New Value* cell, enter the value of this item, $864.

7. In the next *Item* cell, choose the *Sandstone - flat* item. In the *New Quantity* cell, enter the quantity on hand, in this example, *7000*. In the *New Value* cell, enter the value of this item, *$1050*.

8. Figure 13-28 shows the inventory adjustment. Click *Save & Close*.

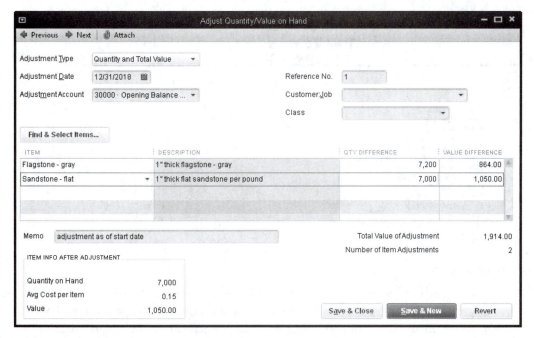

Figure 13-28 Adjusting inventory

Setting Up Fixed Assets and Loans

If you own fixed assets, such as buildings, equipment, and vehicles, you can create *Fixed Asset* items to track their details. If you use QuickBooks Accountant, you can use *Fixed Asset Manager* to calculate and track depreciation on each asset.

If your company borrows money, you can track loan information as well. QuickBooks calculates loan amortization schedules and automatically allocates amortized principal and interest for each payment.

Setting Up Payroll and Year-to-date Payroll Information

See Chapter 10 to learn how to set up payroll and record year-to date payroll in QuickBooks.

Verifying Your Trial Balance

Now that you've entered all the information for your accounts, you can run the *Trial Balance* report to make sure your QuickBooks account balances match the balances on the trial balance report you obtained from your accountant or generated from your previous accounting software.

Computer Practice

To use a QuickBooks *Trial Balance* report to verify your account balances, follow these steps:

1. On the *Reports* menu, choose *Accountant & Taxes*, and then choose *Trial Balance*.

2. In the *From* and *To* date fields, fill in your start date. Figure 13-29 shows the *Trial Balance* report as of *12/31/2018*.

3. Write down the balance for the *Opening Balance Equity* account, and then close the report window.

    If QuickBooks asks if you want to memorize the report, click *No*.

```
7:36 PM                          Stone Wall Construction
10/14/14                              Trial Balance
Accrual Basis                     As of December 31, 2018

                                                      Dec 31, 18
                                               Debit            Credit
             Journal Entries                     0.00
             10000 · Checking                10,850.22
             11000 · Accounts Receivable      6,075.00
             12100 · Inventory Asset          1,914.00
             15000 · Furniture and Equipment 10,000.00
             17000 · Accumulated Depreciation                   1,000.00
             20000 · Accounts Payable                           1,500.00
             24000 · Payroll Liabilities                          350.00
             25500 · Sales Tax Payable                            150.00
             30000 · Opening Balance Equity                     11,339.22
             30100 · Capital Stock                              10,000.00
             45100 · Job Income                                  6,000.00
             51400 · Job Materials Purchased   1,500.00
             TOTAL                           30,339.22         30,339.22
```

Figure 13-29 A QuickBooks Trial Balance report

The *Trial Balance* report in Figure 13-29 doesn't exactly match the trial balance shown in Table 13-3. For example, the report includes the *Opening Balance Equity* account, one income account, and one cost of goods sold account. Income, cost of goods sold, and expense accounts have balances because you entered unpaid bills and open invoices dated during the prior year. QuickBooks automatically closes those balances to *Retained Earnings* at the start of your next fiscal year (in this example, on *1/1/2019*).

> Note: Your QuickBooks *Trial Balance* report could also differ from the trial balance outside of QuickBooks if the reports don't use the same accounting basis (cash or accrual, as described on page 163).

Closing Opening Balance Equity

After you run the *Trial Balance* report in QuickBooks and have the balance for the *Opening Balance Equity* account as of your start date, you can close that balance into the *Retained Earnings* account. This section shows you how to do that.

> Note: If your company is a sole proprietorship, you use the same steps, except that you close *Opening Balance Equity* into an account called *Owner's Equity*. Similarly, if your company is a partnership, you allocate the money in the *Opening Balance Equity* account among the partners' profit accounts.

Computer Practice

To close the *Opening Balance Equity* account (for a corporation), follow these steps:

1. On the *Company* menu, choose *Make General Journal Entry*.

   If the *Assign Numbers to Journal Entries* dialog box appears, turn on the checkbox, and then click *No*.

2. In the *Date* field, fill in your start date, in this example, *12/31/2018*.

3. Record the journal entry, as shown in Figure 13-30.

   Figure 13-30 shows the *Make General Journal Entries* window in QuickBooks Accountant. If you use a different edition of QuickBooks, your window may differ slightly.

4. Click *Save & Close*.

    If the *Retained Earnings* message box appears, click *OK*. If the *Items not assigned classes* dialog box appears, click *Save Anyway*.

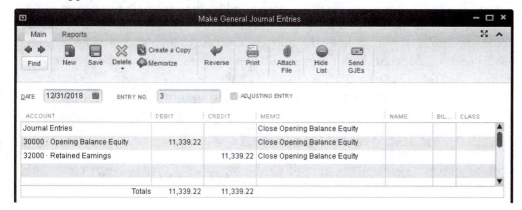

Figure 13-30 A journal entry to close the Opening Balance Equity balance to Retained Earnings

5. To verify your account balances, run a *Balance Sheet* report (on the *Reports* menu, choose *Company & Financial*, and then select *Balance Sheet Standard*. In the *Date* field, choose the day after your start date (in this example, *1/1/2019*, as shown in Figure 13-31).

		Jan 1, 19	
		Debit	**Credit**
	Journal Entries	0.00	
	10000 · Checking	10,850.22	
	11000 · Accounts Receivable	6,075.00	
	12100 · Inventory Asset	1,914.00	
	15000 · Furniture and Equipment	10,000.00	
	17000 · Accumulated Depreciation		1,000.00
	20000 · Accounts Payable		1,500.00
	24000 · Payroll Liabilities		350.00
	25500 · Sales Tax Payable		150.00
	30000 · Opening Balance Equity	0.00	
	30100 · Capital Stock		10,000.00
	32000 · Retained Earnings		15,839.22
	TOTAL	28,839.22	28,839.22

8:28 PM
10/14/14
Accrual Basis

Stone Wall Construction
Trial Balance
As of January 1, 2019

After closing the Opening Balance Equity account, Retained Earning matches the value on your non-QuickBooks trial balance report.

Figure 13-31 The Balance Sheet report the day after the start date

Setting the Closing Date

Your company file setup is complete and you're *almost* ready to keep your books with QuickBooks. Before you begin recording transactions, you should set a closing date for the company file and then back up the file. See Chapter 12 to learn how to set a closing date and closing date password. Chapter 1 describes how to back up a company file.

> Tip: Keep this backup of your company file in a secure location so you have a record of your initial setup transactions.

Creating Additional Users

When you first set up a company file, QuickBooks creates the administrator user, who can access any part of the company file and set company-wide preferences. In addition, if more than one person works on your company file, the file's administrator user can create new users, and assign permissions and passwords to them. That way, you can limit access to sensitive data to keep it secure. You can also keep an eye on what users are doing to check for errors and prevent financial shenanigans. And if you have multiple QuickBooks licenses, several people can work on the file simultaneously. This section describes how to set up users and enable simultaneous access to your company file.

Assigning the Administrator's Password

Because the administrator user can do anything within a company file, you need to assign a password to the administrator user.

Computer Practice

To assign the administrator's password, follow these steps:

1. On the *Company* menu, choose *Set Up Users and Passwords*, and then choose *Set Up Users*. In the *User List*, *Admin* is already selected, so click *Edit User*.

    The *Change user password and access* dialog box appears. The heading is *Admin Name and Password*.

2. In the *User Name* field, keep the name *Admin*, as shown in Figure 13-32. Press *Tab*.

    You don't have to change the administrator user name. In fact, it's less confusing if you keep it set to Admin. However, if you do change it, QuickBooks identifies the administrator by appending "(Admin)" to the end of the user name in the *User List*, such as *Supervisor (Admin)*.

3. In the *New Password* and *Confirm New Password* fields, type the password, in this example, *Admin12345*.

    To keep your QuickBooks data secure, be sure to use a complex password. QuickBooks passwords are case-sensitive and can be up to 16 characters in length. A complex password is at least seven characters long, and includes a combination of capital and lowercase letters, numbers, and special characters.

Figure 13-32 Setting the administrator password and challenge question

4. In the *Challenge Question* field, choose the question you want to answer in case you forget the Admin password. In this example, choose *City where you went to high school*.

5. In the *Challenge Answer* field, type your answer, *Boston*, in this example.

6. Click *Next*. After reading the password reminder message, click *Finish*.

Now that the administrator password is set, you need to enter this password when you try to log into this company file as the administrator.

Setting Up Other Users

To keep your data secure and track what people are doing in QuickBooks, you need to set up a separate user name and password for each person who accesses your company file. That way, each person has to log in to the company file (and QuickBooks can track what they do). In addition, the program limits the functions they can perform based on the permissions that the administrator assigned to them.

Computer Practice

To create a new user in your company file, follow these steps:

1. On the *Company* menu, choose *Set Up Users and Passwords*, and then choose *Set Up Users*.

2. In the *QuickBooks Login* dialog box, enter the administrator password (*Admin12345*, in this example), and then click *OK*.

   Because the administrator is the only user at this point, only the *Password* field appears. When the company file has more than one user, both the *User Name* and *Password* fields appear in this dialog box.

   The *User List* dialog box opens (Figure 13-33).

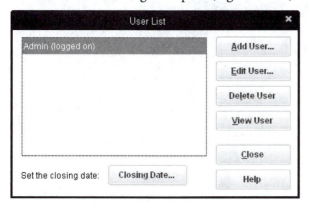

Figure 13-33 The User List dialog box

3. Click *Add User*.

4. On the *User Name and Password* screen, fill in the *User Name* field, in this example, type *Student1*. In the *Password* and *Confirm Password* fields, type the password for the user, in this example, type *Student12345*. Click *Next*.

   After you create a user for someone, that person can change his or her password. To do that, on the *Company* menu, they choose *Set Up Users and Passwords*, and then choose *Change Your Password*.

5. On the *Access for user: Student1* screen, keep the *Selected areas of QuickBooks* option selected, as shown in Figure 13-34. Click *Next*.

   If you select the *All areas of QuickBooks* option instead, the user can change transactions in closed periods. To protect the data in closed accounting periods, it's best to prevent other users from changing that data. If you want to give a user access to all areas except data in closed periods, select the *Selected areas of QuickBooks* option, and then, on the following screens, select the *Full Access* options.

Figure 13-34 The Selected areas of QuickBooks option

6. On the *Sales and Accounts Receivable* screen, select *Full Access* (Figure 13-35), and then click *Next*.

Figure 13-35 Setting user permissions

7. In this example, for the remainder of the screens, click *Next* to accept the default settings.

   When you set up your own company file, be sure to select options to set the appropriate permissions for each new user. If you aren't sure what the options do, click *Help* to find descriptions of each permission.

8. On the final window, review the user's permissions (see Figure 13-36).

   If you want to change any settings, click *Back* until you see the screen you want.

9. To save the user, click *Finish*.

10. Close the *User List* dialog box.

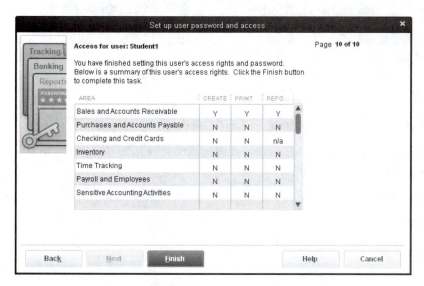

Figure 13-36 Final user screen

Switching Between Multi-User and Single-User Modes

If several people work on your company file simultaneously, you need to change your company file to multi-user mode. However, some QuickBooks tasks require only one person working on the company file, such as merging or deleting accounts and items, setting some preferences, condensing data, and saving an accountant's copy. This section describes how to switch between modes.

Here's how you switch from multi-user mode to single-user mode:

1. Ask other users to close the company file you want to work on.

2. When everyone else has closed the file, open it in QuickBooks.

3. On the *File* menu, choose *Switch to Single-user Mode*. In the message box that appears, click *OK*.

   QuickBooks closes all open windows, switches to single-user mode, and then reopens the windows from the previously saved desktop.

4. After your single-user mode work is done, on the *File* menu, choose *Switch to Multi-user Mode*. In the message box, click *OK*.

5. Tell the other users they can log back into the company file.

Note: In QuickBooks 2015, an administrator user can now close a company file even if other users are logged into it. If you're a QuickBooks administrator user, in your computer's system tray, click the *QuickBooks Messenger* icon (the icon is a stylized person with a green callout). In the *QuickBooks Messenger* window, click the *Actions* down arrow, and then choose *Close Company Files for Users*. Select the users whose company files you want to close. For emergencies, below the *Select users* list, turn on the *Close even if users have unsaved data* checkbox. Click the *Close Company File* button.

Review Questions

Select the best answer for each of the following questions:

1. You are setting up a QuickBooks company file for a company that uses the calendar year as its fiscal year. Which is the best starting date for this company file?

    a) January 1 of the current calendar year

    b) December 31 of the previous calendar year

    c) The first day of the current calendar quarter

    d) The last day of the previous calendar quarter

2. Which of the following setup tasks do you perform in QuickBooks?

    a) Adding accounts to the chart of accounts.

    b) Choosing the type of company.

    c) Registering the company with government agencies.

    d) Recording transactions, such as unpaid bills and open invoices.

3. To record accounts receivable and payable balances in QuickBooks, you should:

    a) Create a journal entry on your start date to set the opening balance for both Accounts Receivable and Accounts Payable.

    b) Create two journal entries on your start date: one to set the opening balance for Accounts Receivable and the second to set the Accounts Payable opening balance.

    c) Record a transaction for each unpaid bill and open invoice as of your start date.

    d) Any of the above.

4. Which method should you use to ensure that your account balances are correct?

    a) Run a *Profit & Loss Standard* and a *Balance Sheet Standard* report as of the start date.

    b) Verify that the *General Ledger* report as of the start date matches the one your accountant gave you.

    c) Run a *Transaction Detail by Account* report and use it to double-check the transactions you recorded.

    d) Verify that the *Trial Balance* report as of the start date matches the one your accountant gave you.

5. Which tasks should you perform after you complete the company file setup?

    a) Back up your company file.

    b) Close the books as of the start date and assign a closing date password.

    c) Record a journal entry to close the *Opening Balance Equity* account.

    d) Run a *Trial Balance* report to verify account balances.

Setting Up a Company File Exercise

Applying Your Knowledge

You don't need to restore a sample file for this exercise. You use the *EasyStep Interview* to create a new company file.

1. In the *EasyStep Interview*, fill in the company information shown in Table the following table.

Table 13-8 Stone Wall Construction company information

Fields	Data
Company name	Stone Wall Construction LLC
Legal name	Stone Wall Construction LLC
Tax ID	99-0000009
Address	1250 Granite St. Rock Island, WI 61201
Country	U.S.
Phone	309-555-1111
Fax	309-555-1112
E-mail Address	info@stonewall.xyz
Web site	http://www.academyphoto.xyz
Industry	Construction Trades
Income tax form	Sub Chapter S
First month of fiscal year	January
Administrator password	Leave blank
Company Filename	Setup-<your name>.QBW Save in your student files folder.

2. Use the settings in the following table to set up the company.

Table 13-9 EasyStep Interview settings

Settings	Data
Products and services	Both products and services
Sales	Charges sales tax Creates estimates Track sales orders (not available in QuickBooks Pro) Use billing statements Use progress invoicing
Purchases & vendors	Track bills Track inventory Track time
Employees	Both W-2 employees and 1099 contractors
Start Date	12/31/2018

3. During the *EasyStep Interview*, accept the default chart of accounts.

4. After the *EasyStep Interview* is complete, turn on account numbers, and then add the accounts listed in the following table.

    Accounts with colons in the names represent subaccounts you need to create. In this exercise, don't enter descriptions or bank account numbers, or assign tax line items.

Table 13-10 New Accounts

Account number	Account Name	Account Type
10000	Checking	Bank
10050	Savings	Bank
10090	Journal Entries	Bank
22000	Visa Credit Card	Credit Card
24020	Payroll Liabilities:Employee Payroll Taxes Payable	Other Current Liability
24030	Payroll Liabilities: Other Payroll Liabilities	Other Current Liability
27000	Equipment Loan	Long Term Liability
40000	Services Income	Income
46000	Product Income	Income

5. Print an *Account Listing* report (on the *Reports* menu, choose *List*, and then choose *Account Listing*).

6. Add the items listed in the following table. Print an *Item Listing* report. If an item field isn't listed in the table, leave it blank or accept the defaults that QuickBooks selects.

    You can add *Service*, *Inventory Part*, and *Non-inventory Part* items using the *EasyStep Interview* or within the *Item List* window.

    Use the *Item List* window to add *Sales Tax* items. (The *EasyStep Interview* doesn't support creating sales tax items.)

Table 13-11 New Items

Type	Item	Description	Tax Code	Account	Cost	Price
Service	05 Masonry: Wall	Construct concrete block wall	Non	Job Income		$85.00
Service	05 Masonry: Wall repair	Repair concrete block wall	Non	Job Income		$80.00
Inventory Part	Concrete block	Concrete block gray 8" x 8"	Tax	Product Income	$1.69	$2.20
Inventory Part	Concrete block solid cap	Concrete block solid cap gray	Tax	Product Income	$1.99	$2.50
Non-Inventory Part	Flagstone	1" thick flagstone – gray per pound	Tax	Product Income	$0.18	$$0.25
Sales Tax Item	Illinois State sales tax	Illinois State sales tax Sales tax is paid to the Illinois Department of Revenue. (Use Quick Add to add as vendor.)		Sales Tax Payable		6.25%
Sales Tax Item	Rock Island City sales tax	Rock Island City sales tax Sales tax is paid to the Illinois Department of Revenue.		Sales Tax Payable		1.25%
Sales Tax Group	Rock Island City total tax	Add Illinois State tax and Rock Island City sales tax to item		Sales Tax Payable		

7. Turn on class tracking and create three classes: *Retail, Wholesale,* and *Overhead.* Delete other classes that QuickBooks created by default.

8. Make sure that the company file includes terms for Net 15, Net 30, 2% 10 Net 30, and Due on Receipt.

9. Use the bank statement in the figure to record an opening-balance journal entry for the checking account.

The Checking account bank statement is dated 12/27/2018. Enter the checking account Ending Balance from the statement as the company file Checking account's opening balance.

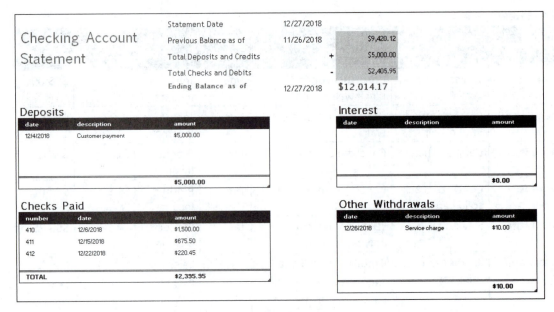

Figure 13-37 Checking account statement prior to start date

10. Record the deposits and checks in the following table to update the Checking account balance through the start date.

Table 13-12 Trial Balance for Stone Wall Construction

Type	Trans No.	Transaction date	Amount	Account or item
Deposit		12/28/2018	1500.00	Opening Balance Equity
Deposit		12/30/2018	2000.00	Opening Balance Equity
Check	1013	12/29/2018	475.22	Opening Balance Equity
Check	1014	12/30/2018	550.00	Opening Balance Equity

11. Record the unpaid bills shown in the following table.

Table 13-13 Unpaid bills

Bill No.	Bill date	Vendor	Amount	Account or item	Customer	Class	Terms
3296	12/29/2018	Hard Rock Supplies	3000.00	Job Materials Purchased	Smith House (non-billable)	Retail	Net 30
5103	12/30/2018	Concrete Construction	1255.50	Tools and Small Equipment		Overhead	Net 30

12. Record the open invoices shown in the following table.

> Note: For this example, assign the *Rock Island City total tax* item to the retail customer.

Table 13-14 Open invoices

Inv. No.	Invoice date	Customer: Job	Total Amount	Items	Qty	Class	Terms
995	12/14/2018	Smith House	6800.00	Masonry: wall	80	Retail	Net 15
997	12/20/2018	Rock Castle Construction	2365.00 (including sales tax)	Concrete block	1000	Wholesale	Net 30

13. Record an inventory adjustment (*2018-2*) to add the inventory physical counts and values shown in the following table, as of the start date (*12/31/2018*). Use the *Opening Balance Equity* account as the *Adjusting account*.

Table 13-15 Physical Inventory as of 12/31/2018

Item	Quantity on hand	Value
Concrete block	1,000	$1,690
Concrete block solid cap	200	$398

14. Use the trial balance shown in the following table to record a journal entry to specify the opening balances for any accounts that still don't have opening balances. Run a *Trial Balance* report as of *12/31/2018* and then *1/1/2019*.

Table 13-16 Trial Balance for Stone Wall Construction

Account	Debit	Credit
Checking	14,488.95	
Accounts Receivable	9,165.00	
Inventory	2,088.00	
Accounts Payable		4255.50
Payroll Liabilities:Employee Payroll Taxes Payable		2,000.00
Payroll Liabilities:Other Payroll Liabilities		925.00
Sales Tax Payable		165.00
Capital Stock		10,000.00
Retained Earnings		8,396.45
Total	25,741.95	25,741.95

Note: The trial balance you see won't exactly match the values shown in Table 13-16. When QuickBooks closes the year, the income, expenses, and cost of goods sold values post to *Retained Earnings*, as shown in the next figure.

15. Generate a *Balance Sheet Standard* report as of *1/1/2018*.

Note: In this report, *Retained Earnings* is adjusted for the income and expenses from the previous year. If you change the report date to *12/31/2018*, *Retained Earnings* reverts to the before-closing value and you'll see *Net Income* in the report.

Chapter 14

Company Startup Case Study

Topics

This chapter covers the following topics:

- Case Study Description

- Company Setup

- Business Transactions

- Analysis and Bank Reconciliation

Case Study Description

Marcus Smith is starting a landscaping company, Greensmith Landscaping. He lives in a mid-sized city in California, where the residents want to make the most of their small yards. He plans to offer landscape design, construction, and maintenance services.

He has hired one full-time employee: Jenny Miller, who will provide the company's design services. In addition, he has hired Duncan Fisher as an hourly employee for construction work. He initially plans to supplement Duncan's time with subcontractors for construction and maintenance services. He also plans to sell a few of the more popular plant care products to his customers.

He has chosen QuickBooks to keep his books and manage his business. In this case study, you will record the initial start-up transactions for the company. You will record one month's business transactions, including purchase orders, checks, and bills for purchases, and sales receipts and invoices for sales. You will also receive payments and deposit them in the bank. In addition, you will process payroll, pay taxes, and track inventory. After recording the transactions for the month, you will reconcile the company's checking account. Finally, you will answer questions about the company's finances.

Company Setup

The company file for this exercise is already set up with accounts, customers, vendors, employees, classes, items, fixed asset items, payroll, and other lists.

Instructions

1. Restore the case study file to a company file, named Greensmith_Landscaping.qbw.

   Restore the sample file, Ch14_casestudy 2015 (Portable).QBM.

   Or, if you are using QuickBooks 2014, restore Ch14_casestudy 2014 (Portable).QBM.

2. Record the transactions for June 2020, which begin on page 429.

3. Reconcile the bank statement for June 2020 (see page 438).

4. Prepare the following reports and graphs for June 2020:

    a. Balance Sheet Standard as of 6/30/2020

    b. Profit and Loss Standard

    c. Profit and Loss by Class

    d. Statement of Cash Flows

    e. Sales by Item Summary

    f. Sales by Customer Summary

    g. View the Insights dashboard for This Fiscal Year (if you run QuickBooks 2015)

    h. Inventory Valuation Summary as of 6/30/2020

    i. Unbilled Costs by Job

5. Create a portable file of your company file and name it Greensmith_Final_[yourlastname].qbm.

6. Answer the analysis questions on page 439.

June 2020 Transactions

When you record these transactions, QuickBooks will display a message telling you the transactions are more than 30 days in the future. Click *Yes* to record the transactions. To turn off this warning, on the *Edit* menu, choose *Preferences*, click the *Accounting* category, and then click the *Company Preferences* tab. In the *Date Warnings* section, turn off both checkboxes.

For some transactions, QuickBooks will ask if you want to change the original record, for example, when you change an item's price. Click *No*.

1. Deposit Marcus Smith's owner investment into bank account to fund operations.

Transaction type: Bank deposit
Deposit to: Checking
Date: 6/1/2020
From Account: Owner's Contribution – Check number 1922
Memo: Deposit Owner's Contribution
Class: Overhead
Amount: $50,000

2. Issue purchase order to Conner Garden Supplies for plant care inventory items.

Transaction type: Purchase order
Vendor: Connor Garden Supplies
Class: Maintenance
Date: 6/1/2020
PO number: 2020-100
Items: Sprkl pipes – quantity 100
           Sprinkler Hds – quantity 200 – Rate 1.10
           Soil – quantity 20
           Pump – quantity 5
Memo: Sprinkler items, soil, pumps order# 2020-100

3. Write check to Nye Properties for office rent plus refundable deposit.

Transaction type: Check
Pay to the order of: Nye Properties
Check number: Set up to print later
Date: 6/1/2020
Amount: $4,500
Memo: June rent plus $2,000 deposit
Expense account: Rent, $2,500, class: Overhead
Expense account: QuickAdd Refundable Deposit as Other Current Asset, $2,000,
Class: Overhead

4. **Issue purchase order to Computer Services by DJ for office computer.**

Transaction type: Purchase order
Vendor: Computer Services by DJ
Class: Overhead
Date: 6/1/2020
PO number: 2020-101
Items: QuickAdd Computer as Non-inventory Part assigned to Account: Office Supplies, Rate 2,000.00
Memo: Computer order# 2020-101

5. **Issue purchase order to Gussman's Nursery for landscaping supplies.**

Transaction type: Purchase order
Vendor: Gussman's Nursery
Class: Landscaping
Date: 6/1/2020
PO number: 2020-102
Items: Lighting – quantity 50 – Rate $6.75
Memo: Lighting order# 2020-102

6. **Record bill from Computer Services by DJ for office computer.**

Transaction type: Enter bill
Vendor: Computer Services by DJ
Class: Overhead
Date: 6/8/2020
PO number: 2020-101
Ref. No.: 2583
Items: Autofill from purchase order
Terms and Bill Due autofill
Memo: Office computer

7. **Record bill from Gussman's Nursery for lighting**

Transaction type: Receive Items and Enter Bill
Vendor: Gussman's Nursery
Class: Maintenance
Date: 6/9/2020
PO number: 2020-102
Ref. No.: 3999
Items: Autofill from purchase order
Terms and Bill Due autofill
Memo: Lighting order

8. Write check to Sowers Office Equipment for equipment rental.

Transaction type: Check
Pay to the order of: Sowers Office Equipment
Check number: Set up to print later
Date: 6/9/2020
Amount: $825
Expense account: Job Expenses: Equipment Rental, class: Landscaping
Memo: Backhoe rental

9. Record bill from Conner Garden Supplies for plant care inventory items.

Transaction type: Receive Items and Enter Bill
Vendor: Conner Garden Supplies
Class: Landscaping
Date: 6/9/2020
PO number: 2020-100
Ref. No.: C-1426
Terms: Net 15
Items: Autofill from purchase order
Bill Due: Autofills
Memo: Landscaping supplies

10. Record bill from Nolan Hardware and Supplies for landscaping supplies.

Transaction type: Bill
Vendor: Nolan Hardware and Supplies
Class: Landscaping
Date: 6/9/2020
Ref. No.: 14-120
Amount Due: 2588.23
Terms: Net 15
Bill Due: Autofills
Expense account: Job Expenses:Job Materials:Decks & Patio
Class: Landscaping
Memo: Landscaping supplies

11. **Record bill from Chris Markley for subcontracted work.**

Transaction type: Enter bill
Vendor: Chris Markley
Date: 6/12/2020
Ref. No.: 167
Amount Due: 2588.23
Terms: Net 15
Bill Due: Autofills
Expense account: Job Expenses:Subcontractors
Class: Maintenance
Memo: Subcontractor for maintenance

12. **Record sales receipt to Chapman, Natalie for plant care products.**

Transaction type: Sales Receipt
Customer: Chapman, Natalie
Template: Sales Receipt – Retail
Date: 6/12/2020
Sale No.: 100
Check No.: 628
Item: Soil – quantity 5
Class: Maintenance
Memo: Soil
Total: 35.94

13. **Record timesheet for Jenny Miller.**

Turn on time tracking.
Do not set up Jenny Miller to use time for payroll.
Name: Jenny Miller
Week of: June 8 to June 14, 2020
Customer: Job: Golliday Sporting Goods:75 Sunset Rd.
Service Item: Design
Class: Landscaping
8 hours per day, Monday through Friday
Make hours billable.

14. **Record invoice for Balak, Mike:Residential job for weekly lawn maintenance**

Transaction type: Invoice
Customer: Balak, Mike: Residential job
Date: 6/18/2020
Invoice #: 2020-100
Item: Gardening – quantity – 12 – Price Each– 50.00
Class: Maintenance
Memo: June maintenance
Total: 600.00

15. Write check for accountant's fee.

Transaction type: Check
Pay to the order of: Campion, Patrick, CPA
Check number: Set up to print later
Date: 6/18/2020
Amount: $675
Expense account: Professional Fees: Accounting, class: Overhead
Memo: Fee for startup

16. Record payment for Balak, Mike: Residential job invoice.

Transaction type: Payment
Customer: Balak, Mike Residential job
Date: 6/22/2020
Amount: $600
Check #: 1123
Apply to: Invoice 2020-100
Memo: Payment received for invoice 2020-100

17. Enter timesheets for Jenny Miller and Duncan Fisher.

Name: Jenny Miller
Week of: June 15 to June 21, 2020
Customer: Job: Golliday Sporting Goods:75 Sunset Rd.
Service Item: Design
Class: Design
8 hours per day, Monday through Thursday
Make hours billable.

Name: Duncan Fisher
Set him up to use time data during paycheck creation.
Week of: June 22 to June 28, 2020
Customer:Job: Crenshaw, Bob
Service Item: Installation
Payroll Item: Regular Pay
Class: Landscaping
8 hours per day, Monday through Thursday
Make hours billable.

18. **Record sales receipt for Golliday Sporting Goods: 75 Sunset Rd. job for landscaping design.**

Transaction type: Sales Receipt
Customer: Job: Golliday Sporting Goods: 75 Sunset Rd.
Template: Sales Receipt – Retail
Date: 6/22/2020
Sale No.: 101
Check No.: 4502
Item: Add billable time to receipt
Class: Design
Memo: Receipt 101 for landscaping design
Total: $3,960.00

19. **Record invoice for Andres, Cristina for landscaping design and construction.**

Transaction type: Invoice
Customer: Andres, Cristina
Date: 6/23/2020
Invoice #: 2020-101
Item: Design – quantity – 24
            Installation – quantity – 80
            Lighting – quantity – 20, Rate – 12.50
Class: Landscaping
Memo: Invoice 2020-101 Design and installation
Total: 4389.38

20. **Record telephone bill.**

Transaction type: Bill
Vendor: Cal Telephone
Date: 6/25/2020
Ref. No.: blank
Amount Due: 112.84
Terms and Bill Due: Autofilled
Expense account: Utilities: Telephone
Class: Overhead
Memo: June phone bill

21. Record electric bill.

Transaction type: Bill
Vendor: Cal Gas & Electric
Date: 6/25/2020
Ref. No.: blank
Amount Due: 201.97
Terms and Bill Due: Autofilled
Expense account: Utilities: Gas and Electric
Class: Overhead
Memo: June electric bill

22. Record invoice for Crenshaw, Bob for sprinkler installation.

Transaction type: Invoice
Customer: Crenshaw, Bob
Date: 6/26/2020
Invoice #: 2020-102
Item: Add time from timesheet
                Sprinkler Hds – quantity – 12, Price Each 5.95
                Sprkl pipes – quantity – 50, Price Each 2.75
Class: Landscaping
Memo: Invoice 2020-101 Design and installation
Total: 1346.14

23. Record payment from Andres, Cristina.

Transaction type: Payment
Customer: Andres, Cristina
Date: 6/27/2020
Amount: $4,389.38
Check #: 1826
Apply to: Invoice 2020-101
Memo: Payment received for invoice 2020-101

24. Record credit card payment from Crenshaw, Bob.

Transaction type: Payment
Customer: Crenshaw, Bob
Date: 6/29/2020
Amount: $1,346.14
Credit Card payment: Visa 1111222233334444 Exp. Date – 7/2022
Apply to: Invoice 2020-102
Memo: Payment received for invoice 2020-102

25. Deposit checks from Undeposited Funds account.

Transaction type: Deposit
Payment method type: Cash and Check
Deposit To: Checking
Date: 6/29/2020
Amount: $8,985.32

26. Deposit credit card payment from Undeposited Funds account.

Transaction type: Deposit
Payment method type: MasterCard, Visa, Discover
Deposit To: Checking
Date: 6/29/2020
Amount: $1,346.14

27. Pay employees for June 8 through June 21, 2020.

Pay period ends: June 21,2020
Paycheck date: June 26,2020
Bank Account: Checking
Jenny Miller – salary for 80 hours
Duncan Fisher – 32 hours
Starting check number: 1501

28. Pay all bills.

Pay from account: Checking
Sort by vendor
Pay bills:
    Cal Gas & Electric $201.97
    Cal Telephone $112.84
    Chris Markley $2,000.00
    Computer Services by DJ $2,000.00
    Conner Garden Supplies $816.00
    Gussman's Nursery $337.50
    Nolan Hardware and Supplies $2,588.23
Total payments: $8,056.54
Payment date: June 29,2020
Checks to be printed.

29. Print checks.

Bank Account: Checking

First Check Number: 2000

    2000 Nye Properties

    2001 Sowers Office Equipment

    2002 Campion, Patrick, CPA

    2003 Cal Gas & Electric

    2004 Cal Telephone

    2005 Chris Markley

    2006 Computer Services by DJ

    2007 Connect Garden Supplies

    2008 Gussman's Nursery

    2009 Nolan Hardware and Supplies

30. Write check to Conner Garden Supplies for landscaping materials.

Transaction type: Check

Pay to the order of: Conner Garden Supplies

Check number: 2010

Date: 6/30/2020

Amount: $99.47

Items: Plants/Trees: Fruit Trees – quantity – 6, class: Landscaping, Customer: Loomis, Anne

Make item billable

Memo: Fruit trees for Loomis, Anne

Bank Reconciliation

Reconcile the Checking account using the statement in the following table.

> Note: QuickBooks uses the tax tables within your copy of the program to calculate paycheck withholdings. Because paychecks calculated with different tax tables will have different net amounts, this bank reconciliation does not include the paychecks you created.

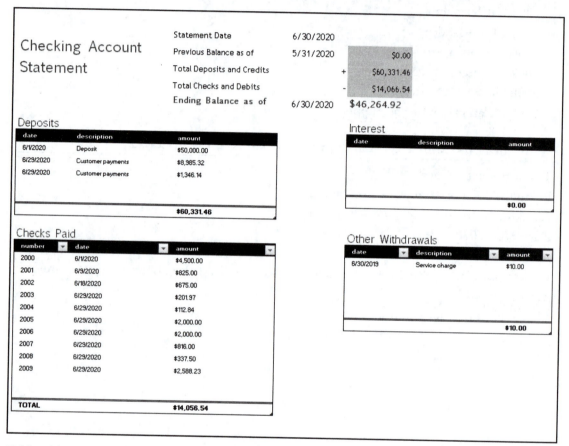

Checking Account Statement		
Statement Date	6/30/2020	
Previous Balance as of	5/31/2020	$0.00
Total Deposits and Credits	+	$60,331.46
Total Checks and Debits	-	$14,066.54
Ending Balance as of	6/30/2020	$46,264.92

Deposits

date	description	amount
6/1/2020	Deposit	$50,000.00
6/29/2020	Customer payments	$8,985.32
6/29/2020	Customer payments	$1,346.14
		$60,331.46

Interest

date	description	amount
		$0.00

Checks Paid

number	date	amount
2000	6/1/2020	$4,500.00
2001	6/9/2020	$825.00
2002	6/18/2020	$675.00
2003	6/29/2020	$201.97
2004	6/29/2020	$112.84
2005	6/29/2020	$2,000.00
2006	6/29/2020	$2,000.00
2007	6/29/2020	$816.00
2008	6/29/2020	$337.50
2009	6/29/2020	$2,588.23
TOTAL		**$14,056.54**

Other Withdrawals

date	description	amount
6/30/2019	Service charge	$10.00
		$10.00

Table 1 June Checking account statement

Analysis Questions

Use the sample file and the reports you ran to answer the following questions.

1. What is the net income or net loss for June?

   _____

2. What is the total for expenses for June?

   _____

3. What are the payroll expenses (gross wages and payroll taxes) for June?

   _____

4. What is June's gross profit?

   _____

5. What is the total for design service income for the month?

   _____

6. What is the total for product income for the month?

   _____

7. What percentage of June sales came from products?

   _____

8. What percentage of June sales came from Bob Crenshaw?

   _____

9. How much are the liabilities as of June 30?

   _____

10. What is the total for unbilled expenses?

    _____

11. How many hours of time are unbilled?

    _____

12. Which class had the highest net profit?

    _____

13. What is the net cash increase or decrease for the month?

    _____

Index